THE DEATH OF
LUIGI TRASTULLI
AND OTHER STORIES

D1190546

SUNY Series in Oral and Public History
Michael Frisch, Editor

Alessandro Portelli

THE DEATH OF
LUIGI TRASTULLI
AND OTHER STORIES

Form and Meaning in Oral History

STATE   UNIVERSITY   OF   NEW   YORK   PRESS

Published by
State University of New York Press, Albany

© 1991 State University of New York

For information, address State University of New York
Press, State University Plaza, Albany, N.Y., 12246

Library of Congress Cataloging-in-Publication Data

Portelli, Alessandro.
    The death of Luigi Trastulli, and other stories :   form and meaning
in oral history / Alessandro Portelli.
        p.   cm. — (SUNY series in oral and public history)
    Includes bibliographical references (p.
    ISBN 0–7914–0429–3. — ISBN 0–7914–0430–7 (pbk.)
    1. Oral history.   2. Working class—Italy—Terni—History—20th
century.   3. Working class—Kentucky—Harlan County—History—20th
century.   4. Terni (Italy)—Social conditions.   5. Harlan County
(Ky.)—Social conditions.   I. Title.   II. Series.
D16.14.P67   1990
907—dc20   89-26260
                                                                              CIP

Contents

Section Two
Harlan, Kentucky, United States

III. THE INTERDISCIPLINARY APPROACH

Introduction

In 1849, Herman Melville wrote in a letter, "Would that a man could do something & then say—It is finished . . . that he has reached his uttermost & can never exceed it." This book brings together essays written, rewritten, revised, translated and retranslated, at different times from 1979 to 1989; they have gone through so many changes that it is hard to think of this as a definitive version.* On the other hand, in *Moby-Dick*, Melville also wrote, "God keep me from ever completing anything. This book is but a draught—nay, but the draught of a draught . . ."

This book, of course, is no *Moby-Dick*. But it tries to convey the sense of fluidity, of unfinishedness, of an inexhaustible work in progress, which is inherent to the fascination and frustration of oral history—floating as it does in time between the present and an ever-changing past, oscillating in the dialogue between the narrator and the interviewer, and melting and coalescing in the no-man's-land from orality to writing and back. The process of memory, the form of oral historical narrative, and the experience of the encounter in the field are some of the themes of this book.

This approach seems to contradict the initial impulse for much of the most worthwhile work in oral history: the search for "more reality," for direct experience, and for first-person "testimony." I do not wish to belittle this impulse, for it is the source of the political, or at least moral, tension which makes oral history attractive in the first place. In a 1989 article, the historian and activist Sergio Bologna reminded us that " 'Oral history' in Italy began between the

---

*Information on publication history is enclosed in the form of footnotes appended to each chapter. It is to be intended that earlier published versions are different—sometimes very different—from the ones which appear in this book.

1950s and 1960s, as an antagonist with the institutions and methods of historical research." Its theme, Bologna continues, was "the denial of memory"; its practitioners, outsiders who "knew that, because they were uncovering a memory suppressed, they would be denied recognition as regular historians, they would be refused access to the essential tools of their art."

I was seeking suppressed memories and forms of expression when, in 1969, I made two decisions which shaped my life: I bought a tape recorder, and I joined a radical group (everything else, from my professional career to meeting my wife, followed). One reason for the title of this book is to repeat once more that the death of an obscure factory worker in an obscure industrial town is a historical fact of great significance and deep implications, and deserves our full attention. Ever since the Federal Writers' Project interviews with former slaves in the 1930s, oral history has been about the fact that there's more to history than presidents and generals, and there's more to culture than the literary canon. Indeed, one of the reasons why oral history has been sometimes less than welcome in some circles is that it has disarranged many accepted truths. The history of slavery had to be rewritten once the ex-slaves' testimony was finally taken seriously; and we can no longer think about Fascism as we did before Luisa Passerini or Ronald Fraser began their work (although, of course, many still do—to their own great loss).

Sergio Bologna regrets that when, in the 1970s, some scholars introduced in Italy a heightened methodological awareness derived from British, American, and French experiences, the political climate did not encourage a dialogue between the new approaches and the political tension of the founders of Italian oral history. Although this is true in general, there are exceptions, and I like to think of my work as a contribution to this dialogue. Though coming from different directions and along different routes, Luisa Passerini, Cesare Bermani, and several others in Italy (including myself) have all worked with different combinations of methodological awareness and political tension. Internationally, this has been true of many oral historians who brought a sophisticated historical training to the study of oral sources from nonhegemonic social groups and the reconstruction of suppressed memories: Ronald Grele and Michael Frisch in the United States, Raphael Samuel, Anna Devin and Mary Chamberlain in Britain, Mercedes Vilanova and Cristina Borderías in Spain, Eugenia Meyer, Annemarie Troeger, Lutz Niethammer and countless others in many different countries.

Rather than replacing previous truths with alternative ones, however, oral history has made us uncomfortably aware of the elusive quality of historical truth itself. Yet, an aspiration toward "reality," "fact," and "truth" is essential to our work: though we know that certainty is bound to escape us, the search provides focus, shape, and purpose to everything we do.

The question is, then, what kind of truth? If I may be forgiven another literary reference, we may take a hint from Nathaniel Hawthorne's classic distinction between "Novel" and "Romance" in the introduction to *The House of the Seven Gables*. The Novel, he says, "is presumed to aim at a very minute fidelity, not merely to the possible, but to the probable and ordinary course of man's experience"; the romance, on the other hand, allows greater freedom to the imagination, but "it sins unpardonably" whenever it "swerve[s] aside from the truth of the human heart." If we modernize Hawthorne's language and adapt his metaphor, we may imagine a parallel distinction between the "minute fidelity" to fact of positivistic history and social sciences, and the special attention to subjectivity ("the human heart") which oral history requires and permits.

"Fidelity" and "subjectivity," however, like Novel and Romance, are neither apart nor antagonistic: each provides the standard against which the other is recognized and defined. I was attracted to the stories of Luigi Trastulli's death because their imaginative errors expressed the shared subjective dreams, desires, and myths of the narrators. But the first step I took when I began to study those stories was to check the archival and printed records, and to attempt as faithful and minute a reconstruction as possible of what had actually happened. This reconstruction, however, was not an end in itself, but a step toward the reconstruction of the subjective truths implicit in the tales and the creative "errors" they contained.

By "subjectivity," then, I do not mean the abolition of controls, nor the unrestrained preference, convenience or whim of the researcher. I mean the study of the cultural forms and processes by which individuals express their sense of themselves in history. Thus defined, subjectivity has its own "objective" laws, structures and maps (what Hawthorne called "the truth of the human heart"). They may be less tangible and universal than those of hard facts, but they can be reconstructed by means of the appropriate scientific tools—which include an open mind and a willing imagination.

When I stumbled upon the story of Luigi Trastulli, I wasn't even looking for oral history: I was in search of folk songs. Had I been trained to stick to the purpose of my research and to take seriously only "minute fidelity," I wouldn't have listened. I would have written the whole thing off as "faulty memories" and the "unreliability of oral sources." But my only training previous to beginning field work was a bit of advice from Gianni Bosio: "Never turn the tape recorder off"—that is never turn your attention off, and always show your respect for what people choose to tell you. This was the first reason I listened; the second reason was that the stories were beautiful and well-told, and knew that there's no beauty without meaning (aesthetics is not merely ornament and appreciation; it is a form of knowledge). Respect for my partners in dialogue and attention to the meanings of verbal form were to be the foundation of my work ever since.

But before I go into that, I would like to make some remarks on the fact that I stumbled inadvertently onto the whole thing: the stories, their meaning, the need for an *ad hoc* approach. I was not a professional historian (or a professional "anything," at the time) testing my training against some research problem. On the contrary, it was the discovery of the problem which caused me to train myself as accurately as I could in oral history and half a dozen other related fields. I tend to favor, therefore, an essentially inductive approach: starting from a specific riddle, creating a method, and discovering new principles to make sense of it, rather than working from general principles through the application of general methods to specific problems.

In a way, this whole book, and most of my other work (including my oral history of Terni, *Biografia di una città*, Torino 1985) has been an attempt to respond to the questions raised by stories heard in my early field experience, like those of Trastulli's death (chapter 1) or of Alfredo Filipponi's mythical adventures with the "Founder" of Italian communism, Antonio Gramsci (see chapter 6). This is another reason for the title of this book: to root the analysis in a specific, concrete event, and go on from there. If the title has overtones of Agatha Christie's *Roger Ackroyd* and detective novels, it is intentional: Carlo Ginzburg (and Edgar Allan Poe before him) has shown brilliantly how much the critic and the historian have in common with the detective.

Some implications of the inductive approach concern the nature of field work and the disciplinary definition of oral history. No one undertakes field work without some conceptual framework, without some idea in mind of what one is looking for and expects to find (in my case, I was concerned with the relationship of folk song to working-class identity and consciousness). But we must bear in mind that the field situation is a dialogue, in which we are talking to people, not studying "sources"; and that it is largely a *learning* situation, in which the narrator has information which we lack. It is part of the interpersonal nature of field work that the agenda of the interviewee be given equal time and respect with that of the interviewer: as I found out in my experience with Maggiorina Mattioli (see chapter 13), there's a lot more to be learned by leaving ourselves open to the unexpected than by a repetition of our own conceptualizations. In places like Harlan County, known to be suspicious of outsiders, "furriners," revenuers, and sociologists, the narrators' sense that I was not *studying* them but *learning* from them projected a degree of confidence, which ultimately also helped further my own agenda.

Another consequence of the primacy of field work and of the inductive approach is that, by having people as sources, oral historians tend to develop a heightened awareness of interdisciplinarity. Human beings do not belong to any one field of scholarly inquiry, and Gianni Bosio's strictures on the separation of history from ethnology and the demeaning image of "folkloric man" (that is, human beings as seen through the exclusive filter of folklore) also apply to the "literary," "historiographical," "anthropological," "linguistic," and all the other scientific versions of the one-dimensional man. Waddy Moore, former president of the United States Oral History Association, wrote in 1978: "Scratch an oral historian and you're just as likely to find a folklorist, sociologist, economist, someone from the field of communications, medicine, government, business, literature, entertainment, and so the list goes on." Moore's intention was to criticize the lack of proper historical training among alleged oral historians, and he was absolutely right. But, from another angle, he was in fact listing some of the things that an oral historian needs to be in order to be good at this trade.

The history of oral history, therefore, is one of convergences: with sociology (the "life history approach," from the Polish heirs of William Thomas and Florian Znaniecki to Paul Thompson or Isabelle Bertaux-Wiame and Daniel Bertaux), psychology (most notably Luisa Passerini and some of the work of Carl Ryant), linguistics (Dominique Willems), ethnology and anthropology (Jan Vansina, Dennis Tedlock, and Elizabeth Tomkin), folklore (Lynwood Montel and a host of others), music (not only as a field of study, but as a broad ability to listen, as in the case of Studs Terkel).

In my own case, my motivation was ultimately political, and my only formal training was in criminal law—which I thought was wholly unrelated to what I was doing (it was years before I realized that this was where I had learned the techniques of formal thinking in the the first place). What I brought to the stories, in fact, was an interest for narrative and linguistic form, stimulated by the fact that my initial corpus contained a number of clearly imaginary tales. Others have written interestingly and shrewdly about the importance of form in the interpretation of oral history: among others, Ronald Grele and Régine Robin. I used literature, folklore, and linguistics to develop a method for the study of subjectivity by focusing on the implications of the verbal strategies used by the narrators. This is another reason for the choice of this book's title: most oral narrators, folk storytellers and working-class historians have a tendency to couch their ideas in narrative form, thus leaving their discourse open to the possibilities of the untold, the symbolic, the implicit, and the ambiguous. So this is a book of stories—and of ideas from and about stories.

The politics, of course, remained. But they acquired another dimension in the discovery of the political consequences of my own presence in the dialogue of the interview. The impact of the field experience on the researcher has long been part of the self-awareness of modern anthropology: from Claude Levi-Strauss's *Tristes Tropiques*, to the type of work represented by James Clifford and George E. Marcus's *Writing Culture*. The ways in which oral history modifies the self-awareness and identity of the historians themselves is an important aspect of the work of feminist, Third-World, and community-based historians. A combination of field work, scientific analysis, and autobiography makes recent work by Katherine Angueira and Luisa Passerini especially relevant. Native anthropology, and the community-based work of John L. Gwaltney, John Kwo Wei Tchen, and Rina Benmayor (to mention only some examples in the United States) have explored links between the personal identity of the researcher and the social identity of the community. Feminist and community-based oral history have also viewed oral history as a consciousness-raising and organizing tool.

When all the necessary caveats are taken into consideration, the fact remains that the self-analysis and the consciousness-raising which derive from the field encounter are shared by both the observer and the observed. Oral history does not begin with one abstract person observing another, reified one, but with two persons meeting on a ground of equality to bring together their different types of knowledge and achieve a new synthesis from which both will be changed. This, at least, has been the lesson I have learned.

The central sections of this book describe two industrial cultures: Terni in Umbria, Central Italy; and Harlan in the heart of the Eastern Kentucky coal fields in the United States. Harlan had been a sort of personal myth for me ever since I first heard the songs of Molly Jackson and Sara Ogan in the 1960s; but it was almost twenty years before I scraped up the courage and resources (both professional and economic) to actually go and find out for myself what it was like. Terni is the place where I grew up; for ten years, I thought I had left it for good and was never going back—until the militant folk singers of the Nera Valley and their stories brought me back. Somewhere in the mid-1970s, I began to wonder why these two places—the Appalachian coal fields and the rural backyard of the Terni steelworks—held such a grip on my imagination. Then I realized I had been attracted by the fact that, more than anywhere else in my knowledge, these two areas had produced songs in which an advanced modern working-class awareness combined with the integrity of traditional forms of expression. This, in fact, was no coincidence.

Though they are worlds apart, Harlan and Terni do share some common experiences. Both underwent the impact of exogenous industrialization at roughly the same time and both have been suffering from the decline of industrialization in recent years. In both places, a thriving traditional, rural culture was suddenly brought face-to-face with full-blown industrial development; there was hardly any gradual process of adaptation, or time for change and growth from within. So one theme of this book is the interplay of traditional cultures and industrialization—the uses of traditional culture by working people as they struggled with and tried to make themselves at home in a world which they built but, to a large extent, they did not choose to make. In both areas, therefore, I do not seek to reconstruct a "pure" working-class culture; rather (and consistently with the overall methodology of the book) I focus on change, and on those aspects of culture where folk and working-class culture overlap, conflict, or mix with the culture of the ruling classes and with aspects of mass culture: sports, music, paternalism, religion, patriotism, and the uses of space.

However, although I believe that bringing together materials and analyses from different cultures is an essential part of my method and project, I do not attempt to push these structural affinities into a full-fledged comparative approach. For one thing, I do not believe in stressing similarities too much, unless one is ready to make a punctual study of differences as well—and, at this stage, I am not. In fact, the Terni essays were composed at a much more advanced stage of field work. They were revised and completed over the years in which I was writing *Biografia di una città* and afterward, while the Harlan essays are the first tentative hypotheses at an early stage of the work (although they benefit from the Terni experience in point of method).

Harlan is well-known for its dramatic history of union strug-gles, culminating in the 1930s, and then again in the 1970s with the Brookside strike reported in Barbara Kopple's award-winning docu-mentary, *Harlan County, U.S.A.* Like most other coal-mining areas, Harlan was hard hit in the 1950s, and again in the 1970s and 1980s by the decline of the coal industry and consequent loss of jobs and increased emigration. Perhaps the best introduction to Harlan avail-able today is Jim Garland's autobiographical book, *Welcome the Trav-eler Home* (1983).

Terni is situated about sixty miles northeast of Rome on the Via Flaminia, along the Nera river. It has a population of slightly less than 115,000. A second-rank agricultural trading center in the Church State, it was incorporated in newly independent Italy in 1861. Giuseppe Garibaldi used Terni in the 1860s as the starting point for his expeditions to liberate Rome. The availability of hydro-electric energy resources, and its strategic position (far enough from the sea and the borders to be protected from enemy invasions, near enough to Rome to contribute to its defense) caused Terni to be se-lected by the national government as the seat of the first large heavy-industry area in Italy in 1885. The steel works were privately owned, but worked mostly for the Navy and the state-owned rail-roads. Earlier, the Italian Army had also established a gun factory in Terni; chemical plants and textile mills (the latter employing mostly female labor) completed the local industrial structure. Grad-ually, the production and distribution of hydroelectric energy be-came a major resource and activity. From the 1920s to the 1960s, steel, electricity and chemical plants were all owned by the Terni Company, which gradually came under government control. Terni grew to identify itself with progress and industry, and with the working class which symbolized both and formed the majority of the population. Important struggles took place in 1907, with a three-month lockout of the steel works; in 1920, when five people were killed by the police after a rally; and in 1953, when the whole town rebelled against the firing of nearly three thousand steel workers. During the Fascist regime (1922 to 1943), a small underground op-position remained active; this was the core of the "Antonio Gram-sci" partisan brigade which fought in the Resistance against the Nazis and the Fascists in 1943–44 and liberated Terni a few hours before the Allies reached it. Since the 1950s, the town's industrial system has undergone a steady decline which has become dramatic in recent years. Since 1916 (with the parenthesis of fascism), Terni has regularly elected Leftist administrations; after World War II, the Communist vote oscillated between 45 and 50 percent.

The sections on Terni and Harlan in this book are framed by a "prologue"—the story of Luigi Trastulli, which sets the tone for the whole book—and two methodological sections which, although always rooted in specific research experiences, reach for some broader general hypotheses. Chapters 2, 3, and 4 deal with methodological problems in the light of field experience: the question of form in oral narrative, the interpersonal nature of field work, and the impact of time. The two final chapters present two interdisciplinary experiments using legal procedure and the theory and teaching of literature—in which, however, the theoretical conclusions are functional to practical application, as in the controversy of political trials and the teaching of literature in universities. The last chapter, on William Faulkner, was written at the same time as the first, on Trastulli. The writing of these two essays focused my thinking on what I was doing both in the field and in the classroom, and it is fitting that they should open and close this book. On the other hand, the last chapter is also the basis of another book about orality in American literature, on which I have been working for some time. So this book is linked both to my earlier work (on Terni) and to my ongoing and future projects (on Harlan, and on orality and literature)—one more reason for thinking of all this work as a continuous flow, in which everything becomes something else before it has time to freeze into a finished, separate stage.

This book would not exist if it weren't for the help, support and encouragement of friends on both sides of the Atlantic.

The research in Terni was entirely self-financed, so the help of friends there became essential. Gianfranco Canali and his family more than anyone else, and Valentino Paparelli, Enrico Cardinali, Gisa Giani, Lucilla Galeazzi, and Renato Covino are only some of those who helped with hospitality, ideas, contacts, and criticism. The local CGIL union (General Italian Federation of Labor) and the ANPI (National Association of Italian Partisans), and the young people of the cultural cooperative *La Strada* have also been extremely helpful.

My research in Kentucky was started with the help of a James Still Fellowship from the Appalachian College Program of the University of Kentucky at Lexington. Transcription was helped by other grants, also from Berea College; travel funds came from the Italian National Research Council and from the English department of the University of Rome "La Sapienza." But I wouldn't be able to work in Harlan County without the extraordinary network of friendship and support that I have found there.

Annie Napier and her family; Bob and Becky Simpson; the Cranks Creek Survival Center in Cranks Creek, Kentucky; and the Earl H. Turner family in Lynch, Kentucky, gave me homes in different parts of Harlan County. Gurney Norman and Debbie Bays provided transportation. Bill Turner, Hazel King, and Annie Napier gave me no end of contacts and joined me in conducting interviews. Appalshop at Whitesburg, Kentucky; the Highlander Center for Social Research at New Market, Tennessee; President John Stephenson of Berea College; Dr. Ronald Eller of the University of Kentucky's Appalachian Center; and Dr. Alice Brown of the University of Kentucky's Appalachian College Program are the most important organizational and institutional supports. Patty Smith and Julia Hairston transcribed some of the Harlan interviews. And it all began with David Walls, who first invited me to Kentucky, took me to Harlan, and encouraged my interest in Appalachia.

If it hadn't been for Linda Eklund, I would never have set my mind on an English version of my work and looked for publication in the United States. She helped me revise the English of some chapters, and gave me essential advice which I followed throughout. (Of course, if the book still reads awkwardly in parts, it is nobody's fault but mine.)

The international oral-history "community" is an essential part of the background and history of this book; it would take too long to name all my debts of gratitude, so I will mention just the greatest, Ronald Grele. Michael Frisch, of course, is the one who made it all come together.

Woody Guthrie says that "the amount that we owe is all that we have." Every book is the work of many people; but this is even truer for a book of oral history. Ninety-two of the people from whom I borrowed the words for this book are in my list of narrators; they are also authors, together with the hundreds of women and men from whom I received the gift of songs and stories in the twenty years since I began the experiment in equality which is field work.

1

The Death of Luigi Trastulli:
Memory and the Event*

MEMORY AND FACT

"For an experienced event," wrote Walter Benjamin, "is finite—at any rate, confined to one sphere of experience; a remembered event is infinite, because it is only a key to everything that happened before and after it."[1] Luigi Trastulli, a 21-year-old steel worker from Terni, an industrial town in Umbria, central Italy, died in a clash with the police on 17 March 1949 as workers walked out of the factory to attend a rally against the signing of the North Atlantic Treaty by the Italian government. The walkout, the clash, and the killing of Trastulli lasted less than thirty minutes; but, from that moment on, the memory of this brief episode has exerted a shaping influence on the town's identity and culture.

This essay is about the way in which this *évenement* was elaborated, changed, and interpreted in the *longue durée* of memory and culture, as shown by oral sources and their interplay with the written record. What makes Luigi Trastulli's death important is not its intrinsically tragic nature (Terni has experienced more dramatic events in its history, including the air raids which killed thousands of citizens in 1943–44 and the mass layoffs of steel workers in 1952–53). Its importance lies, rather, in the fact that it became the ground upon which collective memory and imagination built a cluster of tales, symbols, legends, and imaginary reconstructions. The most widespread and significant "error" (too common to be explained

---

*First published as "La memoria e l'evento. L'assassinio di Luigi Trastulli," *Segno Critico* [Perugia, Italy], II, 4 (1981); in a revised version, "Historia y memoria: La muerte de Luigi Trastulli," *Historia y Fuente Oral* [Barcelona, Spain], 1 (1989), 5–32.

with faulty individual memories) is the shifting of the date and context of the event from the 1949 anti-NATO rally to the street fighting subsequent to the layoff of two thousand workers from the steel factory in October 1953.

"History," says Hans Magnus Enzensberger, "is an invention which reality supplies with raw materials. It is not, however, an arbitrary invention, and the interest it arouses is rooted in the interests of the teller."[2] This is why "wrong" tales, like the many versions of Trastulli's death, are so very valuable. They allow us to recognize the interests of the tellers, and the dreams and desires beneath them. As a steelworker said, after a seminar in 1979 during which I had discussed the "wrong" versions of Trastulli's death, if one tells a story differently from the way it happened, "maybe unconsciously that's what he was trying to aim at; maybe it was a desire he had, and his actions have been based upon it. Though it never became a historical fact, yet unconsciously there must have been something in his behavior that aimed to achieve it and now he makes a myth of it because he never reached it in fact; but surely—who knows—what he is telling us was his ambition."

The oral sources used in this essay are not always fully reliable in point of fact. Rather than being a weakness, this is however, their strength: errors, inventions, and myths lead us through and beyond facts to their meanings.

STRATEGIES OF OFFICIAL MEMORY

In order to assess the departure of oral sources from the events as ascertained, I will start with an outline of newspaper reports and court records. The Rome daily *Il Messaggero* (a conservative paper) reported the event as one of the many anti-NATO protests taking place all over the country that day, under the headline "Rallies, demonstrations and clashes with police."

After the police arrested six young men for posting unauthorized [anti-NATO] posters in the streets, the *Commissioni Interne* [Factory Committees] decided to stage a rally at the *Politeama* [city theater]. Though they were aware that no parades were permitted, the committees ordered the hands to march in formation to the theater. When the *celere* [jeep-mounted anti-riot police] arrived in front of the steelworks, the jeeps were stationed about two hundred feet away from the crowd and two officers dismounted and tried to persuade the leaders to make the workers walk to the theater individually. Some refused and started leading the other demonstrators toward the city center, but the officers still endeavored in vain to avoid a clash. Later, as scuffles began to break out, the men in one of the jeeps were ordered to fire a few rounds in the air. At the same time, other shots were heard, presumably fired from the factory mess hall and from the third floor of a nearby building, and a bottle containing incendiary liquids fell near the officers' jeep, causing a detonation and flame. At this point, the police cars began to circle and drive into the crowd. As resistance continued, a few tear gas cans were used and a few shots were fired.

In the final tally of the clash, there was one person dead (one Alvaro [sic] Trastulli, 21); nine demonstrators were wounded, and ten policemen were bruised by stones. An autopsy on Trastulli's body will establish whether he was killed by police weapons or others. In the evening, the town was calm; but the leaders of the *Camera del Lavoro* [city labor council] held an emergency meeting and announced a general strike for today.[3]

A nearly identical text appeared the same day in the Milan *Corriere della Sera*, Italy's then most important paper: either the two papers used the same reporter or they received the same police handout. The pro-government press implies that the innocent mass of the "hands" were manipulated by callous leaders into a clash with police; that there was an unauthorized march going on; and that Trastulli may have been killed by shots from behind the workers' own lines. Later, these will be precisely the outlines of the police inquest on the episode. Interestingly, they have Trastulli's name wrong (Alvaro instead of Luigi). Apparently, written sources are not always automatically reliable.

On the other side, the Communist party daily *L'Unità* presents a different version, with a radical shift in narrative point of view:

The factory whistle blew at 10:30. Thousands of plant and office workers were already gathered in the courtyards, and now walked out in mass toward downtown. They were going to demonstrate against the war pact [NATO]. They had walked no more than 300 meters when the police arrived—about ten jeeps, the usual frantic dance, the usual clubbing of heads. The workers walked slowly on. Some approached Inspector Pessolan's jeep—"Be smart, boys," he told them. "You must have a permit to parade."

That was no parade, they explained. Did he mean that every day, when the workers walked out at shift end and filled the street, they had to have a permit? But the inspector's driver will not listen; he jerks the jeep forward and then back and the first worker is wounded: Ettore Scatolini, a former partisan, is lying on the pavement with a broken foot, crushed by a wheel.

The workers shout in protest. They do not attack. All they do is cry out their anger. And then the police fire on them; they fire straight into the crowd. Ground-floor windows are perforated by bullets. The volley lasts several minutes. Two tear gas cans explode . . .[4]

As *Il Messaggero* and *Corriere della Sera* anticipate the strategy of the government organs, *l'Unità* anticipates the cultural and judicial strategy of the labor movement. The headline screams: "Terni and Perugia [Umbria's regional capital] strike to protest the police massacre." One dead does not make a massacre; but the hyperbole prepares the shift of Luigi Trastulli's death from news to epic, which is found in many later oral versions, and which is also implicit in the article's sudden shift from the past tense to the historical present. The article already contains the version which the organizers will give in court: there was no march. It was just the workers' mass filling the street as they always do when they leave the factory at the end of the shift. Many oral narratives still hold on to this version:

AMBROGIO FILIPPONI: "You know, when the workers came out of the gates, of course they were numerous, so their impact covered the whole street; it was a stream of people moving ahead. Even nowadays, when they come out of the factory, the workers fill the avenue. And for the police, according to them, this instead was a parade. Not workers who come out and are forced to rub elbows as they walk for practical, logistic, inevitable reasons. They construed this into an unauthorized parade. And this meant, in their minds, that they were allowed to fire into the parade.

Certain narrators reinforce this version by shifting the time of the episode from 10:30, when it happened, to the end of the morning shift:

> TRENTO PITOTTI: It was a matter of three, four thousand workers all coming out together. And, all shifts, you know: Because there you had the first, second and third shifts running into each other. I mean, two shifts plus the extra morning shift they used to have.

The first available official judiciary document following Trastulli's death is the report of Terni's district attorney (*procuratore della Repubblica*) to his superiors in Perugia, dated 18 March 1949. While the conservative newspapers of the same day already reported the episode in detail, the district attorney wrote that he had not yet received a report from the police: perhaps the police informed the judicial authority only after they had determined that the press would carry their version of events. The district attorney, however, also assumed that there was a parade going on: "From verbal information received," he wrote, "it appears that yesterday morning the workers of the local steel factory abstained from work in protest against the N[orth] Atlantic Treaty and left the factory in columns . . . carrying signs, and went toward the city square."

The opening formula deserves attention: "From verbal information received . . ." Although judicial reports are among the standard written sources on which historians habitually rely, Terni's district attorney reveals that, behind the written document, there are oral sources ("verbal information") of which we know nothing, summarized and transcribed by some police official or judicial clerk in ways over which we leave no control. Orality is woven into the very texture of the written official record.

When the police tried to stop them, the district attorney continued, the marchers refused to comply. "As a consequence, scuffles originated, during which at a certain point several shots were fired following which Luigi Trastulli, a factory worker, was killed and the workers Leonello Dionisi and Raul Crostella were wounded and taken to the local hospital, where they are still undergoing treatment." The district attorney knew nothing yet about the alleged fire bombs and shots from the mess hall; he knew that "scuffles originated," but not how and by whom they were started. He knew, however, that Trastulli's death was caused "by an automatic weapon fired from a short distance, the bullet going through the body from right to left and cutting the aorta artery." He was also able to reassure his superiors that "the parade dissolved and order was restored and no longer disturbed."[5]

As we read further into the judicial record, we see how the district attorney's office gradually internalized the police version as described by the early newspaper reports. The first selection of witnesses was hardly impartial: policemen, office workers (at the time, mostly non-union), and government employees whose office windows looked upon the scene of the clash. Within less than a week, on 23 March, the district attorney's version of the event had incorporated the workers' responsibility for the first scuffles; the jerking back and forth of the jeep (reported by *l'Unità*, but described by the magistrate as the driver's involuntary reaction to his fear of the mob's violence); the shots from the mess hall and nearby buildings; and the conciliatory attitude of police. While Inspector Pezzolano managed to persuade some of the crowd to disperse, the district attorney wrote, "certain rowdier elements, armed with bats and sticks previously hidden, who had beforehand limited themselves to insults . . . attempted to break the circle of jeeps[6] and, lifting one of the cars, attempted to capsize it. The driver tried to escape by shifting quickly back and forth." But one of the demonstrators "hit the driver violently with a tin poster"; one policeman "had his helmet torn away from him"; and many were hurt by bats and stones. The Inspector's orders to scatter were answered by more hurling of stones and bottles, "one of which contained a flammable liquid which fortunately did not fire, but whose nature was revealed by the exhalations of acid vapors." Finally, "some sharp shots echoed from the drinks stand in front of the steelworks gate and from a window of the stairs of number 206, a building that had filled with demonstrators, and from which smoke was seen coming out. The shot was answered by rifle shots fired by policemen in one jeep only, in order to intimidate the crowd, and by tear gas cans, which cleared the street of demonstrators."

The court initiated proceedings against parties unknown for first-degree murder, and indicted the members of the Factory Committee for unauthorized demonstration (a charge of which they were later acquitted). Rather than following the trial in detail, I will dwell briefly on the two most controversial points: who fired the shots, and whether or not the workers were already marching on parade.

2 important issues

On the first point, the prosecution heaped testimony of police- |
men and passersby who witnessed, with plenty of detail, that
they saw the shots fired from a window at number 206, from the
drink stand near the factory gate, and from the mess hall. Others
stated that they saw workers carrying clubs, broken bottles, and a
scabbard (later found inside the factory gates). On the workers'
side, the most detailed description of the responsibility of the police
was in the testimony of Raul Crostella, who was gravely wounded
in the clash:

> I was hit in the back. I managed to turn around and saw
> the men on the police truck fire toward me. I was hit before I
> had time to turn around. I don't know who fired on me. I can
> say with absolute certainty that it was someone from the po-
> lice. The policemen were unrecognizable because they were
> wearing anti-tear-gas goggles and helmets. The truck from
> which the shot was fired was about sixty feet away from
> me. . . . No one told me that the demonstration was unautho-
> rized. The police started the manhunt with no warning.

As to whether there was a parade or just a mass exit from the   2
gates, the police insisted that the workers were carrying signs made
of tin (which they later supposedly used as clubs); they also exhibited witnesses who had received fliers announcing the march. Although the signs might have been meant for use later in the
authorized rally, there seems to be little doubt that the workers, in
fact, intended to parade from the factory to the theater downtown.

"Yes, we did strike, and the demonstration was on; we [the
Communist party] had organized this demonstration," says Bruno
Zenoni, then one the party leaders, who criticizes the union offi-
cials for not taking "a clear stand" on this point at the trial ("The
comrades who testified in court were afraid," he says. "It's a fact.
You can see it in the trial record, from the way they answered").
Given the political climate, it was an understandable behavior, and
it did serve the purpose of getting them acquitted.[7]

COLLECTIVE SYMBOLIC ACTIVITY

We can now proceed to the examination of oral sources. The narratives of party cadre and officials are usually exact as to date and
background and, understandably, echo the official defense line.

AMBROGIO FILIPPONI: [I remember] the attack, the actions of the police, which [Mario] Scelba [the notorious Minister of the Interior] had organized, who enjoyed the advantage of riding on top of the jeep, higher than the workers' heads—Scelba's great scientific discovery!—and so could club them more easily. Clashes were frequent and fierce in Terni, and I remember them because I was a part of it. I don't think I missed a single one of those fights. And we had clashes in Terni, with shooting, in the case of Trastulli, Luigi Trastulli, and of others who were wounded later. [Trastulli], it was in 1949, March 17th. You see, we were demonstrating against NATO. The workers had left the plant to go to a demonstration, a rally that was supposed to take place.

ALESSANDRO PORTELLI: Were they carrying signs?

FILIPPONI: I don't remember any signs. I was in school at that time. And we heard, the news came that there had been shooting; I left school immediately, the parade was still coming down, in small groups, the ambulance cars ran back and forth, and then we heard of Trastulli's death and the wounding of several other workers.

Another party official, Alvaro Valsenti, stresses the political background. "In those days, parliament was debating Italy's participation in NATO; and the democratic peace movement—we had committees in every factory and community—organized protests, demonstrations, all over the country." Valsenti, however, is rather ambiguous as to whether the demonstration had already begun when the contact with the police took place:

So, as the workers walked out of the steelworks and other factories, a lineup of police attempted to block the road. There was an exchange, some scuffles, and so on; then, suddenly they began to shoot. This is the story of the death of Trastulli and the wounding of Crostella and Dionisi, this is when it happened. Then others were wounded, because there was a contact, as it were, between policemen, workers, they were throwing things, trying to defend themselves.

Rank-and-file narrators are less matter-of-fact, more epic, and more imaginative. Their stories swell with anger—thirty years after the fact—as if it had just happened.

R & F: anger
e più story

ROCCO BIANCHI:[8] Because you see, Scelba, the police minister, stuffed Terni with cops, with all the trash, all the gangs of Calabria, of Sicily. And he stuffed Terni with *celere.* They came on trucks, they came on trains, by the hour, and for every local citizen there were four cops upon his tracks. *Celerini,* spies, cops, and so on and so forth. Terni was known as the "new Stalingrad." They just flooded the place with jeeps, with machine guns, with clubs, with machine guns. The workers, at the sight of those damn jeeps running all over up and down the avenue and carousing and charging on the yard before the factory,—you know, when a worker sees these people paid with the workers' money, this police that Scelba invented, he becomes bitter and exasperated. And it seems that from somewhere, from some of those small bars and stands outside the gates, some of the workers hurled bottles at them; threw some bottles at the jeeps' wheels—a beer bottle, soda bottle, coke bottle, empty. And you understand, those whores, flesh for sale, with machine guns in their hands, they shoot and they kill Trastulli.

This speaker's shift to the historical present parallels the narrative technique of the *l'Unità* article of thirty years before, and signals a leaning toward the epic. The same verbal form, enriched by a solemn rhythmic scanning and meaningful pauses, turns the narrative of another worker, Ivano Sabatini, into an actual piece of epic poetry:

> Well
> we were walking out of the factory
> we find in front of us
> six or seven police jeeps
> and one of these jeeps rushed against the workers
> with a beastly rage.
> Some of the workers
> managed to stay out of the way
> of the rush of this jeep
> but comrade Luigi Trastulli
> was climbing a wall
> climbing a wall
> and a machine gun volley
> froze him dead.
> And we see Luigi Trastulli

> lose his grip on the wall's edge
> while another policeman
> maybe more human
> lowered his gun.
> But Luigi Trastulli
> fell to the ground
> and was shot dead point blank.

Sabatini's story presents two of the most important symbolic motifs recurring in oral narratives: the placement of Trastulli's death on the factory wall rather than in the middle of the avenue; and the scene of the guard who lowers his gun. One of Terni's greatest folk poets, singers and narrators, Dante Bartolini, reinforces and amplifies both these motifs and adds a third, extremely important symbol: the police jeeps themselves.

> BARTOLINI: It's Trastulli I'm talking about. When we all came down from the factories to protest against war, wasn't it? Against the Atlantic Treaty. And then, at that time, Scelba was in power, and so the jeeps, my son, came on against the workers, and this boy, you have seen the cross, you have seen it, where he was killed, right there at the factory, near the gate, a bit further down. And he, as soon as he came out [of the gate], they went for him with those jeeps, they crushed him to a pulp. It ran him over.
> PORTELLI: What did the workers do then?
> BARTOLINI: Well, what did they do—they struck, there was nothing else they could do. We did fight in the street, you know. With the police. Throwing bricks. One young man, with whiskers, about twenty-five years old; if this guy gets hold of you, he can throw you twenty yards away. They called him Tarzan. So he jumped on a jeep, and each cop he caught he hurled him down to the pavement. He caught one carrying a rifle, hit him on the head, got hold of his helmet, whirled him around like a bowling pin—like that, *brrr*—then he picked up the jeep and pushed it out of the way. Wow! When the people see a thing like that, when they see that kind of thing, they all pile on top, so they couldn't get away. And the army. They called out the army, they ordered them to point their rifles at us; and when he said "Fire!" they dropped the rifles to the ground. That was some demonstration! "Fire!" he says. *Brrrrm*, all the rifles on the ground.

The dubious reliability of this tale enhances its imaginative and symbolic quality. Let us examine the three main symbols—the guard's refusal to fire on the workers, the jeep, and the wall. The refusal to fire, as described by Sabatini, was actually mentioned by a coeval, semi-official source. In a speech on the Senate floor, Socialist senator Tito Oro Nobili said, "At a window of the barracks [along the avenue], there was a nest of machine guns. The terrorized crowd detected a guard preparing to fire on them; but one of his colleagues quickly stopped him by seizing him and pulling him back inside."[9]

Bartolini's more complex version combines this motif with the shift and condensation of two other episodes which, supposedly, took place in Terni in 1948 and 1950. Raul Crostella (one of the wounded in the Trastulli incident), recalls:

> There was an episode where the *celere* came out, and they sent this platoon of soldiers as a reinforcement. In Terni it had never happened, and this was the first time they sent soldiers on public order duty. So the soldiers lined up in front of *Pazzaglia* [a café at the confluence of Main Street and the town hall square]. The soldiers blocked the road, with the police below and the workers above. At a certain moment the police chief orders them to attack; but the army officer in charge of the soldiers said that he had been sent to keep order and order he would keep. And he lined up his men facing the police. In three rows. And there was an incredible scene, the women hugging the soldiers, "long live the army . . ." And the police had to go back to their quarters, melancholically.[10]

Bartolini and Crostella's tales voice the Left's distinction between the army, a "democratic" body comprised of drafted citizens and workers; and the *celere*, a professional police specialized in the repression of the working class—"Scelba's scientific invention," "this police that Scelba invented"—identified with the Christian Democrat government and the hated Minister of the Interior: "Scelba was in power, and so the jeeps came on against the workers." The army represents, then, the "healthy" democratic aspect of the post-Fascist state as opposed to its repressive and reactionary side symbolized by the jeep (just as Sabatini's "human" policeman evokes the essential humanity of even the *celere* as opposed to their role). By having Trastulli killed by a jeep, Bartolini makes him an almost direct victim of the Christian Democrats.

Political victim.

Finally, the wall appears conspicuously in many narratives. Trastulli, recalls Giuseppe Laureti, "was running away. They hit him with a machine gun volley. It nailed him to the wall, there, like that." Other narrators echo the same motif:

> AMERIGO MATTEUCCI: This boy, twenty-one years old, was mowed down by a machine gun volley, which also left a streak on the wall.
>
> TRENTO PITOTTI: If you look at the wall [you can still see the marks of] all the twenty bullets.
>
> MATTEUCCI: This machine gun volley, which was actually lucky that he was the only one climbing the wall at the moment. He was climbing the wall because the police had blocked the gates and they wouldn't let us out.
>
> PITOTTI: You know that wall, over there; he was climbing across . . .

The image of Luigi Trastulli killed on or against the wall originates in traditional religious and political iconography. The machine gun volley that left its streak against the factory wall evokes images of executions, such as those of partisans and anti-Fascists by the Nazis during the Resistance, combined with crucifixion imagery. Trastulli was, in Laureti's words, "nailed" to the wall, and the policeman who lowered his or his colleague's gun is reminiscent of similar stories in folk versions of the Passion of Christ. This imagery is reinforced, in some versions, by placing the victim above the wall, high above the crowd. One narrator, Menotti Zocchi, explains Trastulli's death precisely with the fact that he was standing above the crowd while the police fired in the air: "Trastulli, it happened that he climbed a window, and maybe someone . . . well, they fired high; they didn't fire on the crowd, you see. He had climbed a window, a little bit higher. Maybe they were trying to shoot in the air."[12]

Probably a desire to debunk all this mythologizing is behind other tales, in which some of the same symbols take on opposite meanings. Lucilla Galeazzi remembers two:

> Well, [of] these two versions, I think the first is more reliable because I had it from my uncle, and he was there. The other one, I can't say how credible it is, and who started it. The first story was told by my uncle, and he used to say that they were coming out of the factory because they were sup-

posed to go to this demonstration against NATO. But some of the people were walking out but didn't mean to join the parade, they only wanted to go home. [When the police started shooting, Trastulli] tried to climb the wall to go back inside, and they shot him down on top of it while he was climbing.

The other version comes from my high school philosophy teacher, in 1968. And he says that this man Trastulli wasn't a Communist militant at all, maybe he was even a Christian Democrat, or at least he was nothing but a sympathizer, not a party member at all, and he was climbing the factory wall because he didn't want to join the demonstration, so he was trying to go around the picket line or something. He jumps off the wall, and they kill him. And immediately he was made into the Communist martyr, though according to this person he was no Communist at all.

Giuseppe Laureti also says that "maybe that guy wasn't even in it. Maybe he was just a camp follower." There is no doubt that Trastulli was indeed a member of the Communist party. In fact his widow appeared by the side of the national Communist Secretary Palmiro Togliatti at least once after his death.

The Socialist Tito Oro Nobili, however, said in his Senate speech that Trastulli "was devoted only to his family and his work, and could not bear to be away from his home even for a very short time unless in the company of his family." Therefore, Nobili assumed, he was "among those who had explicitly stated that they wanted to go home and would not be able to attend the parade." On the one hand, Nobili stresses the "innocence" of the victim, making the crime even more shocking. On the other hand, he attempts to deprive the Communists of the "ownership" of their cherished martyr.

A similar debunking intention may be attributed to Lucilla Galeazzi's philosophy teacher at a time—1968—when New Left intellectuals were actively attacking Old Left myths. But the fact remains that at least two of the "de-mythologizers"—Galeazzi's uncle and Menotti Zocchi (who claims that the death was accidental)—were stalwart Communist activists.

DISPLACEMENT AND CONDENSATION

The more remarkable phenomenon in the collective remembrance of Trastulli's death does not, however, concern the sequence of the

1949 or 1953 ?

events as much as their placement in time and context. Many narrators, including eye-witnesses, believe that Trastulli did not die at an anti-NATO demonstration in 1949, but during the street fights which followed the announcement of the firing of more than two thousand workers from the steel factory in October 1953 (following the firing of another seven hundred in December 1952). In this way, the narrators merge the two most dramatic events of Terni's postwar history into one coherent story.

The best version of this kind is the narrative of Amerigo Matteucci, a remarkable example of working-class storytelling.

> Well, practically, when they began to talk of this strike, of this great strike, general strike—you remember, don't you?— Terni went through terrible moments then. The merchants pulled their shutters down, without being even asked to join; without being called to the struggle. It's not as if the workers had gone up to a merchant and told him to shut down shop, you know. But they reasoned this way: "Two thousand and seven hundred people out of a job—and our economy, what's going to happen to it? And us, how about us? What're we going to eat?" So there was this resentment, and they closed down everything, shut down everything.
>
> When the workers walked out of the factory, they came out in groups, because the jeeps were lined up outside. Viale Brin—you know Viale Brin, what it looks like. From the Valnerina gate on up, it was all a storming of jeeps, cops carrying clubs. Anyway, they came out the way workers do, exasperated with worry about losing their jobs, but somehow disciplined, thinking they were going to a rally. Every worker thought he was going to a rally, to hear a speech in the square about what was going on, to make public opinion aware of what was going on. Instead, things turned out different. Out came one group, then two groups, then three groups—at a certain moment, there was gunfire. Gunfire, while this poor guy was walking out . . . twenty-one-year-old kid . . . he was mowed down by a volley that left a streak all across the wall.
>
> But it was a two-edged weapon. Because we saw the blood, the blood. And when throughout Terni, men like us, like other people, began to shout "They've killed the workers", when the people heard the shots—with the memory still alive of the war, because Terni had been martyrized by the air raids—the people went blind with rage. From out the win-

dows, they began to throw—I mean, the women even—dishes, pots, and pans as the jeeps went by. I'm telling you, it was Judgment Day. When we marched along Viale Brin toward the square, it was out of this world; I mean, people along Corso Tacito, the new main street that goes toward Town Hall square . . . hundreds of people on the rooftops, ready to drop tiles on the cops. It was unbelievable, unbelievable. Water hoses . . . pieces of wood to build barricades because they said that the police were bringing in reinforcements from Rome . . . building sites that were emptied and planks placed across the road to block passage.

Well, it was a moment of . . . And it went on, this struggle; it was successful. But, it was successful in that it enabled us to negotiate. Yes, that's the fact. Because of course, in order for that struggle to succeed, it would have had to be a revolution.

Matteucci's story is a faithful description of what happened in October 1953; the only thing "wrong" with it is that this wasn't when Trastulli was killed. The chronological displacement is echoed by a number of narrators: "It was when they fired those two thousand, two thousand five hundred workers (Bianchi); "They were firing people at the steelworks. They were marching down Viale Brin, all together: the workers came out on strike, because they were firing those six hundred people. It was the first set, I think, the first six hundred" (Antonina Colombi); "It was about the two thousand; they killed a man when the *celere* charged" (Laureti); "Trastulli—it was on the day of this big strike, the layoffs" (Zocchi). The causes of this collective error must be sought, rather than in the event itself, in the meaning which it derived from the actors' state of mind at the time; from its relation to subsequent historical developments; and from the activity of memory and imagination.

In the first place, Trastulli's death was such a dramatic shock that it created a need for adequate circumstances, causes, and consequences. It was difficult to accept it as an accident which occurred during a minor scuffle in a routine political protest. Since the firing of nearly three thousand workers in 1952–53 is the most important dramatic event in the town's working-class history and in the personal lives of literally thousands of citizens, it is only appropriate that the most tragic episode should find its place in this context. It also makes sense that, if a worker is killed, this ought to be when there is widespread fighting going on.

[handwritten marginalia:] and from memory and imagination / Cause of error found in meaning derived from actors' state of mind at the time; from it relation to subseq. hist. event.

A first step toward "adequate causation"[13] is the insistence that it was a premeditated murder. "They did it methodically. It wasn't an accident," says Bruno Zenoni. "The prefect [local representative of the central government, in charge of public order] boasted, had boasted a few days before, that he would put the Communist workers in their place—he'd lay a few of them stiff on the street, and that would stop their demonstrating." In fact, stories about statements of this kind by the prefect had appeared in *l'Unità* before Trastulli's death.[14]

The concept of adequate causation is also relevant from another point of view. The struggle against Italy's participation in NATO and, later, to remove Italy from the alliance was a central tenet of Communist party platforms until the 1960s; but, when these stories were collected, it belonged to a bygone era in Party history. In the 1970s, when the strategy was to attempt to seek the United States' toleration in view of possible Communist access to government, Secretary Enrico Berlinguer went so far as to describe NATO as a peace instrument and a guarantee of national independence. As a consequence, it became rather awkward to make a martyr of someone who got himself killed while opposing it. The new situation may have influenced some narrators to shift the story to the context of the struggle for jobs, which was still recognized as a legitimate cause.

AN UNSETTLED ACCOUNT

Shortly after Trastulli's death, a Communist worker, Sante Carboni, wrote a song about it. One verse suggests a deeper, hidden motive behind the chronological shift:

> To you young bride
> And to your little child
> We pledge that the murderer
> Shall not die in bed.[15]

Trastulli's death opened an account which remained unsettled for years. Terni's workers had just emerged from the experience of the partisan liberation war; less than a year before, they had reacted with militant demonstrations and sit-ins to the wounding of the national leader, Palmiro Togliatti.[16] That they would not back down in confrontations with the police was an integral part of their identity and self-esteem: "After our strikes, we took to the streets, we fought some real fights" (Antonio Antonelli); "We came to blows, right in the town square, we sure did" (Dante Bartolini); "I don't think I missed a single one of those fights" (Ambrogio Filipponi).

The symmetry between police offense and popular response is part of a code of behavior which is referred to by many narrators: "When the people heard the shots . . . they went blind with rage," says Matteucci. So the idea of retaliation must have been in many people's minds. A witness for the prosecution told the district attorney, "I have heard that immediately after the event, the Communist [Alfredo] Menichetti harangued the workers with a very violent speech about hatred and revenge against the police, against the government, and against the parties which support it. Among the large crowd, few applauded his words." Of course, Menichetti denied this, insisting that he had told the workers to go home.

But it is a fact that the workers did not intend to let the matter rest. Remo Righetti, then the senior Communist city councilman (and acting mayor, since the mayor happened to be out of town in those days), recalls a significant episode:

> The next day the workers covered Viale Brin with new signs: Viale [boulevard] Luigi Trastulli. That same day—maybe the next morning, I don't remember exactly—the prefect sent a message to the city administration ordering us to send city guards to take down the signs which the workers had put up. [I sent word back:] You tell the prefect that it's the police who fired. They're the ones who fired in Viale Brin. So let the police . . . if that sign bothers them, let them take it down themselves. Tell him to send the police, like he sent them to fire on the workers."

Carboni's song and the changing of the street's name show that, in many minds, the need to "do something" about the murder was very much alive. The crime ought not to go unpunished. The unions and the Left set up an inquest, which supposedly identified the officer responsible for ordering to fire, but no action could be taken upon these findings. And the workers had some more tangible response in mind, anyway.

> PORTELLI: What happened afterwards?
> CALFIERO CANALI: Nothing! Nothing happened. Nothing happened, because—I don't know why. Because maybe the

people, the workers, they'd have been ready to do something, but they were held back by—by the leaders, because . . . it was like when Togliatti was wounded. It looked as if . . . if it had been for the rank and file, there would have been a revolution, right then. Instead, we didn't do anything because—of course, in those days, what could you do? They'd have blown us like bagpipes, if we'd attempted anything. And yet, there was so much bitterness inside your body, so much hatred!

The anger with which, thirty years later, workers still repeat that "Nothing!" was done after Trastulli's death (Canali repeats it three times, pounding the table with his fist) is symmetrical to the complacent tone of the official sources announcing that "in the evening, the town was calm" (*Il Messaggero*), and that "order was restored and not further disturbed" (the district attorney). Enforced peace reigned in the street, certainly not in people's minds.

> PORTELLI: What was the worker's response?
>
> FILIPPONI: The workers, I remember that their response was to proceed to physical retaliation. The majority were on this ground. And Trastulli's funeral, though there was a great deal of fear, of terror, because you could see the machine guns up in the turrets of the prefecture building, and the funeral passed underneath . . . it was raining, that day, and the funeral was an enormous, overflowing mass of citizens, that attended. So there was a reaction in the masses; an intelligent reaction, but a rather intense one.
>
> PORTELLI: You mean, there was a desire to fight, but they didn't act upon it?
>
> FILIPPONI: No, no, no; we didn't. From the mass, here and there, there was so much anger, it would have taken nothing to start a fight. But the consequences would have been disastrous, of course. We weren't in a climate, in a situation, that was favorable . . . that was revolutionary, it seems to me.

All witnesses stress the ferment, the bewilderment pervading the town. "I reached the steelworks' gates," says Bruno Zenoni, "and all the workers were milling around, discouraged, mixed up." Iole Peri recalls the "People who came to the hospital all the time, queueing to see the wounded, and groups of people talking in the streets—it all turned into a march, remember? At the hospital, everywhere, groups of people talking."

One theme ran through these discussions. "I remember the people massed in front of Palazzo Mazzancolli, where the Communist city office was," says Filipponi; "The people had spilled into the building, the courtyard was full, and so was the little square outside, the Via Cavour was full of people and—'Folks, what are we going to do? What can we do? How can we tolerate this?' And so on."

It is intolerable; but the unbalance of power is such that it *must* be tolerated. It is a hard bite to swallow for anyone, but especially so for people whose self-esteem rests on a tradition of militancy and pride. The unpunished murder of a comrade, the impossibility of retaliation, is not only an unbearable physical violence; it is also a deep humiliation, a loss of face. Only five years before, the working-class partisans—had marched into Terni proudly carrying their weapons, convinced that the town and the factory now belonged to them. Now, the killing of Trastulli shows the working class that power relationships have slid back. The prefect's alleged boast, that he would put the workers in their place by laying some of them stiff in the streets, has been made true and there is nothing they can do about it.

Memory goes to work to heal this wound in two distinct ways. Some narrators amplify the description of the episode in order to show that, indeed, the workers did respond immediately; others shift everything to a context—the 1953 layoffs—when a response actually did occur.

The first strategy is used by Trento Pitotti. After Trastulli fell, he says: "the jeeps, I'm telling you, from the middle of the street we carried them all the way to—you know where the old sports field used to be, don't you? Well, try to imagine it, all turned over, upside down, we capsized them, after this business happened, after the police had shot, had killed this man Trastulli. Afterward, the jeeps, turned over, capsized, you understand, it was a real mess." The insistence on "afterward" serves two purposes: it proves that the workers did fight back, but also that they did not initiate the fight.

Dante Bartolini's narrative is a more complex and subtle variant of the same strategy. When asked "What did the workers do afterward," first he says that "there was nothing they could do" but strike. He then goes on, however, to say, "We did fight in the streets." His rapid transition makes it hard to tell whether the scenes he describes (which combine aspects of the Trastulli episode, such as the capsizing of the jeep and the seizing of the policeman's helmet, with events that took place later, in 1950) are supposed to have been immediate reactions to Trastulli's murder or whether he is mentioning them in order to prove that at least in some other occasions the workers did fight, thus compensating the lack of reaction on that occasion. I think this ambiguity is quite intentional.

The chronological shift, however, is the more common strategy. Although they were unsuccessful, Terni's workers still recall their near-insurrection of 1953 with great pride. In fact, the barricades which went up in those days were a response not just to the loss of jobs and power, but also to all that had gone on before: they were a way of settling accounts (with themselves as much as with the government) also for Trastulli's unpunished murder, and to retrieve—if not their jobs—at least their sense of dignity as a class.

How memory operated to heal this wound is shown by the testimony of workers of the next generation. Carlo Martinelli recalls that Trastulli's name figured prominently in the first political conversations he remembers hearing in his family when he was around the age of 12 (he was born in 1940).[17] His contemporary Mario Vella, who went to work at the steelworks in 1954 at the age of 17, recalls: "We younger guys, when we walked out at shift's end, the older men would point out to us: they'd say, do you see that? and there was a wreath [near the spot where Trastulli had died]. He died for you, too; if you have a job at the steelworks perhaps you owe it, you owe it to him."

Typically, Trastulli was being described as a martyr of the struggle for jobs, rather than for "peace," against NATO. The older workers, Vella recalls, "told us about the workers who were being killed in the streets by the police"—as if the murder of Luigi Trastulli was still happening in 1954. Clearly, Trastulli's name was part of the political initiation of working-class adolescents in the factory and within the family. The wreath of flowers (which, together with the memorial marble tablet, may have visually reinforced the idea that the wall was where he died) and the recurring stories on the local page of *l'Unità* especially each year around the anniversary, kept the memory alive. Clearly, even though Trastulli did not die fighting for jobs in 1953, the workers carried him along in their minds when they took to the barricades then.

THE FORMAL ORGANIZATION OF MEMORY

The chronological shift of Trastulli's death concerns, finally, the mechanisms of memory. To date an event is to break down continuous time into a sequence of discrete events, grouped into periods around certain key facts ("before the war"; "after I was married" . . .). This "horizontal" breakdown hinges in turn upon a "vertical" structure: all sorts of events happen simultaneously at any given moment, and the building of a chronological paradigm implies a selection of homogeneous events from among those happening at any given time. Most narrators seek to confer coherence to their stories by adhering to a (relatively) consistent principle or "mode" of selection: the sphere of politics; the life of the community; and personal experiences. Each mode has a spatial correlative the national and international perspective, the town, and the home. Of course, no narrative is ever entirely consistent; on the other hand, a given event can be placed in more than one mode. The identification of an event and of its meaning is, however, usually based on the network of sequential and simultaneous events to which it is linked by means of the narrative and memory mode.

Now, the murder of Luigi Trastulli is a problematic event from this point of view. It does not fit the "political" mode, since its repercussions in the life of institutions, parties, governments, and elections did not go beyond a couple of speeches by Leftist members in Parliament. On the other hand, it cannot be considered as belonging to the personal mode; with the exception of the victim's immediate circle, it did not directly impinge on anyone's life.

The collective, community mode would be the proper collocation, because here is where the event carries the most weight. At this level, however, its only possible meaning is precisely the one that the narrators are trying to avoid: a message of collective powerlessness and defeat. Placing Trastulli's murder in the mode in which it belongs would reopen the wound.

Since, however, it looms so large in memory, narrators must come to terms with its location, both in time and mode. Two strategies offer themselves: a "vertical" shift in modes (upward to pure politics or downward to personal life and affections); or a "horizontal" shift in chronology.

The upward vertical shift extols the roles of government, Party, and local institutions. After being fired from the steelworks in 1952, Dante Bartolini wrote a song in which he grouped Trastulli with other recent working-class victims of police repression in other parts of Italy, claiming that "they were killed by the same assassins, the followers of Mussolini": the removal of the episode from the community mode to the political mode is paralleled by the spatial shift from the local to the national perspective.

Other narrators stress the leadership role of the Communist officials. Filipponi says "And I remember the action of the political representatives of the Left, with rallies, street speakings, to restrain anger to attempt to control the situation, which was creating a danger of a clash."

"We had men with real balls, with balls made of steel," says Rocco Bianchi, describing the role of the local leaders and the party inquest on the murder. Clearly, the idea that the party and leadership were in control is a reassuring factor in view of the fact that control was actually slipping away from the workers and their organizations.

An analogous narrative comes from the other side, in the testimony of a civil servant from the prefect's office.

> SALVATORE PORTELLI: The situation, after Trastulli's death, was going from bad to worse, and things were really dangerous. Police and workers faced each other in the streets and a clash seemed imminent. And I think it was at that time, at that moment, that the prefect—Mr. Mauro, Francesco Mauro—stepped down into the square himself, between the two sides, as it were, of the police and the rebels, and he managed to calm them down. "What're we gonna do?" says he. "You wanna cause a massacre, both of you?" And after this, some contacts started, and talks, whereby, I think, the police were called back to the quarters; and the workers' organization, the unions, they allowed a truce in the agitation. It also seems to me, I don't quite recall now, that the layoffs themselves were suspended. This, at least, I remember.

While the "balls made of steel" retrieve the slipping sense of power for the Communist workers after the setback, the largely mythical story about the peacemaking, folksy, dialect-speaking prefect reclaims the "human" side of the government institutions after the murder. Also, this story claims for the government and its representative a role above the class conflict. This was hardly the case: the prefect was ultimately responsible for law and order in the town and, indirectly, for the use of the police.

The strategy of downward vertical shift is implemented by stressing the narrators' involvement in or perception of Trastulli's death: "Wasn't I there, too?" (Canali); "My daughters were there" (Colombi); "When the news reached the Party office . . ." (Zenoni);

"I was in school at that moment" (Filipponi). Stories in this group make a very vivid use of point of view:

> ALFREDO VECCHIONI: I remember that there was a rally at the town hall, and I was standing right there on the corner by the *Credito Italiano* [bank]. It has two entrances, you know. I was hanging around, minding my own business, peacefully, not imagining a thing. All at once, they start them little motorbikes, jeeps, go to climbing up sidewalks and all, nearly ran me over, like that. Well, I just barely managed to run inside [the bank] by one door and come out the other—on the other side, there was an another column coming. I mean, that day they really were out to get us. "What's the matter," says I, "you out of your minds?" Crazy, for goodness' sake. With their things, sticks, clubs—some of those cops you still see, some of them, around town.

Other stories ply the personal mode by claiming a personal relationship with the victim:

> "Poor boy—he used to work beside me down at the machine shop. We were together, he worked on a milling machine" (Canali); "He was a serious comrade, an honest comrade who didn't mess with anyone. Only, we used, in those days, to bring [party and union] literature into the plant, which we would stick inside our pants to carry it past the guards and then gave it out to the workers inside. But the guards treated us like we were witches, and eventually I was fired, too" (Sabatini).

Trento Pitotti's narrative is a very effective case of personalization, in which the eye-witness motif and a vivid description of the narrator's own feelings are enriched by the "it could have happened to me" motif typical of narratives of work accidents, and by an analogy with the narrator's previous experiences.

> When the Trastulli thing happened, you know—when it was about Togliatti['s wounding], I wasn't scared at all; but *that* day, I sure was. Bullets were a-buzzin' right past your ears—zzzzz, zzzzz. Says I, they're gonna kill us all. We came out, the strike was on, and the police rode up. The police blocked the road, and the workers, by and by, swelled up

against them. They wanted to keep us inside. So we broke through by force. And the police, so it goes, hit this man, this Trastulli. Coulda hit me, coulda hit anybody. I mean, we were a lot. I . . . can you believe it? . . . I was scared stiff. I mean, I had been in the war, I wasn't supposed to have been afraid, but that day of Trastulli, I had . . . I hadn't actually stepped aside, but I was kinda tryin' to . . . I heard them big bullets brush my ears, I said, they're gonna kill us all, goddam the sonofabitches. But eventually it turned out well, it calmed down.

The other strategy which allows to recover Trastulli to the communal mode without hurting the community's pride is the "horizontal" chronological shift, that is, changing the date of the event. This strategy, however, raises the problem of coordinating the new placement of the event with the memory of other simultaneous or adjacent events. In order to preserve the all-important 1953 date and layoffs context, narrators need to rearrange all their personal chronology. For instance, Antonina Colombi discovers a discrepancy between the date which she reconstructs on the basis of her personal and family chronology, and the date which seems "right" to her on the basis of the event's political and social meaning.

"I remember that my daughter had just got her growth—she was so sick afterwards that she didn't have anything for a while." Colombi (who, as we have already seen, personalizes Trastulli's death by saying "my daughters were there") goes on to date her daughter's puberty: "My daughter is now forty-four; when we came back to town [after the war] she was around ten; it [her first period] happened five years later . . ."—so it must have been 1949 or 1950 at the latest.

Interestingly, her selection of period-marking events is very gender-specific. A male narrator, Salvatore Portelli, coordinates the date of the murder with other aspects of his personal chronology: the name of his boss ("It must have been 1949, because the prefect was" [Mauro]) and the purchase of an automobile ("and it was before we bought our first car, too.")

Colombi's chronology, however, clashes with the fact that she is sure Trastulli was killed on account of the layoffs. She knows very well when these took place, because her own husband and brother were fired. Finally, she solves the riddle by recalling that there were actually two waves of layoffs: the seven hundred in December 1952, and the two thousand in October 1953. All she needs to do is expand the interval, by moving the 1952 layoffs back to about 1950—helped by the fact that a policy of mass firings of workers had actually been announced (and partly implemented) as early as late 1947.

Other narrators apply the same solution. Alfredo Vecchioni, who was fired with the two thousand, also places the murder in the context of the layoffs; on the other hand, he recalls that he was still employed when it happened. So, it must have been "between the seven hundred and the two thousand." Although no narrators mention it, perhaps the fact that Trastulli died in March facilitates the placement between the December and October layoffs.

What is at stake here is, in fact, the definition of "event." Standard chronology sees the early threats and firings of 1947, the seven hundred layoffs of 1952, and the two thousand dismissals of 1953 as a series of discrete, if similar and connected events. Subjective working-class chronology perceives them as *one* protracted event— especially the 1952–53 sequence, usually referred to as "the three thousand," as if they had all been fired together—symbolized and unified by the free-floating datation of the death of Luigi Trastulli.

In fact, narrators do not seem to concern themselves excessively about chronological accuracy. Most interviewees, when I got around to mentioning that Trastulli actually died at a peace demonstration in 1949, seemed to take the information in their stride. "Well," replied Antonina Colombi, "they were all coming out of the factory, so they fired into the crowd. I mean, I am demonstrating for peace, and you kill me?" The fact that it happened near the factory apparently confirms that, whatever the details of the episode, its meaning remains the same.

Antonina Colombi is more right than it may appear at first glance. Although the politically educated steel workers of Terni were aware of the distinction between "economic" and "political" strikes (which was to become one of the grounds for the split with the conservative unions), they were also aware of their connection. Whatever the official rationale for a march or a rally, workers generally attend with all their grievances in mind.

The same dialectics can be discerned in another dramatic precedent: when the army fired on the crowd at a rally in June 1920 killing five people, the official record has it that the rally was called to protest Italian military intervention in Albania; but most contemporary narrators remember it as a protest against layoffs at the army's weapons factory in Terni. Thus, though they were called in 1949 to protest against NATO, the workers of Terni were also thinking about their jobs—in fact, they felt that Italy's participation in the alliance and the threat to their jobs were all part of the same framework of restoration of conservative power. NATO was, in a way, only the abstract shape of their very immediate problems.[20]

MEMORY AS HISTORY

To conclude, memory manipulates factual details and chronological sequence in order to serve three major functions:

1. SYMBOLIC. Trastulli's death represents the postwar working-class experience in Terni as a whole. This central symbol generates others (the jeep, the wall, the lowered gun), and finds its own symbolically adequate context;

2. PSYCHOLOGICAL. The dynamics, causes, and chronology of the event are manipulated in order to heal the feeling of humiliation and the loss of self-esteem following upon the impossibility of reacting adequately to the comrade's death (and to the loss of power which it reveals). Also, the narrative structure is rearranged in order to account for the duplicity between the official motive for the protest and the immediate concerns of the workers who attended; and

3. FORMAL. The horizontal shifting of the event endows it with an adequate time-marking function (most life stories hinge on 1953 as a turning point); all chronology is then rearranged or blurred in order to compensate for the shift.

The discrepancy between fact and memory ultimately enhances the value of the oral sources as historical documents. It is not caused by faulty recollections (some of the motifs and symbols found in oral narratives were already present in embryo in coeval written sources), but actively and creatively generated by memory and imagination in an effort to make sense of crucial events and of history in general. Indeed, if oral sources had given us "accurate," "reliable," factual reconstructions of the death of Luigi Trastulli, we would know much less about it. Beyond the event as such, the real and significant historical fact which these narratives highlight is the memory itself.

Memory as history

I. ON METHODOLOGY

2

Research as an Experiment in Equality*

Perception of an object costs
Precise the Object's loss—
Perception in itself a Gain
Replying to it's Price—
Emily Dickinson

"THAT'S WHAT THEY USED TO MAKE US SING"

In September 1974, carrying my tape recorder, I drove into Greve, a small town in the Chianti hills of Tuscany. I was there not as an independent researcher, but as an appendix to the machine. My task was to locate an acknowledged speaker of "pure" dialect, tape him for thirty minutes, and hand the tape to a team of linguists who were doing a dialect atlas of central Italy. It was all very easy—until I sat down with Alfredo Crimi, my informant, in front of the microphone and a glass of wine, and he asked: "Well, what shall we talk about?"

I was stumped. As long as he spoke dialect, the linguists didn't care what he spoke about. So, doing what comes naturally, I asked Crimi to tell me about his life as a tenant farmer on a big estate. While he talked, I asked him an occasional question about aspects that interested me. He gave details freely, but was unresponsive whenever I tried to elicit a judgment, an opinion, or a criticism.

After the required thirty minutes of tape were filled, I mentioned that I was interested in *improvvisatori, the folk poets who make up and sing improvised stanzas on any subject, from contem-

---

*Originally written in 1982; a shorter version appeared in *New York Folklore*, XIV, 1–2 (1988), 45–57.

porary politics to ancient chivalric poetry. They are found throughout central Italy; but Tuscany is the fountainhead of the tradition,
and I had never collected there. Crimi said he knew one, and took
me to his place.

When we arrived, the poet was at work in his orchard. His
name was Ferdinando Bandinelli, but his friends called him
"Dante." He waved and greeted us: "Hello, comrades!" He didn't
know me, but somehow the fact that I was with his friend defined
my politics. For the next two hours, the two men reeled off stories,
songs and poems about unions, politics, strikes, and the Communist party. When it was time for me to leave, Crimi asked the poet,
"Aren't you glad I brought this gentleman over? You see, he never
asked me about priests." It seems that, while I was "studying" him
and his answers, he had been studying me and my questions, and
had found out which side I was on.

This taught me that there are always two subjects to a field
situation, and that the roles of "observed" and "observer" are more
fluid than it might appear at first glance. It was the same lesson I
had learned from another experience four years before. In June
1970, in the hill village of Labro, on the border between Latium and
Umbria in central Italy, I met Trento Pitotti and recorded his repertoire of folk songs. Trento was by far the best folk singer I ever met,
and he knew many ritual, religious, and lyrical songs. He also sang
some "topical" songs, music-hall style, from the 1930's and 1940's.
Only one blemish marred my delight and the "perfect" tape I took
home that night: two of Trento's topical songs (both interesting and
previously uncollected) were unmistakably Fascist.

I liked him anyway. So a year later, when I happened to be
driving past Labro, I dropped by to say hello. We talked a while,
and it turned out that, far from being a Fascist, Trento was a politically active Communist. He had been a factory worker in the steel
mills of Terni twenty miles away, and lost his job in the layoffs of
1953, when the company seized the chance to get rid of most Leftist
and union activists in its workforce. Since then, he had never been
able to get another job and was making a scant living as a cobbler,
waiting to be old enough to collect a pension. I asked him why,
then, he had sung those Fascist songs. "Well," he said, "you asked
for old-time songs, songs from when I was young. That's what they
used to make us sing in those days."

Trento didn't know me, when I first recorded him. His life experience had taught him that he would be safer singing religious,
ritual, sentimental, humorous, or conservative songs to an outsider

who didn't look or talk like working-class and who had said nothing about himself. I had thought I was not supposed to "intrude" my own beliefs and identity into the interview, and Trento had responded not to me as a person, but to a stereotype of my class, manner, and speech. I had been playing the "objective" researcher, and was rewarded with biased data.

This chapter is an attempt to correlate the lessons I learned in field work about the relationship between the researcher and the "informant," with the lessons taught by Italian anthropologists, cultural organizers and political thinkers who have recognized and discussed the political implications of equality and hierarchy, sameness and otherness in field work and in the study of people's culture. The identity and role of "militant," "native," and "organic" intellectual have been crucial concerns in these studies, and in my own experience.

AN EXPERIMENT IN EQUALITY

An inter/view is an exchange between *two* subjects: literally a mutual sighting. One party cannot really *see* the other unless the other can see him or her in turn. The two interacting subjects cannot act together unless some kind of mutuality is established. The field researcher, therefore, has an objective stake in equality, as a condition for a less distorted communication and a less biased collection of data.

Equality, however, cannot be wished into being. It does not depend on the researcher's goodwill but on social conditions. The very need for anthropological research in Western societies implies the recognition and observation of otherness in subjects who are not on the same social and political plane with the observer. As long as informants who belong to oppressed or marginal social groups hesitate to open up to members of the elite, every field worker will be involved in a complicated game of hide and seek. Ernesto De Martino, the scholar and Socialist activist who first created an anthropological awareness of southern-Italian rural culture, once wrote:

> Reopening a dialogue between two human worlds which long ago ceased to speak to each other is a difficult enterprise, and it causes many burning humiliations. It humiliates me to be forced to treat people my own age, citizens of my own

country, as objects of scientific research, almost of experimentation. It humiliates me when they take me—as they have—for a revenue agent or for a show business entrepreneur traveling through Lucania in search of musicians and singers. It humiliates me to be compelled in certain villages to avoid the local Communists, to dissimulate even with them, because otherwise the priest would never tell me things I need to know.[1]

As De Martino points out, not only the observed, but also the observer is diminished and alienated when social conditions make equality impossible—as is the case in most field work experiences. And it is a fact that a great deal of information did escape him, because of the forced dissimulation involved in doing research in the country's poorest and most forgotten region, Lucania.

The field interview, therefore, cannot create an equality which does not exist, but demands it. The interview raises in both parties an awareness of the need for more equality in order to reach a more open communication. As long as the unequal hierarchy of power in society creates barriers between researchers and the knowledge they seek, power will be one central question raised, implicitly or explicitly, in every encounter between researcher and informant. Dealing with power openly makes a field interview an experiment in equality. Gianni Bosio (the founder of a radical tradition in the study of Italian folklore and working-class culture) put it this way:

> Cultural work defines its identity against the logic of assimilation [to the dominant social relationships] by creating the means for its own independent survival. Cultural work cannot help but turn into political struggle for the self-defense of culture; and political struggle becomes in turn the highest form of cultural work.[2]

A JOINT VENTURE

Trento and I became friends, and he introduced me to Dante Bartolini, a distant relative of his who was also a local poet, singer, and storyteller, as well as a symbolic figure of the anti-Fascist Resistance of 1943–44.

From under the coal heaps in his cellar and from the back of his memory, Dante dug out words and music to songs, poems, and stories he had composed or learned in his life as a farmer, steel-worker, underground anti-Fascist activist, guerrilla fighter, herb doctor, hog killer, barkeeper, and all-round village wise man. He in turn introduced me to other comrades.

Amerigo Matteucci was a construction worker, mayor of the tiny mountain village of Polino, and a fantastic improviser of highly political verse in traditional forms.

Pompilio Pileri, an innocent-looking, frail, blue-eyed man in his 70s was a former shepherd who had never owned his own sheep, who was impishly charming as he accompanied his friends' singing on the *organetto* and dramatically imposing when he performed his long song about the hardships of a shepherd's life. Luigi Matteucci, a farm hand, had (like Pompilio) never learned to read or write, but could outsing anyone (except maybe Trento himself). Their valley, the Valnerina, was the rural backdrop to the great steel mills of Terni, and the blend of rural traditional forms with urban industrial politics made the Valnerina singers and story-tellers unique.

For many years, frequent visits to Valnerina were a very important part of my life. I often took friends and co-workers with me to initiate them to this living tradition of working-class culture growing out of traditional folklore. We helped Dante and his comrades put together a program of their songs and stories and arranged for them to travel in Italy and abroad as conscious messengers of the dignity of their culture and the role of their class.

Sometime during this period, a local student who had joined me in the collecting work discovered in the archives of the University of Perugia a set of tapes which these same individuals had recorded in the late 1950s for a team of university anthropologists, conservatory ethnomusicologists and state radio technicians. These tapes contained none of our friends' political repertoire, though that material was all created before the tapes were made. Instead, they had sung only rather innocuous folk songs of love and ritual, old ballads, *stornelli*, and a few satirical pieces about local events.

This was due, in part, to the technological and academic array of the research team. In the 1950s, the radio (a state monopoly) was openly anti-Communist; so Dante and the others sang only "politically safe" material. Also, Italian folklorists had always been more concerned with the recovery of past traditions than with contemporary folklore, and even the very progressive scholars who made those tapes were influenced by this approach.

Other historical patterns were also at work. In the 1950s, workers were still smarting under the setbacks they had suffered in the post-war years. Several of the informants themselves (including Dante and Trento) had lost their jobs in 1953, and were having a hard time finding new jobs in the face of open political discrimination. No doubt they felt they had better keep their protest songs to themselves.

But when I met them in 1970, things had changed. The Left and working people in general had won dramatic gains in 1969, when a season of strikes and revitalization of the unions from below again made labor a central force in Italian society. Dante and his friends were much more secure financially, less easily blackmailed, and more confident, even eager to show their political identity in public. Also, the fact of recording was no longer a strange and intimidating experience: they had cassette recorders in their homes, and my own equipment was much lighter and less obtrusive.

This episode taught me the historically conditioned nature of field work. A changed political climate allowed the Valnerina singers an ampler exercise of free speech in 1970–72 than in 1958–59, and I was able to collect important material which had escaped researchers better professionally qualified than I but who were unable to interact in a mutual fashion with them. It was the same question with which Ernesto De Martino had struggled a generation before.

I wonder—again in view of the historical grounding of field work—how the Valnerina singers would react were I to meet them now for the first time. No doubt the legitimacy of their Communist affiliation had been established, and they would have had no qualms about voicing it. On the other hand, the present crisis in industrial (and therefore, working-class and Communist) culture would perhaps make them relate to those songs differently, as part of their history rather than of their immediate experience.

THE SOUTHERN QUESTION: REGION AND CLASS

. . . I entered those peasants' homes—wrote Ernesto De Martino—as a "comrade," a seeker of men and of forgotten human histories; I went as one who is intent on observing and verifying his own humanity, and wants to join the people he meets in working toward a better world in which we shall all be better—I, the seeker, and they, the found. Our being together as comrades, our attempt to meet within a common history, had never been experienced before in ethnological research . . . A passion to know those aspects of the present which remind us of a recent or distant past can only exist as part of the passion for transforming the present into a reality more worthy of human beings.[3]

This famous quote describes the interaction of scholarship and political involvement that characterized the best Italian anthropology in the late 1940s and 1950s. Social sciences in general had been viewed with hostility by fascism because of their latent critical potential. On the other hand, the best humanist, non-Fascist tradition—as represented by the historian and philosopher Benedetto Croce—dismissed them as "pseudo-sciences."

According to Croce, history alone can perceive the individual event in its inherent uniqueness, and is, therefore, the only true social science, while the search for patterns and the comparative approach of sociology and anthropology is only "positivistic naturalism." Croce's vision of history, besides, focused on what he described as the "ethical-political" dimension: mainly the history of elites and institutions. While it liberated Italian culture from romantic and positivistic residues (and valiantly contrasted the anti-cultural impulses of the Fascist regime), Croce's historicist approach was certainly not conducive either to a systematic interest in folklore or to a recognition of the specific historical presence of the "lower" classes.[4]

After World War II, the contact with American culture, in the context of a renewal and modernization of Italy's intellectual life, brought about the discovery of sociology and anthropology. The American and American-trained social scientists who began to work in Italy in those years found, in southern Italy, an ideal testing ground for theories on peasant societies and modernization. The South was approached more as a "problem" in modernization and uplift than as a culture in its own terms. An unstated but recognizable assumption seemed to be that the backward, underdeveloped condition of the region was, to a large extent, caused by flaws in the culture of its people. The role of "applied" social sciences, therefore, was mostly to gather the data and prepare the ground for policies brought in from above and outside. While individual researchers (such as Edward Banfield, Frederick Friedmann, Robert Redfield, and Tullio Tentori) often did work of very high intrinsic merit, they hardly interfered with the basic subordination of the South to the North, with its class system, and with the perception of the region and of its people in the dominant culture.[5]

In those same years, however, several Italian intellectuals were individually looking at the South not only as a problem in cultural and economic development, but also as a source of cultural diversity and wealth. The encounter with a "Third World" within a supposedly advanced Western nation (the "Indies of our own," as De Martino phrased it), the discovery of the otherness within ourselves, conferred a highly political charge to a small and sometime peripheral but extremely active (and, in the long term, influential) group of intellectuals.

Carlo Levi's classic book, *Christ Stopped at Eboli* (Turin: Einaudi, 1945) had opened the way. A northern, Jewish artist and intellectual exiled by fascism to an isolated mountain village in Lucania, Levi discovered there a world "beyond" everything. There is a mystic quality, as well as an artist's aesthetic vision, to Carlo Levi's South, its remoteness, its distance, and its impermeability to history. Levi is fascinated by the otherness of an apparently unchanging world which exists within his own and yet has hardly anything in common with it. On the other hand, he was in Lucania as a political exile; as such, he was able to see its people also as citizens like himself, endowed with the same rights, and deprived of them by the same oppressive system that persecuted him. They might not be part of "history" as defined by Benedetto Croce, but they certainly were not to be classed as outside humanity.[6] Simply by being there, with all its remoteness and otherness, Lucania showed that the values and principles of high Western culture were not as universal as the idealistic school of thought sometimes seemed to believe.

The most important contribution of Ernesto De Martino (himself a Southerner, a disciple of Benedetto Croce, and a Socialist organizer) was toward a redefinition of the relationship between history and the people which Croce's theory had excluded from it.[7] De Martino inherited from Croce the belief in the primacy of history, and saw himself primarily as a historian. On the other hand, the influence of Marxism and the example of Soviet folklore science made him aware of the need for a history that could account for the presence and role of the majority of mankind. While he shared Levi's deep emotional involvement with the rural South, De Martino's appreciation was not motivated by its otherness from history, but by what he conceived to be the new role of the southern rural masses (and of Third-World peoples) *within* history. "All over the world," he wrote in 1949, "the masses of the people are struggling to break into history, to free themselves of the chains that bind them to the old order."[8] In this historical upsurge, it was impossible for the historian and the anthropologist to remain only an outside observer.

While De Martino's political militancy and regional roots led him to see himself as a participant in this historic change, his consciousness of his role and identity as an intellectual also made him aware of ambiguities. As the oppressed masses "break into history," he said, they bring with them their yearning for justice (often expressed by what he called "progressive folklore," as opposed to a concept of folklore as inherently conservative and archaic); but they also bring the archaic, regressive aspects of their present culture as shaped by the experience of oppression. The rise of the masses will imply, at least for some time, a degree of "barbarization" of culture as a whole.

The intellectual's duty, therefore, is to guarantee some kind of "prophylaxis" by placing this process in historical perspective and providing the "historic pity" necessary for "archaic" cultures to be understood and protected from exploitation by the forces of reaction. The intellectuals' ability to maintain their own otherness, to preserve a distance from the masses even while they share in the struggle for their emancipation becomes necessary not only for their own salvation, but for that of the masses as well.

On the other hand, De Martino realized that this necessary distance is also the result of a historic injustice, and is an injustice in itself. When facing the southern peasants, he wrote, "I am ashamed of my privilege of not being like them, as if I had stolen something that belongs to them as well. Or, rather, I am ashamed that I accepted this filthy concession from society, that I allowed society to use all its arts to make me 'free' at this price."[9]

A complex pattern of identification and difference appears also in the work of another major southern writer, social scientist and political activist, Rocco Scotellaro. Born of an artisan and farming family in Lucania, Scotellaro strove all his life to be true to his class roots while, as a poet, a researcher, an activist and even briefly as the mayor of his native village of Tricarico, he saw a painful distance grow between himself and his own people. On the other hand, he perceived that this distance was not only the negative effect of the intellectual's estrangement, but also a condition for a more effective and conscious participation.[10]

This ambivalence shaped his political and intellectual life. When he went to jail (after leading landless peasants to seize the estates of the local landlords), Scotellaro endeavored to prove to the other inmates that he was one of them, seeking an almost prepolitical, almost paleo-Christian sense of brotherhood and of "likeness." But the inmates attempted to comfort him by telling him that he would get out soon, because "jail is not for the likes of you." Later, when he left Tricarico to study in Naples and thus be better prepared for a role of political leadership, Scotellaro remembered that the landlords and bosses, too, had often "pointed the way to the station" to him, as if to tell him that he must separate his fate from that of the illiterate masses and take his place among the educated, the elite, and the rulers.[11] The conflict between the insider's empathy and the outsider's critical eye gives shape and meaning to his unfinished autobiography as well as to his pioneering collection of life stories of southern peasants.

A double oxymoron—"native intellectual," "militant intellectual"—crosses the lives of Rocco Scotellaro and Ernesto De Martino. De Martino tells the story of the old farmhand who took him aside in an alley of the town where he was Socialist local chairman, recited to him a long poem about life of a poor farm worker, and then told him "You go on—you who know, you who can, you who shall see."[12] This is an ambiguous mandate. It may mean that the democratic intellectual will open the way, but also that the intellectual will "go on" and leave the peasant behind. For both of them, the problematic term *intellectual*—evokes a difference that keeps turning up disturbingly throughout a lifelong search for understanding, participation, and identification.

"WE HAD NO INTELLECTUALS"

As the Valnerina experiment went on, I learned first-hand what De Martino and Scotellaro teach: both the "militant intellectual" and the "native intellectual" are more complicated roles than they appear to be at first glance. Being politically close to the informants did not make me an insider; on the other hand, when the significance of the fact that I had also grown up in Terni dawned on me, this complicated rather than simplified my relationships with the interviewees.

When I met Bruno Zenoni, a leader of Terni's partisan brigade with an incredibly precise historical memory, I introduced myself as a "comrade," explaining that the motivations of my research were broadly political rather than academic. He was pleased, spoke freely, and introduced me to other people. However, I began to notice that, while his introduction was sufficient to guarantee me politically, he still always introduced me as "professor," rather than "comrade." I had stressed political homogeneity; but he was foregrounding my cultural and professional difference and otherness.

The working class of Terni always had a difficult relationship with intellectuals—a rare and mostly hostile species for generations in town, anyway. Merely looking like one had been enough to put partisans and underground anti-Fascists on their guard; more recently, young intellectuals had been easing old workers out of leadership roles in the unions and the party. On the other hand, Zenoni's generation had a high respect for culture, and the lack of education and intellectual professional skills was felt to be a serious hindrance to the growth of the working-class movement. "When we took over the city administration after the war," said Zenoni, "we had no intellectuals, and we had to do everything ourselves, with the little schooling we had." Once he felt that my politics were not antagonistic (though I wasn't a party member), the fact that I was a "professor" intrigued him with the possibility that his history, which he had been telling and reconstructing for forty years, might be collected and told by someone who had the skills to do it professionally. The lesson here was the other side of the medal from those of Greve and Labro: here, I had been displaying my sameness, but (once some kind of equality was achieved) it was my difference that was appreciated.

Meanwhile, I was learning that there was another ground of sameness: the fact that I had grown up in Terni changed the whole relationship, for myself as well as for the interviewees. It had never occurred to me to think of myself as a "native intellectual"—I wasn't born in Terni, I had always felt as a sojourner there, and I had been away for ten years before I came back to interview. Yet, while I gradually realized that I belonged to Terni more than I had ever known, my "informants" developed subtle counterinterviewing strategies to find out who I really was—like dropping names, making allusions and studying my reactions. The pattern of sameness and otherness was reproduced by the fact that I had gone to the same schools, had grown up in a working-class neighborhood, yet I came from a middle-class family. Discovering that we had met as boys on a soccer field sometimes made for a more relaxed exchange. Sometimes, however, my being a native only underscored the class difference. "So we meet again," said a steelworker, after identifying me as a grade school classmate. "Are you still the teacher's pet?"

ORGANIC OR UPSIDE DOWN

Every social group [wrote Antonio Gramsci] coming into existence on the original terrain of an essential function in the
world of economic production, creates together with itself, or-
ganically, one or more strata of intellectuals which give it homogeneity and an awareness of its function not only in the
economic but also in the social and political field.

The most influential theory of the relationship between intellectuals and the working class is the one based on Antonio Gramsci's concept of the "organic intellectual," formulated in his prison
writings. An organic intellectual of the working class is an intellectual who is or becomes part of the working class movement. Just
what makes an intellectual "organic," however, is uncertain, and
the question has been historically short-circuited by the intermedi-
ation of the political party. "The political party," Gramsci wrote,
"for some social groups is nothing other than their specific way of
elaborating their own category of organic intellectuals directly in
the political field and not just in the field of productive technique."
Therefore, "an intellectual who joins the political party of a particular group is merged with the organic intellectuals of the group itself, and is linked tightly with the group."[13]
In the guarded wording he used in order to elude prison censorship, Gramsci seems to draw the outlines of two types of organic
intellectuals: one which originates from within the "social group," a
sort of "native" intellectual with a political consciousness of class;
and another which joins the class by becoming a member of its political party. Though they have much in common, they are not the
same thing, and have been treated differently by the different currents of the post-war Italian Left.
The majority of the official and organized Left has favored the
second type of organic intellectual, in apparent harmony with the
Leninist idea that the revolutionary consciousness cannot arise from
the workers' own experience, but must be brought to them from
outside. Actually, the real roots of this approach seem to lie rather
in the continuing prevalence of a concept of the unity of culture,
derived from Croce rather than Lenin. Culture remained, therefore,
largely identified with the high culture of the ruling classes, with its
modes of production, values, and professional roles—mitigated perhaps by a wider access to education, a more democratic distribution
of information, more progressive contents, and sometimes a less ab-

struse language. Once they certify their political credentials by joining the party of the working class, organic intellectuals need change
very little of their role, status, or *modus operandi;* and they hardly
need question the *type* of knowledge with which they deal. As Gianni Bosio put it critically, the task of this kind of organic intellectual
consists only in "supplying the workers with materials and information for their uplift and improvement, turning them into targets
for a message which is only a reinterpretation of culture *tout court,*
that is of ruling culture."[14]

Bosio's criticism represents a position which was shared by the
libertarian Left minorities in the 1950s and 1960s and by what
would later become the New Left. These currents were more concerned with the first type of organic intellectual, originating directly
inside the class. A programmatic document of an influential New
Left cultural group, which named itself after Gianni Bosio, says:

> By organic intellectual we mean the intellectual which
> the working class generates from within itself. Organic, and
> intellectual, are the strike leader, the shop steward, or the
> factory-council member, because these roles imply knowledge,
> consciousness, decision making, leadership, organization. And
> further back, organic intellectuals are the folk poets and story-
> tellers, the narrators of historical memory, the traditional
> musicians, when they become aware of the meaning and rele-
> vance of their work.[15]

Gianni Bosio took up De Martino's intensely political approach
to anthropology and history, with certain very important
innovations.[16] First of all, he shifted the focus of observation from
the rural South to the industrial North, from the peasant masses to
the industrial working class (though he consistently maintained
that there were links and continuities between the two, and that the
experience of field work in rural areas provided an essential methodological background for "urban" field work). By focusing on the
modern, advanced regions of the country, Bosio gave new meaning
to De Martino's concept of "progressive folklore" and contributed to
the breakdown of the distinction between ethnology and history, replacing the narrow "folkloric man" (relevant only as the bearer of
cultural relics of the past) with the "historical man" endowed with
all his culture, from traditional folklore to progressive folklore and
modern class consciousness.[17]

Bosio's second innovation was his concept of the circularity between cultural and political work, and the consequent view of the researcher as an organizer. "The organization of culture is as important, and perhaps more important, as the production of culture."[18] He was not only the leading figure in a new "school of thought," but also the founder of a cultural-political movement, which positively claimed that the working class was not only part of history (as De Martino had shown), but had a history (and culture) of its own. The influence of this movement would be felt, though mostly indirectly, both in the radical student movements of the 1960s and in the "Hot Autumn" of the working class in 1969.

Bosio's work was based on a view of the working class as "not just an objective datum for a class-conscious culture, but as an active protagonist."[19] The function of an intellectual who sees himself also as a "militant of the working class" is, then, not to bring to the people a modified version of hegemonic culture, but to "arm the class with its own power." He called for an intellectual who should not be "organic" so much as "reversed" or "upside down"; who could "give up the privilege of being a depository of culture and accept the possibility of recognizing and receiving cultural messages from the proletarian world."[20] The upside-down intellectual will not only teach, but also learn; in the field situation, "upside-down" researchers do not *study* informants, but *learn* from them, and allow themselves to be "studied" in turn.

While Bosio's approach deals with the intellectual's relationship with the working class, it fails to face the closely linked question of the relationship of the intellectual with himself or herself. De Martino's achingly personal conflicts between the activist and the scholar, between human sympathy and scientific and critical observation are mediated, and even removed, by political militancy. Bosio's project could function best for a vanguard group, or at times of very intense political activism when a political solution to all problems seemed possible. The "upside-down" intellectual began to appear as emotionally obsolete in the late 1970s, when revolutionary hopes declined and the working class no longer fulfilled all the functions of a cultural and political model, as the organic intellectual had appeared to the radicals of the 1960s.

When the average, "mass" intellectual suffered dramatic changes in employment opportunities, income, and status; when youth culture and women's liberation beset us with the problems of the politics of private life; and when questions of sexual roles and private identity became more and more pressing, then working-class politics and culture could be seen as an answer to *some* problems, but could no longer be imagined as a satisfactory answer to all. Both the "organic" and the "upside-down" intellectual were trained to remove themselves as individuals—the former, so as to keep most of his privileges in the background and implicitly retain them; the latter, so as to set most of his personal contradictions aside. But as that awkward word—"I"—became relevant again, both of these role models and methodological approaches left too much room for false consciousness to be satisfactory any longer.

A NEW RELATIONSHIP

This brings us back to the original problem: the role of equality and difference in field research. The two concepts are related. Only equality prepares us to accept difference in terms other than hierarchy and subordination; on the other hand, without difference there is no equality—only sameness, which is a much less worthwhile ideal. Only equality makes the interview credible, but only difference makes it relevant. Field work is meaningful as the encounter of two subjects who recognize each other as subjects, and therefore separate, and seek to build their equality upon their difference in order to work together.

In these terms, research may help us cope with some of our most pressing contemporary needs: the redefinition of "self" and the crisis of political action. The recognition of the other, which is the foundation of anthropology, is at best limited unless it implies also a questioning and redefinition of the anthropologist's (or historian's) own identity. At a time in our common history when the crisis of radical and revolutionary movements has left most of us alone to face our individual and common problems, the quest for self-definition often takes the form of narcissism, cynicism, downright selfishness, and disregard for general issues. I believe that one possible function of research today is to, once again, place the question of identity on a social and interpersonal plane, and to help us recognize ourselves in what makes us similar yet different from others.

On the other hand, when the encounter takes place in the light of equality, not only the observer, but also the "observed," may be stimulated to think new thoughts about themselves. This throws a new light on an old problem: the observer's interference on the observed reality. The positivistic fetish of noninterference has developed outlandish techniques to bypass or remove this problem. I believe we ought to turn the question on its head, and consider the changes that our presence may cause as some of the most important results of our field work.[21] There is no need to stoop to propaganda in order to use the *fact* itself of the interview as an opportunity to stimulate others, as well as ourselves, to a higher degree of self-scrutiny and self-awareness; to help them grow more aware of the relevance and meaning of their culture and knowledge; and to raise the question of the senselessness and injustice of the inequality between them and us. Political work is work for change, and all these changes are highly political. At a time when politics in traditional terms of propaganda, organizations, and institutions has become unsatisfactory and at times even unsavory, the fact that our presence may facilitate meaningful change in the self-awareness of the people we meet is perhaps one still usable form of political action.

3

What Makes Oral History Different*

"Yes," said Mrs. Oliver, "and then when they come to talk about it a long time afterwards, they've got the solution for it which they've made up themselves. That isn't awfully helpful, is it?" "It is helpful," said Poirot . . . "It's important to know certain facts which have lingered in people's memories although they may not know exactly what the fact was, why it happened or what led to it. But they might easily know something that we do not know and that we have no means of learning. So there have been memories leading to theories. . . .

Agatha Christie
Elephants Can Remember

His historical researches, however, did not lie so much among books as among men; for the former are lamentably scanty on his favorite topics; whereas he found the old burghers, and still more their wives, rich in that legendary lore, so invaluable to true history. Whenever, therefore, he happened upon a genuine Dutch family, snugly shut up in its low-roofed farmhouse, under a spreading sycamore, he looked upon it as a little clasped volume of black-letter, and studied it with the zeal of a book-worm.

Washington Irving
"Rip Van Winkle"

---

*A first version, "Sulla specificità della storia orale," appeared in *Primo Maggio* [Milano, Italy], 13, (Fall, 1979), 54–60; it was reprinted as "On the peculiarities of oral history," in *History Workshop Journal*, [Oxford, England], 12 (Spring, 1981), 96–107.

MEMORIES LEADING TO THEORIES

A specter is haunting the halls of the academy: the specter of oral history. The Italian intellectual community, always suspicious of news from outside—and yet so subservient to "foreign discoveries"—hastened to cut oral history down to size before even trying to understand what it is and how to use it. The method used has been that of charging oral history with pretensions it does not have, in order to set everybody's mind at ease by refuting them. For instance, *La Repubblica*, the most intellectually and internationally oriented of Italian dailies rushed to dismiss "descriptions 'from below' and the artificial packages of 'oral history' where things are supposed to move and talk by themselves," without even stopping to notice that it is not *things*, but *people* (albeit people often considered no more than "things") that oral history expects to "move and talk by themselves."[1]

There seems to be a fear that once the floodgates of orality are opened, writing (and rationality along with it) will be swept out as if by a spontaneous uncontrollable mass of fluid, amorphous material. But this attitude blinds us to the fact that our awe of writing has distorted our perception of language and communication to the point where we no longer understand either orality or the nature of writing itself. As a matter of fact, written and oral sources are not mutually exclusive. They have common as well as autonomous characteristics, and specific functions which only either one can fill (or which one set of sources fills better than the other). Therefore, they require different and specific interpretative instruments. But the undervaluing and the overvaluing of oral sources end up by cancelling out specific qualities, turning these sources either into mere supports for traditional written sources, or into an illusory cure for all ills. This chapter will attempt to suggest some of the ways in which oral history is intrinsically different, and therefore specifically useful.

THE ORALITY OF ORAL SOURCES

Oral sources are *oral* sources. Scholars are willing to admit that the actual document is the recorded tape; but almost all go on to work on the transcripts, and it is only transcripts that are published.[2] Occasionally, tapes are actually destroyed: a symbolic case of the destruction of the spoken word.

The transcript turns aural objects into visual ones, which inevitably implies changes and interpretation. The different efficacy of recordings, as compared to transcripts—for classroom purposes, for instance—can only be appreciated by direct experience. This is one reason why I believe it is unnecessary to give excessive attention to the quest for new and closer methods of transcription. Expecting the transcript to replace the tape for scientific purposes is equivalent to doing art criticism on reproductions, or literary criticism on translations. The most literal translation is hardly ever the best, and a truly faithful translation always implies a certain amount of invention. The same may be true for transcription of oral sources.

The disregard of the orality of oral sources has a direct bearing on interpretative theory. The first aspect which is usually stressed is origin: oral sources give us information about illiterate people or social groups whose written history is either missing or distorted. Another aspect concerns content: the daily life and material culture of these people and groups. However, these are not specific to oral sources. Emigrants' letters, for instance, have the same origin and content, but are written. On the other hand, many oral history projects have collected interviews with members of social groups who use writing, and have been concerned with topics usually covered by the standard written archival material. Therefore, origin and content are not sufficient to distinguish oral sources from the range of sources used by social history in general; thus, many theories of oral history are, in fact, theories of social history as a whole.[3]

In the search for a distinguishing factor, we must therefore turn in the first place to form. We hardly need repeat here that writing represents language almost exclusively by means of segmentary traits (graphemes, syllables, words, and sentences). But language is also composed of another set of traits, which cannot be contained within a single segment but which are also bearers of meaning. The tone and volume range and the rhythm of popular speech carry implicit meaning and social connotations which are not reproducible in writing—unless, and then in inadequate and hardly accessible form, as musical notation.[4] The same statement may have quite contradictory meanings, according to the speaker's intonation, which cannot be represented objectively in the transcript, but only approximately described in the transcriber's own words.

In order to make the transcript readable, it is usually necessary to insert punctuation marks, which are always the more-or-less arbitrary addition of the transcriber. Punctuation indicates pauses distributed according to grammatical rules: each mark has a conventional place, meaning, and length. These hardly ever coincide with the rhythms and pauses of the speaking subject, and therefore, end up by confining speech within grammatical and logical rules which it does necessarily follow. The exact length and position of the pause has an important function in the understanding of the meaning of speech. Regular grammatical pauses tend to organize what is said around a basically expository and referential pattern, whereas pauses of irregular length and position accentuate the emotional content, and very heavy rhythmic pauses recall the style of epic narratives. Many narrators switch from one type of rhythm to another within the same interview, as their attitude toward the subjects under discussion changes. Of course, this can only be perceived by listening, not by reading.

A similar point can be made concerning the velocity of speech and its changes during the interview. There are no fixed interpretative rules: slowing down may mean greater emphasis as well as greater difficulty, and acceleration may show a wish to glide over certain points, as well as a greater familiarity or ease. In all cases, the analysis of changes in velocity must be combined with rhythm analysis. Changes are, however, the norm in speech, while regularity is the norm of writing (printing most of all) and the presumed norm of reading: variations are introduced by the reader, not by the text itself.

This is not a question of philological purity. Traits which cannot be contained within segments are the site (not exclusive, but very important) of essential narrative functions: they reveal the narrators' emotions, their participation in the story, and the way the story affected them. This often involves attitudes which speakers might not be able (or willing) to express otherwise, or elements which are not fully within their control. By abolishing these traits, we flatten the emotional content of speech down to the supposed equanimity and objectivity of the written document. This is even more true when folk informants are involved: they may be poor in vocabulary but are often richer in range of tone, volume and intonation than middle-class speakers who have learned to imitate in speech the monotone of writing.[5]

ORAL HISTORY AS NARRATIVE

Oral historical sources are *narrative* sources. Therefore the analysis of oral history materials must avail itself of some of the general categories developed by narrative theory in literature and folklore.

This is as true of testimony given in free interviews as of the more formally organized materials of folklore.

For example, some narratives contain substantial shifts in the "velocity" of narration, that is, in the ratio between the duration of the events described and the duration of the narration. An informant may recount in a few words experiences which lasted a long time, or dwell at length on brief episodes. These oscillations are significant, although we cannot establish a general norm of interpretation: dwelling on an episode may be a way of stressing its importance, but also a strategy to distract attentions from other, more delicate points. In all cases, there is a relationship between the velocity of the narrative and the meaning of the narrator. The same can be said of other categories among those elaborated by Gérard Genette, such as "distance" or "perspective," which define the position of the narrator toward the story.[6]

Oral sources from nonhegemonic classes are linked to the tradition of the folk narrative. In this tradition distinctions between narrative genres are perceived differently than in the written tradition of the educated classes. This is true of the generic distinction between "factual" and "artistic" narratives, between "events" and feeling or imagination. While the perception of an account as "true" is relevant as much to legend as to personal experience and historical memory, there are no formal oral genres specifically destined to transmit historical information; historical, poetical, and legendary narratives often become inextricably mixed up.[7] The result is narratives in which the boundary between what takes place outside the narrator and what happens inside, between what concerns the individual and what concerns the group, may become more elusive than in established written genres, so that personal "truth" may coincide with shared "imagination."

Each of these factors can be revealed by formal and stylistic factors. The greater or lesser presence of formalized materials (proverbs, songs, formulas, and stereotypes) may measure the degree in which a collective viewpoint exists within an individual's narrative. These shifts between standard language and dialect are often a sign of the kind of the control which speakers have over the narrative.

A typical recurring structure is that in which standard language is used overall, while dialect crops up in digressions or single anecdotes, coinciding with a more personal involvement of the narrator or (as when the occurrences of dialect coincide with formalized language) the intrusion of collective memory. On the other hand, standard language may emerge in a dialect narrative when it deals with themes more closely connected with the public sphere, such as politics. Again, this may mean both a more or less conscious degree of estrangement, or a process of "conquest" of a more "educated" form of expression beginning with participation in politics.[8] Conversely, the dialectization of technical terms may be a sign of the vitality of traditional speech and of the way in which speakers endeavor to broaden the expressive range of their culture.

EVENTS AND MEANING

The first thing that makes oral history different, therefore, is that it tells us less about *events* than about their *meaning*. This does not imply that oral history has no factual validity. Interviews often reveal unknown events or unknown aspects of known events; they always cast new light on unexplored areas of the daily life of the nonhegemonic classes. From this point of view, the only problem posed by oral sources is that of verification (to which I will return in the next section).

But the unique and precious element which oral sources force upon the historian and which no other sources possess in equal measure is the speaker's subjectivity. If the approach to research is broad and articulated enough, a cross section of the subjectivity of a group or class may emerge. Oral sources tell us not just what people did, but what they wanted to do, what they believed they were doing, and what they now think they did. Oral sources may not add much to what we know, for instance, of the material cost of a strike to the workers involved; but they tell us a good deal about its psychological costs. Borrowing a literary category from the Russian formalists, we might say that oral sources, especially from nonhegemonic groups, are a very useful integration of other sources as far as the *fabula*—the logical, causal sequence of the story—goes; but they become unique and necessary because of their *plot*—the way in which the story materials are arranged by narrators in order to tell the story.[9] The organization of the narrative reveals a great deal of the speakers' relationships to their history.

Subjectivity is as much the business of history as are the more visible "facts." What informants believe is indeed a historical *fact* (that is, the fact that they believe it), as much as what really happened. When workers in Terni misplace a crucial event of their history (the killing of Luigi Trastulli) from one date and context to another, this does not cast doubts on the actual chronology, but it does force us to rearrange our interpretation of an entire phase of the town's history. When an old rank-and-file leader, also in Terni, dreams up a story about how he almost got the Communist Party to reverse its strategy after World War II, we do not revise our reconstructions of political debates within the Left, but learn the extent of the actual cost of certain decisions to those rank-and-file activists who had to bury into their subconscious their needs and desires for revolution. When we discover that similar stories are told in other parts of the country, we recognize a half-formed legendary complex in which the "senile ramblings" of a disappointed old man reveal much about his party's history that is untold in the lengthy and lucid memoirs of its official leaders.[10]

SHOULD WE BELIEVE ORAL SOURCES?

Oral sources are credible but with a *different* credibility. The importance of oral testimony may lie not in its adherence to fact, but rather in its departure from it, as imagination, symbolism, and desire emerge. Therefore, there are no "false" oral sources. Once we have checked their factual credibility with all the established criteria of philological criticism and factual verification which are required by all types of sources anyway, the diversity of oral history consists in the fact that "wrong" statements are still psychologically "true," and that this truth may be equally as important as factually reliable accounts.

Of course, this does not mean that we accept the dominant prejudice which sees factual credibility as a monopoly of written documents. Very often, written documents are only the uncontrolled transmission of unidentified oral sources (as in the case of the report on Trastulli's death, which begins: "According to verbal information taken . . ."). The passage from these oral "*ur*-sources" to the written document is often the result of processes which have no scientific credibility and are frequently heavy with class bias. In trial records (at least in Italy, where no legal value is accorded to the tape recorder or shorthand transcripts), what goes on record is not the words actually spoken by the witnesses, but a summary dictated by the judge to the clerk. The distortion inherent in such procedure is beyond assessment, especially when the speakers originally expressed themselves in dialect. Yet, many historians who turn up their noses at oral sources accept these legal transcripts with no questions asked. In a lesser measure (thanks to the frequent use of shorthand) this applies to parliamentary records, minutes of meetings and conventions, and interviews reported in newspapers: all sources which are legitimately and widely used in standard historical research.

A by-product of this prejudice is the insistence that oral sources are distant from events, and therefore undergo the distortion of faulty memory. Indeed, this problem exists for many written documents, which are usually written some time after the event to which they refer, and often by nonparticipants. Oral sources might compensate chronological distance with a much closer personal involvement. While written memoirs of politicians or labor leaders are usually credited until proven to be in error, they are as distant from some aspects of the event which they relate as are many oral history interviews, and only hide their dependence on time by assuming the immutable form of a "text." On the other hand, oral narrators have within their culture certain aids to memory. Many stories are told over and over, or discussed with members of the community; formalized narrative, even meter, may help preserve a textual version of an event.

In fact, one should not forget that oral informants may also be literate. Tiberio Ducci, a former leader of the farm workers' league in Genzano, in the Roman hills, may be atypical: in addition to remembering his own experience, he had also researched the local archives. But many informants read books and newspapers, listen to the radio and TV, hear sermons and political speeches, and keep diaries, letters, clippings, and photograph albums. Orality and writing, for many centuries now, have not existed separately: if many written sources are based on orality, modern orality itself is saturated with writing.

But what is really important is that memory is not a passive depository of facts, but an active process of creation of meanings. Thus, the specific utility of oral sources for the historian lies, not so much in their ability to preserve the past, as in the very changes wrought by memory. These changes reveal the narrators' effort to make sense of the past and to give a form to their lives, and set the interview and the narrative in their historical context.

Changes which may have subsequently taken place in the narrators' personal subjective consciousness or in their socio-economic standing, may affect, if not the actual recounting of prior events, at least the evaluation and the "coloring" of the story. Several people are reticent, for instance, when it comes to describing illegal forms of struggle, such as sabotage. This does not mean that they do not remember them clearly, but that there has been a change in their political opinions, personal circumstances, or in their party's line. Acts considered legitimate and even normal or necessary in the past may be therefore now viewed as unacceptable and literally cast out of the tradition. In these cases, the most precious information may lie in what the informants *hide*, and in the fact that they *do* hide it, rather than in what they *tell*.

Often, however, narrators are capable of reconstructing their past attitudes even when they no longer coincide with present ones. This is the case with the Terni factory workers who admit that violent reprisals against the executives responsible for mass layoffs in 1953 may have been counterproductive, but yet reconstruct with great lucidity why they seemed useful and sensible at the time. In one of the most important oral testimonies of our time, *The Autobiography of Malcolm X*, the narrator describes very vividly how his mind worked before he reached his present awareness, and then judges his own past self by the standards of his present political and religious consciousness. If the interview is conducted skillfully and its purposes are clear to the narrators, it is not impossible for them to make a distinction between present and past self, and to objectify the past self as other than the present one. In these cases—Malcolm X again is typical—*irony* is the major narrative mode: two different ethical (or political, or religious) and narrative standards interfere and overlap, and their tension shapes the telling of the story.

On the other hand, we may also come across narrators whose consciousness seems to have been arrested at climatic moments of their personal experience: certain Resistance fighters, or war veterans; and perhaps certain student militants of the 1960s. Often, these individuals are wholly absorbed by the totality of the historical event of which they were part, and their account assumes the cadences and wording of *epic*. The distinction between an ironic or an epic style implies a distinction between historical perspectives, which ought to be taken into consideration in our interpretation of the testimony.

OBJECTIVITY

Oral sources are not *objective*. This of course applies to every source, though the holiness of writing often leads us to forget it. But the inherent nonobjectivity of oral sources lies in specific intrinsic characteristics, the most important being that they are *artificial, variable, and partial*.

Alex Haley's introduction to *The Autobiography of Malcolm X* describes how Malcolm shifted his narrative approach not spontaneously, but because the interviewer's questioning led him away from the exclusively public and official image of himself and of the Nation of Islam which he was trying to project. This illustrates the fact that the documents of oral history are always the result of a relationship, of a shared project in which both the interviewer and the interviewee are involved together, if not necessarily in harmony. Written documents are fixed; they exist whether we are aware of them or not, and do not change once we have found them. Oral testimony is only a potential resource until the researchers calls it into existence. The condition for the existence of the written source is emission; for oral sources, transmission: a difference similar to that described by Roman Jakobson and Piotr Bogatyrev between the creative processes of folklore and those of literature.[11]

The content of the written source is independent of the researcher's needs and hypotheses; it is a stable text, which we can only interpret. The content of oral sources, on the other hand, depends largely on what the interviewers puts into it in terms of questions, dialogue, and personal relationship.

It is the researcher who decides that there will be an interview in the first place. Researchers often introduce specific distortions: informants tell them what they believe they want to be told and thus reveal who they think the researcher is. On the other hand, rigidly structured interviews may exclude elements whose existence or relevance were previously unknown to the interviewer and not contemplated in the question schedule. Such interviews tend to confirm the historian's previous frame of reference.

The first requirement, therefore, is that the researcher "accept" the informant, and give priority to what she or he wishes to tell, rather than what the researcher wants to hear, saving any unanswered questions for later or for another interview. Communications always work both ways. The interviewees are always, though perhaps unobtrusively, studying the interviewers who "study" them. Historians might as well recognize this fact and make the best of its advantages, rather than try to eliminate it for the sake of an impossible (and perhaps undesirable) neutrality.

The final result of the interview is the product of both the narrator and the researcher. When interviews, as is often the case, are arranged for publication omitting entirely the interviewer's voice, a subtle distortion takes place: the text gives the answers without the questions, giving the impression that a given narrator will always say the same things, no matter what the circumstances—in other words, the impression that a speaking person is as stable and repetitive as a written document. When the researcher's voice is cut out, the narrator's voice is distorted.

Oral testimony, in fact, is never the same twice. This is a characteristic of all oral communication, but is especially true of relatively unstructured forms, such as autobiographical or historical statements given in an interview. Even the same interviewer gets different versions from the same narrator at different times. As the two subjects come to know each other better, the narrator's "vigilance" may be attenuated. Class subordination—trying to identify with what the narrator thinks is the interviewer's interest—may be replaced by more independence or by a better understanding of the purposes of the interview. Or a previous interview may have simply awakened memories which are then told in later meetings.

The fact that interviews with the same person may be continued indefinitely leads us to the question of the inherent incompleteness of oral sources. It is impossible to exhaust the entire memory of a single informant; the data extracted from each interview are always the result of a selection produced by the mutual relationship. Historical research with oral sources therefore always has the unfinished nature of a work in progress. In order to go through all the possible oral sources for the Terni strikes of 1949 to 1953, one ought to interview in depth several thousand people: any sample would only be as reliable as the sampling methods used, and could never guarantee against leaving out "quality" narrators whose testimony alone might be worth ten statistically selected ones.

The unfinishedness of oral sources affects all other sources. Given that no research (concerning a historical time for which living memories are available) is complete unless it has exhausted oral as well as written sources, and that oral sources are inexhaustible, the ideal goal of going through "all" possible sources becomes impossible. Historical work using oral sources is unfinished because of the nature of the sources; historical work excluding oral sources (where available) is incomplete by definition.

WHO SPEAKS IN ORAL HISTORY?

Oral history is not where the working classes speak for themselves. The contrary statement, of course, would not be entirely unfounded: the recounting of a strike through the words and memories of workers rather than those of the police and the (often unfriendly) press obviously helps (though not automatically) to balance a distortion implicit in those sources. Oral sources are a necessary (not a sufficient) condition for a history of the nonhegemonic classes; they are less necessary (though my no means useless) for the history of the ruling classes, who have had control over writing and leave behind a much more abundant written record.

Nevertheless, the control of historical discourse remains firmly in the hands of the historian. It is the historian who selects the people who will be interviewed; who contributes to the shaping of the testimony by asking the questions and reacting to the answers; and who gives the testimony its final published shape and context (if only in terms of montage and transcription). Even accepting that the working class speaks through oral history, it is clear that the class does not speak in the abstract, but speaks *to* the historian, *with* the historian and, inasmuch as the material is published, *through* the historian.

Indeed, things may also be the other way around. The historian may validate his or her discourse by "ventriloquizing" it through the narrators' testimony. So far from disappearing in the objectivity of the sources, the historian remains important at least as a partner in dialogue, often as a "stage director" of the interview, or as an "organizer" of the testimony. Instead of discovering sources, oral historians partly create them. Far from becoming mere mouthpieces for the working class, oral historians may be using other people's words, but are still responsible for the overall discourse.

Much more than written documents, which frequently carry the impersonal aura of the institutions by which they are issued— even though, of course, they are composed by individuals, of whom we often know little or nothing—oral sources involve the entire account in their own subjectivity. Alongside the first person narrative of the interviewee stands the first person of the historian, without whom there would be no interview. Both the informant's and the historian's discourse are in narrative form, which is much less frequently the case with archival documents. Informants are historians, after a fashion; and the historian is, in certain ways, a part of the source.

Traditional writers of history present themselves usually in the role of what literary theory would describe as an "omniscient narrator." They give a third-person account of events of which they were not a part, and which they dominate entirely and from above

(above the consciousness of the participants themselves). They appear to be impartial and detached, never entering the narrative except to give comments aside, after the manner of some nineteenth-century novelists. Oral history changes the writing of history much as the modern novel transformed the writing of literary fiction: the most important change is that the narrator is now pulled into the narrative and becomes a part of the story.

This is not just a grammatical shift from the third to the first person, but a whole new narrative attitude. The narrator is now one of the characters, and the *telling* of the story is part of the story being told. This implicitly indicates a much deeper political and personal involvement than that of the external narrator. Writing radical oral history, then, is not a matter of ideology, of subjective sides-taking, or of choosing one set of sources instead of another. It is, rather, inherent in the historian's presence in the story, in the assumption of responsibility which inscribes her or him in the account and reveals historiography as an autonomous act of narration. Political choices become less visible and vocal, but more basic.

The myth that the historian as a subject might disappear in the objective truth of working-class sources was part of a view of political militancy as the annihilation of all subjective roles into that of the full-time activist, and as absorption into an abstract working class. This resulted in an ironical similarity to the traditional attitude which saw historians as not subjectively involved in the history which they were writing. Oral historians appear to yield to other subjects of discourse, but, in fact, the historian becomes less and less of a "go-between" from the working class to the reader, and more and more of a protagonist.

In the writing of history, as in literature, the act of focusing on the function of the narrator causes this function to be fragmented. In a novel such as Joseph Conrad's *Lord Jim*, the character/narrator Marlow can recount only what he himself has seen and heard; in order to tell the "whole story," he is forced to take several other "informants" into his tale. The same happens to historians working with oral sources. On explicitly entering the story, historians must allow the sources to enter the tale with their autonomous discourse.

Oral history has no unified subject; it is told from a multitude of points of view, and the impartiality traditionally claimed by historians is replaced by the partiality of the narrator. "Partiality" here stands both for "unfinishedness" and for "taking sides": oral history can never be told without taking sides, since the "sides" exist inside the telling. And, no matter what their personal histories and beliefs may be, historians and "sources" are hardly ever on the same "side." The confrontation of their different partialities—confrontation as "conflict," and confrontation as "search for unity"—is one of the things which make oral history interesting.

4

"The Time of My Life":
Functions of Time in Oral History*

STORIES IN TIME

To tell a story is to take arms against the threat of time, to resist time, or to harness time. The telling of a story preserves the teller from oblivion; the story builds the identity of the teller and the legacy which she or he leaves for the future.

In order for the teller to recover himself or herself from time and to move ahead into time, the tale must be preserved. This applies to individual as well as to collective tales: to the myths which shape the identity of a group, as well as to the personal recollections which shape the identity of the individual.

That a tale is a confrontation with time is implicit in the attempt to carve out a special time in which to place the tale—a time *outside* time, a time *without* time. It is the time of myth, and the time of the fairy tale (as in "once upon a time"). It may be the time of certain personal recollections: the "back-in-slavery-times" formula used in black tradition to introduce both folk tales and personal or family narratives; or the "before-the-war" or "before-Fascism" formula which removes events from ordinary chronology in many life histories and personal recollections, and even helps turn a historical figure like Antonio Gramsci into a semi-mythical character.[1]

I will attempt here to explore the relationship between time and storytelling—between time and stories as they are told by oral narrators, as they are shaped by the collector's presence, and as they are written down by the historian—in cultures endowed with and shaped by writing.

---

*First published in *International Oral History Journal*, II, 3 (Fall, 1981) 162–180.

There are times for telling stories. For examples, there are tales—such as the reading of the Gospel in the Mass—which take on a special quality from the context of the telling. There are also favorable and available times for personal stories: family gatherings, corn-shuckings, parties, union or political meetings, or the old men's long afternoons on the park bench or in the tavern drinking wine.

On the other hand, all of time may be storytelling time, in a diffuse, day-by-day construction of a person's autobiography:

> PORTELLI. Your daughter says you have told her a great deal about your life. At what times exactly do you tell her about it?
>
> SOLIDEA GABRIELLI. All the time.
>
> ROSANNA GABRIELLI. For instance, when I come home and I complain that I've had a hard day, and I'm tired, she gets going: "What do you mean? When I was your age . . . this and that . . . you know what kind of life we had to lead," and so on and so forth.
>
> SOLIDEA GABRIELLI. Or perhaps I tell her, you come home nowadays and you find all your clothes pressed and all your things in order; and you don't realize that when I was young, I used to do all these things by myself, and my mother expected me to . . .

Tales go with time, grow with time, and decay with time. This is why cultures develop methods to wrest some independence from time and to preserve words. The formalization of discourse (which also includes poetry) is another weapon in the struggle with time. Poetry is one such method: the formulas used by oral poets are a tool which slows down time and allows them to compose in performance, while speaking or singing.[2] In some societies, specialized individuals, families, and lineages may be entrusted with preserving words, as is the case with the African *griots*.

Still, stories do change. Even myths change and die: not only with space, as Claude Lévi-Strauss has said, but also with time. Fairy tales change, as Propp implies when he mentions genetic relationships at the root of the metamorphosis of the folk tale.[3] Myths change in spite of the fact that their keepers may perceive them as changeless, precisely because their task is to show that it is possible to resist time-change. Life histories and personal tales depend on time, if for nothing else, because they undergo additions and subtractions with each day of the narrator's life. They are much like those medieval chronicles which were, as Lotman says, "isomorphic" with reality because the periodical registration of events made it possible to view them as texts with no final boundary, growing indefinitely along the axis of time.[4] Therefore, a life history is a living thing. It is always a work in progress, in which narrators revise the image of their own past as they go along. The difficulty which collectors (and narrators) often experience in ending an interview shows their sense that the story they have been telling is open-ended, provisional, and partial.

It isn't only a matter of not having reached an end. Myths are about a finished past, yet they also change when the group changes. So do people's versions of their pasts change when the individual changes. Personal change tends to be much more erratic and short-ranged than collective change but, also, often much more conscious and willed. An individual's claim in telling his or her story will often be both to consistency and change, both to coherence and development. Narrators thus establish that they are both the same person they always were, and a different person, too. Thus stories change both with the quantity of time (the amount of experience the speaker had accumulated) and with the quality of time (the aspects which she or he will want to stress at the time of the telling). No story will be repeated twice in the identical manner. Each story we hear is unique.

The researcher's path crosses the narrator's at erratic times, and the collected life history is the result of this chance occurrence. Of course, the researcher may have planned the encounter; but the interviewee hasn't. There is, normally, no reason inherent in the narrators' lives why researchers should knock on their door at any particular time.

At what time in the life cycle the story is told is, however, a crucial factor in its shape. We are all aware that an old person's memory may be damaged and faulty. In the spring of 1980, I interviewed Carlotta Orientali, then ninety-three years old, who had been the secretary of the anarcho-syndicalist union in Terni in the 1910s, and she was unable to tell me anything about her experience. It wasn't only a question of memory; she was physically too weak even to utter what she *did* remember. So her story will go untold, which would probably not have been the case if I, or someone else, had tracked her down and interviewed her twenty years before. Not her memory, but our timing was "at fault."

Time influences the tale in terms of circumstances. I met and interviewed Remo Righetti, a leader of the underground anti-Fascist opposition of the 1920s in Terni—a very good speaker and endowed with a fine memory—on the day his only grandchild had been taken into the hospital with a broken arm. He talked to me for several hours, but he was not as effective as he usually is. Of course, I interviewed him again, but a "twice-told tale" is often a surrogate. One may obtain details and clarify obscurities, but I will never get this man's full personal narrative as it would have been had our first meeting occurred under different auspices.

Repeating interviews does, however, help to fight time. As understanding and friendship grow, details which were withheld at first may be revealed. This was my experience with Tiberio Ducci, a farm workers' leader in Genzano in the Roman hills. He insisted in denying what everyone knew, and what he knew *I* knew—that he and his comrades had used sabotage in a strike in 1906. He could finally bring himself to admit this fact only after three interviews (at first, with tape recorder off). But again, time interfered. When I went back for a fourth interview, this man's memory and lucidity, so bright a year before, had been lost. Again, it was my timing which caused a year to pass between interviews.

This brings up another aspect of the fluidity of oral narratives: the fact that time takes away as much as it adds. There is a limit to how much material can be stored in an individual's or a group's memory. Every time new information is added, old information seems to be discarded in an uninterrupted process of selection. As Lotman and Uspenskij showed, culture is essentially directed against forgetfulness, and it controls forgetfulness by turning it into one of the mechanisms of memory.

The interaction between the historian and the source creates a brand new type of storytelling time. A person may have been telling her or his story for a lifetime, but may never have been asked to spend a whole afternoon or weekend telling it to a receptive, if demanding, professional listener. This of course influences the rhythm and tone of the tale, though not necessarily for the worse. I am not saying that the historian's presence "ruins" the tale, but merely that it changes it. In fact, interview time is felt to be status-loaded time. The fact that the interview takes place means that the narrator is recognized. "Giving" time to interviewers is often a rare opportunity to "take" time for oneself. Often, historians upset an implicit hierarchy: I have seen the look of surprise on men's faces when they realized I also wanted to hear what their wives and children had to tell.

The final result of this encounter is that the oral discourse is transferred on tape and finally into writing. While this assures that the words will be preserved and may be recalled, it also freezes their fluidity. (Italian, like Spanish, has an appropriately metaphoric word to define what happens to sounds on tape: *incidere, grabar*—to carve, as if on stone.) No matter how much we talk about ourselves as "oral" historians, the very technology of our work is to turn the oral into the written word, to freeze fluid material at an arbitrary point in time. This is perhaps neither "good" nor "bad"; there is probably nothing to be done about it anyway. But we ought to be at least aware that this is what we do.

TIME IN STORIES

Historians may be interested in reconstructing the past; narrators are interested in projecting an image. Thus, historians often strive for a linear, chronological sequence; speakers may be more interested in pursuing and gathering together bundles of meaning, relationships and themes, across the linear span of their lifetimes. Much depends on the historian's approach. If the initial question is "tell me the story of your life," the starting point of the tale may be different than if the question were "tell me about yourself." Sometimes, historians will be interested in speaking to a given person about a given event, period, or subject; but speakers will often forcibly reintroduce the time and events in which *they* are interested. For example, in a family interview, in which I was interested mostly in the women's stories about local outlaws of the late 1800s, the husband, Mario Fagioletti, spoke for an hour and a half about his adventures as an orderly in the Navy during World War II. His purpose was to establish his image in the context of the interview: his story began (as an interruption on his wife's) with the statement "I have always been a revolutionary." He probably wanted to establish rank in comparison with the great old-time bandits, and with a relative of his wife's who had been a famous anti-Fascist in the 1930s, and who had also been discussed in the interview. Also, he probably wanted to claim his portion of interview time, since the women of the family had gotten most of the attention.

Time also enters tales in the guise of the "velocity" of narrative: the ratio between the duration of the telling and the duration of the events referred to.[5] Before that, there is a speed of speech— the number of syllables uttered in a given time and the duration of certain nonpunctual sounds. All of this may be quite idiosyncratic. Often, the habit of speaking to a familiar audience will induce narrators to mention long and/or important episodes only in passing, especially if they have told them before; or to allude to them within other parts of the narrative. Researchers will often need to slow the narrator down, or ask for explanations and details, sometimes on aspects or episodes which may be of interest to the historian but may appear marginal to the narrator.

The velocity of speech is also loaded with meaning. One speaker whose speech we measured was consistently faster when the story was personal and in dialect, than when he discussed general and political subjects and used standard Italian. The historian's presence, again, may influence this aspect; for instance, dialect-speakers attempting to express themselves in a language closer to the interviewer's (or endowed with higher status) may slow their pace considerably.

Thus, narrators are often quite creative with their handling of time. One is, in fact, more likely to find narrative devices akin to those of contemporary, even experimental literature, than to the linear disposition of historical narrative time. What has been said about *avant-garde* literature may sometimes be true for oral autobiographies or historical narratives: "traditional art may be said to place the *text in time; avant-garde*, or modern art in general, breaks the tradition and places *time in the text.*"[6]

By way of examples, I will mention some of the ways in which narrative time varies the shape of the oral historical storytelling. In one celebration of the liberation from Fascism, in Genzano, six elderly militants were asked to reminisce in public about their experiences. They tacitly arranged themselves by seniority (expressed by political experience, rather than age). The first (and least-authoritative) speaker described life in Genzano in 1943 under German occupation and Allied gunfire from nearby Anzio. After him, each speaker proceeded to "explain" the anti-Fascist Resistance by setting its roots and origin farther and farther back in time. The second speaker described guerrilla actions in the 1940s; the next explained that these actions could not have been possible without the underground organizations of the 1920s and 1930s—which was, in turn and by successive speakers, accounted for by the strong pre-World War I Socialist tradition shown by victories in local elections; by the farm laborers' strike of 1906; and by the great rebellion of 1898. The circle was completed when the first speaker, Leonardo Bocale, traced in another interview the roots of Genzano's revolutionary tradition to the riots which greeted Pope Pius IX's visit to the town in 1848: thus, the history of anti-Fascism came to be told competitively and backwards.

Bocale's account of the events of 1848 was interwoven with stories of 1898 in a fashion which he described as "shuttlework". "I go back and forth [in time] like a shuttle," he said.

"Shuttlework" is a good description of another typical way of handling time in oral narratives. Solidea Gabrielli used this form throughout her interview:

> We used to have a little grocery store, so we had to get up early in the morning to go and fetch milk, and vegetables, with our little cart; always a troubled life. But we never rebelled. We never did. We took it gladly, philosophically; I was always singing. Today, their life [her daughter's and son's], if they have to get up early once, it looks like they're going through some tremendous kind of trial, a sacrifice or something. And then I think, when I was your age, we'd get up early every morning to gather firewood in the thickets . . .

Both the backward search for roots of the Genzano anti-Fascists and the running educational and admonitory function of the Terni housewife's "shuttlework" indicate that the story is being told with the present in mind. In fact, shuttlework is often linked with the use of history as a repertory of examples, and thus with diffuse storytelling. More than once, in the Genzano town square, I overheard bits of political conversations among old people, in which comparisons and references to the past were interwoven with the discussion of contemporary issues. Later, I was to find that this is an ingrained structure in Harlan County coal miners' discourse in Kentucky.

Another form may be compared to a wheel, with a circular rim and spokes branching out in all directions from one central core of meaning. This was the case of Solidea Gabrielli's husband, Mario. He told his life in a very free manner, moving back and forth along paradigmatic threads (work conditions, police repression, and family matters) and shifting from one to the other in free associative form.

Before the taping began, he had described his first day in the factory, as if it were the first day worth remembering in telling the story of his life. The actual recorded text, however, began with the complaint that, though he had worked in the steel mills for forty years, he had been recently denied a loyalty medal because of his political trial in 1949 during the aftermath of the death of Luigi Trastulli, a worker who was killed by the police during a peace demonstration. He told about the trial, then went on to working conditions and other subjects, often prompted by my questions. After a few hours, when it was time to close the interview and the tape recorder had been actually turned off, Gabrielli repeated the initial sequence. He told again, with more detail, the story of his first day in the factory, and concluded: "This is my life. I'm proud of it. My family is proud of me, and if I don't get the medal next year, they're going to hear from me."

The whole tale might be described as an amplification and demonstration of a central statement concerning his image of himself and the recognition he gets from his family but is denied by his employers because of his political background. In a way, although the interview covered a span of half a century, it was all about this very present dilemma.

All aspects of time in the text as recorded are thus the result of a compromise between two interacting subjects. I will describe here one interview with Bruno Zenoni, another anti-Fascist leader from Terni, noting the compromises achieved in a cooperation which evolved gradually in the course of the interview and can be very clearly reconstructed from the analysis of the tape and transcript.

The final text may be divided, ultimately, into chronological units: family and childhood, beginning of fascism and early work experiences; underground organizing and jail; war and resistance; important post-war events; and the present. The move from one unit to the next is always the result of *my* decision. A question about a new theme signals that I have "had enough" about the period under discussion and we may move forward. (Occasionally a longer pause indicates that Zenoni has exhausted a given theme.) On the other hand, within each section Zenoni moves freely back and forth in time, though roughly observing a basic chronology. This compromise depends on two specific factors:

1. This speaker's sense of time is closer to mine than in most other cases. Zenoni was personally interested in history, and had done some archival research, helped students with dissertations, and met and talked frequently with intellectuals;
2. His long life is all meaningful to him. There is no single event or epoch which may function as a starting point or pivot. This makes it easier to take chronology as the organizing factor.

It must be noted, however, that chronology broke down once the narration reached the present (which, of course, is harder to describe in narrative form). Then, a freer use of time prevailed: the present was discussed in comparative, shuttlework fashion, with constant references to the 1920s and the Resistance. Often, especially with regard to daily life, Zenoni gave more vivid and detailed descriptions of the past in contrastive terms with the present than he had when discussing those times specifically. In fact, his emotional involvement was higher, since the past was being made relevant to the present. He had offered initially a more "bookish" selection of events and narrative approach; only later, he appreciated that I was also interested in personal, everyday details and their historical meaning. Thus, toward the close of the interview he brought up certain aspects of the partisan war, which he had censored earlier. They were now relevant by contrast to the discussion of contemporary political violence and terrorism; also, he felt he knew me better by now and I would use the information "correctly."

One of Edith Wharton's ghost stories begins: "It was the Autumn after I had typhoid . . ."[7] There is no date: this conveys the impression that the narrator is speaking to an intimate circle of listeners who need no other information. The reader, however, does not possess this information; thus, the formula creates for us a sense of timelessness. It might have been *any* time. We are excluded from the narrator's sense of time, and thus from the sense of reality which she shares with her circle. (In fact, she can see ghosts. We can't.) This is a common experience for oral historians. For instance:

> AMERIGO MATTEUCCI: One more thing I remember, about Bianchini's farm. It was a farm with thirty-four hands. On Sunday mornings, the overseer would come in and say, "Say, you guys, no going to town today. We have work to do . : ." Can you believe that? It was slavery. That's what it was, slavery.

This may have been anytime in the first half of the current century. In a way, this is what the narrator expresses by his use of a durational verbal form, the imperfect tense. He wishes us to perceive the slowness of change in the lives of farm workers. Other information in the interview allowed me to place the story in the late 1930s. But to the narrator's immediate circle of friends (one of whom was present at the interview), the place and the superintendent's name are enough to narrow down the temporal range to a significant degree, and to evoke a whole wealth of shared stories and associations from which I was excluded. So, I had to ask, "When was this?" We are always asking people to be more explicit in their time references, reminding them that they are speaking to an audience which includes at least one outsider.

Some narrators (like Bruno Zenoni) pay more attention to dates. James Hall, a miner from Lynch, Kentucky, described a pitched battle with nonunion labor in nearby Benham. When I asked him when it was, he said:

> I think it was along about '37 or '38, along in there, some-where along in there. Now you take old Earl Turner, he should know. He's got memories a whole lot better than mine about these things. He might give you the exact date and time on this stuff. There's one other feller over here, Walt Hammons, he's real good about dates and things like that.

A group of researchers from the *Circolo Gianni Bosio* (a Rome-based organization of militant historians, musicians, and anthropologists) working in the neighborhood of San Lorenzo in Rome were faced with a similar problem with dates. They were trying to reconstruct the daily life of the community under fascism, but kept coming across descriptions and anecdotes which neither they nor their informants could conclusively place before or after the March on Rome (28 October 1922) which is the conventional date of the beginning of the Fascist regime.

This of course was a problem for the historians, since they were trying to identify the changes caused by fascism in people's lives. It was, perhaps, less of a problem for the narrators. They were implicitly saying that—at certain levels at least—the advent of fascism had caused no immediate changes in their lives. This is a common occurrence. In Nuto Revelli's great book, *Il mondo dei vinti*, one keeps coming across passages like this: "Then fascism came, but I didn't even notice. I wasn't concerned . . . fascism did us neither good nor harm, just as if it had never been."[8]

A line about the Depression from a Lonnie Johnson blues song tells it perfectly: "People ravin' 'bout hard times, I don't know why they should/If some people were like me, they didn't have no money when times was good." The distinction between "good" and "hard" times is just as blurred for some black people as the distinction between Fascist dictatorship and bourgeois democracy was for Revelli's poor mountain farmers, or even for the urban proletarians of San Lorenzo. Our partitions of time—pre-fascism, fascism, post-fascism—may not be as universal as we think.

Which of course does not mean that they are meaningless: only, that they operate at certain levels and not at others. To political activists, or to politically-minded individuals, fascism made a difference immediately. They had to give up political activity. They may have gone to jail. They resented the loss of whatever freedom had existed before. For some, on the other hand, fascism really begins in the mid–1920s, with the deflationary policies which curtailed the workers' standard of living, and merges with the memories of the Great Depression. Others realized that times had changed when they were faced with the choice of whether to take a party card in order to get (or keep) a job—or when their neighbor's son was arrested or disappeared mysteriously into exile in France. Still others realized what had happened only with wartime restrictions, when, as Ambrogio Filipponi put it in Terni, the "wartime anti-fascism" of the "housewives who were sick and tired of having to line up for food"geared into the politics of underground opposition.

THE PHONOLOGY OF TIME

Time is a continuum; placing an event in time requires that the continuum be broken down and made discrete. As is the case with other continua—for example, sounds—this process happens at two levels: that of linear succession and that of vertical simultaneity. Periodization—the syntagmatic plane—is the procedure with which we are more familiar: it divides time horizontally into periods and epochs, which are"hung" on key events operating as partitions and interpreters of each sequential unit.

But time is also broken down on the paradigmatic axis—simultaneity—much as a phoneme is broken down into traits or a musical note into harmonics: all happening at the same time, all inseparable from one another, yet logically distinct. If we take a conventional time unit, a second or a year, there is always more than one event happening in it. (To put it another way, each conventional time unit can be used to designate more than one event.) Concurrent events, on the other hand, concern different areas of meaning and experience: the weather, politics, work, sports, family, and the like. They may then be grouped with events which can be referred to the same area of meaning but occurring at other times, thus forming syntagmatic lines running parallel to one another. I propose to call *level* each syntagmatic line, and *mode* the pattern evolved by each narrator in order to combine the events of his or her life into homogeneous levels and to select one level as dominant in the periodization and interpretation of the narrative.

We may roughly define three vertical strata (tentatively geared to space referents) around which levels and modes are arranged in most narratives:

> *Institutional:* the sphere of politics, government, parties, unions, and elections; the national and international historical context; and ideology. Space referent: the nation and the world.
>
> *Collective:* the life of the community, the neighborhood, and the workplace; strikes, natural catastrophes, and rituals; and collective participation in "institutional" episodes. Space referent: the town, the neighborhood, and the workplace.
>
> *Personal:* private and family life; the life cycle of births, marriages, jobs, children, and deaths; and personal involvement in the two other levels. Space referent: the home.

Modes and levels are never entirely separate and discrete, since they all run simultaneously and mix together in the way people think and tell their lives. They interweave, communicate and influence each other. The placing of one event in one level is not intrinsic to the event itself, but to the narrator's perspective. A war may be narrated as the inevitable consequence of imperialistic capitalism; as the catastrophe which caused the destruction of a hometown; or as the personal experience of fighting and the tragedy of the loss of relatives and friends. It may be in no mode at all, as was the case with William Faulkner's character, Rosa Coldfield, in *Absalom, Absalom!,* who perceived the Civil War as "hearing and losing the knell and doom of her native land between two tedious and clumsy stitches on a garment"—a neat contrast between the "institutional" ("doom of her native land") and "personal" modes.[9] On the other hand, love and marriage are quite personal matters, but some narrators may deal with them politically (as in stories about the divorce and abortion referendums of the 1970s). Much the same may be said of health (and the state of the local hospital, or the national sanitary system).

The choice of mode depends on the narrator's intentions. Mario Fagioletti, the former "rebel" navy orderly, spent more than an hour telling us how he manipulated the officers and stole their liquor—meanwhile ("between drams," we might say, following

Miss Coldfield's example) there was a war going on, in which his ship was sunk, which he got around to mentioning in the final five minutes of his long fabulation.

Since the choice of mode determines which events are "pertinent" (that is, endowed with meaning), mode becomes relevant to periodization: to date an event is not just to place it in the linear sequence, but also to decide in which sequence it belongs. Thus, James Hall, who claimed he was no good with dates, managed the following sequence:

> PORTELLI: I think this was around 1935, wasn't it? In 1935, they had a company union.
>
> HALL: 1935 they had a company union, what you call a ULE [United Lynch Employees]. When we got our union shop, I guess that what year that was, it was around about '38. Somewhere along in there. Why, I remember it so well I married on the first day . . . no, on the last day of March in 1938. First day of April, they struck and stayed out seven weeks.

In Hall's story, told in the personal mode, union history is part of family history rather than of "labor history" or some such abstraction; he tells the story of how the United Mine Workers of America came to Lynch in terms of his father's involvement in it, and he "hangs" the crucial episodes on the periodization of private life. In the same way, Antonina Colombi reconstructs the date of the death of Luigi Trastulli with the help of the chronology of her daughter's puberty, while Salvatore Portelli recurs to another personal, but typically male frame of reference (the name of his boss or the purchase of the first family car).[9]

Luigi Trastulli was killed during a peace demonstration in 1949, but many narrators believe that he died during violent protests against loss of jobs in 1953. There is also frequent manipulation of the circumstances of his death and of the narrator's point of view. The widespread horizontal and vertical shifting in chronology and modes reveal the way in which individuals face, in different forms, a crisis of meaning and identity which concerns the community as a whole (and therefore remove the event from the "collective" mode). This shared activity of memory also shows how problematic is our concept of "event," both as an "objective" concept, and as opposed to "duration" (as in the French *Annales* distinction between *évenementiel* and *longue durée*).

From the point of view of duration, narrators do not see the struggles of 1949 to 1953 as a sequence of discrete events but as a continuous whole. One way of looking at the death of Trastulli in 1949 and the barricades in 1953 is as two phases of one event: an offense-response sequence lasting four years rather than a few minutes. Duration becomes secondary, as if time had been suspended in between. To use another literary example (again from Faulkner in *Light in August*): time was suspended for Reverend Hightower between the shot which killed his grandfather in Grant's cavalry charge in the Civil War and Joe Christmas's death in the 1930s. For the workers of Terni, time was suspended by the shot which killed Luigi Trastulli in 1949, and resumed its course in October 1953 when the workers struck back.

Again, the example of phonology may give us some clues. Phonemes (events) break down the continuum of sound (time) into discrete and apparently punctual, durationless units. Phonemes, however, do not exist in and by themselves. They are recognized as such in a conventional pattern of relations with other pertinent sounds; a sound which is a phoneme in one convention (one language) may be mere noise in another. Events also are identified according to a pattern of meaning. What is an event to us (the rise of fascism) may be a non-event to Nuto Revelli's mountaineer (and vice versa). A phoneme and a historical event are not purely "objective" realities, but are constructed as such by the network of relationships in which they are inserted. The attribution of relevance and meaning is a cultural act, depending on a complex interplay of individual and collective patterns. What Alberto Asor Rosa said of contemporary art may apply to this cultural construction of history: "*Conventional* time (the time of the text) keeps replacing *real*, or supposedly real time (history, the existence of mankind), and openly claims for itself a higher degree of authenticity."[10]

Phonemes (and events) are usually conceived as punctual; however, this is only an effect of the convention through which we conceptualize them. In fact:

A. Phonemes (events) are not discrete, but appear to be so because of our need to organize our perception of sound (time). Sounds do not follow one another in neat linear succession, but are often intertwined; a sound which we perceive as coming after another may have been articulated before the other was finished, or even simultaneously. Likewise, before one "event" is finished, the "next" may be well under way;
B. Phonemes have a temporal dimension (*morae* in vowels; "diffuse" versus "compact" in consonants), which confers on them a linear quality beyond the "vertical" traits.

Thus, though the concept of "event" seems to indicate a "point" in time, events stretch in all directions. For example, *when* did the New York Stock Exchange "crash"? As John Kenneth Galbraith noted, before the 24 October date became canonized, dates varying from the twenty-third to the twenty-ninth were also used. The "crash" metaphor implies a sudden collapse, but certain descriptions resemble more of a slow-motion movie. The crashing lasted at least a week.[11]

Thus, both the concept of "event" and "duration" appear to be more a matter of how we look at (and narrate) history, than something inscribed into "objective" reality. One other teaching of the stories about the death of Luigi Trastulli is that the act of remembering is, itself, a historical fact operating in the *longue durée* dimension. It is the task of those who deal with history rather than chronicles, to study, not only the mechanics of the material event, but the events of the remembering and the telling—the patterns of the remembering and the forms of the telling—through which we are able to perceive the "event" in the first place.

MEMORY AS WRITING

A classic science-fiction novel—Ray Bradbury's *Fahrenheit 451*—describes a future in which books are forbidden and burned, while members of the underground opposition each memorize a book in order to save them from oblivion. It is a remarkable description of the relationship between writing and memory, and of the problems faced by a society without writing which aims to save its cultural heritage from the erosion of time.

The first problem, of course, is how to pass on the text of the culture as it was molded by previous generations. Techniques of memory are developed. "All of us," says a character in Bradbury's novel, "have photographic memories, but spend a lifetime learning how to block off the things that are really *in* there . . . we've got the method down to where we can recall anything that's been read once."[12]

Futuristic methods aside, cultures in which writing is absent have been using the techniques of formalization of speech in order to make existing texts more lasting and to recall time-tested materials to build new texts and transmit them in turn. The extent of this process, however, is limited by the extent of the total memory available to the group, whether shared or individually. This is when the concept of "communal censorship" becomes useful.[13] Censorship functions less as a means of ensuring conformity than as a tool of selection, a means of keeping to a workable minimum the extent of the collective discourse which must be borne in memory.

The prevalence of orality in a culture, therefore, implies a basic distinction between ephemeral and permanent texts: the former belong to the time of their creation and utterance, while the latter become (to borrow an expression Kurt Vonnegut's *Slaughter House 5*) "unstuck in time" and can be transmitted down or recalled up. This distinction coincides roughly with that of formalized and informal texts, inasmuch as formalization is a memory device; also, still more roughly, with the distinction between texts belonging to the individual and texts belonging to the group.

A text survives when it can be detached from the person of its first creator and from the time of its creation, and be appropriated (and changed) by the group to be used at another time. Otherwise, it is forgotten and allowed to die. "The chance that [an individual's] creative achievement would survive him depends primarily upon its 'utility'," writes Jack Goody: "it is a now or never matter; there is no chance that his discovery will be acclaimed at a later date; there is no store for subsequent recall."[14] Of course, this is a heuristic and methodological distinction. There is perhaps no "individual" text without communal meaning. On the other hand, all "communal" texts are filtered by individual consciousness. Between "formalized" and "informal" texts, lies a continuum of intermediate forms.

When writing becomes available, the question of the preservation of words is radically changed. More and more texts may be preserved, regardless of their immediate communal "utility." An "unlimited proliferation characterizes . . . the written tradition in general,"[15] write Jack Goody and Ian Watt; an individual's contribution, ignored by contemporaries, may be preserved to be recognized and used at a later time. The possibility of saving individual discourse from time generates new forms of discourse. Examples include the diary, the great written form of bourgeois self-searching; and the novel, the achievement which marks the hegemony of the written and printed word and of the individualistic values of the bourgeoisie. For centuries, from *Robinson Crusoe* onward, novels have been bearing individuals' names and telling individuals' stories. This became possible because the individual *counts*—or is *said* to count—both socially and politically; and because individual stories can be saved and therefore become worth saving. If people are, in Bradbury's words, "dust jackets on books," the book inside may now be their own.

The presence of writing liberates orality from the burden of memory. The preservation of texts, the certification of contracts, the chronicle of events are all performed more efficiently by writing. Social and individual memory is thus relieved of the task of preserving "communal" texts to be handed down in time, and orality is freed (precisely when individual texts become worthwhile) for individual and ephemeral discourse. Time, once an obstacle that oral discourse needed to overcome, turns into its main asset. The link between oral speech and time enhances the values of immediacy, improvisation, and spontaneity. Because writing has taken up its burdens, orality can be free to flow and change with time rather than attempt to resist it at all costs. Freed from responsibilities toward social memory, speakers are allowed to place their own subjectivity and experience at the center of the tale.

Again, it is more a matter of degree than a "yes-or-no" alternative. Oral speech remains impregnated with memory; otherwise, even the most common conversation would be impossible. But it is no longer obsessed with it. Formalized speech forms, rather than the main task of cultural preservation, carry out specialized tasks with their aesthetic functions often prevailing over more directly practical ones. (Again, a caveat is in order: the inculturation of children is still carried out orally for the first few years of their lives.)

Writing gives orality back to time, and time back to the individual. It introduces into oral discourse certain cultural characteristics of written culture: the interplay of the individual with society which shapes the novel and is the basic pattern of autobiography and fiction film. So, when people use the time-worn (*time* worn) cliché "my life is a novel" (which I heard, among others, from Maggiorina Mattioli—whose life story, discussed in chapter 13 in this book, did indeed resemble *Absalom, Absalom!*), they mean at least two things:

1. My life is worth telling. This has become more true since the novel has been concentrating on common people and experiences rather than on larger-than-life heroes and adventures. The legitimation of the telling, in fact, no longer lies in the exceptionality of content alone, but also largely on the mastery of storytelling form. Hence,
2. My life is told like a novel, and for the same reasons. The very act of telling it shapes my identity; my handling of time, point of view, and motivation are not unlike those found in novels (especially contemporary ones). We might reverse the formulation and say that it is the modern novel which is much like oral auto-

biographies, thereby proving correct Alberto Asor Rosa's provocative statement that *avant-garde* art is "the only mimetic, i.e. realistic, art of our time."[16]

Thus, our effort to make life histories, oral narratives, and personal tales fit into the pattern of historical discourse—or at least to read them in such terms as to conform to the pattern—does worse than overlook the form of these stories: it ignores their meaning. But once we are aware of this, what do we do about it? Removing the problem at the root—at the time of the interview—is, as we have seen, impossible. We should rather recognize this fact and work with it at the level of our writing, where the narrators' words are appropriated into the historian's text and become part of our discourse.

There is no question of not meddling with the form of the source. Even if we tried to print interviews in their entirety, we would end up with lengthy and almost unreadable texts (in which the mechanical fidelity of transcriptions thinly veils the qualitative betrayal of turning beautiful speech into unreadable writing); and we would be turning oral into written discourse anyway, which is no minor interference. No, the problem cannot be faced in terms of purity—of saving the sources' "authenticity" from the "infection" brought by contact with the historian. Rather, we ought to work it the other way around: let our discourse be infected—hybridized, mongrelized, and "miscegenated"—by the novelistic quality of the narrators' storytelling.

This blending of discourses and narrative styles is not achieved by merely quoting the sources. It is, rather, a matter of modifying our narrative approach, our own handling of time and point of view. Let our history be as factual, logical, reliable, and documented as a history book needs to be. But also let it contain the dialogic history of its making, and the experience of its makers. Let it show how historians themselves grow, change, and stumble through the research and the encounter with other subjects. Speaking about the "other" as a subject is far from enough, until we see ourselves as subjects among others and we place time in ourselves and ourselves in time.

II. TWO INDUSTRIAL CULTURES

Section One
Terni, Umbria, Italy

5

Dividing the World: Sound and Space in Cultural Transition*

SOUNDS

According to Roman Jakobson and Morris Halle, musical scales and phonological structures are devices which culture uses to shape nature by imposing rules of distinction on the natural continuum of sound. Roland Barthes also describes linguistic articulation and signification as acts of "cutting out" the "amorphous masses" of continuous matter. Turning *continua* into *discreta* appears to be a basic operation of language and culture.[1]

There are, however, more than one set of rules by which the natural world may be divided into culturally meaningful segments and grids. When different systems of division meet, clash, or overlap, crises occur—more so if the encounter does not take place on a basis of equality. In this chapter, I will try to explore how contradictory and changing rules for the divisions of sound and space have affected folk and working-class culture in a specific industrial and urban context.

Music

Describing a recorded performance by Amerigo Matteucci, a folk singer from Polino, a hill village near Terni, Giovanna Marini notes that the singer stays outside any established harmonic-modal sys-

---

*Presented at the Fourth International Oral History Colloquium, Aix-en-Provence (France), September 1982. Translated as "Geteilte Welt. Laute und Raume in Kulturellen Ubergang," in L. Niethammer and A. von Plato, eds., *"Wir kriegen jetzt andere Zeiten"*. *Auf der Suche nach der Ehrfahrung der Volkes in Nachfaschistischen Länderen*, Verlag J. H. Dietz Nachf, Berlin-Bonn 1985, band 3, 220–231.

tem and rhythmic pattern, until a guitar accompaniment (played by an urban folk musician) "chains him down" to the chromatic scale and a 4/4 pattern. Traditional music in the Terni area is mostly unaccompanied singing, influenced by archaic modal scales and by the bagpipe styles of nearby Abruzzi and Sabina. The voice and the bagpipe (like the old-time fiddle) are "continuous" musical instruments, which can generate a progression of sounds rather than the distinct intervals of a musical scale. Thus, they allow for the preservation of archaic modes and for a great variety of intonation, glissando, approaches to peak notes, and noncanonic intervals.[2]

The advent of radio and recorded music, and the introduction of industrially produced, fixed-intonation instruments (such as the small, accordion-like *organetto* which replaced the bagpipes in most of central and southern Italy) impose modern scales and stable rhythmic patterns. In the *organetto*—which was described as the "rural instrument of the industrial age"—notes are mechanically determined and placed along a discrete categorial scale; nonstandard, traditional intervals cannot be played. The *organetto*, however, also has a continuous bass note, which can be used to accompany singing in the old modes. Ignoring the *organetto's* fixed intonation, the voice moves freely between the tones and semitones of the diatonic scale. Many performances of traditional singers accompanied by the *organetto* are struggles for mastery between different cultural systems—even when the singing and the playing are performed by the same individual.[3]

These cultural systems, however, are not endowed with equal prestige and power. Their encounter may result in a fascinating "otherness" comparable to the Afro-American "blue note" (itself the outcome of a similar overlapping of cultures); more often, however, it results in sheer heterophony, total assimilation, or silence. However, even when trying to sing modern pop songs, traditional singers still reveal their cultural history in their singing style. The resistance of the "vernacular" culture to assimilation is couched in one of its less-conscious (and most deep-rooted) elements—the human voice—and is revealed by the "deviant" rural use of an industrial artifact, the *organetto*.

Speech

The poem *"Il Partigiano"* ("The Partisan") was found among the papers of Dante Bartolini, the singer, poet and storyteller from Castel di Lago near Terni. The first verse reads (line numerals added, punctuation simplified):

1. *Cari lettori mi perdonerete*
2. *se qualche sbaglio lo vinissi a fare*
3. *che poca scuola o fatto lo sapete*
4. *ecco perché mi venco a lamentare.*
5. *La colpa chi la há lo indenterete*
6. *quelli che ci fan sembre tribolare*
7. *notte e giorno a tutte quante l'ore*
8. *per colpa di chi è sembre traditore.*

[Dear readers, forgive me / if I make mistakes. / You know I had little schooling, / and this is why I complain. / You know who is to blame: / those who always betray us / and make us suffer / each hour, night and day.]

A thorny problem in oral history is the translation of speech (especially nonstandard speech) into writing. Transcription cannot avoid obliterating some meaningful marks of regional, class, or personal identity and history. Therefore, it is interesting to see how informants themselves deal with the problem, and this poem is a good starting point. The problem of having had "little schooling" was a recurrent theme in the poetry and speech of Dante Bartolini, who remained steeped in oral culture while aspiring to the mastery of written forms and attempting to imitate the poetic models he had learned in elementary school. Thus, his poem is addressed to "readers," and was probably laboriously composed while he sat at his kitchen table. On the other hand, it was couched in the *ottava rima* (eight-line stanza) which, though derived from literary poetry, is used in the folk culture of central Italy for public improvised singing rather than for private reading and writing. This is reflected by the fact that each line, as is customary in oral composition, is a distinct semantic unit. Bartolini probably thought out each line mentally before setting it down on paper. In setting down his poem, he was therefore faced with some of the same difficulties which I had in transcribing his interviews.

Bartolini's written text diverges at several points from standard spelling. Some errors are grammatical, with no phonetic implications, resulting from the widespread difficulty with the use of accents or *h*'s in auxiliary verbs (*o* for *ho* or *ò*; *hà* for *ha* or *à*). In Italian, however, most spelling differences imply phonetic ones, and therefore the pattern of errors reveals some of his problems with sounds. The most relevant pattern is the following:

Line	Bartolini	Standard	Translation
4	ve*n*co	ve*n*go	I come
5	i*n*de*n*terete	i*n*te*n*derete	you'll understand
6,8	se*mb*re	se*mp*re	always

In many central and southern varieties of Italian, the contrast between voiced and unvoiced stops (which holds for most Romance languages) is neutralized following a nasal consonant: it is impossible to contrast a minimal pair such as, say, *quanto* ["how much"] versus *quando* ["when"].[4] Usually, this confusion is not crucial: non-standard varieties which lack the nasal + unvoiced stop cluster generally recreate the distinction by assimilating /*mb*/ or /*nd*/ clusters as /*mm*/ and /*nn*/:

Standard	Central Italian Vernacular	Translation
qua*nd*o	qua*nn*o	when
qua*nt*o	qua*nd*o	how much

In the process of cultural change, vernacular speakers learn from school or the media that Standard Italian possesses both the clusters between nasal consonants and unvoiced stops which are absent in the vernacular (*quanto*), and the nasal + voice stop ones (*quando*) with which they are familiar. There are, however, no set rules to discern whether a word including the latter is the correct Standard norm or a carryover from vernacular use (and therefore "wrong"). Where they had no problem in discriminating between *quanno* and *quando,* they are now confronted with one form—*quando*—which is both Standard Italian for "when" and vernacular for "how much." All words with an *nt, nd, nc, ng, mb, mp* (and sometimes *nn, mm*) raise the same problem. The only thing speakers know for sure is that their former use is wrong; the loss of the comfortable haven of vernacular speech is not compensated by full mastery of standard forms. Especially in situations where they feel they must prove themselves culturally (such as writing a poem or releasing an interview), many speakers will reflect in the uncertainty of their speech a deep-set cultural uncertainty about themselves.

In Terni, the tension is heightened by the fact that the local dialect is even less respectable than that of other towns. Terni had a relatively obscure history before industrialization, and so never developed an educated, dialect-speaking elite. On the other hand, all the technical and much of the political cadre which came after the founding of the steel mills in 1885 originated from outside and spoke with other accents. Vernacular poetry and dialect are, indeed, still very lively and appreciated; they reflect, however, more of a defensive reaction than an adjustment to modernization, and, in fact, there is broad gap between this sub-literary written dialect and the actual speech of the majority of the population. Dialect, therefore, bears a more than the usual connotation of class and geographical subordination. A writer in a Fascist youth paper complained in 1943 that "Our dialect has neither the precious style of Siena, nor the sweetness of Venice or the aristocratic poise of Piedmont. It is rough, ordinary, full of phonetic distortions."[5] Self-deprecation is thus built into the language. The nasal/stop cluster becomes a crisis point, which speakers (and transcribers) face with a diversified set of strategies. What makes Bartolini's poem interesting is that he uses all these strategies in one context. Let us examine the existing strategies, confronting them with uses in the poem.

1. *Preserving vernacular pronunciation* (lines 6 and 8: *sembre*). Straight vernacular is used mostly by individuals who do not have to prove their status, either because they have none (which is the case I encountered more often in Terni), or because their status is otherwise assured;

2. *Hypercorrectism* (line 4: "ve*n*co). Reversing the vernacular rule, all nasal consonants are followed by unvoiced stops, even in words in which voiced stops would be the required Standard form. This practice is found mostly among mobile, status-conscious groups, or in individuals with "little schooling" in places of authority. I found many examples in police records, or in the speech and writing of local government officials and union officials.

3. *Blurring the distinction* (line 5: "inde*n*terete"). This is the most dramatic strategy of all, because it reveals that the speaker is afraid of committing himself or herself. This may be achieved in two ways:

a. Using the two spellings and sounds interchangeably, as if they were not linguistically pertinent. This may be the function of the reversal of the two clusters in this example. In several interviews, the Standard Italian *andiamo* ("let's go") is rendered phonetically, by the same speaker and in the same context, but in several different ways—*annàmo, anniàmo, antiàmo, andjàmo*—as if he or she were putting out feelers to test which use meets with the most favorable reaction.

b. Blurring the sound itself. In verse 10 of the same poem, Bartolini rhymes *conto* ("account") with *mondo* ("world"). Apparently, the contrast does not hold for him, and the two words are actually pronounced as if they rhymed. The blurring of the sound may also be part of the reason for most inconsistent or reversed spellings.

The plurality of strategies in very brief contexts shows that the one certain factor is uncertainty.[6] When working-class speakers blur the contrast between *nt* and *nd* by uttering a sound placed somewhere along the theoretically empty continuum which separates a full *t* from a full *d*, they attempt—either consciously or unconsciously—to escape the disruptive consequences of the overlapping of two sets of rules for the division of sounds. Since they cannot find a rule for the Standard Italian distribution of phonemes, they abolish it. The result is similar to the noncanonic sounds of singers who are unaccustomed to the diatonic scale; but, in this case, the blurring is conscious, and therefore much more anxious.

The resulting "lax, half-voiced" sound[7] they utter is a good metaphor of a cultural condition. The lax rendition is achieved by withholding energy, as if the speaker were trying to become invisible. The hesitant, whispered, in-between sound (especially in a language like Italian which has no *shwa* sounds) is one step removed from silence. The feeling of having lost one language without mastering another, with the consequent loss of meaningful social presence, is often expressed by the interviewees. In wistful, faultless old-time dialect, Elchide Trippa says that he "would speak less and say more" if he could carry on the whole interview in pure dialect. Bruno Zenoni, in another context, formulates the problem in terms of political as well as cultural deprivation:

> We didn't used to have intellectuals in the [Communist] party. So they didn't used to do as they do now. When at meetings with workers they'll laugh and make fun of you if a comrade says a word wrong or he doesn't know what it means. When this happens—you know, we're not in this for money, for a career—you just give up and keep quiet. Leaders didn't used to mind the propriety of language; now they rub it in. And, you know, I'm a volunteer, so I just shut up and go home.

Propriety and *property* in Italian, are the same word; and language is one of the forms of property with which social historians ought to be concerned. Oral historians in particular do only half their job if they concentrate on *what* people say and ignore *how* it is said—the narrative form, the sound shape of the narrative. A slurred, half-voiced consonant may contain information which a detailed life story might not explicitly reveal.

SPACE

Urban Space

RICCARDO DE CESARIS: The part of town I live in is kind of strange because it's the periphery of two different neighborhoods—*Le Grazie* [working class] and *Città Giardino* [middle class]. And all around, it was rural, which has been a great influence to me, growing up. I mean, I was pretty close to the places where young people meet, school and everything; and yet I had a chance to be in touch with the old rituals of harvest, sowing, the vintage season, right with these generations of rural families that were living next door. People who really lived only on agriculture, you know; and they had a whole ritual, timed their lives differently, the day was made up of different relationships. It allowed me to be in touch with the two dominant cultures in Terni, the dominant industrial and the peasant one, too, which today are fairly mixed, though I remember that ten, eleven years ago they were quite distant. And then, two hundred meters south, *Quartiere Giardino*—white-collar people. I mean, three realities within three hundred meters from each other.

Rural and urban space form in Terni an uneasy continuum rather than a sharp discrete. Industry was not a spontaneous local growth, but was dropped in wholesale from the outside. For several decades, the new factories and the industrial neighborhoods grew outside the town's walls while local townspeople still went to work in the surrounding fields. On the other hand, a large portion of the working class was composed of rural immigrants or commuters who continued to live in the villages nearby.

While immigration and commuting created complex networks of kinship between the town and the country, urban industrial workers were variously influenced by the rural environment. They learned from their rural comrades how to grow orchards to supplement their incomes. They also used the countryside for hikes and picnics, as well for hunting; and took to the hills in mass during the war either as refugees or partisans. While voicing hostility to "rural" factory workers whom they accused of unfair competition for jobs and political and professional incompetence, industrial workers also learned from them forms of workplace sociability and alternative uses of time which helped counteract the hegemony of industrial ideology. The geographical continuum between town and country created economic and ideological divisions between different groups of workers; and yet, across these divisions, they shared an unrecognized cultural continuum.

While town and country maintained this intense communication, boundaries grew within the urban space itself. Perhaps the most crucial one was the invisible line which divided the older and poorer parts of town from the new middle-class sections inaugurated after the 1870s. This line ran at the corner where Corso Tacito (the "new" Main Street, inaugurated in the 1870s) enters Piazza del Popolo (Town-Hall Square, traditionally known as "People's Square"). Some of the most dramatic events in the history of Terni took place there: from the killing of five workers by the police in 1920, to the barricades after the layoffs in 1953. "That point, was like a nerve center; it was a division between the bourgeoisie and the proletariat," says Arnaldo Lippi.

The evolution of folk rituals marks the recognition and successive blurring of this geographic class boundary. Lippi recalls that this "was the place of the *merancolata*. In this carnival ritual named after the *merancola*, a stone-hard hybrid of orange and lemon, groups of working-class youths would gather on one side of the square and middle-class youths at the other, pelting each other with *merancola*: "It was neat, precise, a neat cut: on this side you'd see us, on the other all those . . . ," Lippi said. The ritual reflected a perception of Terni as split along class lines, by representing a discrete urban space, crossed by an ideal barrier. "I mean, divided by class! Don't forget that that's where the *Circolo dei Signori* [Gentlemen's Club] was—gentlemen's club, can you believe it?" Lippi asked.

The *merancolata* lasted until the 1940s; by then, however, it had been gradually replaced by another ritual, the *Cantamaggio*. This was originally a rural wassail ritual, which the local petty bourgeoisie revived at the turn of the century as a symbol of their identity which was threatened by industrialization. It soon began to gravitate toward the town, and, in the Fascist period, was appropriated by the authorities. It became a representation of the town's new identity, from rural roots to industrial present, in the form of a parade of decked floats and a vernacular song festival. The ritual now culminates, every May Day, in the symbolic crossing of the old border in front of the authorities. The class division of the *merancolata* is thus replaced by the continuity of urban space, representing the continuum of a fluid citizenry instead of the discrete of conflicting social classes.

This move from class to citizenry can be seen both as a loss of class identity and as a sign of social mobility. Let us compare the ways in which two former factory workers of different generations describe the changes taking place between the 1950s and 1960s:

> BRUNO ZENONI: Workers have been expelled from the center of town. The [Town Hall, or "people's"] square used to be full of them, in their overalls, every morning. They were proud, not ashamed, of their overalls. Since the new housing projects were built in the periphery, workers were kicked out of the center. They don't live there anymore.
>
> MARIO VELLA: The generations before me, they would go strolling in the square—[proclaiming] "I work at the steel mill." Those people went out in their overalls, maybe a bright colored sweater underneath, but the overalls on top, because they were rooted, their marrow was rooted, their very being, in the factory. My generation, you don't find us goin' around showing off—[saying] "I was hired at the steelworks." No, I am a person, and I don't want the factory to dominate me, to haunt me all the time.

Different though they are, both narratives reveal how the abolition of one visible barrier—urban space or a dress style—resulted in the creation of other, more subtle ones. The earlier class separation of urban space had resulted in homogeneous neighborhoods, often company-owned villages whose residents belonged to the same class and worked for the same employer. When class barriers were lowered, the town as a whole became more indifferentiated, but individual neighborhoods became more internally divided. Working-class children went to school, and rose to higher status or higher aspirations than their parents; and middle-class and petty-bourgeois families were drawn in by the low rent. The working class, expelled from the center of the town, mixed with other social groups in the suburbs. Elderly retired workers, who used to live in the center, routinely complain of the anonymity and heterogeneity of their new environment. While the new areas and even the projects are much better than the old rundown environments, the working class no longer has "a room of its own."

On the other hand, the younger generations felt that they were reclaiming the right to stand in the center of town, in a new form. When young workers replaced the overalls with suit-and-tie, they walked the city streets as citizens and equals of the managers from whom they took orders at work. The working-class presence could not be recognized because visible discriminations had been abolished.

In the terms of our analysis, this means that what used to be a spatial continuum between the factory and the town was replaced by a discrete, while the discrete classes now appeared as the continuum of a democratic citizenry, which no longer extended workplace hierarchy into codes of social deference. However, as Vella very lucidly describes, the democratization of urban space generated by the new distinction between town and factory was compensated by a tightening of class boundaries in the workplace. "Certain borders," says Vella, meaning those between workers and managers, had been tolerable "partly because the class distinction continued outside the factory." The overall-clad workers showed pride in their identity but also recognized a status hierarchy which satisfied those members of the ruling class who needed the gratification, as Vella puts it, of showing their status by "crushing someone" in public. But when workers began to wear suits and ties and go to the same cafés, managers resented it. "Watch it now, I'm not saying that the workers gained anything; all I'm saying is, the bosses lost something. And they took it out on you once you were back inside the gates," so that "when I walked through the gates, [they made me feel] potentially defenseless."

The achievement of social homogeneity in the sphere of consumption, a symbol of the equal rights of democratic citizens, allowed Vella's generation (the first one raised in democracy) to represent themselves in terms other than their class. But class boundaries, removed from the visible space of the street, were sharpened in the enclosed world beyond the gates. Also, as in the pattern of urban living space, apparent social homogeneity *between* the classes tended to create a new boundary *within* the working class—detaching the individual worker from the class as a whole. Individual workers were freed from the restraints of class identity, but could no longer rely as much a they had on the collective strength of their class and organization. Free and alone, their autonomy outside and their defenselessness inside were the outcome of a unitary process of change.

Metaphors of Space: Family and Class

The erosion of class codes in life styles was part of a dramatic improvement in standards of living and social equality which took place especially between the late 1950s and early 1960s. It also exacted, however, a heavy price in confusion.

For one thing, the advances determined by the so-called "postwar boom" of the national economy coincided locally with a crisis of industrial employment and union work-site power; thus, the national boom and the local crisis sent contradictory messages to the local working class. One meaning, however, was shared by all messages: the reduced centrality of working-class identity, as consumption became as important as production, and Terni's industrial system was fragmented and reduced.

Inasmuch as equality took the form of assimilation, the very strength of the organized working class, in helping achieve equality, helped erode identity. In Terni, as in other parts of Italy where the Left retained a strong organization and held local power, unions, parties, and the local administration became channels of social mobility, co-opting working-class individuals in position of leadership and in intellectual roles.[8] These individuals rose above the working class while representing it. The division took place, not only between leaders and the rank-and-file, local administrators, and party activists, but also among the individuals involved in this process. While their political allegiance—indeed their professional life—belonged to the working class, their lifestyle, their white-collar duties, and their limited but real power placed them squarely within the middle class. The price, for many of them, is a serious identity and role crisis.

Beginning in the 1970s, the distinction between manual and intellectual work was blurred also at the workplace, as the national steel contract created a unified career ladder for blue- and white-collar workers, thus abolishing a historic partition within the labor force. Individuals could now move along a continuum of labor from the shop to the office, from blue collar to white. Again, the removal of outside barriers originated barriers inside. As office workers began to unionize, the antagonism between unionized blue-collarworkers and formerly anti-union white-collar employees was replaced by divisions within the union, and between groups with different outlooks and interests. What used to be a sharp conflict between "comrades" and "scabs" became a painful contradiction among "comrades."

The distinction between working- and middle class in Terni was complicated by the consequences of the layoffs of 1953. While many of those who were fired suffered a severe downward mobility (including emigration and permanent unemployment), several former factory workers used their severance pay to start small businesses. Many failed, due to inexperience; but others thrived in the subsequent boom of the 1960s. "There was a [Communist] Party meeting the other day, to discuss our policy for the middle classes; and I could physically recognize that many of those who came— merchants, small businessmen—were former factory workers who had been fired in 1953." (Ambrogio Filipponi, 1979)

Economic survival, or even success, has not removed these individuals from their class roots and political allegiance. Alfredo Vecchioni, the owner of several stores and a supermarket, was still angry and nostalgic in the 1980s about losing his factory job twenty-five years before, and automatically described himself, not as a merchant, but as "one of the workers who were fired in 1953."

Yet, although they have not subjectively joined the middle class, these individuals are no longer fully part of the working class. "There never was much contact between workers and the new sectors of the bourgeoisie, former workers who became bosses. They may live in the same building, go out hunting together; but the problem is deeper. Socially, culturally, there never was a real exchange." (Luigi Castelli)

Shop-floor workers who have become clerks or technicians with the new contract; party, union, or local government cadres removed from the shop floor to administrative duties; merchants and entrepreneurs who came from the ranks of the laid-off workers of 1953—these groups are the most numerous components of a stratum of no-longer manual workers, not-yet middle-class citizens, partly nostalgic and partly striving individuals, uneasily located between classes like the intermediate sounds between *t* and *d* which they are the most likely to utter in interviews.

We might add another group which was just becoming visible at the time these interviews were collected: male industrial workers married to women in white-collar jobs such as teachers, social workers, and nurses. The blurring of class boundaries has resulted in the diminution of the class homogeneity of the family unit. Until two or three generations ago, it was taken for granted that workers' children would follow their parents' footsteps. In fact, the steel company, until the 1960s, had a policy when a worker retired of hiring one of his sons. "I am third generation in the factory. My grandfather drove the oxen when they were digging the foundations. My father worked in it, and I did, too." (Settimio Piemonti)

This, however changed radically with the generation of the 1960s:

> GIORGIO RICCI: I was born in Terni. In Terni, there are fifteen, twenty factories; and for eighty percent of the people here, a job at the steelworks means you give a party and pop a bottle of champagne. This, I couldn't accept.
>
> SANDRO PORRAZZINI: My father's dream used to be that I'd grow up and settle down to a job at the steelworks. Now [1982], I talk to older people at work, and hardly any of them—either blue-collar or office workers—have children who expect to go to work there.

These changed expectations add class overtones to the generation gap, as families are now crossed by class and status lines, with education being the most important factor. While I have found no instances in which this interfered openly with the bonds of affection, upwardly mobile children feel that their parents can no longer share their knowledge and experiences, which results in a sort of paternalism in reverse:

> DONATELLA MONTINI: My parents sent me to a classical high school. Typical: you don't send your daughter to a teacher's training or to a vocational school and then to a job. You want her to get ahead. And now of course, I can't talk to them about my interests—like structuralism or what. I know they haven't had the same experiences, and I don't relate to them on this level. It's rather paternalistic. But there's no reason I should tell them . . . "You're not dressed right," or some such thing. I know who they are, I accept them that way.

Differences between the children's lifestyles and that which they inherited from their parents can become metaphors for larger patterns of cultural conflict:

> ALDO GALEAZZI: My brother and I built this house with our own hands, with pick and shovel. It was destroyed during the war, [and] we built it up again. And now my children look down on it. My daughter says: "Do you expect me to live in a house like this? Is this all you got for all the work you did?" I

mean, it's like Khrushchev did to Stalin. If we hadn't built the house, she'd have nothing. Instead, she's been living rent-free for years. See what I mean? Like Khrushchev did to Stalin.

Stalinism, indeed, was often a reaction to the blurring of the distinction between "them" and "us." The Communist party's "historical compromise" policy of the 1970s (when they sought in vain for an alliance with the Christian Democrats) was often described by the image of the unfinished fording of a river, a metaphor of "in-between-ness" which persisted when the historical compromise was replaced by a loosely defined "third way" (neither capitalism nor Soviet Socialism) and culminated in the recent change of the party's name. In a way, the Communist party's perpetual wading in troubled waters—losing touch with the familiar shore without gaining a foothold on the other side as between East and West, class opposition and national unity, or socialism and "improved" capitalism—is both a reflex and a cause of the uneasy "in-between-ness" of the class it used to represent. One is tempted to say that, in the last fifteen or twenty years, the discourse of the Communist party has often had a "lax, not fully voiced" sound.

Metaphors of Space: Consumer Culture

MARIO CONTI: We ought to bear in mind the TV commercials [of the 1950s] with the young executive on his sailboat or private plane, and the woman in heat waiting by the fireplace . . . We all used to play the football polls then, and we still do; we'd buy lottery tickets by the hundreds, because we all wanted that two hundred, one hundred millions, to get ourselves a sailboat and even more, to get that woman in heat . . . It was a consumerism which was foisted on us by the bosses and the government. They kept building freeways and churches; and the unions were too weak to struggle for a different use of social wealth, for a different society.

To this socialist factory worker, the higher standards of living achieved in the last decades are, at least in their present form, as much a consequence of the weaknesses as of the strength of the working class. Change is determined by forces over which workers have little control, and their only option is to make the best of their side-products. Thus, he does not moralize: he knows that what the system offers is desirable and "good"—if it weren't, it could not produce its "bad" results. Styles of consumption are both the rewards and the symbols of social mobility. But because they are signs, they can also become detached from their referent, and be used to replace social facts rather than represent them. While the tensions generated by the achievement of social mobility only concern a limited portion of the working class, the tensions of consumerism have an impact on everybody, including those whose mobility is nil.

This helps explain why a dissonance "in excess" is found in much of the lifestyle of the working class. The "sprawling, highly ornamental, rococo extravagance," the "abundance of odds-and-ends" which Richard Hoggart describes in British working-class homes[9] can be seen also in the overfurnished *sala* (a combination parlor and dining room) of Terni's working-class homes, revealing an anxious, overzealous imitation of incompletely mastered and already obsolescent codes:

> DONATELLA MONTINI: When we moved to town, we found ourselves surrounded by the middle class—it walked the floor above our heads, it lived next door. And they had codes that were very clear, but not to us. Their homes always looked neat and tidy; ours . . . My God, what if the bell should ring? The house is a mess, the dishes are not done . . . Always the image of the neighbors, all neat and clean . . .
>
> MARIO VELLA: You talk about why we bought a chandelier with hanging crystal drops. Ah, it's all about mother and the day we got rid of that old lamp, that painted tin plate hanging from a wire off the ceiling, with a bulb underneath. Nowadays, people put them in barns, but that's what we grew up with. That kind of lamp. And the day we were able to afford the luxury of changing the lamp and getting [the drops] it was a conquest, that is, the symbol through which we gratified the great step forward [which] we were taking.

While the improvement in standards was real, its sign was dubious. The crystal chandelier satisfied, as Luisa Muraro put it in a famous and controversial essay, a right and need for "sensuality and aesthetic pleasure."[10] On the other hand, by the time the Vella family got around to buying it, more sober styles were in vogue among those—including radical intellectuals—who derived their sensual and aesthetic pleasures from other sources and didn't have to prove (to themselves in the first place) that they were not really poor. The dissonance in excess of working-class furniture is an equivalent of linguistic hypercorrectism—the same as those eternally over-sugared cups of coffee one is always offered during interviews. It didn't take me long to realize that my taste for sugarless coffee was a luxury reserved to those who don't have to prove they can afford an extra lump of sugar.

Private Space and Public Space: The House and the Street

In the older working-class neighborhoods of Terni, one can still see people sitting on their doorsteps, halfway between the house and the street: the men sometimes reading the paper or chatting with neighbors (or looking inside at the TV); the women often sewing, knitting or husking beans—doing *house* chores in *public*. Orchards are still often in front (as opposed to *back*yards), and display an economic rather than only ornamental use of the land. Ground-floor windows are very low so people can poke their heads in from the street and talk to the families inside. The transition from the public space of the street to the private space of the house is a gradual continuum, rather than a sharp discrete:

> LUCILLA GALEAZZI: I never felt I was living among strangers until we moved to a new place and I started carrying my own house key. We had never used to lock the door, even at night. By day, the door stood open, with the key outside. And now, I had this strange sensation of the key in my hand, and I could not get into the house without it, because there was no key outside the door.

The relocation, in the 1970s, of the residents of a company village (Villaggio Matteotti) to new, modern apartment buildings generated an obsession with keys, bolts, locks, and hedges. The old village had been built during Fascism, and it reflected the "ruralistic" ideology of the regime: each house was a separate unit, with a wide orchard and a large cellar so that each family could raise some of its own food and make its own wine, relieving pressure on the state and the company for higher wages. To a working class that was partly influenced by rural culture, this also seemed in keeping with the traditional way of life. The houses, though, were built cheaply, and had become rundown by the time the company decided to relocate to a new village which was planned by some of Italy's best progressive architects.

The new apartments, conceived with an urban lifestyle in mind, were much nicer than the old houses, but more impersonal. The families missed the personalized changes and improvements they had wrought over half a century. Most of all, they missed the cellars and orchards where they could employ their time, take pleasure from the land, and see the neighbors and be seen in turn while yet standing on their own ground.

The architects had provided public spaces for socialization, but hardly any intermediate ground between public and private spaces. The people were used to both communication and distance; now, distance was built into the very ideas of living in *apart*ments, while the visible artificiality of the "social" spaces became less a compensation than a threat to privacy. The old houses were separated from each other by the orchards; the new apartments were so close that distance had to be created by the people by locking themselves in and staying away from all the nice public grounds. As in other cases of modernization from above, the new Villaggio Matteotti came— (to borrow a concept from Marshall Berman)—to "incarnate the paradox of public space without public life."[11]

The new boundary between outside and inside also caused boundaries to be rearranged on the inside. It was hard, in the new apartments, to preserve the traditional distinction between the "public" *sala* and the "private" kitchen: "The *sala*," a worker said, "is a useless expense for us; family life takes place in the kitchen. We take all our meals there, and only use the *sala* if there's a visit. Modern kitchens are too small, and a worker can't afford to eat in the living room every day."[12]

The *sala* furniture is often bought only once in a lifetime. One can't afford to put it to everyday use—and certainly one doesn't wear work clothes while sitting on it. As Benjamin Franklin once said, one does not dress in private as for a public ball. The families in the new Villaggio Matteotti—as well as most families caught in the transition between rural and urban uses of domestic space— seemed to feel that this very elementary distinction in their lives had collapsed.

ACHILLES AND THE TURTLE

In modern societies based on class—as opposed to traditional societies based on caste—identity and status are *achieved* rather than *ascribed, fluid* rather than *fixed*. Individuals are allowed—and therefore expected—to create their own identities. Because class boundaries are less rigid than caste ones, individuals are expected to move across them as if they were no boundaries at all. The more society assumes the appearance of a *continuum* rather than a *discrete*, the greater is the gap between social mobility as a norm; and its availability in practice. This contradiction harps upon individual consciences and is anxiously overcompensated in cultural practices— from language to furniture, from music to the uses of urban space and the spatial metaphors of social structure.

For each boundary that is blurred or ironed out, new ones arise or old ones are revived; for each new boundary across an old continuum, a distinction is abolished elsewhere. But the rules regulating the new boundaries which divide the world are more elusive than the old ones. They are made and re-made elsewhere, and they change too fast for people to keep up with them. Social mobility and cultural change, then, are not be seen as a transitional process from one identity to another, but as a permanent condition. Working-class people race to adaptation and assimilation much as Achilles raced the mythical turtle: no matter how fast they run, they never catch up. As that ubiquitous blues line puts it, they keep stumbling, but have no place to fall.

6

Uchronic Dreams: r—⟶Imaginary tales

Working-Class Memory and Possible Worlds*

There are always several contradictory trains of
events happening. There are always several contradictory histories of what has happened. And one of
them is only more real than the others because more
people, or animals, or plants, or rocks, or machines,
believe that it is the real one. All sane things sup-
press the memory and recognition of all the trains-
of-events except one. But not all persons or things
remember and recognize the same train-of-events.
That's the difficulty. Most of the persons and things
accept the same events and conditions most of the
time, but all do not accept them all the time.

Raphael Aloysius Lafferty
The Three Armageddons of Ennyscorthy Sweeney

If it had been me, if I'd been the father, I wouldn't
have allowed him to die, up there hanging on that
cross.

Maddalena, textile worker
Terni, Italy

THE MEANINGS OF UCHRONIA

This essay is about a type of imaginary tales which I propose to call
"uchronic." Uchronia has been defined in science-fiction criticism as
"that amazing theme in which the author imagines what would

*First published as "Una storia sbagliata: memoria operaia e mondi possi-
bili", in *I Giorni Cantati* [Firenze, Italy], 1 (June 1981), 13–31; a revised text
in Paul Thompson, ed. *Myths We Live By* (London, England: Rutledge and
Kegan Paul, 1989).

have happened if a certain historical event had not taken place"; or as the representation of "an alternative present, a sort of parallel universe in which the different unfolding of a historical event had radically altered the universe as we know it." The word itself is coined after "utopia," replacing the Greek *topos* (place) with *chronos* (time): utopia is a nowhere place, uchronia a "nowhen" event.

While both definitions refer to science-fiction novels, I will try to show how similar tales are found in oral historical narratives. I will discuss mostly oral testimonies collected in the 1970s from old-time Communist activists in Terni, an industrial town in Umbria, central Italy. These stories often emphasize, not how history went, but how it *could*, or *should* have gone, focusing on possibility rather than actuality. They offer glimpses of favored alternatives which their narrators believe might have resulted if appropriate leadership had caused specific events between 1919 and 1925, and again between 1943 and 1953, to occur differently. They contrast the existing world against a desirable world, and claim that, only by accident, their hopes and dreams were derailed.

My first encounter with—and discovery of—uchronia in oral history occurred in a 1973 interview with Alfredo Filipponi, a former factory worker, tramway driver, coal merchant, and local secretary of the Communist party during fascism and military commander of the partisan brigade "Antonio Gramsci" in 1943–44.[2] I had asked him the usual question: "During the Resistance, did you have in mind only national liberation, or were you also hoping for something more?" This was his reply:

> Well, we thought of national liberation from fascism, and, after that, there was the hope of achieving socialism, which we haven't achieved yet. At that time, with the partisan struggle, we should almost have made it. After the partisan war was over—Terni was liberated eleven months earlier than the rest of the country—Comrade Togliatti spoke to us. He called a meeting of all the partisan commanders and party leaders from every province and region of Italy. He made a speech. He said there was going to be an election. "You have prestige, Omega," (that was my party name. Gramsci himself had named me that way. My partisan name, instead, was "Pasquale"). "The reason I asked you to come is, you must get to work for us to win the election." Four or five others spoke, and they agreed. I raised my hand: "Comrade Togliatti, I disagree." "Why. Omega?" "I disagree because, as Lenin said,

'when the thrush flies by, then it's the time to shoot it. If you
don't shoot when it flies by, you may never get another
chance.' Today the thrush is flying by: all the Fascist chiefs are
in hiding and running away, in Terni as well as everywhere
else." All the others said it was the same in their parts, too.
"So, this is the moment. Weapons . . . no need to talk about
it, we know where they are" (we had hidden them). "This is
the time: we strike, and make socialism." He put his motion
and mine up for a vote, and his got four votes more than mine
and was passed. But they got the warning; they had to admit I
was right, later. [Umberto] Terracini and [Luigi] Longo [two
national leaders] were there when I was speaking—I stood
here talking, and they were sitting there in front of me, ten
feet from me. When I spoke, they got up and said they agreed.
Togliatti disagreed, but he learned his lesson, because he had
seventy-six votes and I had seventy-two.

This confrontation between Filipponi and Palmiro Togliatti,
postwar Communist party secretary, never took place. Filipponi
was giving here his imaginary version of a crucial event in the
history of the Italian Communist movement: the so-called *svolta di
Salerno* the political "U-turn" in which Togliatti (just returned from
his exile in Russia) announced to the party cadre at a meeting in
Salerno that socialism was not on the immediate agenda, and that
the party should cooperate with anti-Fascist forces toward the creation of a Western-style democratic (and "progressive") republic.
Reactions to this announcement ranged from opposition to in-
credulity, and old-time activists still debate whether Togliatti's line
was correct.

In this story, Filipponi suggested that history might have been
different if another road had been taken. The shape of the tale depends on personal and collective factors. Filipponi was old and ill
when he was interviewed, and died shortly thereafter; he had long
been removed from active party leadership, against his will and following a dramatic confrontation. As the conversation went on, the
epic and detailed (though factually inaccurate) style he had used in
the beginning to describe his partisan experience gradually broke
down, and he slid deeper and deeper into fantasy and fabulation.
First, he claimed a central role in the founding convention of the
Communist party at Livorno in 1921, which he actually did not even
attend. Then, he told a detailed story of how he escaped from
prison with the party's founder, Antonio Gramsci, and hid with him

for months in the mountains—which also never happened. Finally, he ended his story with the imaginary confrontation with Togliatti.*

It was as though, as the weariness of age and illness and the fatigue of the long interview eroded his conscious controls, the censorship of rationality gave way to dreams and desires long buried into the subconscious in a process much reminiscent of an open-eyed dream. This dream gave vent to the personal desires and frustrations of the narrator. Although he had devoted most of his life to the party, Filipponi felt he had never been properly rewarded and recognized. Thus, he placed himself in imagination at the very center of the party's history and at the side of its "founding father," from whom he claimed to have received, in a sort of baptismal investiture, his party name and his political identity.[4]

But there is more than a personal frustration to this story. Filipponi also voiced a collective sense of disappointment in the shape which history took after the great hopes aroused by liberation from fascism.

A 1947 report of the Terni Communist federation says: "Among the rank-and-file, there is a widespread disappointment

---

*Filipponi was expelled from the party in 1949. According to some witnesses, his ambition played a role in his conflict with the new party leadership; also, his fighting partisan mentality was considered unfit for the postwar political climate. When he was expelled, according to Mario Filipponi (no relation) "there was a sense of loss, like at the death of an important person." Comunardo Tobia remembers him on the barricades in the 1953 strike: "he was beside me and I didn't look him in the face." Filipponi was later quietly readmitted, but never given any responsibility.

The name "Omega" was used in the 1920s not by Filipponi, but by the party's regional secretary, Filippo Innamorati; by appropriating the name, Filipponi also appropriates Innamorati's historical leadership role.

Antonio Gramsci (1891–1937), one of the major Western Marxist thinkers, is usually referred to as the founder of the Communist party. Although he was one of movers of the Communist separation from the Socialist party (Livorno, 1921), Gramsci did not become party secretary until 1924. He was arrested by Fascist authorities in 1927; released on parole because of his health conditions in 1937, he died shortly afterward. During the Resistance, many brigades, including the one active in the Terni area, were named after him.

Palmiro Togliatti (1893–1964) became secretary of the Communist party while in exile in Moscow in the 1930s (his compromises with Stalinism have been the object of much controversy in Italy recently). In the postwar years, he shaped the Italian Communist party and formulated the theory of "national roads" to socialism.

for the way in which democracy has evolved so far. It must be recognized that we have relied too much on institutional and legal action, waiting for solutions from above, and have not given the workers enough responsibility in solving their own problems."[3] Stories of disappointed expectations caused by the restoration of class relationships in the factories and in the state are common in the generation of the 1940s. As the desire and hope for revolution and socialism were removed from the party's agenda and eliminated from open discussion, they were gradually buried deeper and deeper into the activists' memories and imaginations, to re-emerge in fantasy, dream, and folklore. Filipponi's "wrong" tale was less the result of imperfect recollection than, ironically, of a creative imagination. It was the narrative shape of the dream of a different personal life and a different collective history.

Such stories do crop up occasionally in different parts of the country. A construction worker from Subiaco in Latium used to tell a story about himself that is very much like Filipponi's. An artisan from the San Lorenzo neighbourhood in Rome also described a confrontation between himself and Togliatti (or Togliatti's "representative," as he put it sometimes). Diname Colesanti, niece of the Terni anti-Fascist exile Giovanni Mattioli, also talks about a "quarrel" between him and Togliatti about the Salerno line: "Had Togliatti followed Giovanni's advice, things would have been different." Sometimes, such conflicts did not happen only in memory and imagination: in Calabria, local party cadre refused to believe the party documents describing the new line, and thought they must have been forged by "provocateurs."[4]

Two other aspects enhance the meaning of Filipponi's story. One is the structural relationship of the episodes about Togliatti and Gramsci. Stories about Gramsci are even more common than stories about Togliatti, which is understandable given the former's "founder" status. Most stories about Gramsci mythically associate the speaker and the place where the story is told with the founding hero's presence; as such, they have much in common with stories about the other national founding hero, Garibaldi. Most stories about Togliatti, on the other hand, tend to differentiate the speaker from him. As founder, Gramsci represents the ideal reasons at the roots of the party's identity; Togliatti is remembered most as a shrewd, "realistic" political tactician. Therefore, Gramsci's role in folk versions of history is to reinforce identification with the party's origins; Togliatti's, sometimes, is to express disappointment with its historical action. Filipponi's testimony is a thorough example of this process.

The second aspect of his tale is the presence of a material correlative to the post-liberation stories: the practice (mentioned by Filipponi and widespread in the 1940s) of hiding away the weapons used in the Resistance, expecting to take them out again sooner or later for the revolution (or, as some speakers say, to defend democracy against expected attacks of reaction). Arms were found hidden in the factories of Terni as late as 1949; and one informant told me he had kept his until the 1970s. The preservation of arms meant that the job begun with the anti-Fascist Resistance had been left unfinished and would have to be completed someday. In a way, the revolutionary desire buried in the subconscious of activists like Filipponi is another hidden weapon, left to rust unused.

This feeling was bound, on the other hand, to come to terms with the personal and collective need to survive, to rebuild, and to defend and expand the limited but concrete gains of the postwar years, within the existing framework. Revolution or not, life has to go on. As the party leadership declared that revolution and socialism were out of the question and increasingly identified itself and the class it represented with the values and the machinery of Italian democracy, it became increasingly difficult to express—or even to entertain—the frustrated hopes and desires. The result was a deep-seated conflict between the rationality of the world as given and the dream of another possible world.

Filipponi managed to voice this conflict in a more recognizable form because his personal disappointment coincided with his view of history, and, most of all, because in many ways he embodied the relationship between the political vanguard consciousness and the folk roots of working-class culture. Born in Valnerina, the mountainous backyard of Terni's steelworks, he was always more at ease with dialect than with the standard Italian of political parlance (although his sixth-grade education made him one of the best-schooled Communist activists in the underground generation). He was a tolerable player of the *organetto*, the small accordion which dominates folk music and folk dancing in his region. Filipponi's description of how he was fired from his tramway job is patterned after a folk tale.* The advice to "seize the time" in the post-

---

* "After I had been working [at the tramways] for several years, Mussolini wrote a letter to the manager and told him: 'Within five days you must fire the famous Communist chief Filipponi Alfredo and send word to me about it.' The manager sent for me, read the letter, and said: 'I don't have the

liberation period was couched in a proverb about hunting, a very popular sport in Umbria: "When the thrush flies by, then it's the time to shoot it." Like other working-class activists who justify their politics with proverbs and folk songs, Filipponi attributes his proverb to Lenin, in an attempt to reconcile his class-conscious folk wisdom with the theoretical prestige of the founding heroes of the Communist movement.[5]

WHEN HISTORY WENT WRONG

The cluster of stories about the missing revolution of the 1940s are not an isolated instance. The motif of "history could have gone differently" is found in narratives dealing with all the major crises of working-class history, both local and national. Many stories concern the period between the end of World War I and the advent of fascism. Describing the cost-of-living strikes of 1919, Arnaldo Lippi says "The leaders of those struggles had no authority on the working class; we didn't have the true class that the Communist party created later, in spite of all its shortcomings. If there had been a Communist party then, there would have been a revolution."

The 1920 sit-ins in the factories are one of most commonly cited unseized opportunities. According to Remo Righetti, "We should have gone on to the insurrection, I mean, because this is what we had in mind—we're going to make a revolution, we used to say then. But the union leaders had other ideas in mind, they weren't going to make any revolution." Gildo Bartoletti reiterates: "The Socialist party had 157 members of Parliament; power should have been in hands of the Socialists. But [Socialist Secretary Filippo] Turati wouldn't take the responsibility. He should have taken power, but wasn't man enough.[9]

When Giacomo Matteotti, a Socialist member of Parliament, was murdered by Fascist killers in 1924, the regime suffered its first (and last) serious crisis. "The Fascists," says Arnaldo Lippi, "were

---

heart to fire you.' After ten days or less, there comes another letter from Mussolini: 'I have heard that Filipponi is still employed. If you don't fire him within three days, I'll fire him myself, and you'll be fired too.' He sent for me, and said, 'What must I do?' 'What can you do,' said I: 'Go ahead and fire me'." The archetype is the story of Snow White, with Mussolini as the evil Stepmother Queen, and the manager as the hunter who is supposed to kill the princess but is reluctant to do it.

scared. But we had no leaders. The Communist party was still weak, and the leaders who had a following among the people— [Claudio] Treves, Turati—were all in exile abroad; ours were all in jail. If we had had the right leaders then, maybe fascism wouldn't have lasted twenty years." Lippi's facts are wrong: during the Matteotti crisis, Socialist leaders Turati and Treves were still in Italy, and Gramsci had not yet been arrested. But the political analysis is serious: at that all-important moment, the working class had no leadership.

Stories about the 1920s explain the missing revolution by citing lack of leadership, thus blaming the Socialists from whom the Communist party split in 1921. But the history of the 1940s cannot be "justified" by the lack of a legitimate Communist leadership. Therefore, uchronic tales focus on specific events and individual decisions, reiterating one motif—"they told us to keep calm"—to describe the implicit contrast between the "political," tactical approach of the leadership and the state of mind of the rank-and-file. But the meaning is the same: at one point (which varies with each narrator), history went needlessly wrong.

In a typical uchronic statement, Settimio Piemonti associates two major crises of the decade—the day of Italy's separate peace with the Allies in 1943, and the attempted murder of Palmiro Togliatti in 1949: "I still can't believe 8 September [1943]: that day, we could have picked hairs from the Germans' asses one by one; there was nothing we couldn't have done. Instead—be calm, be calm, be calm . . . Just the same as when Togliatti was shot: calm, calm, calm . . . And the cops at the arms depot had already handed their guns over to us . . ."

The construction-worker and folk-singer Amerigo Matteucci (mayor of a hill village near Terni) improvised *stornelli* on the national reconciliation and amnesty to the Fascists as promoted by Togliatti which, thirty years later, he still saw as a mistake which prevented the revolution:

> Caro compagno te lo voglio dire
> l'errore fu la gente perdonare
> l'errore fu la gente perdonare
> E condannato sia il traditore
> se bene vòi ave' all' umanitàne
> se bene vòi ave' all' umanitàne
>
> Scusate amici mia se sto a sbagliare
> io sono sempre alla rivoluzione
> io sono sempre alla rivoluzione.

[Dear comrade, I want to tell you that it was a mistake to forgive those people: traitors must be condemned, for the good of mankind. Forgive me friends, if I'm wrong; but I am still for the revolution]

"The next day [after Togliatti was shot]," Matteucci muses "he began to speak, to say a few words, and he always recommended the same thing—calm down, calm down, calm down . . . But I think it was a moment when . . . I may be wrong, but at the moment I think all our problems could have been solved." The wounding of Palmiro Togliatti is only one of the many stories about the unseized chance which could have generated an alternative history. Other episodes include the police killing of the Terni steelworker Luigi Trastulli in 1949 and the firing of three thousand Terni steel workers in 1953. Calfiero Canali recalls that, after Trastulli's death, "the people, the workers, were ready to do something, but were held back by—by our leaders, because . . . it was like after Togliatti was shot. If it had been for the rank-and-file, it looked like revolution would break out any moment." According to Antonio Antonelli, "On the third night of street fighting [after the 1953 layoffs] all the people were ready, with gasoline tanks and other stuff, to wipe the cops out. But they promised they would hire two hundred men back, and things calmed down after these promises. But the workers weren't ready to give up the fight. What the workers said was, 'All our jobs back or let's fight, our jobs back or let's fight.' After things ended that way, the working class lost faith, and never gained it back, because they were disappointed."

Another narrator, recorded in 1973 (whose name I withhold to protect his identity), told a dramatic uchronic story, which was later substantially confirmed by other narrators:

The night after the layoffs were announced, we took a stand. "Tomorrow morning, we said, "we're going to do an action in the factory. We're going to kill fifty of the bosses." We were all set, all our minds made up and everything. We had filed iron bars to a point, real sharp. But the unions called us in. "Look," they said, "things are looking good. The struggle is won. You're ruining everything. Don't do anything rash . . ." So we had to give it up. I mean, fifteen of us might still be in jail today, but I still believe that if that morning we had cut down . . . I mean, we wouldn't have had to stop at fifty, we'd make it a hundred, once we got going, it wouldn't make any difference. And once you had a hundred dead bosses in there—I guess things would have been different. Perhaps after they'd buried those fifty, sixty bosses, they would have gone on and fired the workers anyway. But at least there would have been fifty vacant jobs. I admit it might have been the wrong thing to do; but I am still convinced that they would have re-opened the gates to all the two thousand.

These stories show the role of uchronia as one possible narrative expression of the refusal of the existing order of reality. The uchronic form allows the narrator to "transcend" reality as given and to refuse to be identified and satisfied with the existing order. Through uchronia, these speakers said that the most desirable of possible worlds (which to them was still identified with communism) could be created someday, if the right chances are seized. And the old textile worker with the appropriate name of Maddalena carried uchronia to a further and more radical point when she said that, had she been God (had God been a woman . . .), the most crucial event in our history might also have gone differently. And who knows what the world would be.

POSSIBILITY AND DESIRE

We could dismiss these stories saying that there are at least ten times as many stories that go in the opposite direction: stories that deny that history ever went wrong and claim that not only did it go the only possible way it could have gone, but that this outcome was also a just and satisfactory one. But the relevance of an imaginary motif cannot be measured on statistical grounds alone.

For one thing, we must consider the quality of the narrators. Among the sources of the stories discussed here are a high proportion of activists who held places of responsibility and prestige in the party, unions, and local governments. These stories are not the mumblings of isolated and disgruntled old men, but a rationalization of their past by individuals who were the backbone of the working-class and Communist movement in Terni for three generations.

Also, we must consider the place of the motif within each individual life story. In almost every case, the uchronic turn is placed so as to coincide with the peak of the narrator's personal life, with the moment where each of them played the most important role or was, at least, most actively involved as a participant. Paradoxically, the "inaccurate" motif tends to be linked with the best-remembered historical episode as though the "wrongness" of history became most evident when seen at the closest range.

Finally, we may take a hint from the autobiography of Frederick Douglass. "I have been frequently asked, when a slave," he says, "if I had a kind master, and do not remember ever to have given a negative answer; nor did I, in pursuing this course, consider myself as uttering what was absolutely false; for I always measured the kindness of my master by the standard of kindness set up among slaveholders around us."[7] A negative judgment on the slave's condition was not only dangerous to utter, but also difficult to conceive: the slave would have had to evaluate the master on a scale other than that of the existing order, a scale which not all were strong or imaginative enough to envision. Also in less dramatic situations, the voicing of a critical view of one's own experience against the prevailing interpretations of history runs against outer and inner sanctions. It takes a much higher emotional investment to admit to oneself that things are wrong, than it takes to consent to conventional truths. Doubt and dissent can only surface when they possess a high degree of intensity; and then, those who express them are often also partly speaking for the majority who dare not admit their doubts even to themselves.

Yet, the common sense of history does say that this is the only possible and the only desirable world. Against hypothetical, conflictive stories like Filipponi's, stands the running argument: there could have been no revolution in Italy in the 1940s, because the Allies would not have allowed it—look what happened to Greece. "They would have blown us like bagpipes," says Calfiero Canali. As we have seen, in another context, Canali also tells a uchronic story of his own: the same speakers who say that history went wrong at the crucial moment of *their* lives, accept the common sense of the inevitability (and justness) of history in other respects. The conflict, in fact, is not between irreducible rebels and passive conformists, but runs within each individual in ever-changing shapes and terms.

The inner, personal nature of the conflict is paralleled by the frequent narrative contrast between the party—bearer of reason and knowledge—and the instinctive, angry rebelliousness of the masses. Arnaldo Lippi says, "We were nothing but fighters. We were not armed with the politics of knowledge; we wanted a fight, which the party knew we couldn't sustain, being too few." Lippi makes a spontaneous distinction between *us* and *the party*: and the party, not "us," is right. Though the speaker meant to underline his allegiance to the party, somehow the subjectivity of desire smoulders under the objectivity of reason and clamors for recognition. How do we reconcile the fact that we know that the party was right, with the fact that we irrepressibly feel that history has been wrong?

THE MYTH OF INEVITABLE PROGRESS

In order to deal with this contradiction, rank-and-file narrators must deal with the image of history which they have absorbed in school and which the party itself has reinforced—a linear process of growth and progress toward some desirable end. "History, don't you see, marches toward liberty," says a song by Silvano Spinetti, a Communist farm worker from Genzano. This vision was articulated by the elites in order to legitimize their role and strategy; it was subscribed to by the Socialist and then the Communist leaderships in order to raise hope in the rank-and-file, and again to legitimize their own leadership. If history is directed either by providential guidance or by the lights of reason and objective socio-economic forces, then the existing state of things is only a necessary stage in a process both inevitable and desirable. While uchronia claims that history has gone wrong (has been *made* to go wrong), the commonsense view of history amounts to claiming that history *cannot* go wrong—and implies that what is *real* is also *good*. History tailors the desirable to the given: as Russell Kirk once said (*apropos* the conservative mind . . .), "the test of a statesman is his cognizance of the real tendency of Providential social forces."[8]

Togliatti's *svolta di Salerno* is a case in point. Though it may very well have been, in itself, quite wise, this choice retains legendary overtones because it is described as *both* a free choice and an enforced one—the result, at the same time, of Togliatti's subjective wisdom (his concept of the "mass party" and the intuition of the "Italian road to Socialism") and of objective circumstances (the Allies) which allowed no other course. The historian Claudio Pavone has noted that "Togliatti often presented as successful initiatives actions that which were, in fact, only defensive moves," and "this was to be among his more lasting contributions to the party's mentality."[9] The practice of representing setbacks and defeats as victories was often used in the 1970s, especially during the "historical compromise" and "national unity" phase of the 1970s, when the Communist party seemed to be approaching state power in partnership with the conservative Christian Democrat party. When work-ers' rights that had been hailed as historical conquests a few years earlier were jeopardized, Luciano Lama, secretary of the left-wing unions, described them as undesirable "barrels of ashes" to be left behind on the road of power and modernization. Enrico Ber-linguer, Communist party secretary, masterfully tailored the "desir-able" to the "possible" when he said that "a Leftist government would not be a good solution for Italian democracy at this time" because it might tempt conservative forces to a *coup*. Both Lama and Berlinguer would, clearly, have preferred to preserve the union rights and to achieve a Leftist government; but, rather than admit that they lacked the power to make these things possible, they chose to claim that they were *undesirable*: pretending that factory councils were destroyed and the Left kept out of power, not because the party and the union could not help it, but because they chose not to.

In the 1970s, as the Communist party increasingly tried to identify itself as a "responsible," "acceptable" political force, it be-gan to take responsibility not only for the future but also for the past. All the historical events preceding (and, implicitly, leading up to) the imminent accession to power were now to be seen as posi-tively good even if the Communist party had originally opposed them. Thus, Berlinguer described NATO—once fiercely opposed by the party—no longer as a vehicle of imperialistic hegemony but as a "guarantee" of Italian national independence.[10] (Incidentally, the Communist party was never allowed access to state power; but the ideological price paid in the attempt remained.)

This approach was reproduced at the local level. While all Terni workers describe the 1953 layoffs as a major and lasting de-feat, the local historian and Communist party Senator Raffaele Rossi described them in the 1970s as an almost unadulterated good:

> The great layoffs of 1952–53, and the struggles that fol-lowed (in various forms, including grave street fights, a state of siege, the use of firearms, barricades, many wounded and hurt) preserved and increased the unity of social and political forces (the all-parties Terni Committee), promoted research and ideas on the relationship of state-owned industries to re-gional economy, and hastened a deep reorganization of the factory which prevented its closure and changed it, for the first time, from war to peace production.[11]

This description (which literally puts what happened to the workers in parenthesis, and credits the layoffs with a sequence of positive verbs—"preserved," "increased," "hastened," and "prevented" . . .) has hardly more factual credibility than Filipponi's uchronic dream.[12] But it squares with the need to imagine a progressive history leading up to the progressive "historical compromise" (anticipated by instances of cooperation between what used to be described as antagonistic forces: the "all-parties" committee).

This version of history is so far from the direct experience of the majority of the population that it takes no hold on rank-and-file imagination; but the process functions more effectively when it deals with distant events on a national scale, which individual narrators have little opportunity to verify against their own first-hand experiences. The encounter between the imagination of the historical compromise and the folk imagination of the rank-and-file creates utopian visions of a triumphant present. "All our struggles did serve a purpose," said Alfeo Paganelli, a factory worker, "because the working class has prevailed, and they [the ruling class] have been forced to give in. They may rule in the House or in the Senate, up there; but down here, inside Italy, they don't. If they want to rule, they must apologize to Berlinguer and place him on the chair, the first one, where the crown used to be once. Now it's gone. There's a hammer-and-sickle in its place now, and nothing else."

This vision has much in common with Filipponi's stories about Gramsci. The speaker establishes a relationship between himself and the political hero by pointing out that "our" struggles helped enthrone him; he thus manages to give meaning not only to party history but to his personal history as well. If the past is to justify the present, a life of struggle can found self-esteem and personal identity only if these struggles are described as a success. The need to claim something for oneself, to defend one's own dignity and historical presence, is often at the root of a "consensus" version of history: by saying that history was "good," we claim that we have made something of ourselves.

On the other hand, however, each time I asked old activists whether their present lives correspond to what they struggled for, the answers were reluctant and dubious. "No, it doesn't because all of our leaders own their own houses, and I'm still renting," says Agamante Androsciani. "We might still lose everything we have," said Arnaldo Lippi, who was living very scantily after holding important offices in the city government for twenty years: "Today, I have a small pension, just enough to buy me and my old woman a piece of bread, so we don't have to beg. But it could happen yet," because the ruling classes, he says, will always try to take back what they were forced to give.

Personal experience, then, both reinforces and limits the affirmative view of history. On the one hand, it prompts narrators to insist on the usefulness and success of their lives, by stressing the positive aspects of reality. On the other, it forces them to come to terms with the deferral or cancellation of their ultimate goals, with the limited and precarious nature of actual gains, and with the personal sense of discontent and loss of meaning.

The affirmative discourse is sanctioned by the political leadership and by the power establishment; it is available, ready-made, and articulated. The discourse of negation, on the other hand, must piece itself together from scratch every time, and is burdened by the fear of disapproval and isolation. "I'm sorry, comrades, if I'm talking wrong," apologizes a defiant and timid Amerigo Matteucci, "but I'm still for the revolution."

Therefore, the conflict between the affirmative and negative impulse often results in silence, passivity, and assent without participation—"a passive, often merely formal agreement with the party line, a tendency to delegate to others, which prevents dissent from coming to the fore," as a panel of national leaders put it in 1977.[13] The discourse of negation is distorted, buried, deviated, and allowed to emerge only between the lines, as dream, metaphor, lapses, digression, error, denegation, and uchronia—all forms which give vent to the narrators' feelings and yet control the tension by means of the formal organization of discourse.

WHO MAKES HISTORY

The means of control embedded in the narrative correspond to two major motifs: the "wrong turn" of history is traced to a single event, and the blame is laid to errors or failures of the leadership.

The latter motif is frequently found also in New Left historiography, where it is used to support the image of a revolutionary working class regularly betrayed by reformist and "revisionist" leaders.[14] Uchronic tales, while apparently taking the same approach, in fact perform an opposite function. Blaming the "wrongness" of history on "our" side means, for one thing, that it is still our side that makes history. It is the same frame of mind which inspired the Pueblo myth which attributes the creation of white men to Indian black magic, or the black nationalist myth in which the white race is invented by the mad black scientist Yacub.[15]

These myths reinforce the group's sense of its central role in history, and suggest that if the group had power to generate the evil powers it also has power to eliminate them: "if Indian magic has created white people, an Indian ceremony will control them."[16] "If natural disasters were caused by something he had done," says Matt Witt about a Navajo Indian, "then there was hope: perhaps he could prevent future calamities by not making those mistakes again."[17]

Likewise, the function of the uchronic motif is to keep up hope. If our past leaders missed their chance to "shoot when the thrush was flying by," better leaders in the future won't. The world of our desires is possible: we needn't even change the magic but only work it more correctly, and perhaps replace a few magicians at the top.

The leadership plays, in uchronic tales, a role similar to that of mediators in Claude Lévi-Strauss's structural interpretation of myths: two-faced creatures that hold together conflicting but equally necessary presuppositions. In this case, the contradiction— we, the makers of history, must be right, and yet history is wrong— is explained through the agency of individuals who are *with* us and stand *for* us (in the party, which they represent) but are not *of* us (not members of the working class in terms of status, power, education, language, life-style, and sometimes income: as Androsciani says, *we* rent, *they* own). The ambivalent, internal/external position of the leadership keeps it all in the family, and yet saves the family from guilt and blame. Allegiance to the party was not based (as outside critics often claimed) on a mythic faith in its infallibility, but rather on the ability to shift its failures to the sphere of myth.

This is where the factual inaccuracy of most uchronic tales becomes relevant again.* If Italy did not become socialist after World War II it was for reasons quite removed from the fact that Togliatti's

---

*I say "most" because there is one event to which the "hypothetic" approach to history might be applicable. The Fascist march on Rome of twenty-eight October 1922 might have easily been stopped "if" the King and the government had used the army against Mussolini. Perhaps history *would* have been different. No narrator, however, uses this event as the start of a uchronic chain: the failure must be on "our" side, not the King's. Incidentally, uchronic versions of history are found also among the Fascists.

line overcame Filipponi's (imaginary) opposition; and the triumph of fascism after World War I was not caused by Turati's hesitancy in seizing a power which was never within his reach.[18] The uchronic motif removed the presence of social and political adversaries. It reduced complex historical processes to single events, and complex situations to yes-or-no dilemmas. Thus, it saved the narrators' self-esteem and their sense of their own past, but made it much more difficult to evaluate the party's actual role in those crises and its long-term identity, culture, and strategy. Everything was brought back to the merely tactical plane.

The consequences can be seen at both the levels of everyday politics and political imagination. Most rank-and-file reactions to the historical-compromise policy tended to be couched in tactical terms. "We gave them too much leeway, and were punished in the election" (Veniero Moroli); "Berlinguer offered the Christian Democrats an alliance because he knew they would never take it, and then the blame would be on them" (Amerigo Matteucci); "Look, Berlinguer is no liar. He did it to race faster to our goal" (Dante Bartolini).

But the historical compromise was much more than a tactical move. It was a symptom and a cause of deep changes in the identity, class composition, and political role of the Communist party. This process marginalized many old-time activists, whose identity was so tightly knitted to the party that, while they hurt personally, yet they recoiled from acknowledging what it meant politically. Tactical criticism allowed them to voice their discontent, and yet remove its deeper and most disturbing sources.

The primacy of tactics goes hand-in-hand with an image of history as a series of discrete "turning points," crises, and crucial moments, which dreams of the revolution as a single, traumatic, and violent confrontation, rather than as a slow and deep process of social change. Though all these narrators dreamed of a new world, they were all but incapable of imagining it. They concentrated on the revolutionary seizure of power, but were extremely vague when asked to describe what kind of society they expected afterward. The closest they would come up with was a reference to the Soviet Union—that is, to another *existing* world. No wonder that, when in

---

Mario Sassi, an unreconstructed supporter of Mussolini, told a story meant to prove that Italy would have won World War II had not Enrico Fermi and other nuclear scientist defected to the other side.

the 1980s the world of existing socialism collapsed, the party's identity was shaken to its foundations.

The uchronic imagination, thus, reveals the inability of a significant part of the traditional Communist rank-and-file to acknowledge that basic aspects of the structure and theory of the Communist party (and thus of their own identity) may have contributed to the "wrongness" of history. It also reveals that, for many of these activists, it was too painful and difficult to admit—and even to imagine—that the party was becoming something quite other from what they had known and lived for. On the other hand, the uchronic imagination also reveals the failure of official history to explain the existential experience of a majority of the rank-and-file. Uchronia, thus, saves the precious awareness of the injustice of the existing world, but supplies the means of resignation and reconciliation. While it fans the flames of discontent by uncovering the contradiction of reality and desire, it helps to keep this contradiction from breaking out as an open conflict.

The Best Garbage Man in Town: Life and Times of Valtèro Peppoloni, Worker*

> To add interpretation [to the spoken word] which
> would convey the right meaning is something
> which would require—what? An art so high and
> fine and difficult that no possessor of it would ever
> be allowed to waste it on interviews.
>
> Mark Twain, *Letters*
> Edited by A. B. Payne

> They would teach us even if you were gonna be a
> garbage man, you be the best garbage man you can
> be. This is what we were taught. If you can't learn
> to do anything but haul garbage, you be the best
> garbage man you can be.
>
> Willetta Lee
> Harlan County, Kentucky

REPRESENTATIVE STORIES

A question which is frequently raised in discussions of the bio-
graphical approach and of oral history concerns the relationship between individual documents and trans-individual realities. I would
like to approach this question by analyzing how a single life story
relates to broader and shared patterns of culture, and how the common, shared elements relate to what makes this story both representative and unique.

---

*Published as "The Best Trash-can Wiper in Town. The Life and Times
of Valtèro Peppoloni, Worker," in *Oral History Review*, 16/1 (Spring, 1988),
58–69.

When we speak of life stories, much depends on whether we mean *life* stories or life *stories*. We may insist that these stories are true—these people exist, and they relate events that actually happened—and, therefore, interviews allow us to glimpse the actual experience (life). Or we may work with the assumption that we are dealing with verbal artifacts (stories) shaped by the narrators' self-perception, by the encounter with the interviewer, and by the interviewer's perception and interpretation of them and their words. The impossible dream of attaining absolute "authenticity" and "lived experience" blinds us to the fact that we have, at hand, something which bears at least a formal relationship to the subject's experience. After all, the telling of one's life, is *part* of one's life. To paraphrase Walter Benjamin, the problem is not what is the relation *between* life and story; but, rather, what is the place of the story *within* the life.

THE ADVENTURES OF A WORKING MAN

The life story I will discuss is that of Valtèro Peppoloni, a factory worker and jack-of-all-trades from Terni. It was recorded in April 1981 at his house. The interview lasted about nine hours, from 10:00A.M. to 1:00P.M., and then from 8:00P.M. to 2:00A.M. The transcript runs to almost one hundred typewritten pages. I had approached Peppoloni at the suggestion of his sister's son, a childhood friend of mine, who heard I was collecting oral history in Terni, and insisted I should, by all means, talk to his uncle. Besides myself and my friend, Peppoloni's daughter, her husband and their children were present throughout most of the interview.

Valtèro Peppoloni was born in 1916 at Palazzolo, a village near Citta della Pieve in Northern Umbria. His father owned a small farm and was a Socialist sympathizer. He was not actively involved in politics; yet, the naming of his son with the Italianized version of "Walter", rather than by a Catholic saint's name, was perhaps a "political" act in the anti-clerical tradition still very much alive in what used to be the Church's temporal domains. Valtèro's father was arrested in the 1920s, under some political excuse, and, when he left jail, he was out of a job. The family moved fifty miles south to Terni, where factory jobs might still be found, even in 1929 at the beginning of the Depression. Valtèro's father died shortly after the move, and the family went to live and work as sharecroppers on a wealthy family's property at the outskirts of town.

"The landlady was horrible, a real killer," Peppoloni says. "There were three of us children; my sisters worked as maids in the house, and our poor mother worked a little piece of land on shares."

There was a fruit orchard, and Peppoloni says the fruit was:

> . . . half and half, with the landlady. But, the best fruits were hers. Out of three trees, she would say, "two are mine and one is on shares." As a matter of fact, one night—I remember it well. I'll always remember!—there were these beautiful apricots, so me and a friend of mine—my mother scolded me for this afterwards, but there was nothing she could do about it—I got up in the middle of the night with this friend, and we stripped that tree. And then we took the apricots to Ernesto's, the ice cream place in Via Garibaldi, and sold them. Wow! I gave my mother some of the money, later.

After his father's death, Peppoloni took a job selling tickets at a movie theater in town, for two *lire* per week. "And then it happened that one week [the owner] didn't pay us those two *lire*. I remember that they were showing *Aroldo e il fratellino*, Harold Lloyd and his little brother. And out of spite, I threw open the back doors of the theater, on the post-office side. Some people gave me two pence, some gave me a penny, some gave me sunflower seeds or anything, and I let everybody in free. Everybody."

His next job was at the Papigno fertilizer plant, which had recently merged with the Terni steel company. "I got this job. I was only 15, and I went to work. I was making good money, twelve hours a day. But after eight or nine months, my growth had stopped. The calcium cyanamide was hurting me. So someone told my mother, 'Look, you'd better take your son out of there before he dies.' "

He was then promised a job with the company that was laying the new sewer system in town, but the Fascist employment office let someone else with less rights get ahead of him. So Peppoloni had a talk with the Fascist union secretary.

> I pushed the door in with my shoulder, and broke into his office. And he was so scared that he climbed up his desk. By then, I was 19. I wasn't a child anymore. And besides, there was this fighting spirit, which I still have, which I never lost. Be it good or bad, I don't know, let others judge; but the

fact remains. We began to wrestle, I got hold of him and was getting ready to throw him out of the window. But there was a balcony beneath, so he only fell a few feet. Anyway, they called the police, wrapped me up and took me to Via Carrara [to jail].

He finally got the job with the sewer company, but it was only temporary. "And then, unemployed again. So it happened—look, honestly, I was in the Fascist youth organizations though I never ran around with them. Why? I don't know. I was a Young Fascist—I won't hide it. If this is history, we must tell it like it was. Anyway, one day I found myself inside the Mussolini Army Barracks, and I signed a paper that said: 'I, Peppoloni Valtèro, apply to enlist for unlimited time and destination unknown.' I signed it, and that was it. Three days later I was on my way"—to the Spanish Civil War.

"I must have been reckless, or I didn't know the meaning of fear; anyway, I was always on the front line." He was decorated, but was shocked by the discovery that hierarchy, promotions, and rewards were based on political considerations rather than merit. "So one day, there was this officer—an officer—and I and others tore his silver medal off his chest, right in front of the French generals. Why? Because he hadn't earned it in combat." Peppoloni also had his first political doubts: "I discovered the nature of fascism. I could see it was trampling on people who were trying to live their own lives."

On his return home, Peppoloni was hired at the steel mills as a Spanish War veteran. The Fascist local asked him to pay his party dues, from which he claimed exemption because of his veteran status. There was a quarrel, and the secretary threatened him:

> Oh, he says, "I'm going to show you—I'm a *squadrista* [a member of the original Fascist terrorist squads]. I'll show you!" I says, "I know you, you *squadristi*: you were good to fight ten against one [beating political adversaries], but when there was some real shooting going on [in Spain], I didn't see any of you around." Heavens! He tried to grab me, and then, a couple of friends and me, we did a revolution—we tore up the whole local. Chairs, mirrors, bottles, flying all over the place . . . So the next day the *federale* [city secretary] summons me: "We're going to show you, you're in trouble." "Look," says I, "leave me alone or I'll kill you, no doubt about it." [A guard] came at me, and I grabbed him—I opened the door,

and said, "Look, I'm gonna send you flying all the way down these stairs." And I told [the *federale*]: "Look, if you care for your life, remember, I work at the steel mill. If you touch me, I don't care what happens to me, but you'll never forget who I am."

Peppoloni married just before the beginning of World War II, and was drafted to the Greek front. "I was a rebel spirit," he says, so he had trouble with the brass, but fought well, and was seriously wounded in the attempt to save one of his officers' life. He was given a home leave, refused to go back, was jailed, escaped, and was finally granted a disability discharge. After Italy's separate peace (September 1943), Peppoloni refused to join the Fascist-Nazi army. He took his family back to his home village after the Allied air raids on Terni, traded in the black market, joined the partisan underground, and was caught and tortured by the Nazis, but did not speak. At the end of the war, he resumed his job at the steelworks.

When I began to work there in 1939, it was full of company guards. The guards were the real bosses in the plant, then. They would stand behind your shoulder and watch, even if you were doing your work all right. Because, in those days, we really worked—we w-o-r-k-e-d. We worked: [After the war, however,] the factory was full of guys who, because they had been partisans, had become arrogant. And I would say to them, "No, this isn't right." I had a different mentality, right or wrong. They said: "We must get rid of the bosses, kill them all—isn't this what we fought for?" Myself, though I never could stand the bosses, yet I always tried to do my duty, everywhere I've been. I never shirked. I have changed many bosses. Sometimes I quit, sometimes I had them fire me. But as far as work was concerned, they always carried me in the palm of their hand. I always wanted to be right, in front of the boss.

Anyway, the factory was still full of guards, and they were after us all the time. If you took a minute to rest—when there was a breakdown or something—if they saw you, they'd cry out: "You're sleeping! I'll have you fined!" They saw you wash your hands a minute ahead of quitting time—you were docked. It was oppression, really. In fact, once—there was this guard, the notorious . . . and this friend of mine and I grabbed him and pushed his head into the water tank, and, the bubbles floating up were getting mighty scarce. You know, we went that far—we were ready to drown him, and we were capable of doing it, too.

Peppoloni joined the Communist party, but was critical of slack leadership ("Once I had to kick [a well-known union official] to get him to strike") and of rank-and-file irresponsibility:

People were taking advantage of the situation, in those days. They would bring newspapers inside the plant, and sit down and read [instead of working]. I wouldn't stand for that. Before the war, we weren't free. But after the war, we were the masters, somehow. But, masters, not in the correct sense of the word: because it wasn't the correct thing to do, in those days, to just do whatever we wanted to do. Especially if, when you don't do your work, someone else has got to do it.

"When we were supposed to fight for our union," says Peppoloni, "when there was something which I understood and which was right [I would be there]. Because, if it wasn't right, you wouldn't see me in it. Nor do you see me now." On the other hand, he also says: "I was one of those who took part in every single strike—all; all, all, all of them. All. Even the wrong ones, maybe. I may have been in some of the wrong ones. It's all right; all right. But I was in all of them."

In 1948, when the Communist party Secretary Palmiro Togliatti was shot and critically wounded by a political adversary, an apparently pre-insurrectionary situation developed all over Italy. Peppoloni and some of his comrades disarmed the company guards and organized the occupation of the steel works.

You see, I still go out and fight; even though, nowadays, I could afford not to give a damn. I get nothing out of it. It's my consciousness. But one thing I never did—I must say this—I never went with three or four other guys to get hold of someone and beat him up [He alludes to the beatings administered immediately after the war to former Fascists]. Never, never, never: And I never accepted it. It was done, yes, it was done. But I never dreamed of doing it, and whenever someone suggested it, I said no. Because it would have been like going back to fascism. The Fascists, yes, they used to do this sort of thing.

In 1953, three thousand workers were fired from the steel company and, though he wasn't one of them, Peppoloni joined the barricades. "The police hit me on the head, in the street, they did. But others, who had been fired, I still tell some of them today, 'You guys were staying home weeping between your wife's legs, while we were out in the streets fighting for your jobs."

At work, "everybody thought highly of me." He won a prize for inventing a labor-saving device, but a month later was fired. His helper had made a mistake which damaged a kiln, and Peppoloni had covered up for him and taken the blame. When it happened again and the foreman threatened to fire him, however, he told him whose fault it was, and the helper called him a spy.

I went blank. I was carrying my lunch pail, and banged him on the face with it. I broke him up. I stepped on him, and if the other guys hadn't taken me off him I would have killed him. As a matter of fact, I broke his nose and knocked off some teeth. I went blank, you know. I all but lost my mind. After I had tried to cover up for him, the first time! Later, he said he was sorry he called me a spy, though I'd broken him up.

After the fight, Peppoloni was reported to the chief of personnel.

I had nothing to lose. My wife had died a few months before, less than a year. So, I had nothing left to lose. The chief of personnel was sitting behind his desk, in front of me, and two guards a little to the side. "At last I got you, Peppoloni," he says. I stuck out my hand and caught him by his necktie. If the tie hadn't snapped, I would have choked him. The guards grabbed me, but couldn't take me off him. Why, if the tie hadn't broken, I'd have choked him.

After losing his job at the steel company, Peppoloni took whatever jobs were available in the hard times of the 1950s. "I was a skilled worker—and, two days later, there I was, working on the road with pick and shovel." He managed to rise because he was skilled and a hard worker, but after an accident which partly disabled him he found himself unemployed again at age forty-nine. The Communist party had tried to help him get a city job, but bureaucratic complications got in the way. So "one fine day, I went to see [a Communist city councilman] at City Hall. I was carrying all my cards: union, party, and partisan veteran card. And I said, 'Take them back, I don't need you anymore. And I don't need your party, either. I thought it was a different party.' " The man told him that the only job available was in the sanitation department, as a street sweeper. "I never asked you for an office job, did I? I never asked you to make me work in an office. All I want is work." Now Peppoloni remembers:

> People see me downtown today, and they can still bear witness wherever I go: I really cleaned those streets. I really did, honestly. I *liked* being a street sweeper. They said I cleaned the streets with my tongue, I swept them that clean. There—but I sweated on them, you know. Yes, I did. I used to work the trash-can washer, the dirtiest filthiest job in Terni. The most terrible job there was. You know what it means, to scrape garbage cans in the month of July or August? You open them, and scrape them with a knife. It means you need a stomach stronger than tempered steel, to stand that kind of work. And from forty cans a day they were cleaning before I arrived, between me and another fool like myself, we raised production up to sixty-five cans a day. And they were done clean, neat.
>
> One day, in the middle of the summer, in Viale Carducci. It was so hot—you'd open a can . . . my God! And I was wearing a T-shirt, damp with sweat, so I took it off. Next, I took off my undershirt, too. And went on working. The foreman happened to pass by, and started screaming at me: "Indecency! You're a public officer, a city employee," so on and so forth . . . in the middle of the street. I had the scraping knife in my hand, sharp as a razor. And I told him, "Get away from me, or I'll cut your throat." I had sweat dripping all over my body. Even my pants were wet, everything. And that was the end of it.

After this confrontation, Peppoloni was transferred to another city job, as a janitor in an elementary school. On his very first day, he had a shouting argument with the headmistress, over a matter of overdue vacations.

After that, she respected me. She meets me on Main Street, downtown, when she's out walking with her friends, teachers and everything, and she says "Hello." "This man," she tells them, "is a comrade, a supporter of [Enrico] Berlinguer [the Communist party secretary in the 1970s]. Awful. But I respect him, because he got my school working like clockwork." I must admit it: the best-kept school, the best-organized school in town, was mine.

His last two years of work were spent as an usher at City Hall, where he managed to quarrel with office workers who came to work late or left early:

"Do your job, you bum! Don't be here stealing your wages!" I mean, I didn't come here to shirk or bum. Like in the party. I didn't join the party to [get something out of it]. The party helped me raise my consciousness, helped me struggle as a worker. It taught me much, I must admit it. But when they want to take the easy way out of their problems, like they're doing now, blaming Stalin for everything . . .

I'm a Stalinist. That's the way I am. The party taught me to be that way, and I can't change so easily. No, not me. My comrades often tell me: "Things are different now, Peppoloni. Times have changed." And I say: "How come you, who are an officer, don't go out and sell the party paper door-to-door on Sundays anymore?" [This used to be one of the basic duties of Communist party activists.] I still do it. How often have I neglected [my children], and they didn't complain? They respected me for it. I still go out and do that job on Sundays. Nobody pays me for it. Nobody. I always gave all for the party, and never asked for anything. And I still do, gladly.

For being the best peddler of the party paper, Peppoloni had just received his latest award: a book and a key holder. Since his retirement, he spends much time carving wood. His masterpiece, displayed in his living room, is a life-size head of Lenin.

SYMMETRY

I have selected the episodes (respecting the chronology) so as to show the skeleton of the story's basic structure. In fact, there are three integrated structures: a structure of linear growth, a structure of circular recurrence, and, underneath both, a thread of stability and permanence.

The linear structure begins with Peppoloni's definition of himself as *scavezzacollo*: a "breakneck," an unruly brat. "I was rough. I had no one to guide me," he says. At this stage, he waters the milk he is supposed to sell in order to raise money for movies and ice cream, raids the apricot tree, and takes revenge on the theater man by opening the doors to all comers. With his first jobs, he graduates from this generic unruliness to what he calls a "rebel spirit," a "fighting spirit" (also, "spirit of adventure," or just "spirit"). He will take no abuse from anyone. He stands for his personal rights against Fascist officials and factory guards, and fights daringly as a soldier. Finally, he achieves what he describes with a very important word in the Italian political lexicon: *coscienza*—"awareness," "consciousness," "conscience." When he says that he joined strikes because "it was my *coscienza*," or that the party "helped me raise a *coscienza*," he means that political consciousness and moral conscience are the same. The pattern of change from *scavezzacollo* to *spirito ribelle* to *coscienza* is the linear, logical growth from an unruly child to a rebel and fighting young man—to a conscious (and class-conscious) worker and a responsible person.

The circular structure is also very clear. Political, personal, and professional relationships develop into conflicts and finally come to a verbally or physically violent showdown. It happens with the Fascist employment office, the Spanish Army, the Fascist local—as well as with the Communist councilman, the chief of personnel, the sanitation foreman, and the school headmistress. This represents the conflict between Peppoloni's rebellious righteousness at its different stages, and the basically unjust structure of society, as well as the lack of adequate *coscienza* in other people. Although he grows, the world around him remains the same. He is always the moral winner, and then moves on to another relationship, confrontation, and showdown. The combination of the two patterns describes a sort of *Bildung*: the process whereby a person becomes, gradually, what he is, in conflict with the world outside.

However, these stages of development do not really *replace* as much as *build* upon one another. For instance, when he tells of the fight with the chief of personnel after being fired from the steelworks, he repeats that his wife had just died and he had nothing to lose. It is as though, now that he is no longer responsible to her and to the institution of marriage, one of the agencies that held his riotous rebel spirit under the control of *coscienza* as responsibility was removed, and he was able to revert to an earlier stage of pre-adult rebelliousness (much as the loss of his father made it easier for him to grow up a *scavezzacollo*). This confirms that the story is not so much one of linear growth and change as one of cumulative building of personality.

In spite of his changes, however, Peppoloni insists, at another level, that he never really changes: the politicized worker is the same person as the boy who raided the apricot tree ("there was this fighting spirit, which I still have"). The deeper level of the narrative, therefore, is one of consistency and continuity. The basic value, which is never explicitly defined (although it has to do with the obsessive theme of "respect"), but which holds the entire story together, might be called *symmetry*. Nello Innocenti, a folk singer-improviser whom I recorded near Rome in 1970 described Lenin (in a perfect, Dantesque line) as "colui che mise il mondo in simmetria"—"he who put the world in symmetry." Lenin's head is displayed in Peppoloni's living room, and symmetry is the basic principle of order in his ideal world. The first episode he tells of his life—the jailing of his father, is about this. Ostensibly, his father was arrested for political reasons: actually, Peppoloni says, it was because a local Fascist official had borrowed some money from him and didn't want to pay him back. It was a breach of symmetry that started the whole chain of events.

The principle of symmetry operates on two levels: words and work. The first meaning of symmetry in words is symmetry between words and facts. Words must correspond to facts ("If this is history, we must tell it like it was"), and facts must correspond to words: an aspect of symmetry is keeping one's word. The Fascist local had said that he would be exempted from dues; but they broke their word, and he punished them. In his quarrel with the Communist councilman—although he insists that he expected no gains by joining the party—he discovers that he cannot rely on the party as much as the party relies on him, and he throws his party card back.

Finally, symmetry in words is consistency: "I'm a Stalinist: that's the way I am. The party taught me to be that way, and I can't change so easily." The leadership, in fact, has not been consistent: first, they set up Stalin, and then they took him down. In the 1970s, Peppoloni actually returned his card for a while. "I don't need a card to be a real Communist," he said, meaning that the party was inconsistent, not him. His criticism of the party leadership also concerns an inconsistency between role and behavior: union officials ought not to be "kicked" into joining strikes, party officials ought to do their duty and go out and sell papers like the rank-and-file. The same applies—symmetrically—to the rank-and-file: if I am out on the barricades fighting to save your job, you ought to be out there, too. This "political" symmetry is the bridge between symmetry in words and symmetry in work. Both concern the symmetry between rights and duties.

First of all, there must be symmetry between work and pay. The landlady did not share the trees symmetrically, and he takes the fruit. The theater owner does not pay him, and Peppoloni stops doing his work for him. He is hurt financially, and causes his employer an economic loss.

The symmetry of work and pay is part of the symmetry of rights and duties: " 'Let's do our work first, our duty,' I used to say. Then we'll claim our rights and struggle for them." At another level the synthesis is defined when, in terms which summarize much of the tradition of the Italian working class, he says: "I always wanted to be right, in front of the boss." ["Ho voluto avere sempre ragione di fronte al padrone."] By this, he means that, if he is to claim his rights successfully, then his employer must have no claim or complaint on him. This puts the worker in a strong bargaining position.

This attitude seems to be based on the unstated assumption that the relationship with the company is basically fair: they never fail to pay him, and the pay is ultimately fair. When it isn't, or when the company does not live up to its obligations, symmetry is re-established by struggle. This is why Peppoloni claims, at one level, that he only participated in strikes when he felt they were justified. Of course, this view of symmetry does not coincide with the Marxist concept of "exploitation," a breach of symmetry implicit in capitalism in the form of unpaid labor (when Italian workers say that they are "exploited," they usually mean that their employers are "unfair" under existing relationships, leaving the nature of the relationship itself in the background. This terminological difference has created untold misunderstandings between workers and political activists in the 1960s and 1970s).

On the other hand, Peppoloni is also aware that what keeps the relationship "fair" is a symmetry of power. This is why, immediately after saying that he joined only justified strikes, he contradicts himself and says that he "took part in every single strike . . . Even the wrong ones, maybe." The only way symmetry can be maintained between employers and workers is by balancing the employers' power with the organized strength of the working class. Inasmuch as they serve this end, all strikes are "justified." When this balance of power is upset, employers tend to crush the workers'

rights and workers tend to neglect their duties, unless they are controlled by "consciousness": "We were the masters, somehow. But,
masters, not in the correct sense of the word."

As the episode of the guard that he almost drowned shows,
Peppoloni reserves the right to define for himself what is fair in
terms of duties. To a certain extent, he takes work for granted. Most
workers in Terni answer the question "What was work like during
Fascism?" in tautological form: "You just had to work"; "We were
really working"; or "Work is work." Peppoloni puts it this way: "In
those days, we really worked—we w-o-r-k-e-d. We worked."

Work is work: there's a hard core to work, which cannot be
compressed. But there is also a hard core to a human being that
cannot be compressed either. The episodes of the near-drowning of
the guard and the near-knifing of the sanitation foreman show the
awareness of this limit, which had been anticipated by the early experience in the chemical plant where long hours and unhealthy conditions had stopped the boy's natural growth. The nature of work
and human nature must be symmetrical and compatible. Otherwise, rebellion and refusal are "justified."

Finally, there must be symmetry between work and recognition. Peppoloni's almost obsessive theme is one of "respect." Over
and over, he says, "m'hanno portato in palma di mano"; employers,
foremen, and co-workers "always carried me in the palm of their
hands." The visible signs of this symmetry are the prizes (the reward
for his labor-saving invention, and the book and keyholder for selling the party's paper), and, even more, the fact of literally being
recognized and greeted by his peers and superiors (the headmistress
and her socio-professional group) "when people see me downtown."

What keeps together the two motifs—the linear development
and the symmetrical structure—is the concept of the unity of the
self. Again and again, Peppoloni insists that he still has the same
rebel spirit of his youth, that he cannot change and does not wish
to. We are a long way from modernistic fragmentation of self. On
the other hand, this insistence on unity is determined precisely by
the powerful impulses to fragmentation which are present in modern industrial society. The tracing of the unity of one's self thus becomes one of the most powerful impulses behind the telling of
one's life story.

CONSCIENCE AND CONSCIOUSNESS

The story, then, has a very tight and recognizable structure.
Though it was a long, spontaneous interview, Peppoloni never lost

control of the pattern. He had certainly thought about this for a long time, and had told his stories over and over (the reason I interviewed him was that my friend, his sister's son, had heard them before), but never as a coherent whole, at one sitting. The interview gave him a chance to connect coherently a repertoire of stories that had been told many times but separately. However, he could not have improvised the overall shape if he hadn't thought about it and had not told them before.

The fact that the stories had already been told also makes them more than individual property: they have been shared. His family takes pride in them, so they are also family property. Then too, they have probably been shared and exchanged with comrades of his own generation.

An oral speech act, to a higher degree than a written one, is implicitly social, because it requires an audience: the fact that these stories had been told often means that Peppoloni's circle found them, at least, congenial—and, perhaps, that they were more or less consciously shaped or selected to meet the expectations of that particular circle.

A more explicit social element is the presence of motifs, themes, and patterns of plot and performance which can be compared with other stories told in the same environment. When we analyze life stories this way, we are in a no-man's land between folklore, which is largely a science of analogies, and literature, which is a science of individuation, concerned with what makes each literary work different from all others at least as much as with trans-individual concepts such as genre or motif. The problem, here, will be to identify both what is "communal" and what is "individual" in Valtèro Peppoloni's story.

Of course, one thing that this story shares with all the others is that none of them is exactly like the others. No individual statement fits entirely into the grid of the culture to which it belongs. In fact, a culture is not a *grid* (which is only a useful theoretical device) but a *mosaic* in that each piece fits in with the others but is different from them all. The fact that a culture is made up of individuals different from one another is one of the important things that social sciences sometimes forget, and of which oral history reminds us.

I will start with the stealing of the apricots, because it has the stature of a founding myth. The same motif is found in several other narratives. My interview with Iginio Vella began with a question about a raid on a cherry tree which was a famous event in our neighborhood. Vella says:

So we went to make this experience, on a tree near our house. There was a bunch of friends, and we went to rob the cherry tree. We stripped it bare, completely. With a certain style and with the patience of a monk, we actually stripped the pulp from the stones, one by one, and left the stones hanging on the branches. Just to give the whole thing more character, to make things more stylish.

Another narrator, Alvaro Valsenti, recalls:

After I began to work at Alterocca's print shop, [in the 1930s], I began to meet other anti-Fascists. There was this constant sense of rebellion, comparing ourselves with others, the first stirrings of class hatred. We saw people eat fruit—as for us, all the fruit we had was what we could steal in the villas. We had the map of Terni in fruit. We knew where and when we could get pointed grapes, and when right here, beyond the fountain in Piazza Tacito, there were medlar trees, or another vine of raisins under the balcony of Palazzo Spada.[1]

We may find other examples, but these two along with Peppoloni's story of the apricot tree are worth comparing because they tell us a great deal about how each narrator connects them with his own personal growth.

Vella's is the tale of a youthful escapade: you haven't been a child unless you've stolen fruit at least once; you haven't been young if you haven't been at least a little bit unruly. (If I may add a personal recollection, the reason I wasn't asked to join fruit raids by Iginio and our common friends was that, as the only middle-class child in a working-class community, I was considered to be outside—not above—this sort of thing.) Vella's insistence on style shows that it was more of a joke (some famous historical practical jokes have had to do with stealing fruit) than a matter of redressing class wrongs. The tree, in fact, belonged to an equal, a neighbor, a co-worker of his own parents.

On the other hand, Peppoloni's stripping of the apricot tree is the crowning of his *scavezzacollo* phase. It prepares his future awareness of social injustice which, at this stage, is still implicit. It is more a breach of deference than a class-conscious act, although it violates the owner's property rights.

Finally, Valsenti also describes himself at length as an unruly, daring, working-class street urchin. ("So our life was always in the streets. We did the craziest things, the most terrible, dangerous inventions . . .") However, he places the habit of stealing fruit in a broader context of class relationships symbolized by his topography. The raids on orchards and vineyards take place in the very center of town, below the Prefecture and City Hall, thus making a statement about the overlapping of urban and rural space and about the invasion of the urban center and the institutional space by working-class "ghetto" kids.

At this stage, Valsenti describes himself as already a "rebel"—a term that, for Peppoloni, designates a higher stage of development. In fact, while Peppoloni stole the apricots before he had his first job as a factory boy, Valsenti associates the fruit with his print shop job and the first awareness of anti-Fascism. We may conclude that the three narratives share the same motif (the stealing of fruit) with the same function (founding the narrator's relationship with deference, hierarchy, and property). But each narrator tells it with a different intensity, places it at a different stage in his personal development, and varies its meaning accordingly.

This story also has another trans-individual dimension. It ties in with a collective tradition which is common enough to have a name in history books: *furto campestre* or "rural theft." The theft of the landlords' fruit, crops, and produce by poor farm hands or sharecroppers was an aspect of preindustrial class relationships as "normal" as shoplifting is in contemporary consumer societies or stealing the master's hogs on slave plantations. It did not express a full-fledged class consciousness or an open rebellion, but rather a weakening of private property as a principle, which might—or might not—lead to further developments. This behavior characterizes an early, preindustrial stage of the history of modern popular classes; but, as Herbert Gutman pointed out, attitudes developed in this phase were effective in shaping the mentality of industrial workers.[2] The majority of Terni's factory workers consider stealing company property a terrible thing to do. However, after World War II, when electricity was expensive, the workers of the Papigno chemical plant—including the most righteous ones—used to take home a *pallocco*, a fistful of cyanamide, and used it for lighting at home. Pre-industrial traditions have been used to erode company time (like having parties on Christmas Eve, cooking meals on steel kilns, and going to sleep at night if the work allows it). So, there is a dual attitude: company property is sacred because "we must always be right in front of the boss" (and also because it is, at least in principle, also *our* property); but there is nothing sacred about company time and even the sacredness of property can be put aside in an emergency.

Many narrators establish an explicit parallelism between the individual life cycle and phases of collective history. Thus, the rural-theft stage may be compared to a preadult phase of the history of the working class, where consciousness is not yet formed, but there is a general unruliness which foreshadows things to come. Arnaldo Lippi, one of Terni's best folk historians, neatly divided the history of the town into periods—rebel spirit (*spirito ribelle*) and workers' consciousness (*coscienza*)— which coincide with the next two stages of Peppoloni's life and of his own:

> We were under the Church's rule. My father, the worst insult you could make him, was to call him a subject of the Pope. He was a republican, but he'd rather be under the king than under the Pope. This shows you what kind of environment we grew up in. Of course, growing up in this environment, I could only grow up a rebel . . . mostly by instinct, because my family was poor. I wouldn't call it anarchism. It was a sense of independence, without a real outlet . . .

After industrialization and the first strikes, this "*rebelliousness* inside us" grows into "an emancipation, a more mature *consciousness*." And yet, like in Peppoloni's story, consciousness could not exist without the foundation and the persistence of the rebel spirit.

Both Lippi and Valsenti associate the independent, unruly rebellious spirit with the Anarchist movement which existed in Terni since before industrialization, and left an important trace in the Communist rank-and-file. The level of individual and collective "consciousness" is related, on the other hand, with the leadership of the vanguard party. "The party helped me raise my consciousness, helped me struggle as a worker," says Peppoloni. This parallels Peppoloni's idea that he was "unruly" because he had no guidance, no father.

In fact, in certain cases, it is the same story. Angela Locci, who used to work beside her father in the Centurini jute mill, recalls the noise, the screams, the throwing of bobbins, and the beating of scabs during the strikes by the women who worked in the plant. Although she was a Socialist, she says, "I wouldn't join them. I didn't like to go and throw bobbins, raising a ruckus and everything. My father used to say, 'Don't go, there's no telling what they'll do.' Sometimes we would go and watch, and our men would tell us 'How can you go and throw bobbins, and still call yourselves Socialists? What kind of doctrine is that?' "

These women—like Peppoloni—had "no one to guide them," neither the family nor the party. Only with the assistance of "our men" and of the Socialist leadership do they graduate from "ruckus" to "doctrine." The party's fatherly wisdom is the other side of moderation: thus, many narrators say half regretfully that, at crucial moments in class-struggle history, the rebellious but immature workers were told to "be calm" by their leaders (see chapter 6). Thus, Peppoloni's life story follows the same pattern as the town's history as told by other narrators: from the unruliness of rural theft through instinctive, unguided anarchic rebellion to the consciousness of working-class organization.

The other important motif is Peppoloni's confrontation with his superiors: Fascist officials, army officers, company brass, the sanitation foreman, and the headmistress. Several other narrators tell similar episodes, in which they face representatives of authority—government, company, party or union.

"I had a confrontation with the prefect," says the former partisan Bruno Zenoni. Just after the end of the war, the prefect summoned him and asked him to stop a demonstration of unemployed veterans, which he refused to do. The prefect began to shout—"Look, says I, these are Fascist methods—you can't use them anymore," Zenoni said. The prefect tried to throw him out bodily, at which people came in from the offices down the hall to separate them.

A typical tale in this vein concerns union negotiations, a standard setting of confrontation. Arnaldo Lippi speaks of when he was one of the worker's representatives who, briefly after World War II, were added to the company's board of directors. "One day, I had the guts to tell the biggest, the most worshipped [of the administrators], the head of the management board. 'Look, you only have one advantage over me, that you are educated and I am not. Otherwise, I'd tear you to pieces.' We had engineers, technicians, with us; but when we walked into that big room, when we discussed the problems, it was always Lippi who spoke." A variant of this theme is found in stories in which local rank-and-file Communists "stand up" to national party leadership. The most representative of these tales is Alfredo Filipponi's story of his confrontation with Togliatti over revolution or elections (see chapter 6).

Now, part of the meaning of these stories is revealed by the fact that—like the moments of truth in Mark Twain's novels—they

Public Confrontation

always occur in public and before an audience. Peppoloni tears the medals off the officer's chest in front of the French officers. His confrontation with the foreman who screamed at him for not wearing his shirt takes place in the middle of the street, under the town's eyes. He fights his helper who called him a spy under the eyes of two shifts of workers at the factory gates. When he breaks into the offices of the Fascist secretary or the chief of personnel, there are always at least a couple of guards standing by to witness what he does. Zenoni's confrontation with the prefect is also witnessed by the office staff, Lippi faces management before the entire union delegation, and Alfredo Filipponi faces Togliatti under the eyes of the Communist leadership.

What is important, then, is not only to *confront* authority, but also to be *seen doing it.* Confrontation is both a challenge to authority and a metonymical appropriation of it. This is why the manager confronted by Lippi needs to be "the biggest, the most worshipped"—and why, in the next scene, Lippi is no longer pitted against the administrators, but seated beside them: "At the inauguration, next to the president, I was sitting here and he there, and I was with them, managing, inaugurating the school."

As we have seen from Peppoloni's story, the motif of confrontation is balanced by the motif of respect represented by his superiors' greeting when they meet him—on Main Street, not just any street. The spatial opposition between working-class peripheries and the middle-class center of town implies that "respect" must be manifested there to be really visible. Says Mario Gabrielli, "When my children come to Terni [downtown] with me, they can see who their father is. I ought to carry a tape recorder with me, to greet back all the people who greet me."

These stories show that there is a personal, even physical relationship between workers and management. The dialectics of public confrontation and public respect describe a paternalistic environment, where hierarchy and deference extend from the workplace to the street.

This does not mean that there has not been a great deal of hostility and conflict—in fact, the sometimes frightening violence of these stories of confrontation is also shaped by the paternalistic relationship. The "unfairness" is seen in personal as well as in class terms, it involves an element of personal disappointment with superiors often respected for their professional ability. There is a wealth of stories about workers facing the man who fired them in the street, walking into his office, going up to his house, and confronting him with the personal effects of his impersonal management decisions.

A typical story of personalization is that of Alberto Petrini. One day, he and some of his co-workers read a notice that they had been fired. "When we saw the notice, we up and went to the head manager's office. 'Did you sign this paper?' we asked. He tried to stall . . . 'I don't know' . . . So we picked him up and carried him to the personnel office; with him ahead of us we went to the department head, then to the foreman. Always with the same question: 'Are you the one who signed this paper?' Finally, we came to the kiln engineer. 'Did you sign this?' 'Well, you know, boys' . . . 'All right. Call your wife at home, and tell her to set five extra plates for dinner and five for lunch. Until we get our jobs back'."

Peppoloni, then, is not an exceptional case. Several of these stories are set in the climate of the immediate postwar years, when partisans were still powerful and feared. Vero Zagaglioni, a former partisan, tells of the day he walked into the office of the secretary of the factory manager and demanded his old job back. "Hurry up, or I'm gonna stick two fingers inside your throat and turn you inside out like a sock." The story of Aldo Galeazzi—the athlete who went to the chief of personnel's house after being fired with the three thousand in 1953 and let him know that he would break his arms and legs if he didn't get his job back—has become something of a local folk tale, complete with variants (see chapter 8, page 258). Of course, Galeazzi, Zagaglioni, and Petrini all got their jobs back.

One last point concerns work ethics. Peppoloni's story is reminiscent of Max Weber's concept of *Beruf*, which he discusses in his work on the Protestant ethic and the spirit of capitalism; however, Peppoloni is neither a Protestant nor a capitalist. A more appropriate precedent might be the story in Ralph Ellison's *Invisible Man* of the educator who works his way up to college president from being "the best slop dispenser" to hogs in the history of the college (a parody of the life of Booker T. Washington). Ellison says here that the myth of personal mobility ("the black rite of Horatio Alger") does not apply to a group of people which has been held down collectively.[3] Something like this has shaped class relationships in Terni. In 1881, the paper of the local "liberal" bourgeoisie reprinted Benjamin Franklin's "Advice to those who would be rich," but changed the title to "Advice to workers."[4] Franklin's virtues of thrift, temperance, and hard work were originally listed as "ways to wealth," but here they have been turned into items of discipline. The work ethic is no longer linked to individual social mobility: workers will not become rich that way; they will merely keep their jobs.

In Peppoloni's case, the individual work ethic becomes a collective work ethic: "Being right in front of the boss" will not make workers rich, but will put them in a better bargaining position and give them moral strength. Peppoloni insists that he does not want to become rich, personally; but that if his class and movement appropriate this ethic, everybody's life will be better. The religious sanction of the Protestant work ethic, in turn, is replaced by a political sanction: the value system of the class and of the organization promises him that, though we may not go to heaven, we will gain a better world here.

SHARED POSSIBILITIES

By way of conclusion, most of Valtèro Peppoloni's story, as we have seen, falls into shared narrative patterns, structures, and motifs. There are enough collective and shared elements in this story to justify viewing it as a representative document of the local working-class culture.

But then the question becomes: if it is so typical, what is individual about it? We may deal with this at two levels—one of content and one of form.

On the level of content, we may relate the culturally shared metaphors of the company's paternalism and the party's "fatherly" role with Peppoloni's early loss of his father, which he explicitly associates with the troubled relationship with authority which runs across his life. Thus, "collective" cultural traits acquire for him an intensely personal meaning.

On the level of form, Peppoloni's story is made up of culturally shared traits to such an extent that it becomes *too* typical, so much so that there is no other story quite as typical. No other story contains such a proportion of shared cultural traits, and organizes them so tightly: the extent of "collectiveness" is absolutely unique. What makes this story intensely personal is, in the end, the fulness, depth, and intensity of its personal use of shared cultural traits. That is why I would call it "representative," rather than "typical": like a "grammar of motifs," like a repertoire, it does not describe the "average" experience, but lists the ingredients of shared possibility. And it tells us, in a paradoxical way, that even those persons who are most shaped by cultural patterns are, on that very account, uniquely individual.

8

Sports, Work, and Politics
in an Industrial Town*

John Henry told his Captain,
Man ain't nothing but a man,
And 'fore I'll let that steam drill beat me down
I'll die with this hammer in my hand,
Die with this hammer in my hand.

John Henry, in Zora Neale Hurston,
Mules and Men

TIMEKEEPERS

Let me tell you how the story went. The company began to bring in those timekeepers, with stopwatches—American style, you know. The famous [Frederic W.] Taylor. Then the engineers, in order to apply this Taylor [method of scientific management] 100 percent, would call in six men they knew they could trust, and put them to work on the machines—bending iron. "You've got to make us look good, see, because people are coming, and they're going to watch every move we make." So these men would work and work and work. They didn't realize the harm they were doing, you understand. After that, they'd call in other workers [saying] "If those men could do this much work, so can you." And if you didn't do it,

---

*Presented to the conference on "Working-Class Memory and New Class Composition", Rimini, 23–25 October, 1981; published as "Sport, lavoro e politica in una città industriale," in C. Bermani and F. Coggiola, eds., *Memoria operaia e nuova composizione di classe*, (Rimini, Italy: Maggioli editore, 1986), 263–292.

they'd put you to sweeping floors—ten *lire* per hour. You understand? So you'd work yourself sick over those machines, you did. It's not that the workers did it because they wanted to . . . to show off, understand. They only wanted to take a few extra *lire* home.

The narrator, Mario Gabrielli, describes here the reorganization of work at the Terni steelworks in the late 1940s. After the demise of fascism and the end of World War II, the workers had gained some control over working conditions and hiring policies, even the selection of management personnel. The aftermath of the Left's defeat in the 1948 national elections favored the restoration of traditional power relationships in the factories, and the workers' gains stood now to be repealed all over Italy. The Terni steel company claimed that it had been forced to hire too many workers, and began to fire men (three thousand in 1952–53 alone) and to restore hierarchy, piece-rate pay, and speedups. Political discrimination and repression became rampant.

The company, however, was not content with discipline: it also aimed to gain the workers' consent. One of the more effective strategies it used was to appeal to aspects of their own culture. This process is shown in an implicit contradiction in Gabrielli's story. On the one hand, he insists that workers worked harder only because of economic pressures (low pay and fear of losing their jobs). On the other, he remembers that the engineers appealed to the test team's desire to "look good." The same ambivalence is apparent in the testimony of another worker, Calfiero Canali:

Well, in those days they sent those timekeepers around, to time people's work. And teams competed with one another: first shift, second shift, night shift. When the second shift came in, first thing they'd do, they'd look up at the blackboard where the other shift had marked how many ingots they'd made. "How many did they get? Two hundred? We'll do two hundred and ten, then." Next shift comes in—"How many? Two hundred and ten? We'll make two hundred and twenty." And they'd work until they could work no more, because they had incentives—a pittance, but we needed that money, and we all wanted it.

PORTELLI: I wonder if there was something else, besides money—some kind of competitive team spirit?

CANALI: Yes, yes. Competitive team spirit, yes, because every shift had a leader, a boss, and they always tried to compete with each other.

PORTELLI: Did it also have to do with the professional pride of skilled workers?

CANALI: Well, of course that was part of it, too. But the fact is, when those steel bars went through the hewers, well, there were a lot of accidents then. Over at the coils, they did everything by hand then. Have you ever seen what it's like? There's a white hot steel bar coming out of the train, and you're supposed to catch it with a pair of tongs and turn it around and pass it on to the next man and he puts in inside the other side of the train. And every once in a while someone would put this white-hot steel bar right through their leg, or their feet would be sawed off. Why? Because they were working too fast.

Canali and Gabrielli refer to the late 1940s and early 1950s, which were supposed to be exceptionally tough times. But things were not much different in the 1960s, according to Francesco Proietti. "It was a matter of prestige for the foremen. If one's team had made 450 tons, the other had to make 451." The team, Proietti says, participated because "it was a matter of money. The more you produced, the more you earned." When asked specifically, however, he also admits to other motivations. "Work has a financial side, but often it's also a matter of satisfaction, somehow. That was part of it, too. Yes, it was. The bosses insisted on this more than the workers; but the workers did, too, because—you know: 'They did so much. We've got to do more.' That exists, too."

This experience, of course, is not restricted to Italian steelworkers. Earl Turner, a coal miner from Lynch in Harlan County, Kentucky, had a foreman who "could run more coal than anybody on the section, man. He got so-and-so many tons yesterday. Well, you know, try to beat, do more tomorrow." But the men would "take chances," do "some dangerous things, some crazy things" also because of their own "pride" in workmanship:

Competition between the men. I'm gonna beat . . . I'm a better mine operator than you . . . shuttle car operator, operating them shuttle cars on rubber tires. Man, I got the best coupé and I cruise good. Everybody tryin' to show. And all the time the boss is gettin' a big bonus and we didn't know it. They makin' the money.

The workers' attitude, then, seems to have been shaped both by a need and a desire. Material need (the "financial side") caused them to literally work themselves nearly to death; the desire for respect, "satisfaction," and "pride" caused them to compete with the other workers. By encouraging them to think in terms of a competitive race, management channelled their motivations through the chain of command into more productivity, cooperation and discipline.

Interviewees always describe the situation in terms of races and competitions but are reluctant to admit that this approach struck a responsive chord in the workers' own attitudes. In most cases, they only acknowledge this idea when suggested by the interviewer, which may parallel the fact that the concept of "race" and "competition" was initially suggested by management. (Johnny Jones, also from Lynch, says, "We had a lot of bosses that was trying to get promoted, you know, get ahead. Run more coal than the other boss.")

However, this technique would not have been effective if the workers had not been receptive to it. They had little opportunity to refuse to do more work, but, by viewing it as a competition, they "justified" exploitation in terms acceptable to their own culture. As terms like "team" and objects like the stopwatch suggest, the ideological framework was that of sports.

Descriptions of work often use sports terms and metaphors. "In our team," says Vittorio Giantulli, a young forging technician, "we had a pressman and a dial-man who could have been world champions." In 1948, while management was presenting over-exploitation as an exciting competition, the unions were applying the same logic to vocational training. According to the former youth leader Raul Crostella, "We were the first in Italy—the national unions actually criticized us for it—who tried to give a new impulse to vocational training, by organizing competitions--*Ludi iuveniles*, we might say—among workers. All the young workers who had a skill, we made them compete in those games."

The Latin expression (meaning "youth games") shows where the idea came from: the *ludi iuveniles* were part of the *Littoriali*, a ritual created by fascism in the 1930s, in which students would compete in academic subjects and workers in trades and skills. In Terni, the *littoriali* involved construction workers, lace makers, olive pickers, butchers, mechanics, and several groups of skilled factory workers. In one event, three-man teams of skilled workers competed in the construction of a shooting mechanism for a piece of artillery.[1] Later, when low pay and management pressure "invited" workers to push themselves to the limit for piece-rate pay and to compete with one another to keep their jobs, it would be easy for them to interpret this experience in the light of those precedents.

This attitude was reinforced by the mass popularity of sports in the 1940s, and by the use of sports metaphors in popular speech. The Communist daily paper *l'Unità* filled the local pages with announcements of all sorts of competitions among readers and party members: the best recruiter, the prettiest girl, the loveliest child, the best peddler of party literature. The language was lifted from the sports page, mostly metaphors from the then extremely popular sport of bicycle racing: "Vanda Vanni rushes into second place" was the headline for a beauty contest. The ranking leader was always described as the wearer of the "yellow shirt" or the "pink shirt," which are the symbols of victory in the cycling tours of France and Italy. Again, there are precedents from the Fascist era: a work-safety drive in the 1930s was described and carried out with all the formulas and trappings of the long-distance bicycle races.[2]

Thus, while competition was encouraged by management, it was also actively sought by the workers; both sides invented similar events and used the same metaphors. The language of sports was a signifier capable of conveying two distinct sets of signifieds: discipline and productivity, or self-expression, sociability, pride, and identity. Both sides coexist, potentially, at all times; but either one prevails according to cultural power relationships. In the rest of this essay, I will try to trace some of these shifts by describing the role of sports in the workers' culture, its use by management and by the state, and the ways in which the coexistence of a shared signifier and opposed signifieds becomes a disrupting element in the workers' sense of their own identities and culture.

SPORTS IN THE WORKING-CLASS COMMUNITY

Alvaro Valsenti, a former factory worker and Communist official tells a story of growing up in the 1930s as a working-class child in Sant'Agnese, the "Red" proletarian neighborhood where even fascism could never gain a real foothold.

We used to go swimming along the factory canals. We would dive in and swim the underground canals, three or four hundred meters in the dark—we didn't even know what was there, in that water—and then we'd swim by the tenements, all the way to Sant'Agnese. It was a great adventure, like going on a cruise. That cool water, channelled down from the hills [to carry hydraulic power to the factory], filled with the refuse and oil dumped from the chemical and steel plants . . . We used to swim naked; the canal was our sea. Those of us who had summer jobs would go swimming as soon as they got off work; the rest, would be in the water from morning 'til night all summer. We all knew how to swim, which kids no longer do anymore; but we taught one another. We ran our own Olympics in 1936. Even before that, Sant'Agnese gave a great contribution to Terni's sports: soccer players, boxers, runners, swimmers, gymnasts, all kinds of athletes came from there. We were all in great physical shape. I can still dive from the ten meter platform, because we all learned by diving into the river from the iron bridge. We played soccer, went hunting—little kids, we'd take our fathers' rifles, hide them in burlap sacks, and out to the fields we'd go. Working-class boys aren't afraid of anything.

Though hunting is popular among all classes in central Italy, it has a strong connection with working-class life. A feature story in the Terni page of *l'Unità* in 1946, told how workers made their own bullets and went hunting every Sunday "oblivious of foremen, bosses, work, lack of money, inedible bread, the many problems of daily life." According to the paper, there were about fifteen thousand hunters in Terni province.[3] In the 1970s, Terni overwhelmingly rejected a referendum proposal to abolish hunting (the Communist party had come out officially against abolition); and about 10 percent of the population of Umbria was then estimated to be actively involved in hunting.

Hunting is a male sport, and Valsenti appropriately talks of working-class *boys*. Other traditional, pre-industrial sports—*bocce* (a kind of bowling) and *ruzzolone* ("rolling stone")—are also linked to male environments: the tavern, the wine cellar, and the *Dopolavoro* (the workers' "after-work" clubs created by fascism which were very active in the promotion of sports.[4] Though *bocce* and *ruzzolone* were often played (and still are occasionally) during the outings and picnics which were the favorite working-class Sunday activities involving the whole family, even then the games were played almost exclusively by males.

Sports connected with the daily experience of workers in many other ways. The popularity of competitive cycling coincided, in the 1940s and 1950s, with the long rows of bicycles parked by the factory gates or lined up at shift changes. Guido Perona, who won the gold medal in the pursuit race at the London Olympics of 1948, was raised in the crumbling alleys of Terni's old downtown area and worked at the steel plant. *L'Unità* described his career as a "back-and-forth between the track and the factory." One of the few female sports stars, the cyclist Diname Binarelli, also came from a working-class background and bore a name shaped by the industrial cultural tradition of the so-called "dynamic town."[5] Terni's greatest sports culture hero, world-champion motorcyclist Libero Liberati, began his career driving a motor van for the Terni steel company. The great auto racer Baconin Borzacchini came (as shown by his first name derived from the founder of international Anarchism, Mikhail Bakunin) from an anarchist family and (like Liberati, whose first name means "free") became acquainted with engines by working in a local motor repair shop.

On the other hand, Borzacchini, Perona, and Liberati belong to a different realm than the Sunday *bocce* players: that of spectator sports. Watching has always been more common than practicing sports in Italy, where three national sports dailies routinely sell more than most "regular" papers. Terni is no exception: *Il Corriere dello Sport* is the best selling paper at the stands near the steel factory's gates, and sports is the workers' main subject of conversation. "Sports talk," wrote Umberto Eco, "is outwardly similar to political talk . . . and turns out finally to be the parody of political talk. Since the parody absorbs all the energies that citizens have available for political discourse, sports talk is the *Ersatz*, and finally the replacement, of political discourse."[6]

Though there is truth in this statement, field work shows that the relationship between sports talk and political discourse is more complex. Sports, in fact, sometimes supply working-class citizens with language tools for political discourse. The partisan commander and Communist leader Alfredo Filipponi used a hunting metaphor when he urged his comrades to revolution after World War II: "Lenin said, 'When the thrush flies by, then is the time to shoot it. If you don't shoot when the thrush flies by, you may never get another chance'." Riziero Manconi, the last anarchist delegate to Terni's labor exchange in the 1940s, described his difference from the Communists by means of another hunting metaphor: "They always think in terms of numbers, numbers. There's more to it than numbers. I mean, if you have five hundred cartridges, and the other man only has twenty or thirty, but two or three hundred out of yours are no good, then the man with fewer cartridges may be better off than you are."

Sports also supplied metaphors of identity. In the 1920s, workers often rooted for cyclist Alfredo Binda, against his rival Leandro Guerra, because the latter was a Fascist while Binda came from a working-class, anti-Fascist family. In the 1940s, they rooted for the apolitical cycling star Fausto Coppi in opposition to his conservative-Catholic rival, Gino Bartali.[7] Alfredo Provantini, a party official and member of Parliament, wrote that, as a working-class boy in the 1940s, "I rooted for Torino and Fausto Coppi."[8] Torino was an almost invincible soccer team, based in industrial Turin and supported almost exclusively by Fiat workers. Also, Torino's colors happened to be deep red.

There were also deeper roots to the communication of sports and politics. The first gymnastics clubs created in Terni in the early 1900s were based in working-class neighborhoods. While one was established by Cassian Bon, a paternalistic Belgian industrialist,[9] others bore names like "Andrea Costa" (an early Socialist organizer), or "Giuseppe Garibaldi" (at the time, a radical anti-church symbol at least as much as a patriotic one). Leftist activists were commonly active in sports: Carlo Farini (son of the Socialist leader Pietro, and later a prominent Communist figure) played center-half for the Terni soccer team in the 1910s, and was noted for his rough play.[10] Young communists in the anti-Fascist underground in the 1920s used the Garibaldi gym as a meeting point; they insist, however, that they attended the gym for its own sake, not merely as a cover. "Sports was what kept us together," says a former activist and athlete. They all came from the same neighborhood, and the gym was their natural meeting point. When independent gym clubs were eliminated and replaced by the Fascist-run *Dopolavoro*, this function was lost. As late as 1938, however, a group of conspirators chose a boat race on the lake of Piediluco as the occasion for a meeting.

The partisan Bruno Zenoni says that the Gramsci partisan brigade was helped in its guerrilla operations in the Valnerina hills in 1943–44 by the fact that many of its members had hunted there before, and so knew the ground well. Earlier, many narrators remember the "Red Guards" toting hunting rifles as they watched at the factory gates during the sit-ins of 1921. "One day, this guy steps up to me and says, 'Have you got a hunting license?' I say, 'Yes, I do.' 'Well', says he, 'you go and stand guard over the power-house, then'," remembers Settimio Piemonti.

Calfiero Canali is one of the many narrators who hint at the possibility of using hunting weapons in class struggle—if only to reject it. "We all had weapons," in the riots after the firing of workers in 1953. "I mean, I didn't have anything. I was a hunter, I had my hunting rifle. What use is that, in front of a machine gun?"

STRENGTH AND WORKMANSHIP

In 1948, after the workers reacted violently to the wounding of Communist party Secretary Palmiro Togliatti, several rank-and-file activists from Terni were forced to seek refuge abroad to escape arrest. Claudio Locci, who spent several years in Czechoslovakia, proudly recalls becoming "a *udernik* and a *stakanovist*. A *udernik* is a worker who boosts production by way of strength; and a *stakanovist* is one who does it by way of ideas."

This distinction parallels the stratification of professional pride. "I always mixed with very highly skilled workers," says Santino Cappanera, "and in those circles the most respected person was the one who had ability to do jobs that others couldn't do. In other groups, whose work wasn't as skilled, maybe they had more feeling for the person who worked hardest physically with strength, for the person who would not tire easily. They were proud of that."

The stratification of pride parallels the stratification of the work force and the stratification of sports heroes. Some are linked to machines and technology, and represent the values of progress together with the "workmanship" which both Thorsten Veblen and Christopher Lasch identify in sports.[11] Others are linked to the body, and represent the values of physical prowess, strength, agility, and endurance. The first group includes world-famous auto and motorcycle racers like Borzacchini and Liberati; the second, the dynasties of wrestlers, shot-putters, discus-throwers, long-distance runners, and gymnasts, who came from the ranks of Terni's labor and achieved a more local but lasting fame. Though there is no one-to-one correspondence between types of workers and types of sports heroes, this pattern assures that the entire range of working-class identifications is represented in sports mythology.

As one enters Terni from the Rome motorway, one drives along Borzacchini Boulevard right by the Liberati Stadium. Both were inaugurated in the 1970s, and the names show how important these two heroes still were long after their deaths. At the end of the boulevard, a third artifact completes the town's self-presentation: a huge steel forge removed from the factory and mounted as a monument. Terni greets travelers in the name of sports and work, united under the aegis of progress and technology. "It is only right," someone wrote, "that an industrial town like Terni should give birth to motor aces like Liberati and Borzacchini."[12] Alvaro Valsenti also agrees that "the passion for engines, progress, technology, and mechanics" is one reason for Terni's workers' cult of Borzacchini and Liberati. In fact, early interest in automobiles was shown in Terni by Socialists and Anarchists; and in the 1940s factory workers raised money to buy Liberati a competitive motorcycle.[13]

While Borzacchini and Liberati embody the modern world of the skilled workers, a long list of wrestlers and gymnasts represents the culture of the body in which the unskilled workers also could identify. The clearest case for this relationship can be made through what *l'Unità* described as "the great, good, and popular figure" of Aldo Galeazzi, who won several national workers' competitions in the 1930s. Galeazzi participated, as he recalls, "in almost every sport: boxing, wrestling, discus throw, shot put, and weightlifting." "If you ask around among the old comrades in the industrial neighborhood," says his niece Lucilla Galeazzi, "you'll find that they all remember [Aldo] Galeazzi. He was renowned mostly for his size and his strength. They remember him because he was active in sports, and later because he joined the Communist party and became an activist. Everybody remembers him on the front row at every demonstration, every battle, and every struggle."

The episode which consigned Galeazzi to folk legend (complete with many variant versions) concerns his response in 1953 to finding his own name in the list of men fired from the steelworks. Several workers, at the time, reacted by physically attacking the members of the company hierarchy whom they held responsible for the loss of their jobs. Galeazzi went straight to where the personnel manager lived, knocked on the door, and asked the man's wife to let him speak to him. He knew he was at home, so, when she told him he was out, Galeazzi simply raised his voice and said: "Well, should he ever come back, please tell him Aldo Galeazzi was here and will be waiting for him outside. If I'm not hired back immedi-

ately, I'll break both his arms and legs." The threat carried more
conviction because of his athletic record. And he got his job back.

The Italian language uses the same word—*lotta*—for "wrestling" (as in sports) and "struggle" (as in "class struggle"). This
coincidence reinforces the physical dimension of social conflict,
symbolized by the Galeazzi legend. Often, street fights also involved authentic athletic feats. In the 1953 general strike, Bruno Zenoni recalls that "There was this other guy, a butcher—he had been
a shepherd, I guess—who threw stones from the barricade all the
way across the square at the police. Can you believe it?" Dante Bartolini remembers a young man, "they called him Tarzan," who
"jumped on a [police] jeep, and each cop he caught he hurled him
down to the pavement. He caught one carrying a rifle, hit him on
the head, got hold of his helmet, whirled him around like a bowling
pin—like that, *brrr*—then he picked up the jeep and pushed it out
of the way."

In 1927, after the execution of Sacco and Vanzetti, the anti-
Fascists decided to black out the town in protest. One man tied a
piece of wire to a brick and was supposed to throw it across the
high power wires. "Workers are strong. Workers can do it," says
Arnaldo Lippi. Unfortunately, he forgot to let go of the wire and
was electrocuted.

WHO OWNS SPORTS

In 1925, the Terni company announced that it was building, across
the street from the steelworks, "the largest sports field in Central
Italy." This was a public-relations move on the part of the company,
which had recently been involved in controversy with the local Fascist officials over the control of the regional hydraulic resources
(Mussolini had finally decided the question in the company's favor).
At the same time, the building of the new sports field sanctioned
the newly-expanded company's domination over the town's leisure
as well as over its work. It was also the first sign of the primacy of
spectator sports over participatory practice. The local press described it as a token of the "noble feeling of love which binds the
company to the town."[14]

The new stadium was built on company-owned land. The
money, however, was docked out of the workers' pay envelopes,
without bothering to ask for their consent. While many workers
might have given gladly for better sports facilities, some resented it.

"Sports are but another excuse for vampirizing the employees," said a letter to a newspaper. Another complained that, because of high seasonal unemployment in the chemical and electric sectors, many "are out of work and have other sports to worry about."[15] Some workers, however, took another attitude: the new stadium was built with their money and labor, and therefore it rightly belonged to them rather than the company. "The field was made by the workers," says Augusto Cuppini, a steelworker, athlete and sports organizer. "We had to pay one *lira* a month. What that means is that it was made by the workers, not by the company. It was made by the working class."

The building of the new stadium introduces a new relationship between sports and workers: supply from above. Until then, sports had been largely a voluntary, self-run activity. With the onset of fascism—and especially with the establishment of its welfare, educational and leisure-time agencies—sports were brought to the people by the state, either directly or through the increasingly state-controlled company. Apparently, the state and the company were only giving the workers a chance to do better and with less effort what they were already doing or would have liked to do anyway. Even present-day Communists who were then involved in the *Dopolavoro* still fail to see it as part of the regime's strategy. Aldo Galeazzi (whose photograph in all the regalia of Fascist athletic glory figures prominently in the *Dopolavoro* publications) claims that the company was "forced" to cater to the workers' sports needs in order to prevent mounting discontent. Augusto Cuppini remarks that, "aside from all the mistakes that fascism made, sports during fascism were well organized. In those days, a worker or a worker's son had access to sports. Today, they don't." Lowering the threshold of access to sports—and other services and forms of consumption—allowed the regime to relieve pressure from wage levels and to reap a precious harvest of propaganda.

The question whether this new access was a concession from above or a gain from below ties in with the question of who "owned" the new stadium morally. As to the legal side, there never was any question. The workers, the state and the company all had a stake in sports; but the shared signifier was being used by implicitly conflicting sides to satisfy divergent ends and to carry divergent messages. The 1941 company yearbook declares that *Dopolavoro* sports change the workers' and the nation's spirit, and improve the race "shaping the new Military Nation."[16] The same line is echoed by all the institutions (schools, media, and army) which deal with sports. On the other hand, none of the working-class interviewees mentions race-building or military prowess; what they gained from sports was pleasure, self-realization, and companionship.

The middle class was more receptive to the ideological message. Laura Galli, who came from one of the town's "best" families and was active in school sports in the 1930s (women's access to sports was another effect of the lowering of the threshold), says that sports are one of the reasons why she associates fascism with her "happy youth." Young people, she says, "were kept busy at all levels," so they stayed away from drugs and other modern dangers. Her father insisted that she practice sports. "I was his first child, and he wanted a son, so he used sports to train me in courage and bravery. He took me hunting along with him; when I was 18, he got me a license for a .24 [caliber] rifle. I was on my high school track team—javelin throw and relay run. I took part in the national student games, trying to uphold my school's name."

Anna Santini, from a family of small merchants, also recalls:

> I was happy, because fascism gave us some satisfaction, too. I was an athlete, and we had a chance to go skiing for free. I was ten or twelve, and at that age, you understand, I was happy. Everything was paid for, everything was all right. Of course we wore a *fasces*, the Fascist symbol, on our sweaters; and we had to do the Fascist salute all the time. I was the youngest member of the team, and once I won the long-distance race in a competition up North. Then the Fascists began their shout—*"eia eia alalà."* That was their cheer—and their salute, and we had these big *fasces* on our backs which at the time didn't seem to weigh too much—nowadays perhaps they might, but then we didn't . . . . It was good. And all ended when Fascism fell.

While sports were part of the regime's attempt to monopolize people's leisure, their organization through the *Dopolavoro* contributed to the remaking of Terni into a company town. "The company took over all branches of sports," says Cuppini, "boating at Piediluco, skiing, swimming—they made a new swimming pool by the chemical plant at Nera Montoro in 1935, I think. They used to hire all the best athletes, like Fiat does nowadays."

The joint strategy of company and government preempted all leisure time and space. Any activity which took place outside this control was suspect—including perfectly innocuous church-youth activities, which eventually goaded even the Church into some sort of opposition. Poliuto Chiappini, a Catholic activist, remembers with delight "how mad the Fascists were when athletes from our oratories beat them in sports, where the superiority of Mussolini's new generations was supposed to shine." In fact, sports, especially soccer (which requires space, of which the churches had plenty) were one of the attractions that the Church offered to young people. Even some Communist workers chose to send their children to the parish rather than have them join the Fascist youth groups (Valsenti, however, remembers that, at the oratory, he was subjected to constant preaching in favor of the Fascist regime and against Communism).

The real conflict, however, did not lie so much in the creation of alternative institutions as in the attribution of meaning to the existing ones. As is often the case with paternalistic relationships, what the rulers saw as a generous gift appeared to the ruled as some kind of negotiated right.[17] Thus, the workers also saw their participation in sports sponsored by the state or the company as a service rendered to their employers, and expected some kind of compensation. Reporting a game played by the Terni soccer team, a northern newspaper wrote: "What the Terni athletes had in mind was a job at the factory first, and a place on the team second." Working-class athletes felt that the time they devoted to company sports was a sort of "overtime," which compensated all the services and opportunities they received. This is evident in an episode recalled by Aldo Galeazzi. In order to protest for the unhealthy conditions on the shop floor, he stopped showing up for training and competitions at the *Dopolavoro*. He returned only after being moved to a less unhealthy job with better hours and conditions.

The struggle over meanings also invested the cultural symbols derived from sports. Terni's greatest sports glory in the 1920s and 1930s was Baconin Borzacchini, named after Mikhail Bakunin by his father, a fervent Anarchist. When Baconin became a famous champion, his name became a problem, until at the age of twenty-six he allowed himself to be formally baptized and renamed Mario Umberto, after the king's son, Umberto, and his bride, Maria Josè. A symbol of working-class revolutionary ideals was thus appropriated and subverted into a symbol of monarchist loyalty. His funeral, not long after his change of name, was a great ritual of unity among all classes, gathering an immense crowd under the eyes of Church and state dignitaries in the town square. The regime capitalized on its new ownership of its name, when the names of the Garibaldi gym

club and of the *Ternana* soccer team were both changed temporarily
to *Mario Umberto Borzacchini*.

SPORTS AND LOCAL IDENTITY

"It was after the Ethiopian war [in 1936]. They played this soccer
game in Terni—Rome against Turin. Most people here rooted for
Rome. But when the Romans came into town, they began to insult
us . . ." (Valtèro Peppoloni). Terni was very proud of its new dignity
as a province seat, to which it had been raised in 1927, and of its
foremost symbol: the new fountain in the center of the new square
surrounded by all the new government buildings. The fountain's
thin and tall spout of water gushing high from a low circular base
was intended as a symbol of Terni's water resources, but it also lent
itself to jokes and ridicule. When the Rome supporters reached
Terni and saw the monument they began, with their traditional ar-
rogance toward "hicks," to make jokes about the fountain ("It looks
like a pen in an inkstand . . .") and other landmarks, enraging the
local people. Peppoloni says "As soon as word got around, it was
like a flood, like lightning, and friendliness turned to hostility. And
bedlam broke loose." Emilio Ferri recalls that "There was fighting
in the streets—along Main Street and all around the railroad station. It seemed that it would never end. It went on for hours."

Most narrators make a point of stressing that everybody joined
in: Fascists, anti-Fascists, and there's a legend that even the Bishop
broke a chair over a Roman's head.[19] Some link the episode to hostility toward Rome as a symbol of the fascist regime and of the new
Italian colonial Empire. Others, who identified with Terni's proletarian and productive image, were hostile to the Romans as bureaucratic parasites ("They do nothing all day and eat; while we work
and have nothing"). Others joined in for the sake of a good fight, or
reacted to the insult to local pride. People joined in with different
meanings in mind—mostly, with mixed meanings in each mind.
But it makes a great deal of sense that the most serious breach of
law and order in the years of fascism derived from an insult to local
identity linked to a soccer game.

Local pride was rooted deep in the workers' culture. "No matter what party you belong to", says Cuppini, "when someone hears
Terni's name. . . . I'm from Terni too. You see, Liberati was known
all over the world, and so was Borzacchini." Terni always suffered
from a sense of isolation and obscurity: away from main routes of

trade with no tourist attraction and hardly ever mentioned in the news, it is made visible by its industries (which also "bear Terni's name") and by some sports heroes. When the *Ternana* soccer team made the major league in the 1970s, Terni's name got more airplay and press coverage each week than in any other year of its history.

For some time, certain sports events also ritually joined Terni to the rest of the country. The most important were two motor races which gained a mythical status mainly because they crossed all of Italy, North to South: the *Mille Miglia* ("Thousand Miles") auto race, and the Milan-Taranto motorcycle race. They came through Terni each year, and they became a sort of modern seasonal ritual. People would gather early along the route of the races, and spend all day making out names of competitors from newspaper lists and calculating times and rankings.

Sometimes, the cycling tour of Italy also came through Terni to put it in the news and make it feel in touch with the world. "The Tour of Italy would come right down our street," says Vincenza Giontella, "and we would stand there and see the stars in person, and everybody cheered. . . . Then, the *Mille Miglia* . . . Borzacchini was in it, and he lived next door. The *Mille Miglia*, too, drove right through Main Street."

The visibility which sports confers to the local community is a powerful antidote to internal conflict. Its meaning, however, changes with power relationships. In the 1930s, these rituals helped unify Terni under a supposedly paternalistic company. In the 1940s, when the workers thought they "owned" the town through the election of a Leftist administration, the same rituals became functional to the dream of a community unified behind its vanguard of industrial workers. In the 1950s, after the workers had been again defeated, they helped unify the town, both as a consolation for its losses and as a harbinger of the rising consumer culture.

When Guido Perona won his gold medal in the London Olympics in 1948, *l'Unità* wrote that sports in Terni were "reborn from the ruins of war just like, through the will of the workers, the town itself has been resurrected": the working class had political control of the town, and therefore identified all the town's symbols with itself.[20] Alberto Provantini writes that Liberati's victory in the *Circuito dell'Acciaio* (the symbolically named "Circuit of Steel" which Terni had created to give him a chance to shine in his home town) was "a symbol of redemption."[21] The workers took over the *Dopolavoro*, and renamed it as "Unione Sportiva Lavoratori Società Terni"—literally, "Terni Company Employees Sports Association."

However, "Società" was commonly left out, "Terni" was understood to refer to the town rather than the company, and the club's name thus designated the *town's workers* rather than the *company's employees*. (I remember perceiving these class overtones as a middle-class child, when reading the name of the track team in sports papers. No other team bore *lavoratori*—workers—in its name.) Factory workers raised money for the soccer team and the union initiated a drive to buy a competitive engine for Liberati. *L'Unità* used the same word—"dismantling"—to denounce the threats to the steel plant and to the soccer team, calling workers to defend both of these precious communal properties.

A sign of return to normality after the war was that, as Provantini remembers, "Across the street from the steel plant, people began once more to crowd the stadium for soccer games." Calfiero Canali recalls that, when he was on the Sunday shift, he would just cross the street from the plant to the stadium in his work clothes. "Nobody thought anything about it, then. Nowadays, if you don't wear good clothes at the game, they look down their noses at you, but then it was all right." This stadium filled with workingmen in overalls often witnessed clashes not unlike the then frequent confrontations of workers with the police in the streets. "Yes, fans were very hot," says Canali, and often "the air was thick with bricks. You know, tempers were hot. We were always struggling, always fighting with the cops when we went on strike. As soon as you stepped out of the gates, there they were with their jeeps and their clubs, beating you up. So we had caught the habit." The crisis of authority spread from the factory both to the streets and the stadium.

After the workers' defeat in 1953, the unification of the town behind its sports symbols took on another meaning. This is how Bruno Capponi, a Socialist unionist and former vice-mayor, describes the symbolic importance of Liberati in those lean years: "When Liberati began to appear and win his first races, the *workers* raised money to buy him a good motorcycle. This shows how our *Citizens* wished to make their town known and appreciated also through sports."[22] [my italics]

The shift from lower-case "workers" to upper-case "Citizens" in the space of three lines parallels the shift in the meaning of sports: what had been a symbol of the working-class leadership in the reconstruction of the town was now a consolation for defeated workers and the offer of an alternate, identity as classless citizens. Radio news of Liberati's distant victories generated waves of excitement and a sudden increase in traffic accidents; but their ultimate role was as an outlet of frustration. "Those were hard times," continues Capponi, and Liberati "meant for us in Terni what Gino Bartali's victory in France had meant for the whole country in 1948.

Capponi refers to a semi-legendary episode in the history of politics and sports in Italy. Bartali's sensational victory in the 1948 Tour of France, amplified by the radio, was supposed to have helped allay the tension following the attempted murder of the Communist party Secretary Palmiro Togliatti a few days earlier. "Bartali's victory had a lot of influence," says Valtèro Peppoloni. "I was a fan, and all the fans, when the radio brought the news, felt some kind of a let-down. As I listened to the radio the anger for Togliatti's wounding simmered down."

Capponi suggests that Liberati functioned locally in the 1950s much like Bartali had functioned nationally in 1948. Workers who identified with him because he was one of them (they had paid for his machine) now identified through him with the town, and could still believe that the town belonged to them. The continuity of the signifier—Liberati—smoothed the reversal of the signified.

YOUNG FANS

The 1970s and 1980s have been a time of crisis for Terni. The gradual closing down of factories and loss of employment opportunities for young people weakened the cohesion of working-class culture and made room for marginal youth cultures and countercultures. Among the spontaneous groups, one of the more visible were the so-called *Ultras*: soccer fans, mostly from working-class backgrounds, who formed something resembling a social club, a youth gang, and a political collective. Marcello (*Ultras* chose not to give their last names), one of the leaders, explained:

> They keep telling us, you know—with all the problems we have, why are you wasting your time worrying about the soccer team? What kind of nonsense is that? All right—and yet, I worry about it anyway, because, just as you worry about politics, and it's only a masturbation of the brain, I might as well worry about the team. It's masturbation, too, but at least it gives me something, a group of people to be with, a social life, things to do.

The so-called *Ultras* are both similar and different from traditional working-class fans. Many come from the same neighborhoods as the old athletes of the 1920s and 1930s (most of my informants were from Sant'Agnese), and turn to sports, like their elders did, in search of sociability. "The game isn't what really counts; what really counts in the stadium is that we are together, enjoying ourselves," says one of them. Their sociability, however, has shifted from participation to spectator sports.

Of course, hundreds of young people do participate in sports today in Terni; the building of sports facilities is one of the achievements of the Leftist administration. Sports, however, are looked at mostly as services rendered individually to citizens, a leisure activity with no political or social identification. Only the *Ultras* keep alive the old connection of sports and class, if ambiguously. "Youth movements in Terni never amounted to much," said Marcello, "so all the marginal proletariat joined up with us." "In the beginning", another boy recalled, "Leftists and Fascists were together in the *Ultras*. Then the Fascists were pushed out, so now it's only comrades. They carry five-point star banners [the symbol of the terrorist *Red Brigades*], and have names like the Red and Green Panthers [the town's and team's colors grafted onto the Black Panther Party name]. They draw hammers-and-sickles on walls, and so on."

One sign of continuity with the past is that sports continue to be seen as a symbol of the town's destiny. In 1983, the local page of *Il Messaggero* complained about an unfair referee, and wondered whether "there is a plan somewhere to destroy this team, and this town," as if the crisis in steel and the decline of the team were part of the same dark conspiracy.[23] The *Ultras* also perceive analogies between the stadium and the world at large. Marcello describes the division of seats and the patterns of behavior at the game as a metaphor of the split between older, securely employed workers, and the young, marginal unemployed. He points out, however, that occasionally the more respectable and older fans also participate in outbursts of violence, and links this behavior to a widespread sense of uneasiness and discontent.

> They say we are the scum of Terni—trouble makers, scum, all sorts of things. Terni wears a front of respectability, but underneath it's one whole big problem: it has an extremely high occurrence of drug addictions, mental illness, nervous stress. But they say we're the ones who are the scum. Like, when the team walks out into the field, we have this ritual of firing colored smoke signals, and it's always a hassle with the people because the smoke bothers them. They breathe poison

all week in the factory; the air pollution in this town is frightening, sometimes if you go up the hills and look down it looks like a dome of smoke—and yet smoke only bothers them in those five minutes before the game. So it used to come to real fights, real blows, with the workers. You see, those who have regular jobs usually don't join our group; they sit quietly and watch the game. They only let go and scream along with us when we are away, but at home games they are quiet. And then, suddenly they explode. I've been through two times when the fans broke out of the hustings and into the field and began to destroy everything. Of course, we joined in, but we didn't start it. It was started by people in their fifties, in their sixties; people who would never dream of doing a thing like that, and yet there they were. They are apathetic, you understand—and then, they just explode.

SHARED SIGNIFIER, SPLIT SIGNIFIED

It is a commonplace to say that the ideas of the ruling class are the ruling ideas in society. There are, however, no satisfactory explanations of just how dominant ideas become dominant. While behavior may be imposed and controlled from above, ideas can only be validated from inside. I would submit that one of the most effective strategies consists in presenting the dominant ideology not as an imposition, but as an *offer*. We have seen how management and the political system were able to use sports to promote their ends precisely because sports were part of the workers' own spontaneous values and practices. If the offer is to be accepted, it must be credible; it can fulfill its function in the strategy of power only if it caters in part to some authentic need of the subordinate groups. The result is more in the form of a negotiated (and unbalanced) tension than of a one-directional domination.

The offer from above is always selective. While it necessarily legitimates some aspects of the people's culture, it implicitly and effectively de-legitimates others and, by the very fact of its selectivity, it fragments the unity and coherence of the culture. Rather than a paradigm of values and meanings, culture may be seen as a structured field of forces, in which every value and meaning coexists with its opposites in a shifting balanced tension. Without recurring to Lévi-Strauss's structural analysis of myth, which describes culture much in these terms, we may observe how proverbs, which formulate many values of folk and working-class culture, always tend to run in opposing pairs: "unity makes strength"/"who does alone does for three"; "when there's a will there's a way"/"man hopes and God decides"; "who sleeps late catches no fish"/"who goes slow goes safe and far."[24] In the nineteenth century, educational booklets destined for workers often used proverbs as their titles, so that workers could identify with the "folk wisdom" they expounded. However, out of each "pair," they would use only the ones that expressed values approved and promoted by the bourgeoisie: the checks and balances of the proverb system were destroyed and the opposing values were dropped out of sight.

Such balanced pairs may be detected in industrial culture as well. Values like independence, solidarity, and prudence, are balanced against individualism, ambition, and the work ethic—both sets being functional to the culture. Work is both satisfaction, and alienation, both achievement, and exploitation, sociability and danger. According to a Newcastle miners' song, for instance, the ideal "collier lad" "knows how to work/and he knows how to shirk."[25] While knowing how to work is essential to group loyalty and self-respect, being able to "shirk" is essential to the preservation of physical integrity. We must always remember that John Henry did beat the steam drill, but "He drove so hard that it broke his poor heart/ He laid down his hammer and he died."

In Terni's working-class history, the coherence of the workers' attitude toward sports and work is fragmented in three ways by separating (1) productivity from safety, (2) class identity from community, and (3) competition from sociability.

In the production contests, productivity prevailed and, as shown by the accidents described by Canali or by the "chances," and the "dangerous things, crazy things" mentioned by Earl Turner, the balancing value—defense of physical integrity—had to be disregarded: the work/shirk equilibrium had been broken. In fact, we might look at sports as one way of separating the care of the body from the realm of work and moving it into the realm of leisure. Galeazzi's "strike" was a successful attempt to keep them together, as he could not cultivate his body as an athlete if it was being destroyed in the factory as a worker. The different reactions to smoke in the factory and in the stadium, on the other hand, are a result of the separation of the two spheres.

On another level, the desire to be a full-fledged member of one's whole community coexists with the need to recognize the differences within it. Local versus class identity, and citizen versus worker status form another balanced structure of valued identities. At certain times, especially in the late 1940s, workers were able to keep local identity and class identity together: in this working-class town, *ternano* and worker were almost synonymous. The manipulation of cultural heroes like Borzacchini and Liberati, the shrewd use of the town's name, and the recurrence of sports rituals broke this unity: origins and class again became separate concepts. Factory workers were promoted to upper-case "Citizens" and were encouraged to look at themselves as *ternani* like all others, including the plant hierarchy or the local bourgeoisie, and forget their differences.

Finally, competition and sociability are another pair of contrasting and yet necessary values, and sports are one way of keeping them together. While not all social activities are competitive, the pleasure and meaning of sports is in the competition. Only when competition alone is stressed and sociability downplayed, sports begin to look like a rat race for success or a desperate struggle for jobs. In the factory contests, though workers fell back on the team spirit to make sense of what they were doing, the aim was not to be together but to keep their jobs—necessarily, at the expense of their less competitive co-workers who were fired.

Workers identified with sports because they recognized in them meanings which they considered their own. But these meanings are separated from their defining context. Most important, they were offered from above rather than created from below; and the workers' very sense of being the creators of their own culture was undermined.

At them same time, new meanings—nationalism and militarism—were introduced. This process was made possible by the fact that the public articulation of the meanings of mass culture is always reserved to the elites. Workers (avid consumers of sports papers and televised sports) hear their own practices and interests explained in the terms of the dominant culture and of its values, and find it more difficult to articulate what they originally meant to themselves. The outward events—the signifiers—seem the same; it may be difficult or impossible to detect and resist the shifts of meanings behind them.

Sports, then, help unify and pacify a socially divided society not because they mean the same thing to all people and all classes, but precisely because they mean different things to different groups, but manage to keep diverging or conflicting meanings together under the same set of signs. This, I would argue, is a basic mechanism of mass culture.[26] When signifiers are shared, the difference of signifieds is hard to detect. The people's culture loses coherence and is turned into a fragmentary subculture bearing all the negative characteristics which Antonio Gramsci recognized in primitive folklore: a contradictory, non-self-conscious, simple, and unsystematic array of heterogeneous practices and ideas.[27] In the light of the process we have described, however, folklore no longer appears as the residue of an archaic past, but rather as the contemporary, constantly renewed product of the permanent disruption of the culture of working people in the encounter with the cultural messages of the elite—and of its remaking in cultural resistance. But that is another story.

9

Typology of Industrial Folk Song*

COMMUNITY AND FORMS

The expression "folk song" implies at least two factors: a *source* located outside the culture of the ruling elites (in Antonio Gramsci's terms, outside the "hegemonic culture"); and a form of *transmission* based mainly on orality. These conditions, in turn, imply the social context of a *community* or a chain of interrelated communities, conceived to be essentially homogeneous, based on face-to-face contact, circumscribed in space and stable in time, and endowed with specific and shared *forms* of expression. The concepts of non-hegemonic source, oral transmission, community and shared forms are the cornerstones of the standard definition of folk song.

The songs of the urban, industrial working class do not fit this definition completely. The source is still nonhegemonic, and often related to the more traditional folk cultures; but the dissolution of traditional communities in the urban context and the growth of literacy and other media often make pre-industrial forms of expression and communication obsolete or unnecessary. Also, the relationship of the nonhegemonic subject to the elite culture undergoes change. Rather than being "outside" (as the rural traditional folk are conventionally supposed to be), the industrial working class is clearly inside and antagonistic. Thus, cultural differences caused by lack of contact are minimized, while differences caused by intense contact and conflict are stressed. I would not, however, subscribe to the view that there is no such thing as an industrial, working-class folk song. I think it is more productive to revise our definition in order to catch this elusive concept, close enough to folk

---

*Published as "Tipologia della canzone operaia," in *Movimento operaio e socialista* [Genova, Italy], VI, 2 (May-August, 1983), 207–224.

song proper to warrant analogies, but different enough to make all assimilation unsatisfactory.

I will attempt here to sketch a typology of the ways in which the music of Italian industrial workers is shaped by the search for community and for adequate forms. In order to limit the abstract nature inherent in any typology, I will use mostly examples from one specific place, the industrial town of Terni in Umbria, Central Italy. I will also, however, occasionally draw from other sources. The final section will be devoted to the close analysis of an individual industrial folk song.

THE RESIDUAL COMMUNITY

Persistence of Pre-Industrial Forms

Industrialization develops against a rural background. Often, as in Terni's case, it is dropped wholesale from outside into an unchanged environment. The steel factory that was built in Terni in 1885 employed immigrant workers, often from rural areas, and many commuters from nearby villages. Pre-industrial culture and forms of expression, thus, survived even inside the factory. The repertoire of Trento Pitotti, a farmhand, shoemaker and steelworker, who has lived most of his life in the hill village of Labro, includes traditional ballads, ritual and religious songs, popular songs, and political songs learned in the factory. Persistence is facilitated by individual and family memory, and by the fact that, in the early industrial age, the uses of leisure time changed more slowly than those of the working day. Taverns, wine cellars, and country outings (as well as jails) preserve old forms; traditional villages and neighborhoods retained much of their original character long after the arrival of the factory, and industrial workers lived at close contact with people employed in more traditional trades (artisans, cart drivers, and the like). In Terni, the local petty bourgeoisie resented industrial culture as an outside encroachment, and sponsored the revival of certain traditional forms, including singing May Day rituals, as an affirmation of local identity and roots.

Changing Rural Forms

When rural workers enter the factory, they often forsake their traditional forms of expression. Sometimes, however, when these forms are still lively, and when industrialization is a very rapid process, they modulate them to suit the new situation. This is the case for much of the traditional culture of the Valnerina (the Nera River valley), a rural and hill area from which many workers commuted to the steel mills of Terni.

The process can be seen at work in the history of a single *stornello* (a lyric verse), which was originally brought to the valley by shepherds who wintered with their flocks in the Roman *campagna*. The original *stornello*, as sung by former shepherd Pompilio Pileri, went: "Dormo fra le pecore e li cani/pe' fa' magna' l'agnello a li Romani" ("I have to sleep with sheep and dogs to feed lamb to the city folks in Rome"). When shepherds brought it back to the Valnerina, the farm workers and tenant farmers changed it to fit their relationship to the landlords: the version sung by farm hand Luigi Matteucci replaces "the city folks in Rome" ("li romani") with "the rich gentlemen" ("li signori"). Finally, the commuting construction workers introduced union terminology and industrial class relationships. The version sung by construction worker and Communist official Amerigo Matteucci replaces the Romans and the gentlemen with "the bosses" ("li padroni") and has become a sort of unofficial folk anthem of working-class Valnerina. But even in this version, the first line is unchanged: sleeping with the sheep and dogs is no longer a reference to actual living conditions, but rather a metaphor grounded in the industrial workers' still vivid memory of their recent pre-industrial past.

Sometimes, in fact, the words and music remain the same, but their meanings change. This is the case of traditional southern songs found in Rome's *borghetti* (immigrant shanty towns) in the late 1960s and early 1970s. Loreta Lippa and Antonia Grande, who had come to the Rome slums from an Abruzzi mountain village, took a verse from a love ballad (which was originally concerned with Turkish raids on Italian coasts), and used it to voice their alienation from the city and nostalgia for their roots. "If the Holy Pope gave me all of Rome / And asked me to forsake the ones I love / I would answer him, no, Holy Crown / I'd rather have my loves than all of Rome." Tommaso D'Agostino, a construction worker from Calabria who had participated in the squatters' and homeless people's movements of the late 1960s, sang another archaic southern folk song as a metaphor of the expropriation of workers who cannot afford to live in the houses they build. "I worked so hard to build a castle / Thinking that I would be its lord / After I made it beautiful and rare / Someone took the keys away from me."[1]

"Imperfect Monostrophism"

The two Abruzzi women sang the lines about Rome and the Pope as a *stornello*—an independent, one-verse lyric piece—but it was originally a verse of a long ballad. The weakening of traditional community makes long performances more difficult, offers fewer occasions to learn long songs, and therefore favors fragmentation. New compositions also tend to be short, often only in one verse. Ever since the early collections of Costantino Nigra in the 1880s, folklorists have described the one-verse lyric piece (*stornello* or *strambotto*) as characteristic of southern folk singing, as opposed to the longer, northern narrative ballads.[2] We will see that the new, urban one-verse piece both resembles this "monostrophic" form, and diverges from it.

Many such pieces (which, for lack of a better term, I will call *strofette*, a generic word for "short verses") were sung in Terni in the early phases of industrialization. The best-known described the different status of the local factories. "Here comes Grüber [wool mill] carrying an umbrella / Next is Centurini [jute mill] with patches on / Then the steelworks with no breeches at all." Or "The steelworks wear a cap / The Royal [gun factory] wears a tub hat."

In 1907, during a long lockout, steelworkers sang verses against the head manager. "With Spadoni's whiskers / We'll make ropes / To hang those rascals"; "With Spadoni's whiskers / We'll make brooms / With his skin, / we'll make dancing shoes."

These verses show a characteristic which is typical of this stage of industrial folk song: the anaphoric repetition of the first line as the matrix of a paradigmatic multiplication. Thus, there are endless possibilities for verses about what workers would like to do with Spadoni's whiskers and with other parts of his body. One verse suggests using his blood to sign the contract.[3] In fact, the one-verse, "monostrophic" label does not fully describe the operation of this form (and it may not fully apply to traditional *stornelli*, either). Although each *strofetta* or verse is a self-enclosed metric, musical, and semantic unit, they are seldom sung separately. They are more likely to be performed in associative strings of partly remembered, partly improvised pieces, free from narrative sequence and strict logical ties, but often linked by the anaphoric first line. During the squatters' two-night sit-in beneath the horseback statue of the emperor Marcus Aurelius on Capitol Hill in Rome, Tommaso D'Agostino made up a *stornello*: "I've been here tonight / Sitting underneath the horse / And I won't go away / Even if they lock me up in jail." He then went on improvising more verses, all based on the repetition of the "I've been here tonight . . . And I won't go away" pattern, until his powers of invention were exhausted. Then he simply went back to *stornelli* from oral tradition, unrelated to the theme and context.

We may define this form as "imperfect monostrophism": an amoebic form in which each verse is independent and may be performed individually, but is, in practice, always joined to others. Traces of this structure may be detected also in the traditional blues. Many early Italian labor and revolutionary songs are based on this form. The most famous, of course, is *Bandiera Rossa* ("The Red Flag"), the folk anthem of the working class, with its endless stream of verses all beginning with "*Avanti popolo*" (forward, people).

Imperfect monostrophism is suited to an environment of quick change, when conflict is endemic, sharp, and brief, and takes the form of personal resentment against individual bosses rather than deep-seated class antagonism. One aspect of the fluid nature of the *strofette* is the way in which they interchange with other folk forms (such as proverbs, as in another verse sung by Loreta Lippa). The verses about Spadoni became graffiti, then slogans, then *strofette* again. Deeply rooted in the ancient tradition of monostrophic lyric folk songs, aphorisms, and proverbs, these humble verses also anticipate future urban forms such as the chanted slogan.

THE SUBSTITUTE COMMUNITY

Workers' Organizations and the Proletarian Anthem

The *Inno dei lavoratori* ("Workingmen's Anthem") was for a long time the "official" mass marching song and brass-band standard of workers' parties, associations, and unions. It is still used as such by the more reformist wing of the Left today. The words were written by Filippo Turati, who was the leader of the Socialist party until the advent of fascism and the split with the Communists. The tune came from the social song of a workingmen's bowling club.[4]

The connection is apt. Participation in athletic clubs, brass bands, mutual assistance societies, brotherhoods, cooperatives and other associations were some of the means by which industrial workers tried to fill the void created by the loss of traditional communities. Early proletarian organizations were meant to provide for all the social, political, and economic needs of their members; they created a community of sorts, where workers would defend their rights together, but also play, eat, and make music together.

During the 1907 lockout of the Terni steel factory, the workers' children left town to stay with families of supporters all over Italy (a strategy which Italian workers later imported to the Lawrence textile strike in Massachusetts in 1912). As the children marched to the station, they were accompanied by a workers' *fanfara* (marching brass band). Meanwhile, a *concertino* (a sitting brass band) toured industrial communities to raise money and encourage solidarity. Earlier, in 1887, the town's *concerto* (a larger sitting brass band) was listed among the organizations making up the anti-clerical Democratic front in the local elections (the anti-clerical connection of brass bands is a tradition going back to the French revolution).

Fanfara and *concertino* are as respectable as the *strofette* are plebeian. They represent the Organizing Committee of moderate Socialists and Republicans, which oversaw the 1907 conflict, just as the *strofette* represent the sudden, improvised, and unruly general strike triggered by the working-class women that was the struggle's turning point. The *strofette* represent the sudden, short-lived explosions of anger that the organization cannot contain; the brass band represents the continuity, the staid bureaucracy, but also the staying power that only organization can give.

Organization is not a "natural" community, in which membership is by birth and descent. The lack of natural boundaries is compensated by the intensive use of writing, whether it be in cards, statutes, by-laws, programs, minutes, and the like. Since membership is by access and consent, the organization also includes individuals from different social backgrounds, some of whom may be trained to deal with the languages and forms of expression of dominant cultures. A 1925 report of the Terni Communist federation recalls how "workers and peasants would seldom take part, in their native jargon, in the political debates [of the old Socialist party], awed as they were by the speech-making of lawyers, teachers, and doctors."[5] This type of membership is bound to influence the writing and singing of songs, too.

Workers have no stake in orality per se: recourse to oral communication is as much a matter of necessity as of choice, and, once education makes writing available, it is taken up enthusiastically. Education and self-improvement were prominent goals of the early workers' movements; and the imitation of the speech, poetry, and music of the more educated classes is part of this pattern. Thus, many organizations take up anthems written by activist intellectuals in the flowery language of late Romantic middle-class poetry; and working-class authors often attempt to reproduce this style, with uncertain results.

As the children marched to the station in Terni in 1907, they were singing a song which may have been the one written by the factory worker Romolo Romoli. It is a text notable for its attempts to poetic diction and literary allusions: "An creduto oltre ad essere schiavi / Di fiaccare la nostra energia / Ci han trovati più forti che pria / Non ci piega d'Orlando il furor" ("They thought they would not only enslave us, but also break our strength; but they found us stronger than ever, because we do not bend at Orlando's wrath"). "D'Orlando il furor" ("Orlando's wrath") is a literary pun, between the name of Giuseppe Orlando (chairman of the steel company) and *Orlando Furioso*, Ludovico Ariosto's sixteenth-century epic. "*Pria*" is archaic poetic diction. But "*an*" ("they have"), is also an attempt to poetic diction, but is misspelled. It ought to be *han*, for the more ordinary *hanno*. Also, the syntax of the first two lines is out of joint. Literary allusions notwithstanding, Romoli's command of writing and poetic diction was still far from perfect.[6]

The relationship between song, writing and organization has important consequences. Composition is separated from performance, music from text. The circulation and persistence of the words no longer depends on music as an aid to memory: all it takes is a piece of paper. Romoli's song is all but forgotten by the people of Terni, but it has reached us because one of his relatives kept his notebooks. Songs become independent of collective memory; they tend to hang around their authors. They are less subject to variation, either as deterioration or as creative elaboration.

The music is also upgraded. Romoli's song is to be sung to an air from Giuseppe Verdi's *Nabucco*, "Va pensiero sull'ali dorate," one of the most popular opera melodies. Pietro Gori, the anarchist leader, lawyer and song writer used this air for his widely known "May Day Anthem." Gori had lectured in Terni a few years before the lockout, and local anarchists were no doubt familiar with his songs. On the other hand, opera was quite popular among those sectors of the working class who could afford the season at the municipal theater (in certain parts of Italy, though not in Terni, one may occasionally still hear opera pieces sung in taverns). Gori and Romoli were aware both of the popular culture potential and of the high-culture credentials of the *Nabucco* air, as well as of its patriotic Risorgimento connotations. They used these cultural factors to convey the workers' sense of dignity and righteousness in a form which all workers would understand and share, and which the other side would also be bound to respect.

The impact of organization and writing loosens the relationship between music and everyday speech. Anthems associate singing with special, ritual situations. They reflect the ethical-political rather than the personal mode; national rather than local perspectives; and leadership rather than rank-and-file. Songs tend to drift away from daily life, toward more abstract and ideological "politics," and contribute further to the separation of politics from the everyday experience of common people.

Finally, the community control (or "communal censorship," as Roman Jakobson and Piotr Bogatyrev once called it)[7] is replaced by the sanction of the organization. Contents and forms which do not reflect the organization's needs and views are dropped—not necessarily through willful censorship, but often simply because they are considered unsuitable, "anachronistic," or counterproductive. Romoli's song, too closely associated with a specific event, was bound to disappear, in spite of its use of apparently durable cultural materials. In the same way, in the 1960s and 1970s, the Leftist parties and unions weeded out of their repertoire all the songs that appeared "obsolete"—often, a euphemism for "too radical." On the other hand, writing gives a song a degree of independence: folk memory and political organizations may have dropped Romoli's song, but it has reached us anyway. Thus, writing protects a song's life—if life is that of "songs / that voices never share."

The Workplace

"Our society is the textile mill/Where forty rascals look over us," says a mill women's song from Bergamo, Lombardia, in northern Italy. Music does not thrive easily in a textile mill: noise, discipline, speed, and the very position of the body militate against it. "Morning 'til night/Tic-tac, tic-tac/Until Saturday we have to put up with this," sang the women workers of the Centurini jute mill in Terni.

Only certain types of industrial work leave room for singing. According to a construction worker who commuted each day from Abruzzi to the Tecnedile building site in Rome, "we sing all the time, also at the site." The open-air environment, low noise level, residual craft workers' control on time and motions of work, along with the rural background of a majority of construction workers, make singing possible.

Singing was occasionally encouraged by management in nothern textile mills to ensure discipline and prevent workers from talking to each other. In the rural South, a woman from Calabria told me grape pickers were requested to sing so they wouldn't be able to eat the grapes. Among the songs she remembered from that situation was a rare and wonderful version of *Lord Randal*. The opportunity to communicate, in conversation or in music, is found more easily in times and places related to but distinct from work. The Terni jute mill workers did not sing at work, but sang on (and of) Saturday nights. They sang during the long walk to the factory and back ("When the whistle calls, early before day/You can hear us walking all across town"). They sang in the dorms where some of the out-of-town workers experimented with new forms of community and new values ("If someone gets ideas/Just because we are mill women/Let them know that if we make love/It's only because we like it").[8]

Whether it includes music or not, the "society" of the mill induces an ambivalent sense of belonging, expressed by the possessive forms used in the workers' language and songs. "Workers *of the Breda factory*/Ring the bell for the struggle," says a 1969 strike song from Milan. "We are *the workers of Centurini*/Make way for us," sang the Terni textile workers. The problem is who belongs to who; and the song does not say whether the "forty rascals" overlooking the mill women also "belong" to the factory in the same way as the women themselves do, or whether they are also members of the "society" of the mill.

In fact, "society"—a new sense of common purpose—often arises when owners and overseers are excluded. Sit-ins and occupations, where workers live and sleep together in the factory, enhance the sense of community and exalt the workers' pride in their skills, in the machines, and in production. If the workers belong to the factory, as some of the songs produced in these context seem to say, it is because the factory belongs to them. One anthem written by the workers during the occupations of the Reggiane factory in Reggio Emilia in the 1950s expresses the sense of belonging and pride of the workers who designed, produced, and marketed a new type of tractor, the R60. The anthem says, "Great and glorious working class/Bravely struggling at the Reggiane/In the mines and in the rice fields/You can hear the sound of the new machine. Stand ready comrades/The yoke is breaking/Let us raise the flag/Of the R60."[9]

Often, however, the communal pride also includes the management and the boss, and it may even be inspired by them. This was the strategy used by Alessandro Centurini, owner of the Terni jute mill, a ruthless and yet paternalistic employer. His women workers sang their songs of defiance and pride; but when he was elected to Parliament and celebrated by giving them a bonus and half a day off, they marched out of the mill singing his praise (much to the dismay of the great Socialist leader, Maria Goia). The song they sang may have been the following: "We make sacks and jute thread/And the machine that helps us makes us happy/When the Centurini whistle blows/We forget our miseries/Happy is the countryside/And happy is the town."[10] Here, the whistle blow is no longer (as in the other Centurini song) the symbol of the violent arbitrariness of industrial time, but becomes the modern counterpart of the church bell, uniting the community around the factory and the machine.

The Electronic Village

The "village" metaphor in Marshall McLuhan's *Understanding Media* suggests that, as modern mass media undermine one type of community, they also create a new one: the *audience*. Electronics replace the horizontal, face-to-face flow of communication with a basically one-way flow of discourse carried by the media. This generates three types of response: silence; textual or stylistic interference; and selective appropriation.

a. *Silence*. Like orality in general, the making of one's own music is a matter of need as well as choice. Once a great deal of music is offered from a variety of sources, homemade sounds seem less necessary. Traditional singers invited comparison only with their neighbors and peers; but media-offered music challenges them to an unequal competition with the best professionals anywhere. As music is increasingly perceived to be associated to show business, singing appears more and more as a conspicuous act of self-exposure. In the electronic village there is much more music, but less singing: it is less necessary, and also slightly embarrassing.

b.1. *Textual Interference*. A strategy often used in the unequal conditions of the electronic village consists of relying on the very power and pervasiveness of the media, "riding" them and distorting their meaning, even turning it back against its source. Parody is the most frequent embodiment of this strategy.

Parody is a junction of opposites: protest or class-conscious words are set to music produced by the capitalistic culture mill. The effectiveness of parody depends to a large extent on the degree of awareness of the intertextual dynamics originated by this paradox. We may identify three forms of parody, according to the use of intertextual relationships: reversal, appropriation, and neutralization.

b.1.1. Reversal consists in openly recalling the original message, indeed leaving it unchanged as much as possible, in order to set off the touches that reverse and deny its meaning. The fewer the changes, the sharper the opposition. A late 1940s pop hit, which described a sailor's departure at dawn (*"All'alba se ne parte il marinaio"*) was used very successfully for a parody which merely replaced *marinaio* with *operaio* ("worker") and implicitly changed the connotation of all the rest. The second-rate romantic associations of dawn and the sea were replaced by the image of the beginning of the long working day in a pallid urban dawn; and the hints of nostalgia in *"se ne parte"* ("away goes") turned into a sense of repetitive weariness. A fine touch, setting off the contrast, is the similarity of the new word, *operaio*, to *marinaio* which it replaces. It is the same device that works so effectively in Joe Hill's replacement of "You will eat" for "We will meet" in *The Preacher and the Slave*, the wobbly parody of a Salvation Army anthem.

b.1.2. Other parodies strive, instead, to appropriate the positive connotations of the original. This was, as we already noted, the case of the political texts set to the *Nabucco* air. The same applies to songs which "ride" religious or patriotic anthems, from *Miner's Lifeguard* to *Solidarity Forever*. The Communist songwriter Raffaele Offidani (active in Rome from the 1910s to the 1950s) turned a World War I patriotic rouser, *Leggenda del Piave*, to the *Leggenda della Neva*. Piave is the river where the Italian troops made their last, successful stand in that war. Neva is the river that runs through Leningrad. Thus, in Offidani's parody as in Lenin's slogan, the Russian revolution replaced the "imperialistic" war. Offidani here used both reversal and appropriation. The river of revolution replaces the river of nationalism, while the patriotic and soldierly connotations are retained in another context. Most of all, the tune is an extraordinarily singable one.

b.1.3. We may finally speak of "neutralization" when the parody ignores the intertextual associations altogether, merely using only the popular tune as a convenient vehicle for new words. It is a tricky thing to do, though, because the memory of the original text never entirely disappears, and the connotations linger in the singer's or the listener's mind, often reversing the interference. When the early Socialist leader Camillo Prampolini attempted to set his own May Day anthem to *Funiculì Funiculà* (a very singable and popular, but also very funny Neapolitan song), the result was ludicrously self-defeating. The same applies to a 1973 parody that used the same tune to commemorate the murdered Chilean President Salvador Allende. When Raffaele Offidani set the fierce text of his *Red Guard* song to the languid French tune of *La Valse Brune*, Lenin himself is said to have winced, and suggested a more suitable Russian folk tune (to which the song was finally sung).[11]

To parody a song is to criticize it, but also to recognize its power. At the least, it is an acknowledgment of its popularity; and at the most, it recognizes the fact that mass-produced popular music is considered by the workers themselves to be more functional than their own. Parody therefore creates a sort of semiological "leopard-spot" battleground, where words and sound change meanings and hands all the time, and no one is safely in control of anything. The guerrilla metaphor is pertinent, because guerrilla is the strategy of the weak and small who fight a big and powerful adversary—which is what happens in the electronic village.

b.2. *Stylistic Interference.* Popular music does not go unchanged through the mouths of working people. Some of the changes are subtler, but more radical, than those merely affecting the text.

During a 1972 strike at the Crouzet factory in Milan, the women on the picket line not only made up new, fighting words to pop tunes; they also shouted these songs all together in the streets. Corny, sentimental, crooning tunes were delivered in harsh, aggressive tones reminiscent of rural archaic styles. It was as if the ultimate resistance to the encroachments of mass culture lay in the less conscious layers of expression: the body, the breath, and the voice.

Dante Bartolini, a Terni steelworker and Resistance fighter, set his song about a partisan battle to a sentimental Neapolitan melody with a tango tempo; but he sang it unaccompanied, with a great show of *rubato, recitar cantando,* rhythmic irregularities, pauses, and tone shifts in the solemn and detached style of the great ballad singer. He did try to sound like a pop singer, and to accompany himself on the guitar; but he was both not good enough and just too good to succeed in this attempt. The original melody became almost unrecognizable, and the final result was a memorable ballad performance.[12]

c. *Selective Appropriation.* In December 1948, *l'Unità,* newspaper of the Communist party, described the troubles of music-hall singer Cecé Doria with the Rome police. One of Doria's songs, a satire of the government's low-income housing plan, had been censored. Music-hall and vernacular songs often blended nostalgia for the past (often a Fascist past) with a broad and angry criticism of the present state of things, which struck a responsive chord in popular audiences. Thus, while some of the songs learned from those sources were picked up and later forgotten in the fashion of pop songs, others were actively incorporated in working-class repertoires.

This was, of course, a highly selective process. The fragments that were remembered and reused were the ones that best fit in with the workers' experiences. Thus, out of the vast production of Furio Miselli, a vernacular poet and musician from Terni, the one song that stands out in oral tradition is his satirical piece on rents and the cost of housing, written in 1926 when the country was already under the Fascist regime.

In Rome, the music-hall song most often found in oral tradition is a description of life in the city, originally composed by Lorenzo Peppi (known as "Pepparello"), an early 1900s street singer and music-hall artist. The verses from this song which working-class informants remember best refer in wryly humorous terms to unemployment, homelessness, poverty, and hunger. Other verses, which are merely comical, are forgotten.[13]

Selective appropriation solves the ambiguity between conservative nostalgia and radical protest, by means of selective forgetfulness, slight but crucial textual alterations, or by changes in contextual connotations. One of Cecé Doria's songs, still found in oral tradition in Rome, is a string of parodies recapping the city's history from the Fascist march on Rome in 1922 to the 1950s and the atom bomb. The first verse says:

> In 1922 we had a government—I don't remember who
> There was a march—I don't remember where
> Which was known as—I don't remember what.
> For the next twenty years we were in trouble
> With so many wars—I don't remember which
> But then one day we were liberated
> By whom?—I don't remember who.

Doria's text may be read as an invitation to forget the past, or as a satire on those who would like to forget. As the song descends into workers' memories, the second meaning prevails: we may speak of a metonymic mutation, as songs change meaning simply because they change communities. In the last couplet, Doria probably referred to the liberation of Rome from German occupation by the Allied troops in 1944, and "who" meant the Americans; but to the Communist informant who sang the song for me in 1976, the word "liberation" referred to the liberation of Italy from fascism, and "who" referred to the partisans (often designated as the "liberation movement").

THE TEMPORARY COMMUNITY

The Event and the Ballad

Both songs of the Centurini jute mill workers (and countless other early industrial songs) mention the factory whistle as the symbol of the artificial regulation of industrial time from above. The changing nature of time is a key theme of industrial folk songs. One stylistic trait which reveals this preoccupation is the fact that many industrial folk songs include a date in their first line, as if to place events in a punctual linear history rather than in the cyclical time of traditional societies. The *Gruppo Operaio di Pomigliano d'Arco* (a group of auto workers from the Naples Alfa-Romeo factory who performed traditional and contemporary topical songs in traditional style) had a song about an explosion in a fireworks factory in which twelve workers were killed. The song begins with the date of the disaster—"Vernarí unnece aprile," Friday, April 11. Dante Bartolini's partisan song also opens with a date ("Don't you remember the tenth of March?") We could mention many other examples, also from American tradition—Della Graham's *Ballad of Barney Graham* ("On the thirteenth day of April/Of 1933"); Woody Guthrie's *Dust Storm Disaster* ("On the fourteenth day of April/Of 1934")—or from Britain: "It was in November and I never will forget" (a song about the Oakley mine strike by miner-poet Tommy Armstrong), and "On the twenty-sixth of August/Our fatal moss gave way" (a mine disaster song).[14]

Historical events—strikes, murders, and disasters—create an emotion which is shared by many people at the same time, thus either reinforcing the existing community ties, or originating a temporary "community" of feelings and of shared emotion. This "emotional community" is represented by the narrative ballads that are quickly made up whenever an event disrupts the continuity of ordinary time; and they are forgotten or radically changed when the emotion disappears or a new event replaces it with another emotion. These songs are generally strophic in form, sometimes with chorus. Their language is highly charged with sentiment; and the music is either adapted from earlier narrative folk songs or (less frequently) appropriated from popular music. Their ephemeral and shifting nature expresses a close adherence to the mutability of history and life.

War

The army is the perfect temporary community. It involves individuals for a limited period of time, but throws them together at very close quarters, and makes them share very dramatic experiences, such as those of wartime, or the subtler emotions of coming of age in peacetime military service. Barracks and trench songs, therefore, are bound to have an influence on all other folk song repertoires.

This is especially true of songs associated with World War I, when for the first time working people from all over recently unified Italy were gathered together. They had had very little contact with one another before, and sometimes could hardly understand each other's dialects. They came mostly from rural backgrounds; and they were thrown together in the face of a modern technological war and of the modern state in its most frightening aspect—the military. They were bound to seek a common expression, and songs supplied at least some of this. Starting with World War I, the northeastern choral singing style and ballad repertoire spread to the rest of the country, often replacing or coexisting with the more archaic, dramatic, and individualistic southern forms. Not only were these songs easier to sing together, but they sprang from the very same ground—the mountains where the war was being fought—and seemed to have a special appropriateness to that region. They became a sort of musical koine, to be heard whenever a temporary community comes into being—be it workers occupying a factory or a busload of kids on a skiing trip. The event-oriented ballads also tend to use these tunes.

Soldiers' songs also influenced one of the most important working women's repertoires: that of the rice-field workers. These women, mostly northerners, went to work in the rice fields during the harvest season and lived together in barracks in conditions very much like those of military service. They developed a song repertoire which blends the choral harmonies of World War I mountain songs (which are often adopted and adapted) with a harsh vocal emission and, often, a radical political message. These songs influenced all the post-World War II tradition of political singing in Italy.

War songs and rice-field songs—together with anthems, popular music, and other song forms—coalesce in the most important modern Italian folk song tradition, the partisan songs of 1943 to

1945. These songs were used by the Left, the unions, the student movement, and the folk revival. Some of them (such as the famous *Bella Ciao*, a traditional ballad which was later adapted by the rice workers) were "sung to death" as patriotic anthems.

The partisan movement brought together urban and rural people, workers and intellectuals, political activists and young people just trying to escape the Fascist draft. The Gramsci brigade, which fought in the mountains around Terni, was led by factory workers with mostly rural or village backgrounds. They lived and fought among rural people with whom they had a difficult but close relationship. The social context and composition of the brigade's experience is reflected in its song bag. It includes anthems reflecting the organization ("Workers and peasants/Let's fight together/At Stalin's call/We are the first partisans"); event ballads reflecting the emotional community generated by military action ("Don't you remember the tenth of March?"; "Don't you remember, mother, that night/ When the Fascists came to raid our home?"); parodies of popular songs, representing the "electronic village" which the advanced use of the radio by the Fascist regime had already brought into being; *stornelli*, both traditional, representing the rural element in the brigade, and new, composed by the partisans themselves; and traditional dance tunes and folk instruments, which were played both by the partisans during moments of rest and by local people at festivities given occasionally by the village communities for the brigade.

Industrial Conflict

Strikes and sit-ins are events which recreate not only an emotional, but also a physical community. Like the rural ritual holiday, they create a space and a time which is related to, but distinct and freed from work. In this context, face-to-face communication is accelerated. Strikes originate many songs because, during a strike, people communicate more—but also because, as in ritual holidays, slightly tabooed activities (as singing as it tends to become in modern urban culture) again become normal and permissible.

Like most temporary communities, strikes and sit-ins do not generate a specific form, but readapt all the existing ones. The workers who occupied the Tecnedile building site in Rome sang anthems (*Inno dei lavoratori*), parodies, *strofette*. They marched in parades preceded by an *organetto*, the small accordion used in rural folk music and dance. During the 1975 sit-in at the Filati Lastex factory in Bergamo, workers sang everything: strings of *strofette* against the boss; anthems (sometimes fragmented to "imperfect mono-strophic" form); parodies; traditional ballads; new protest songs composed by themselves; and topical songs composed by a sympa-thizing folk-revival group. It was as though they were summing up and welding together all the types of community they had known before. This could also be seen in non-musical forms of expression. While they used all the techniques of modern trade unionism, they did not consider themselves above a recourse to traditional magic (which seems to have worked, as the boss had to be hospitalized).[15]

Another fine example of a temporary community generated by an industrial conflict is the Camp Solidarity, created by the striking Pittston miners in Virginia, in 1989. Here pickets were organized and fed, rallies were held, visitors and sympathizers entertained. Once again, all forms of industrial folk song played traditional gos-pel and bluegrass music related to the still vivid rural background (but also to the electronic village of country music), sometimes with slight adaptations to relate to the ongoing struggle; strikers created parodies of Christmas carols (not unlike another, very different struggle, the Berkeley Free Speech Movement of 1964): union songs were taught by visiting and sympathizing folk singers; anthems—from *Solidarity Forever* to *We Shall Not Be Moved*—represented the continuity and strength of organization, as they were performed at the end of rallies, with union officals standing on the platform be-hind the musicians and all the audience joining in.

Demonstrations

A rally or a march is an emotional community based on an organi-zation, all of whose members are gathered at the same place and time. It is a community which moves and speaks collectively, and generates specific oral forms in order to synchronize these actions. The most important form is the chanted slogan, perhaps the only oral folk form exclusively related to an urban, contemporary setting. A slogan is a self-contained metric and semantic unit which is al-ways chanted in a sequence of other slogans or of repetitions (the canonic number is three) of the same one. It also may be viewed, therefore, as another form of "imperfect monostrophism."

Like all true folk forms, the slogan is bound by strict formal requisites, including metrics and rhetorical devices. Its most com-mon form in the Italian language is a three-line verse of 3/3/7 sylla-bles, based on a rhetorical binary opposition, usually with rhyme and/or repetition: "E' ora/è ora/potere a chi lavora" ("It's time. It's time. Power to the workers") as used by factory workers; "Lo stato/ borghese/s'abbatte e non si cambia" ("The bourgeois state must be torn down, not changed") from students; "Tremate/tremate/le streghe son tornate" ("Shiver and shake, the witches are back") from the women's movement.

The folk nature of slogans is also proved by the creative use of "communal censorship." During a 1977 demonstration called by the metal and mechanical workers in Rome (from which all the above examples are taken), a union official shouted into his megaphone the following slogan: "Dal settentrione/al meridione/lotta per/l'occupazione" ("From North to South, struggle for jobs"). Though politically "correct," the slogan was not taken up by the marchers. The expression was rhetorically flat; the metrics were wrong (the form was the five-syllable quatrain, but there are two syllables missing in the third line), and the enjambment between the third and fourth line broke down the correspondence of metric and semantic units. After a few seconds, however, the slogan rose back from the ranks, with slight but decisive improvements: "Dal settentrione/al meridione/un solo grido/occupazione" ("From north to south only one shout: We want jobs"). The new version filled in the missing syllables, resolved the enjambment, and replaced the banal "struggle" with the more dramatic "shout," thus introducing a metalinguistic dimension (the slogan becomes a shout about shouting). Finally, "only one shout" reinforces the binary opposition between North and South and its reconciliation in struggle. Thus, a living oral tradition could be seen at work that day among two hundred thousand marching industrial workers and sympathizers, all from urban environments apparently not conducive to the creation of folklore.

(We may introduce a brief comparison with the slogans chanted at the Solidarity Day march in Washington, D.C., on 19 September 1983. The texts of the slogans were much less poetically and politically elaborate than the Italian ones. On the other hand, their rhythmic performance was much more advanced. A rather weak line like "We can't take it no more/We'll fight 'em" became extremely powerful when a group of black women syncopated it into "We can't/ Take it no more/We'll/fi-i-ght 'em," almost dancing to the rhythm. In a rather oversimplified way, it might be said that the "otherness" of the politicized Italian industrial workers was made explicit by their articulate use of words, while the "otherness" of the rank-and-file American workers was implicit in their creative uses of the body and the voice).

The flexibility and vitality of slogans as a folk form may be briefly illustrated by subsequent occurences of the North/South slogan. In 1982, after the Rome soccer team won the national pennant, the slogan appeared in the form of graffiti on the city walls (the temporary community of fans in sports arenas often adopted forms from political discourse), restating the continuity of graffiti, slogans, *strofette* we noted in the Spadoni verses from Terni, eighty years earlier, and reinforcing the geographic symbolism with the allusion to Rome's central position: "from south to north/only one shout/Rome is the champ." In 1989, a student movement spread from Palermo, in Sicily, as campuses nationally were occupied in protest against poor facilities and archaic power relationships. In January, 1990, student demonstrators in Rome chanted: "Da Palermo al settentrione/ un solo grido/ occupazione." The specific "Palermo" stood for the more generalized "south" of earlier versions; the north/south line repeated the actual geographic direction of the movement (for once, the south was the vanguard). Finally, the word "occupazione", while textually unchanged, no longer meant "employment" as in the older labor version, but referred to the student sit-ins, literal "occupations."

THE PARTIAL COMMUNITY

Where Languages Meet

In the city, no one belongs to a single, tight-knit, all-encompassing community (the extent is also debatable to which this was true even in pre-industrial villages). Identity becomes an idiosyncratic combination of factors: age, sex, education, residence, politics, religion, occupation, leisure habits, relationship to the media, and many more. Although some factors may still be seen as dominant (age, sex, class, and, more recently in Italy, race), the combinations are much more variegated than in the pre-industrial past.

The creation of music reflects through a plurality of languages the plurality of "communities" which cross and overlap inside each individual. The history of working-class music would not be complete if it did not take into account all the workers who make music only partially as workers (or, conversely, all the musicians who just happen to be workers or to have a working-class background). Alfeo Paganelli, a Terni steel-worker and guitar player, used to play *stornelli* at May Festival parades; love songs for serenades, usually for money; jazz classics like *In the Mood* or *The Man I Love* in the *Dopolavoro* dance band; and still plays dance music from waltzes to *Rock around the Clock* in dance halls around town. His own family is steeped in the urban folk tradition. His sister sang a fine version of the Centurini protest song and of Miselli's cost-of-housing piece; and his niece is one of the finest Italian folk revival singers.

Paganelli is not an isolated instance. Many other industrial workers draw their music, as he does, from the residual folk community, from the political organization, and from the electronic village. The relationship to work, however, sets the underlying tone for most of these musicians. Augusto Cuppini, another skilled worker and musician from Terni, boasts of his manual ability as a riveter as well as a guitar player in the same terms of "virtuosity." The manual aspect of art is consciously stressed by many of the several musicians (and painters) who worked in Terni's factories.

The connection may be illustrated, in reverse, by the story of Paganelli's brother-in-law, Aldo Galeazzi, a well-known wrestler and discus-thrower, who started work as a bricklayer in the steel factory. Galeazzi came from a musical family, and his parents insisted that he learn to play the guitar. His teacher was his father's foreman. Galeazzi didn't make much progress, and the teacher/foreman finally told him that his hands were good for nothing but laying bricks—in other words, that an unskilled manual worker could not possess the skill to play music. Finally, like Hercules in the mythological tale, Galeazzi could take it no longer, and smashed his instrument on his teacher's head.

As workers begin to share cultural experiences with other social classes through education or the media, their forms of expression become less distinctive, but they gain access to forms from which they had previously been excluded. George Lipsitz has described early rock-and-roll as essentially working-class music (noting that Elvis Presley, Fats Domino, Little Richard, Muddy Waters, and many others all came from working-class backgrounds and had experiences of industrial work). The proletarian experience is a source of the music and poetry of Bruce Springsteen as well as Bob Seger, John Cougar Mellencamp and others. The involvement of British rock groups in the miners' strike is recent history, and Billy Bragg has emerged as a significant British "proletarian" musician in recent years.

Young rock groups in the peripheries of industrial towns in Italy today show an interchangeability between authors, performers, and audiences which resembles folklore more than the division of labor typical of show business and the Taylor system. Marino Severini, a rock musician from Filottrano, a small town in Marche, identifies very closely with his working-class background. "I chose rock because to me it is an international, urban, subcultural folk music." This band patches together Latin-American sounds learned from their relatives who emigrated temporarily to Argentina; the local folk music they grew up with; and The Clash.[16]

Rock does flourish in industrial towns. The semi-company town of Pordenone in the North is one of the most creative places in Italy's youth culture of today. Terni also has rock, punk, and heavy-metal groups; and they are sometimes fairly good. They relate to the factory in negative terms, as a metaphor of destiny: it is the place they are struggling to stay away from, and whose values they reject. But it also is the most likely place where they will eventually wind up working anyway, and where their parents work or worked. They fail to see any connection between the "heavy metal" sound of their music, and the heavy steel which has been the life of their town for a hundred years. But the experience of steel making, as if in the negative, sets the tone of their entire attitude.

ANATOMY OF AN INDUSTRIAL FOLK SONG

An Historical Ballad

No individual event or person ever conforms entirely to the abstract models of a typology; but typologies may be used to understand what makes each individual unique. The application of the model I have sketched so far to an individual song will show how the types I have described in methodological terms cross and overlap in "real life."

On 17 March 1949, the 21-year-old steelworker Luigi Trastulli was killed by the police during a demonstration against NATO. Sante Carboni, a mechanic, former railroad worker and draftsman, wrote a song about this event.

Born in Ancona in 1901, Carboni has lived in Terni (with an interval of a few years after retirement) since 1929. An anarchist in his youth, he joined the Communist party in the 1930s, and was active in the Resistance movement.

The available sources for the song are:

1. The original typewritten text;
2. Verses remembered and sung (at two separate sittings in 1974) by Iole Peri, who was helped to remember the song by her husband, Alvaro Valsenti, Carboni's closest friend and associate at work and in politics;

3. A letter from Carboni to Valsenti, written in 1979, in which he discusses the song; and
4. An interview with Carboni and Valsenti in 1982.

The tune (transcribed from Iole Peri's performance) is from a traditional northern ballad of the type which became popular after World War I (*Il ventinove luglio*).

The text as given here is the one written by Carboni; the verses omitted in Iole Peri's performance are in brackets; and the ones she sings are italicized. I have also added the numeration of the verses.

The text was typed on the back of a ballot sheet for the election of workers' representatives to the short-lived Management Councils which were established after World War II. "In those days," says Carboni's letter, "as you remember, we didn't have much paper available. We used any blank space we could." The title is given there as "Terni, remember March 17." On another line, it says, "Sung for Luigi Trastulli, the first martyr for peace." The seventh verse is crossed out in the manuscript. In performance, the last two lines of each verse are repeated.

1. [Non è canto di gioia,
nemmeno d'allegria
pur non vi sembri triste
questa canzone mia:]

[This song of mine / is neither for joy / nor for glee; / yet let it not sound sad to you.]

2. [E' nata dal dolore
ma canta la speranza

del popolo che lotta
e sanguinando avanza.]

[It is born in sorrow, / but sings the hope / of the people
who struggle / and shed their blood as they march on.]

3. *Il 17 Marzo*
lasciammo le officine
per dire a lor signori:
Mai più morte e rovine.

[On March 17, / we walked out of the factories, / to tell
those in power: / no more war and destruction.]

4. *Il "Patto" che firmaste*
è un tradimento nero
che renderà l'Italia
schiava dello straniero;

[The Treaty you have signed / is a dark act of treason, /
which will make Italy / a slave to foreigners.]

5. [E Terni laboriosa,
Terni degli operai,
ve lo dice fin d'ora,
non l'accetterà mai!]

[And hard-working Terni, / Terni the workers' town, / is
telling you right now: / we'll never let it be!]

6. [E andavam cantando
sotto il bel sole d'oro,
i canti della pace,
i canti del lavoro!]

[And as we marched, we sang / under the golden sun, /
our songs of peace, / our songs of labor.]

7. [Ma l'eccellenza e soci,
facendo colazione
avevan già deciso
di "darci una lezione".]

[But the prefect and his partners / as they sat down to eat, / had already made up their minds / to teach us all a lesson.]

8. *Inermi marciavamo*
quand'ecco la sbirraglia
ci affronta con le jepi,
i gas e la mitraglia.

[Unarmed we marched, / when the dirty cops / rushed against us with jeeps, / tear gas, and machine guns.]

9. *Noi le gridammo: pace!*
Ma ci risposer guerra
e di sangue innocente
si fè rossa la terra!

[We shouted to them: Peace! / But they answered us with war, / and the earth was reddened / with innocent blood.]

10. *O guardia scellerata,*
celere maledetta!
il sangue di Trastulli
dal ciel grida vendetta!

[You heartless guard, / you accursed cops! / Trastulli's blood / from heaven cries for vengeance.]

11. *Aveva ventun anni*
ed era ardito e forte
pace! vi disse, o infami,
e voi gli deste morte.

[He was twenty-one years old, / and he was strong and bold; / he offered you peace, / and you, rascals, gave him death.]

12. [Padre e sposo felice
gli rideva la vita
ma voi gliela troncaste
con raffiche di mitra!]

[A happy father and husband, / life smiled on him; / but you cut him down / with a volley of your machine gun.]

> 13. *O Sposa giovinetta!*
> *a Te e al tuo pargoletto*
> *giuriam che gli assassini*
> *non moriran sul letto!*

[To you, young bride, / and to your little child, / we swear that the killers / shall not die on their bed.]

> 14. *E tu Gente Ternana,*
> *che sulla bara hai pianto*
> *raccogli il giuramento,*
> *propaga questo canto!*

[And you, people of Terni, / who wept upon his grave, / take up this oath, / and teach the world this song.]

> 15. [S'intenerisca il cuore
> anche a chi l'ha di quarzo
> ricordando l'eccidio
> del 17 Marzo! . . .]

[Let every heart be melted, / even if made of stone, / remembering the massacre / of March 17!]

> [Terni, ricorda! . . .
> Terni ricorderà!. . . .]

[Terni, remember! Terni shall not forget!]

Composition

"I remember," says Sante Carboni, "that we held his wake at Palazzo Mazzancolli [Communist party headquarters], in a little room to the left of the ground floor. It was the partisans' office, remember? Well, one evening around midnight, I went inside, and I saw this boy lying there, bare faced. And I was moved, when I looked at him. So I began to ruminate these verses in my mind, and then wrote them up on the partisans' bulletin board. I made this thing up and I pinned it up. For no reason at all, as I said: just because I was moved by that boy, that's all." When asked whether he was thinking of his composition as a song or as a poem, Carboni answers, "I don't know. Maybe I just began to make it up, and then I realized that it could be sung."

Carboni's process of composition began with the "ruminating" of the verses in his mind. The poem was written down only after it had been completed mentally. Writing, however, was used immediately for communication and circulation. Although his mode of composition was that of an oral poet, Carboni did not sing or recite his poem, but pinned it up on the bulletin board. The lavish use of punctuation marks also shows the dominance of writing as a model.

This process makes music an accessory; like writing, it comes *after* the text, and does not directly influence its composition. Carboni, however, does not just happen to conceive his verse in ballad meter; he is steeped in these forms, and the poem sounds like a ballad whether he planned it that way or not. A typical sign of oral composition is the coincidence of metric units (lines and verses) with semantic units. This song, then, is a written text based on an oral method of composition: a process which is typical of cultures (and individuals) in a phase of change, in which codes and media mix and overlap.

Communities

In his letter and interview, Carboni reiterates the fact that he felt "moved" by Trastulli's death and by the sight of his body. He also says that the source of all poetry and song is always "an emotion," which arises when "an event strikes our soul deeply with sorrow or joy." The ballad of Trastulli is thus associated, first of all, to the *emotional community* generated by the event. It is composed under the impact of the emotion and immediately communicated to the mourners at the wake (the wake itself, on the other hand, is reminiscent of the rituals of an older, pre-industrial *residual* community). Given the priority of the emotional community, it is logical that Iole Peri should drop the first two verses of Carboni's original text, so that the song, as she performs it, begins, as is appropriate to an event ballad, with the date.

After the song is finished, Carboni entrusts it to another, *substitute* community: the political organization, symbolized by the bulletin board. Of course, the political, residual, and emotional community overlap to a large extent, as the wake is held at the party headquarters. They are, however, logically distinct. It was not party members only who were moved by Trastulli's death, and not all members reacted the same way.

Once the organization receives the song, it performs the task of spreading it, and does so by putting it through other, *temporary* communities: a train trip and a demonstration. "We sang it immediately," says Alvaro Valsenti; "We took it up, and made it known. I was in the youth organization, and we went to a peace rally at Assisi—there was a great demonstration there. I still have pictures of it. We chartered a train, and, on the way to Assisi on the train and with all the peace flags flying in front of us, we sang this song. We turned it into a mass song. All of us [were] young people. In fact, those who were twenty years old then, still remember it, even if they don't know how to sing it anymore."

The organization turns the *ballad* into an *anthem* (a "mass song"). But it does not guarantee that it will survive the event. The reliance on writing has loosened the hold on people's memory (the activists of Valsenti's generation know of the song, but can't sing it anymore); and the song is too closely associated with a specific event to serve the general, abstract purposes of a lasting anthem. In fact, although the emotional community which generated the song is apparently the most ephemeral, it is also the one that guarantees whatever life the song has had. It is remembered by people of Trastulli's own age and generation who knew him as a friend as well as a comrade and a co-worker. The song lives in the memory of an emotion.

We need mention only briefly that memory does change the song. The only oral version we have, Iole Peri's, includes just eight of the original fifteen verses—a selection which improves the song immensely. Peri changes only very slightly the verses which she does remember. The most significant change turns the plural "murderers" of verse 13 into "murderer," perhaps reflecting the fact that the guard who actually shot Trastulli had been identified since the song was written.

Verse 5 suggests another type of community—"hard-working Terni, Terni the workers' town." This is a complex image. On one level, it reflects the post-war perception of Terni as socially and politically homogeneous, identified with the workers' politics and culture and with their representative organizations, and emotionally gathered around the young victim. It suggests that those who are not workers and do not share in this collective emotion are not really part of the town. On another level, though, the image echoes the remnants of the residual community: the small town where everybody is everybody else's neighbor, relative, and friend. This perception was, ironically, reinforced by the industrialization which turned Terni into a "company town," where "everybody" worked for the same employer. The *workplace* as a substitute community expanded to include the whole town.

Languages

"The form and tone of everyday language," writes Carboni, "seem inadequate to express sensations that yet must be brought into the open because they cannot be restrained. This is when song, theater, and perhaps poetry are born. My humble verse, though stimulated by a strong emotion, surely cannot be counted among such superior orders . . ." Carboni uses here the apologetic tone of many working-class writers. The anarchist worker Riziero Manconi introduced the reading of a play he wrote, saying, "Written by me—not very good; not very good." The final lines of Dante Bartolini's partisan song say, "Please forgive me / I am not a composer / This song was written by a worker, / I can do no better."

Self-deprecation, however, may be an implicit avowal of ambition. That Carboni was indeed striving for "superior orders" is shown by his intensive use of capital letters, ellipses, and exclamation marks, all intended to underline the emotional and solemn quality of the text. There are also several attempts at poetic diction: *pargoletto,* instead of the more common *bambino* or *figlio,* for child, is the most notable example. A desire to upgrade the song is also the cause of the crossing out of verse 7. The reference to the prefect's threat to the workers gave the song a local flavor and timeliness that would hinder its transformation into a durable anthem. (Carboni confirmed this explanation in a letter to me after the original publication of this essay.)

A parallel process can be detected in an American murder ballad from the labor movement, Jim Garland's "Ballad of Harry Simms," concerning the death of a union organizer in Harlan County, Kentucky. As originally composed in 1932, the song ended with a call for "a million volunteers / To sink this rotten system / In the deepest pits of Hell." In later performances, the volunteers were invited, instead, "to travel 'round this country / And Harry's story tell." While this change may reflect more political moderation on the author's part, it also represents the shift of the song's status. As it travels in space and time from the immediate community of the striking miners to the radical wing of the national labor movement and the folk revival, from immediate emotion to mediated memory, Harry Simms (like Luigi Trastulli) becomes a symbol, and the fighting ballad takes on some of the ritual connotations of the anthem.[17]

Carboni's insistence on "remembering" and the recommendation to "spread" the song show that—like everything which is emphatically *written*—it is intended for the future. "I always loved to read," says Carboni, "so I learned a few words above my level of education and used them occasionally. I had the ambition to say something striking, convincing, well-phrased." This ambition reflects the worker's desire that the effort and ability he puts into his work be visible. The conquest of language is hard work, and it must give tangible results. We can see here a relationship to Carboni's professional skill as a technical draftsman and mechanical tracer. A tracer literally *writes* on steel, copying from the blueprint the shape of the piece he is supposed to finish. These work attitudes and experiences influence Carboni's pride in writing and knowledge. "I always had jobs where some studying was involved. As a tracer, you must know how to draw, you must understand certain problems of trigonometry, study them over. For instance, I had discovered a formula for the division of the circle, which you couldn't find in regular handbooks. Now I don't remember it anymore . . ."

In his text, however, poetic diction meets the resistance of oral and vernacular speech. "*Sul* letto" ("*on* his bed") rather than "*nel* letto" ("*in* his bed") is one example of vernacular diction. The misspelling of "jeep" in the written text, and its mispronunciation by Iole Peri in performance, show that foreign terms penetrate the vernacular with some difficulty and distortion. The many commonplace terms (the "golden sun," and the "smile of life") are somewhere between the formulaic expressions of oral poetry and the cliches of mass culture from popular songs, schoolbook poetry, and newspaper writing. The "happy father and husband" also evokes the style of funeral notices and graveyard signs.

The relationship to schoolbook poetry is complex and interesting. "*Pargoletto*," for instance, evokes the famous line "la pargoletta mano" ("your childish hand") from Giovanni Pascoli's poem on the death of his child (*Pianto Antico*), which everybody memorizes in elementary school. The rhyme between "*morte*" ("death") and "*forte*" ("strong") is in turn derived from *La spigolatrice di Sapri* a patriotic piece by Luigi Mercantini, which is also compulsory elementary school fare. What makes the relationship complex is the fact that both Pascoli's and Mercantini's poems imitate the rhythms of folk poetry and use a relatively plain diction. In fact, the reason they are supposed to be suitable for very young children in non-elite schools is that they come as close as any to what the elites imagine folk poetry and sentiment are, or ought to be. We may describe the relationship as a process of mutual selective appropriation. Elite poetry appropriates aspects of folklore that suit the romantic image of "the people" in the Risorgimento era of national independence movements; and this image is fostered through the school system, where working-class poets like Carboni select those texts which retain traces of their own language and sensibilities but which are sanctified as "high" culture.

Music

Pargoletto also evokes another range of sources: melodrama. The word is used, for instance, in a well-known aria from Vincenzo Bellini's *Norma*. Carboni's line where Trastulli's blood cries vengeance from heaven, "dal ciel grida vendetta," is a well-worn cliche, but it also echoes operatic memories, such as in Verdi's *Rigoletto*, where the words "vendetta, tremenda vendetta" resound memorably. Like many older workers, Carboni is familiar with operas; as a former anarchist, he is also well aware of Pietro Gori's use of operatic melodies for workers' anthems. And he knows Gori's May Day song based on *Nabucco*.

While the influence of melodrama is found at the lexical level and in the general dramatic tone of the song, other stylistic elements reveal the influence of popular music. (Carboni was a constant radio listener. During the years he spent in Paris as a political refugee, he used to go to clubs and heard Maurice Chevalier several times.) The influence of popular music is visible in the *coda finale* ("Terni, remember! . . . Terni shall not forget! . . ."), where the non-strophic structure, the exclamation mark, and the ellipses suggest the long, ornate *belcanto* endings of the sentimental pop singers who were popular in the late 1940s. Finally, Carboni's use of a northern ballad tune identified with the World War I repertoire indicates that folk music was also an influence.

The end result is a blending of all these forms: *belcanto* voice, sentimental finale, and folk strophic form. "I asked a comrade who had a good voice to sing it," says Carboni. "The verses were supposed to be sung solo, and the choir was to take up the repetition of the last two lines. But the verses were supposed to be solo." The ballad was never performed that way. On the train to Assisi, it was sung as all the ballads in the style of World War I are sung on trips, in a spontaneous and unarranged choral form, basically in unison, and possibly with a good deal of heterophony. Only in a later phase, when the folk revival took it on stage, the ballad was performed in ways approaching Carboni's solo / choir idea (but minus the pop finale).

There are hints of another, more ambitious idea, in the ambiguous subtitle. *Cantata per Luigi Trastulli* may be read to mean "Sung for Luigi Trastulli," but also "a *cantata for* him." The second interpretation suggests echoes of a solemn, religious form: a requiem for a "martyr" (which is how the subtitle calls Trastulli) to be sung at his funeral. Thirty years later, however, Carboni visualized the song in yet another form: that of the long narrative ballads on tragic news events, illustrated by colorful placards, and sung by street singers. Carboni may have seen some singers of this kind at his factory's gates. Only a few months before Trastulli's death, a street singer with his placard is said to have appeared at the steelworks to sing about the wounding of Communist party Secretary Palmiro Togliatti. In his letter to Valsenti, Carboni wrote: "My humble verse might perhaps be used as the illustration of a street-singer's placard. Think about it: the workers coming out of the gates, singing, with flags; the police charge, the victims, and the singer pointing with his stick as he sings. It might be like some kind of theater." Behind the street singer, Carboni envisions the combination of theater and music: a humble form of melodrama or perhaps the *sceneggiata*, the Neapolitan folk play based on the dramatization of popular songs. High culture, mass culture, and folklore, all blend in the same image once more.

History and Song

This song is a crossroads of cultural diversity. It combines orality and writing in terms of sources, composition, circulation, performance, and influences. It blends the musical influences of anthems, ballads, melodrama, and pop songs. It addresses different communities, from residual (the wake, the village) to substitute (the party, the workplace, the electronic village of the folk revival) and temporary (the event, the train, the peace parade).

After we take it apart to examine its multiple components, however, we realize that the meaning of this song lies in the interaction and mutual influence of these different components. This song can be seen, then, as a hybrid, in which all the experiences and forms which workers accumulated during the history of industrialization are used and blended together.

This suggests some tentative conclusions on the relationship of folk songs and history. First of all, a song is not a primary source of information about events. We don't need Carboni's song to know about the killing of Luigi Trastulli. On the other hand, we learn a good deal about the history which is *inside* the song.

This typology has attempted to link certain forms to certain phases of the history of the working class. That the relationship is not on a mechanical one-to-one basis, and that no song fits precisely and completely within any one "type" are not shortcomings, but precisely the most worthwhile result of this analysis.

When a song is born, it reflects the moment of its birth, but also much of the history of its creators. It then continues to live and to react to history. The geological layers of forms inside Carboni's ballad teach us about history because the song is not merely a description of a historical event, but a summary of the identity of those who were involved in and who reacted to it. The song is also a synthesis of the event's meaning for those who lived on to sing the tale.

Section Two
Harlan, Kentucky, United States

10

Patterns of Paternalism:
From Company Town to Union Shop*

A ROPE AND A JAIL

This chapter describes the perception of power relationships in a company town in Harlan County, in the coal mining region of Eastern Kentucky, from the middle 1930s to the end of the 1940s—a time and place characterized by dramatic industrial conflict as coal operators resisted the drive to unionization. It is based on analogies and discrepancies between three sets of sources: testimony to a Senate investigating committee, given in the 1930s; interviews collected by myself, in 1986–1989; and a reading of the *United Mine Workers Journal* for the postwar years.

In April 1936, a subcommittee of the United States Senate, known as the "La Follette Committee," investigating violations of free speech and rights of labor, opened hearings at Harlan, Kentucky.[1] Rev. Marshall A. Musick, a United Mine Workers of America field worker and a Missionary Baptist minister, was among the first to testify. He told the committee that, before leaving the county, he had been living at Louellen, a coal camp owned by the Cornett-Lewis Coal Company on the Clover Fork of the Cumberland River, approximately fifteen miles from Harlan. The conditions he described were in many ways typical of a company town: the company owned the houses where the 375 miners (60 of them black) and their families lived. All services were supplied by the company, which deducted costs from the miners' pay. A close watch was also kept over the miners' lives and their organizing efforts. A

---

*Presented at the European Association for American Studies biennial conference, Berlin, April, 1988; published in *Appalachian Journal*, Fall 1989.

union had been established in 1933, but, by 1935, it had all but disappeared.[2]

Other aspects of Louellen, while by no means unique, were somewhat extraordinary. According to Musick, the camp "had steel ropes locked over the streets where they left the highway," so that no one could go in or out of the camp without the management's knowledge. In later testimony, Musick described another remarkable fixture. "They had a place under the concrete steps of the office building that was called the jail . . . It is a space under there in a sloping form under the steps. It is possibly 18 feet one way, and smaller the other way . . . 12 by 12, possibly, approximately . . . It is a kind of a cage . . . It was used a while to lock up United Mine Workers in. Often, men that became intoxicated were put in there temporarily until they were removed to Harlan town jail." With a steel rope and a private jail, Louellen had some traits which reminded outside observers of a penitentiary or a concentration camp.

Louellen's General Manager Robert E. Lawson was also called to testify at the La Follette committee hearings.

A resident of Harlan County since 1922, he was a stockholder with $90 thousand worth of stock in the Cornett-Lewis company. He confirmed the details in Musick's testimony, but denied any anti-labor intentions and practices. He said the rope and locks (the only key for which was kept at the company office) were meant to prevent miners from carrying away furniture bought on credit from the company store before they finished paying for it. The private jail (which Lawson also called "cage") was, he said, even smaller than Musick claimed—only 10-by-12 feet. However, Lawson stated that it was never occupied by more than three persons at any one time. It was intended mostly for drunks. He said, "We have [saloons] thick in that country." Basically, he claimed the steel ropes and jails were only means by which the company protected property and maintained law and order.[3]

Judging from the evidence of other company towns in Harlan County, these fixtures—ropes, locks, and jails—may have been less innocent than Lawson claimed. This is how union organizer George B. Titler describes Verda, a coal camp owned by Harlan-Wallins Coal a few miles from Louellen on Clover Fork: "Across the highway a large tree towered by the road. Fifty-feet high in its branches was a tree house. This was no children's playground, however. It was a pillbox where the Harlan-Wallins gun thugs stationed themselves, like guards on a penitentiary wall, to guard the camp." Titler explicitly assimilates Verda to Louellen.

Although it is unclear which camp she is referring to, Julia
Cowans, whose husband is from Verda but who also lived for several years in Louellen, says, "They had fences. They had guards to
let you in there . . . like a concentration camp or something like, of
that sort."

Even at the "model" company town of Lynch, owned by U.S.
Steel, on the other side of Black Mountain, company guards es-
corted all strangers who arrived at the train station to the company
office. There, they were asked to justify their presence in the camp
or leave. Lynch was surrounded by a wire fence, explicitly intended
to keep the organizers out.[5]

As for the "cage," in Louellen, no doubt drunks were kept
in it. However, according to the song "Harlan County Blues" (by
coal miner George Davis, from nearby Hazard in Perry County)
in Harlan:

> You didn't have to be drunk, they said
> To get throwed in the can
> The only thing you needed to be
> Was just a union man.[6]

In 1986, I began collecting interviews toward an oral history of
Harlan County. The project does not focus specifically on either the
1930s or the Louellen coal camp. That historical period, however,
figures prominently in most recollections; and some of the interviews recorded so far have been collected in the Clover Fork section
of the county in which Louellen was located (the camp called
Louellen has since been dismantled). In this chapter, however, I
will concentrate on one specific interview, notable for the precision
of detail and perceptive analysis. The narrator, Lloyd Lefevre, a retired coal miner, was born in 1913 in nearby Bell County, started
working in the mines there at the age of 15, moved to Harlan
County in 1934, and (except for one year in Leslie County) lived
there ever since in Louellen or its immediate vicinity.

Lefevre described Louellen in detail, and volunteered a description of the steel rope and the "cage" before I even realized that
this was the area of the Louellen coal camp of which I had read in
the LaFollette proceedings.

> They didn't have a fence around [the camp], they just
> had a big post on each side, [where] you pulled off the high-
> way and went over in the camp; they put a big cross tie on

each side of the road, and then they had a steel rope, stretched across there, and they kept a lock on it, you see. And if anybody, if you see any people come, why you had to [get in touch] with the watchmen, and they'd let you in and then he'd lock it back.

Right down in Louellen, right by the theater, they had this little jail there, right under the steps before you went up in the building. It had a steel door, on it. And every time they'd arrest a drunk they throwed him in there. Then next day, they'd take him up here to [the judge in town] and he'd fine him and cut his fine off in the office.

Lefevre thus described the function of the jail in the same terms as had manager Lawson: no mention is made of its being used "to lock up United Mine Workers in," as Musick had testified. The same holds for Lefevre's description of the gate. "Well, mostly now what they done that for, they was people that was going down to the commissary for a lot of furniture and stuff. Maybe one or two had sneaked out and moved out of the mines and they kept them with them. They did it to keep them from getting out with it, I believe that's all it was." Rev. Tom Sweatt, a coal miner from Lynch, Harlan County, also recalls that a co-worker told him that "At night at a certain time they closed the fence and they had a guard, and they said jokingly, I don't know how serious it is, that when he left from there, he sneaked out at night so he could move and go somewhere else."

A PRETTY ROUGH TIME

If we assume consent and harmony between management and workers to be the rule, it may be quite normal for a miner to share the views of management on a specific issue, and to present a favorable image of conditions under the company-town system. Consent and harmony, however, were emphatically not the case in Harlan County in the 1930s, and Mr. Lefevre's personal background reflects this fact.

On the one hand, as already noted, management and workers were, at the time, going through a dramatic conflict which is what prompted the La Follette committee investigation in the first place. On the other hand, Lefevre himself was never what he would call "a company suck." He was active in the union organizing effort, remained a union member in good standing, and was actively involved in the 1970s in support of the Brookside strike which was memorialized by Barbara Kopple's award-winning documentary *Harlan County, U.S.A.* He is not likely to buy the company's story; yet, the fact remains that he corroborates the manager's version, rather than the description given by his neighbor Musick and other fellow unionists, and in many other ways he departs from Louellen's "penitentiary" image.

As is always the case with oral sources, contradictions and the verbal strategies used to keep them under control reveal a great deal about cultural attitudes and power relationships. In order to extract as much meaning as possible from this story, we must cast aside simplistic explanations, such as faulty memory and romanticization of the past. Lefevre's memory is vivid, and he does not gloss over unpleasant aspects of his life and experience. The way he tells it, organizing the union in Louellen was no gala affair.

> They [the company] didn't want no union here; you'd say union, they'd run you out of here. We had . . . we had to sneak around, have union meetings just anywhere you could hide.
>
> Well, we had a pretty rough time, had it rougher than anything else here, had men try to cross the picket lines trying to go to work . . . throwed them over them railroad bridges, [they] never tried it again. We caught one woman one day over the bridge. She and her old man . . . she was trying to push him across the bridge and make him go to work, and they grabbed him, throwed him under the railroad bridge, and throwed her in the river too.
>
> Yeah, we baptized them [scabs] "in the name of the Father, the Son, and John L. Lewis." Okay. We had it pretty rough getting it in, we finally made it.
>
> Hanged cowbells on their [scabs'] necks, take 'em off down the road, told them not to come back. If you come back here we'll kill you. Take them up across the railroad, turn 'em over toward Virginia, tell them not to come back. Yeah, we had it pretty rough.

Ironically, Lawson underplayed this aspect. In fact, he told the LaFollette committee that the miners told him that they had been able to walk around the pickets without harassment.[7] He thus tried to convey the impression that business was pretty much as usual, that "his" miners were content and that the union was only a minor outside interference. But Lefevre and his follow workers and union members knew that their effort to organize was being carried out at the risk of their lives.

The Black Bottom Baptist church where union members used to meet was dynamited and the church's minister, Rev. B. H. Moses, a blacklisted coal miner, was run out of the county. "Brother Moses lived up there," recalls Debbie Spicer, one of his neighbors:

> And they put dynamite to it. He lived up there, and the dynamite burned up pretty close and went out. You can't destroy a child of God as long as the Lord's got something for him to do, you can't do nothing with him. They didn't do nothing with Daniel, they put him in the lions' den but the lions wouldn't eat him, they just laid down. And they throwed the Hebrew children in the fiery furnace and it didn't burn them a bit. Didn't even singe the hair on their head. It didn't blow Brother Moses up. Brother Moses was a real man of God, a real preacher.

Rev. Marshall A. Musick was arrested, charged with "cryminal syndicalism and run out of the county. In 1934, miners marching from the Highsplint and Louellen area toward Harlan were pushed back brutally by deputy sheriffs, and Rev. C. E. Vogel, a Harlan Methodist minister who saw the affair and complained was removed from the area due to complaints from his middle class congregation.[8] Samuel Boggs, a member of the Louellen United Mine Workers local, reminisced about those days in a song:

> I remember one night back in thirty-four
> When two gun thugs had knocked on my front door,
> So I opened up, this is what they said:
> "Join the Union and we'll blow off your head."[9]

During a strike in November 1934, John L. Smith, a black union member, was abducted by deputy sheriffs, "whipped with a hickory limb one inch in diameter and about eight feet long" and dropped across the Virginia line. When Musick questioned him about it, Sheriff Middleton replied, "What is this damn nigger to you?" In January 1937, a car loaded with deputy sheriffs fired into Rev. Musick's home and killed his young son Bennett.[10]

Lefevre knew the Musick family and remembers the murder and the violence. He knew what he was getting into when he joined the organizing effort. It is unlikely that miners like him would have taken such risks if their living and working conditions had made any other choice possible. When describing the Louellen camp, however, Lefevre says that Cornett-Lewis had "a nice camp down there, they [had] a nice place to live. They [the company] kept the camp cleaned, and the people that had the prettiest yard, he'd [Robert Lawson, the company's general manager] give them a little prize. He believed in keeping it cleaned up." The houses had "electric," and a few had running water. Though they were made of frame, at least they were plastered. "They kept 'em painted, you know. They painted them inside and out. They had this ceiling, not that thick, just slapped over, it was kind of thin. They were pretty nice houses."

As of General Manager Lawson, "Oh, he was a good feller. He was good to the men. He knowed, if you would work and do your work every day, he never would say a word to you. But they had a bunch of these drunks, on the week ends, and they'd lay off, you know, Mondays, and he was pretty rough on fellers like that. But if a fellow would work, and do his job, he wouldn't say a word to them."

In a later conversation, Lefevre recalled that a black man had frozen to death in the Louellen private jail. His evaluation of Lawson and of the way he ran his camp, however, is echoed by his neighbors.

> DEBBIE SPICER: [Mr. Lawson] was a wonderful man. He kept a good clean camp. He tried. He wanted everybody to do good. He'd invite people to come to church, Sunday school. He had the yards fenced up . . . pretty flowers, he'd give prizes for which one had the prettiest yard, and—he was just a wonderful man.
>
> HAZEL KING: The Mr. Lawson I knew was a very likable person. He was very fatherly like, I would call it, and he knew every one, and all the children. He was always willing to assist 'em, you know, especially in their interests of having flowers and everything there, neat, and . . . I liked Mr. Lawson. I may be a little bit prejudiced, but I think we had one of the best coal camps in Harlan County. They were some people that really seemed to care about what happened to their people, their workers.

Julia Cowans, who lived in the black section of the camp and had fewer personal contacts with Lawson ("you'd probably see him get out of his car and go up in the office and he'd spend several hours up there and he'd get in his car and he's gone"), also has memories of his paternalistic attitude:

> Well, listen. Personally, I never had any contact with him. But [my first husband], he..he drank a lot. And I've heard him tell it a many a times, he'd leave home and go down to Harlan, and he'd be runnin' out of money; he'd see Mr. Lawson riding down the street, stop him and get money from him.

KIND MASTERS, PROUD WORKERS

The contrast between the conditions which made the unionizing effort necessary, and the often positive description of the environment in which these conditions prevailed, is not unlike the paradox described by Frederick Douglass. When he was a slave, Douglass recalled, he always said (and partly believed) that he had "a kind master" because he "always measured the kindness of my master by the standard of kindness among slaveholders around us."[11]

Kentucky coal miners were not slaves; in fact, one of the reasons for presenting their lives under the best possible light is the desire to protect the image of their own independent manhood, and maintain the appearance and belief of having had some degree of free choice of environment. Frederick Douglass's psychology, however, is not inapplicable to their narratives.

Several factors converge in generating harmonious descriptions of the social environment in which such dramatic conflicts took place. Among the most important are: personal pride; limited horizons and expectations; the mediation of class conflict through personal relationships; and conscious manipulation enacted by management.

Let us begin with pride. Harlan County miners, like most American workers, do not primarily think of themselves as members of an exploited class—as opposed, for instance, to Italian workers, who have often been influenced by some concept of class struggle. Thus, while Italian workers are likely to draw a pessimistic image of their condition in order to project an image of militant pride, Harlan county coal miners seem often to feel that there is something personally demeaning—rather than collectively legitimizing—in appearing to be or to have been exploited.

A coal miner from Lynch, for instance, described in conversation the crowded conditions in some of the company houses even in this "model" town, and the wire fence which used to surround it. When asked to repeat the same things on tape thirty minutes later, he talked his way out of it. Clearly, he felt that it would have been demeaning to his dignity if he had admitted that he had "consented" to live under what might have been construed as humiliating circumstances (and it would have been even more offensive to suggest that he had been forced to). The same process may explain why Lefevre mentioned the man who froze to death in Louellen's jail only a year after our first interview—and then with the tape recorder off.

In the absence of a vision of class conflict, there is little space for self-validation of the workers' identity. Recognition must be confirmed by "significant others," and management is as "other" and as "significant" as they come, especially in the semi-feudal layout of a coal camp. The fact that most of the fiercest struggles were waged about the issue of union recognition reinforces this attitude. This is why it is very important that Lawson, stern but just, "never would say a word to you" if you worked satisfactorily every day and didn't get drunk. He could tell a good worker from a drunkard and a shirker, and gave that worker pride and security. Of course, in order for Lawson's recognition to mean something, he must be "a good feller" and "a wonderful man."

One reason why the manager's attitude is so important is that, in the relatively isolated and literally fenced-in environment of the coal camp, he is the only standard available. Like Frederick Douglass and his peers, Harlan County coal miners had little opportunity to assess their conditions on a universal standard of citizenship or human rights, rather than against their immediate surroundings (or, in the case of immigrants, their backgrounds). And it seems that very elementary rights—houses with plastering and wiring, and respect for men who were doing their work—were not to be taken for granted in Harlan County. In fact, the Clover Fork area in which Louellen was located ranked with Lynch in offering "accommodations far above average for the nation's coal fields."[12] Therefore, Lefevre is reasonably proud of having lived and raised his family in a relatively decent environment: although these advantages depended more on the company's goodwill than on the miners' initiatives or power to enforce them, yet he can at least claim that he was recognized as a good enough worker to be kept on.

And yet, Louellen and Lynch were above average "for the nation's *coal camps*." As the palpably shocked tone of the La Follette committee's questioning shows, to observers living in more usual and democratic environments (or like the union leaders with a broader knowledge of national standards), Louellen looked indeed like a penitentiary. To those whose choice was between Louellen and another coal camp, it looked at least like a clean and orderly one.

Under this light, the question of the steel rope and the cage takes on another meaning. Whether they were used only for drunks or debtors or also against the UMWA is not the real issue. The questions is, rather, what right has a private organization to own a jail, arrest citizens, and deduct fines from their paychecks for misdemeanors not related to their work? And how normal is it for working people to be in constant debt to their employers even for their house furniture? These questions are never raised.

It is very difficult for the miners to view themselves as *citizens*, endowed with equal rights with the Cornett-Lewis Coal Company and its representatives on their country's territory, rather than as *employees* subject to private rule on private property, and, implicitly, as dependents whose personal life is under the control of a stronger power. After all, one cannot very well complain of company "thugs" once one grants the company police power over drunks.

When I naively remarked that Lawson looked like "a dictator over the whole place," Lefevre replied: "Well, yeah, all of the mines was that way back then." Like Douglass, he measures "the kindness of [his] master by the standard of kindness" among masters around him. But it is a peculiar standard. Lawson, Lefevre says, was "a good feller"; but so was a local deputy sheriff ("He was a pretty good feller as far as I knowed him") who Lefevre believes to have been among the murderers of Rev. Musick's son. ("He shot a man's house down here and killed a fellow's boy. [The boy's father] was a preacher.") Being "a pretty good feller" must have been a very relative affair in Harlan County in the 1930s.

ABSENTEE OWNERS, FRIENDLY NEIGHBORS

Back then [says Lefevre] people that owned the mines . . . they just about run the courthouse down there, see. They do anything they want to and get away with it. They had gun thugs, they called 'em, in the camp; they would, they did what the coal operator said and if you don't [accept it], they took and run a man out of the camp. You just had to get up and go. So it was.

At another point in his interview, Lefevre says:

> The strikers, before they got the union in, he [Lawson] allowed them to trade so much a day, you know, and live in the camp, so their kids wouldn't go hungry, you see. And he allowed them to trade at least two dollars a day back when the stuff didn't cost that much to live, you know. So these two dollars a day, he allowed everybody living in the camp to trade at the commissary. But when they got the contract signed and we went back to work, they cut you so much a month to pay them back. He was pretty fair, pretty good to his workers, the men.

These two passages display the verbal strategy used by the narrator in order to reconcile the representation of an abstract class power with that of harmonious personal relationships in the camp. On one side is an impersonal "they" ("they do anything they want to. . ." and "they had gun thugs . . ."), endowed with distant and total power. On the other, a neighborly, personal "he," identified with "Old Man" Lawson, the visible mediator, who was "pretty good to his workers" and kept them from starvation even at the peak of conflict. The combined picture is the essence of paternalism: a personal bond between the oppressors and the oppressed, which obscures under a veil of human relations, even of affection and friendship, the nakedness of exploitation and the totality of power.

Cornett-Lewis may very well have chosen to extend credit to the miners because of humanitarian concern for their children's welfare; after all, it was common for other companies to evict their striking workers (a practice which, if Rev. Musick's testimony is to be believed, in Louellen was limited to union activists). Also, the company may have expected that the strike would, sooner or later, be over, and they would get their money back. That there was a strike on was no reason to stop making a profit from the company store. In fact, although the prices at the company commissary were not higher than those of outside stores (where miners could "redeem" company script at a loss of about 15 percent), Lawson testified that Cornett-Lewis made a profit of 17 to 21 percent from the commissary.

Possibly, both humanitarian and economic motives may have been at work. Here, however, we are not as concerned with the management's intentions as with the verbal structure of Lefevre's narrative, and what it reveals to us about cultural attitudes. He describes a situation where there is a giving (credit) and a taking (the cut); and then he proceeds to assign the giving to Lawson, and the taking to the impersonal "they." "He" fed the miners on credit; "they" docked them afterwards.

This strategy occurs at other points in the interview. At Louellen, "they"—not "he"—didn't want no union"; and "If *they* caught you trading, going out to Harlan and tradin' in the store, instead of tradin' in the commissary, why, *they*'d run you off from here, *they* didn't take you back." Other speakers also use this strategy. Hazel King, whose father owned a small store just outside the camp, speaks favorably of Lawson in the singular "he," but shifts to the plural "they" when remembering how miners were discouraged from trading at her father's store. "*They* didn't always like to share *their* money or resources or what-have-you with anyone else. *They* liked to keep a captive audience with *their* miners."

It may be useful to reiterate, at this point, that Lawson was also a stockholder in the company, not just an employee. *He* is one of "*them,*" to all practical purposes. But *he* is *their* visible, human, and personal presence ("*They* keep the camp clean," but *he* physically hands out the prizes). *He* is the only part of *them* that Lefevre and his fellow miners actually see and meet. Thus, Lefevre says that "*they* controlled the courthouse"; but the testimony of the union leaders who had direct dealings with the courts show that it was Lawson *in person* who took care of this aspect of business. According to Musick's testimony (which Lawson, however, denied), when he was arrested for "criminal syndicalism" pending contract negotiations, Judge Morris Saylor asked the prosecuting attorney to "call up Mr. Bob Lawson, and see what he wanted done about the case." Musick testified that:

> Mr. Middleton went to the telephone booth and returned within a few minutes and told the judge that Mr. Lawson said to set the case for 1:30 and he would be there with his witnesses and proceed with the trial. [In the afternoon, however] the County judge and the County attorney called us into the consultation room, and the judge told us that Mr. Lawson was willing to dismiss the case, all of the cases, if we would go back to the camps and be nice men as we usually had, and go back to work.[13]

Only a restricted group of union leaders, however, dealt with Lawson in his capacity as "super-judge." Lefevre and his peers may never have known him in this light; they met him only in his paternal role, not only inside the camp but also outside.

In the everyday context of the camp, "Old Man" Lawson was half boss and half neighbor. Though he lived above the miners' houses, he still lived in the camp for most of his tenure. He was a church member, shared in social activities, and taught Sunday school. The title "Old Man" seems to go, rather than with age, with the office of camp manager; it also extends to Lawson's successor, "Old Man" Scott. As implied by the etymology of "paternalism," the manager takes on the hue of a fatherly figure: a teacher, a father, a supervisor of morals, and an advisor.

Hazel King, who lived just outside the camp, does not hesitate to apply the cliche: he was "very fatherly like," she says. And Lefevre recalls:

> [At the camp theater] they'd show westerns, good movies. Then old man Lawson would have a safety meeting as he would call it, oncet a month. First Monday in a month. Tried to caution the men about how to take care of theirselves in the mine, and be careful, and he'd give a little prize of some kind every time they had the meeting [usually a sack of flour]. I got it, I don't know [how many] times. He'd get up and make him a little talk.

Lefevre remembers carrying many a dead man out of the mines in his lifetime, crushed by motors or slate falls. "Old Man" Lawson's little talks and encouragement prizes, while worthwhile in themselves, seem to imply that most of the accidents were caused by the workers' carelessness. In fact, at least until the union came in, the companies did not bother much about safety standards. Miners had to "take care of theirselves," and they had to be taught to do so.

The subordinate subjects of a paternalistic relationship have no rights, but they may receive gifts. The exchange of the right to a safe mine with the gift of a sack of flour paralleled the prizes for the better-kept gardens awarded to families who could be evicted any moment at the company's will. This strategy promoted gratitude to management and competition among employees. Besides the immediate gain, recipients were made to feel that they had been recognized; since the prize only went to a chosen few, it gave them the pride of feeling somewhat special, in management's eyes and in their own. Elsewhere, the strategy was less subtle and more exploitative. At the Harlan-Wallins Coal Company, the manager would raffle off (at a profit) used cars belonging to the company or to its officials; and miners were under pressure to buy tickets. This practice gave individual miners the feeling that they had been lucky or at least that they had had a chance; also, as Senator Thomas of the La Follette committee remarked, "it does satisfy a gambling instinct."[14]

The supervision of morals contributes both to the maintenance of discipline and to the image of the manager. When they weren't dynamiting churches for hosting union meetings, as was the case with Rev. Moses' church in Black Bottom, companies encouraged their construction in the camps, though—in Louellen, at least—at no cost to themselves. "They had a big church in here," says Lefevre. "They didn't build it though; the men built it. Cut 'em so much a month to build a church. The men paid for it, that worked here." Like the Terni sports arena built by the steel company with money docked out of the workers' paycheck, the church in Louellen, then, "wasn't built by the company. It was built by the working class"—but in both cases the companies took the credit.[15] The school also worked the same way. Contemporary narrators seem to assume that the school was provided by the company. "We were allowed to go to the school, which the company did furnish," says Hazel King; "and, I don't think we could have had a better school than we had in Louellen." In fact, the company furnished the building, but the teachers were paid by the county or the state for seven months, and by the miners themselves for two (the miners also paid the preacher).

Moral supervision makes for better accounting, as in the case of the controversy over payments due to survivors of a black worker killed in a mine accident. Lefevre recalls:

> He was living with some woman over there in the camp. Old Man Lawson thought she was his wife. He went and settled with her. I don't know how much he paid her, but anyhow he carried her on compensation. He paid her. Later on there was another one come in and brought her lawyer with her from Alabama; this was his real wife. And he had to pay her, too. I don't know what she collected, but now she collected the money out of him, and he put a notice at the office down there, and said everybody that had lived over in the colored camp that can't show a marriage license, said he wanted

them moved out. They just hired a truck, and hauled the furniture down there and around here and yonder, just set it on the road, buddy, all of them that couldn't show marriage licenses. Said he was tired paying the niggers. They wasn't gonna gyp him again. They moved them out, buddy, they went everywhere. Well, there's some white people down there the same way. They sneak out and get married. He was rough on them, that old man Lawson, that way.

The company's moral supervision takes on a different meaning when viewed from Julia Cowans's black woman's perspective:

And the company, the coal operators, if [a woman's] husband was killed in the mine, they had lawyers that would beat that widder out of her money. They would bury him and give her a few dollars, but beat the lady outa money that was rightfully hers.

According to the testimony of James Westmoreland, a miner and union field representative, after the 1934 strike was settled and Cornett-Lewis signed a contract with the union, Lawson requested miners to go and sign the union checkoff in his office. He interrogated union members, and threatened to fire them for being in debt with the company—possibly due to the credit kindly extended to them during the strike. In fact, many did not eventually sign. "Mr. Lawson, you signed this contract," Westmoreland said he told him. "I understood that you, as a church member, go to Sunday school and teach a class. Do you think that it is right after you sign these agreements, not to recognize the correct situation, as you signed it?"

Lawson is said to have replied, "I am not going to have anything to do with the union."[16] Apparently, Lawson was concerned with his workers' welfare as long as they did not take it into their own hands (and perhaps as long as this concern put them in debt to his company).

We have no information as to how the conversations were carried out between Lawson and the miners in the company office. Lefevre mentions the episode briefly, almost gliding over it, as if it did not square with the symmetry of personal relationships and class antagonism he has established in his memory and narrative strategy. "Old man Lawson," he says, "called up everybody up at the office building, wanted to see everybody down at the station." Two factors, however, must have been at work at the same time: fear of company reprisals, as mentioned by Westmoreland, and the fact that individual miners found it easier to confront collectively an impersonal company than to say "No" personally to "Old Man" Lawson.

Lawson, in fact, insisted on the "fatherly" relationship. Sometimes, like children, the miners may be led astray; but a stern hand and a forgiving heart will bring them to their senses. When Musick and other union men were under indictment at the Harlan court house, the judge told them that "Mr. Lawson was willing to dismiss the case, all of the cases, if we would go back to the camps and be nice men as we usually had, and go back to work." Lawson insists that the reason why there was no checkweighman at Cornett-Lewis was that miners did not want to go to the expense of paying one. After Lawson's talks to the workers, the number of checked-off union dues began to drop. By the end of the year, Lawson took the initiative. He described his actions in his testimony to the La Follette committee:

> [In December, 1934] our men met in a body and with a secret ballot voted 275 to 5 that they wanted no union here.
> SENATOR LA FOLLETTE: Who called them in?
> MR. LAWSON: I think I did . . .
> SENATOR LA FOLLETTE: And did they sign the [ballot] slips?
> MR. LAWSON: Yes; they signed their names to it . . .
> SENATOR LA FOLLETTE: And you call that a secret ballot?
> MR. LAWSON: Yes; if a man had a ballot and did what he pleased with it.

THE PRESIDENT WANTS YOU TO JOIN THE UNION

A final comparison between Lawson's and Musick's testimony to the La Follette committee points out the origins of a new form of paternalism which became, in later years, as a result of these struggles, both a counterpart and a parallel to the power of the companies': the paternalistic pattern of the union.

According to Musick, a few months after the 1934 strike, Cornett-Lewis stopped applying the contract, evicted field representatives, and fired about fifty union activists. The union responded by calling a strike. According to Westmoreland, deputy sheriffs were "going from house to house taking the men out . . . I saw revolvers and shotguns and their pistols . . . they had the men by the arms."

Musick also testified (and his testimony coincides with the verse in Samuel Boggs' song) that:

> There were about a hundred men that ceased or refused to go back to work in sympathy with the men that were cut off or discharged . . . There were a bunch of deputy sheriffs went in and forced a number of men to go back to work—made them put on their bank clothes, two or three hours later than the ordinary shift went on, and thus driven at the point of guns to the main hoists, where they were loaded up and taken to the mines.

On the other hand, Lawson testified that it was the union which went from house to house forcing the men to strike, in violation of the contract. "They delegated certain men for certain streets in town to go there and call the people, knock at their door, at midnight, especially the colored people, and tell them not to be found on the job the next day."

What is remarkable about these conflicting versions is not their contrast, but their parallelism: both sides say that the miners were *forced* either to strike or to work. It is a vivid picture—more symbolic than real, perhaps—but more telling for that. The miners do not decide for themselves to go on strike or to go to work; they are *made* to do either one, by the union or by management, fighting over them like God and Satan over the soul of man. Some of the questions of identity and pride, limited horizons and expectations, and tension between personal identifications and abstract institutions which we have identified in the miners' attitude toward management, are transferred, in new but recognizable forms, to their attitude toward the union.

Let us go back to Lloyd Lefevre's narrative.

> We had a hard time getting it [the union] in, but we finally got it. We wouldn't have got it though if it hadn't been for the President, and John L. Lewis. They worked together on that. I heared President Roosevelt makin' a speech one time, he said he was a worker hisself and he wouldn't work for nobody he had [not] hisself agreed to work with. That's when we got it in.

[After the union came in] everything worked just fine. Just normal, everybody got along good, they were better to the men, kept the mine in better shape, you know, [kept] the rock dust [down] and everything. Never did have trouble until lately: the mines is pulling out, they've got no union.

Once again, the structure of pronouns is the cue. The union is never "*we*," but always "*it*," "*they*" or "*he*," meaning John L. Lewis. It is never a first person, always a third. One does not have the sense that the miners *are* the union, but that they *have* a union or that they *belong* to one. The spatial imagery goes in the same direction: the union is perceived as something which the miners "brought in," and which therefore existed somewhere else and independent of them. The miners do not appear to have acquired power and autonomy on their own; rather, there is now above them another power, benevolent and protective, which balances the omnipotence of the companies. "It" makes "them" behave and "be good"—but the miners are still "their" men.

The substitution of protection for power can be seen in the question of safety, which is foremost in Lefevre's narrative as well as in the pages of the *United Mine Workers Journal*, especially in the post-World War II years, when the union had become established and the war emergency was over. On the one hand, the union makes it now clear that death in the mines is not due only to the miners' inability to "take care of theirselves": it is a matter of safety measures, rock dust, ventilation, roof bolting, and many other factors. On the other hand, the union also takes on management's didactic role (often in cooperation with it), teaching miners how to avoid accidents with the same strategy of competitive incentives and rewards. Thus, the *United Mine Workers Journal* for the late 1940s and early 1950s carries several stories describing the outstanding safety instruction programs at Closplint and Highsplint, resulting in Closplint's victory in the Kentucky mine safety championship.[18] However, the miners themselves have hardly any independent means of directly enforcing the new safety measures; they must rely on the union's protection and go on learning how to "take care of theirselves."

Although the accident rate tends to decrease after the advent of the union, "The mining industry of the United States has more fatalities, more disabling accidents, and a higher incidence of pneumoconiosis ("black lung") than that of any other Western industrialized nation."[19] On this point, however, Frederick Douglass's law of comparative, restricted standards, is applicable. Coal miners in the United States are likely to ignore what goes on in other countries; like most of the general public in the United States, they take it for granted that their country's standards can only be the best. They evaluate the union's performance on the standards of previous conditions, and find that it is a great improvement.

Although the union is an abstract entity, it becomes tangible and human in the person of John L. Lewis, just as the company did in the person of "Old Man" Lawson. Samuel Boggs's song says:

> Then along came a man . . . brave as any lion.
> He called us together and asked us to join.
> Long as we may live we'll love "Daddy John"
> For the many good things that he has done . . .

Lloyd Lefevre's account of the origins of the union starts on a note of first-person pride: "We had a hard time bringing it in, but we finally got it." Immediately after, however, he tones it down. "We wouldn't have got it though if it hadn't been for the President and John L. Lewis." *They*, rather than the miners, are the heroes. Lewis campaigned for the UMWA in the 1930s under the slogan "The President wants you to join the union." The personification of the nation in the person of the President shaped the personification of the union in John L. Lewis; and the miners' highest act of self-assertion, joining the union, somehow becomes another act of obedience.

The *United Mine Workers Journal* edition of 7 July 1948 carried two letters from Harlan County miners. One is from Wallins Creek: "I am so grateful for the Welfare Fund . . . I will be for John L. Lewis 'til my dying day and stand for the union and my rights. Bless him, he has stopped the starving here in my home as well as kept others from starving." The other letter is from Highsplint:

> I certainly wish to express my most sincere appreciation and thanks to Mr. Lewis for making it possible for me and mine to have a swell time each year on my ten days' vacation and $100. For, having spent approximately 25 years in the coal mines and having worked for as little as 28 cents per ton, I think it is something to be mighty thankful for.

Again, the benefits of union protection and of the newly created Welfare Fund are quite real; and miners' letters are often structured around the contrast between the past and the improved present. In the published letters, however, miners never say that it is *they*—their struggles, courage, endurance, the violence they suffered and the violence they used—who stopped starvation and made John L. Lewis the president of a powerful union. "He [Lewis] has stopped them working us twelve hours a day," sang Samuel Boggs.

The pride in having established the union is all concentrated in the President; and the miners glory in being represented by a powerful leader of their own. Gratitude, appreciation, thanks, faith, loyalty, lauds, praises, and blessings for John L. Lewis are standard terms in the published miners' letters. Pensions and welfare are usually described not as rights they have conquered, but gifts they receive from the union or personally from John L. Lewis.

Cover after cover of the UMWA *Journal* (at least three in 1948 alone) show miners or widows in the act of receiving a check from John L. Lewis or some other high union official, or John L. Lewis in the act of signing or handing out much needed relief or pension checks.[20] The amount of the check is often prominently indicated; and the opening headlines of three issues in the first five months of 1949 remind readers of how much their welfare payments are costing the union treasure.[21] A photograph shows union officials dressed up in Santa Claus suits handing out fruit and candy to miners' children in Lynch, in a telling continuity of union and U.S. Steel Company paternalism.[22]

"I am thankful for a man in this unfriendly world such as John L. Lewis," writes a miner's widow from Straight Creek, Harlan County[23]—after a rock dust explosion resulting from the failure to respect safety measures killed several miners. Meanwhile, of course, John L. Lewis was getting ready to sign the Bituminous Coal Agreement of 1950, which exchanged hundreds of thousands of miners' jobs for the consolidation of union power in the coalfields. But that is another story.[24]

"I will stand for John L. Lewis 'til my dying day and stand for the union and my rights," wrote the Wallins Creek miner. The seeds of drama lie in this progressive identification of his rights with the established union, and of the union with the union establishment. Increasingly, "standing for the union" came to be identified with uncritical support of its top leadership.

Harlan County was one of the areas where support for the Miners for Democracy movement in the 1970s was lowest. In fact, when Lewis' successor, Tony Boyle, hired thugs to kill Jock Yablonski, the "insurgent" candidate for the union presidency, and his wife and daughter in 1969, funds for the crime came from the district which includes Harlan County. In Harlan, loyalty to Boyle remained high to the end. John Gaventa attributes this attitude to the deep-set identification of the union with its leadership, to an inbred feeling of dependence on the union, and to the reiterated (by the leaders) need to defend the union from its internal and external enemies, branding all criticism and opposition as treason.[25]

Harlan County was the last coal county in the United States to accept the union-shop clause. The cause for this delay was the powerlessness of the miners, which made unionization efforts difficult and dangerous and generated a sense of subordination, dependence, and fear. Some of the powerlessness which militated against unionization, however, was continued within the union. The company town and the union shop—both of them self-enclosed and literally and/or figuratively fenced in—restricted horizons and expectations, and hindered autonomous definition of identity and rights.

FATHERLY ADVICE

One of Boyle's staunchest supporters during the first Yablonski campaign was George J. Titler, who led the union campaign in Harlan in the late 1930s. The final lines of his autobiography, *Hell in Harlan*, warn the opposition that Boyle is "carrying out the principles enunciated in 1936 by the GREAT John L. Lewis when the union gave Franklin D. Roosevelt $500,000 and it is not wise to attack the name of the great Legendary John L. Lewis among the coal miners of America."[26] The threatening tone and the benevolent image of Lewis, and the personal link with Roosevelt were still being used, long after the death of both, to quench dissent and opposition.

"As I retire after 59 years on the firing line," Titler's book begins, "I wish to give the young coal miner some Fatherly advice . . .". The autobiographer's fatherly stance, casting readers (in this case, miners) as children, goes back to the roots of the American autobiographical tradition, the "Dear Son" opening of the autobiography of Benjamin Franklin. But this tradition receives a new twist: the paternal old leader is not only a direct descendant of "Daddy John," the "Legendary" John L. Lewis, but also an indirect heir of "Old Man" Lawson's paternalism.

11

No Neutrals There: The Cultural Class Struggle in the Harlan Miners' Strike of 1931–32*

FLAGS

In 1921, twenty thousand armed miners marched upon Blair Mountain in Logan County, West Virginia. They were stopped by a private army owned by the operators, which did not hesitate to bomb them from airplanes. The marchers were patriotic citizens, and many were veterans of World War I. The American flag waved at their head. The operators' private army also claimed that they stood for principles—free enterprise and private property—which flourish under the American flag. To prevent these two armies from destroying each other, federal troops stepped in. No need to ask which flag this third army was waving.[1]

Let us leave for the moment these three armies under one flag, and move forward ten years and a few miles further southwest. At the end of the winter of 1930–31, the miners around Black Mountain in Harlan County, Kentucky, began to organize and plan a strike. Wage cuts and unemployment following a slump in the already severely depressed coal industry had brought thousands of families to the verge of starvation, while deputy sheriffs and company guards and created a "virtual reign of terror"[2] that effectively frightened the United Mine Workers of America away from the area. "You could talk with any of these [miners] about striking," says Tillman Cadle, a retired miner and organizer, and "they'd say it wouldn't

---

*Presented to the conference on "Working-Class Culture: Memory and Change," Alessandria (Italy), 14–16 March 1985; published as "Con inni e bandiere. Il conflitto culturale nello sciopero di Harlan" in the proceedings, R. Botta et al., eds., *La cultura delle classi subalterne fra tradizione e innovazione* (Alessandria: Edizioni Dell'Orso, 1988), 151–168.

make any difference: if you struck, you starved; if you worked, you starved. There's no difference. So it had just come down to just a matter of starvation and war against starvation, that's what it all come down to."

Miners evicted from the company coal camps at Black Mountain moved to the "free" town of Evarts, where rank-and-file leaders like W. B. Jones, William Hightower and others continued independently to organize. Up to two thousand miners marched through the county to demonstrate and recruit, walking "behind Jones and his organizers riding in an open car with the American Flag."[3] On 5 May 1931, gunfire opened at Evarts between a police-escorted convoy of nonstrikers driving toward Black Mountain and a group of union men. In the battle, three deputies and one miner were killed. Kentucky's governor sent in the National Guard; and Jones and the other rank-and-file leaders were jailed and later tried and sentenced to death (they were finally freed in 1941). A few weeks after the "battle of Evarts," organizers from the National Miners Union, a Communist-led dual union, came to Harlan, and began to organize around the Straight Creek area.

Aunt Molly Jackson, a midwife, daughter of a fundamentalist preacher, and wife of a Harlan miner, worked around the union soup kitchens, spoke at meetings, and wrote songs which later became well-known among urban radicals. One of her songs, based on a hymn tune, said:

> The bosses ride their big fine white horse
> While we walk in the mud
> Their flag's the big red, white, and blue
> While ours is dipped in blood.[4]

CHARACTERS

The Appalachian Mountains have been discovered twice in their history: first, at the turn of the century, as a precious reservoir of natural and cultural wealth—timber, coal, ballads, stories, and crafts; and second, in the mid-1960s, as a problematic "pocket of poverty" and a testing ground of the "culture of poverty" theories which were then popular.[5] Thus, while the federal government created programs of economic opportunity, sociological and anthropological research sought in the people's culture the causes of their poverty.

In one of the most authoritative sociological syntheses, Thomas R. Ford summed up the region's cultural characters under such headings as "Individualism and Self-Reliance," "Traditionalism and Fatalism," and "Religious Fundamentalism."[6]

While empirical surveys appear to support these conclusions, it is not easy to reconcile these terms with the Logan and Harlan Counties scenarios of conflict. Again and again, in the course of their history, these "individualistic" and "fatalistic" people have combined to try to change their fate. In less dramatic but more pervading forms, these traditionalistic people turned, in the course of one generation or less, from "self-sufficient" farmers to wage workers in the industrial context of mines and railroads. Later, they moved in mass to northern cities. Many mountain people from the mining districts have probably gone through more changes in their lives than the supposedly mobile urban middle class.

Individualism is just as problematic (for one thing, it is not easily reconciled with traditionalism and fatalism). Thomas R. Bethell wrote about the family of Jim Garland (Aunt Molly Jackson's half-brother): "[They] prided themselves on their independent thinking, but his father had understood enough about the impersonal economic weight massed against them to join the United Mine Workers of America."[7] To a foreign observer, the puzzling word here is "but." Trained as we are to believe that the first thing an independent-minded worker does is join the union, we would expect a "therefore" instead. In the relatively egalitarian context of pre-industrial Appalachia, however, "self-sufficiency" meant that one was independent not of one's (nonexistent, invisible, absentee, or "impersonal") superiors, but of one's neighbors and peers. Husking bees and roof raisings notwithstanding, the "proud mountaineer" needs no one's help and solidarity. Thus, by joining the union and trying collective action (perhaps encouraged by their new and less "individualistic" immigrant neighbors), mountain people declared that these earlier ideologies were no longer adequate.

On the other hand, the empirical evidence of Ford's traits cannot be disregarded. It may reveal a discrepancy between subjectively articulated attitudes—values, desires, or nostalgia—and collective practices. Or it may reflect the fact that these values are being held onto *as values* precisely because the practices were by necessity so different, the changes were so dramatic, and choice and need were so inextricably interwoven. Tradition and change, plus individualism and solidarity may stand in a more complex relationship than sheer opposition. Tradition may supply—as in Molly Jackson's song—the linguistic forms enabling the expression of new ideas. On the other hand, the discrepancy between values and practices may deprive individuals of the means to recognize and even to name their own actions, and thus to legitimize and consolidate them.

In this essay I will try to analyze how, in the face of unprecedented conditions and finding themselves led to unprecedented actions, miners attempted to legitimize their choices in terms of their traditional culture, of religion, and patriotism. The symbols, words, and sources of legitimacy of this culture were shared with the operators, and the institutions of the state. The consequence was a fierce class struggle for the control of meaning; and this aspect of the conflict influenced the outcome and aftermath of the struggle as a whole.

CONSTITUTIONAL RIGHTS

In 1932, Arthur Garfield Hays, on behalf of the American Civil Liberties Union, wrote a letter to the Bell County Attorney Walter B. Smith expressing concern for the violations of civil rights in Harlan and Bell Counties. In his reply, Smith wrote: "The people of Bell County are fundamentalists in politics, religion, and social economies. They are perfectly satisfied with the government of the United States as it is now administered."[8]

Walter B. Smith was one of the fiercest opponents of the strike. His formulation of beliefs, however, might have been shared by the strikers themselves. As one writer for the *New York Times* put it, "The rise and decline of the coal industry in Harlan and Bell County have not erased the religious and patriotic tenets of operators or miners."[9] The rulers and the ruled, operators and miners, appear to share a common cultural substratum, based on patriotism and religion in their "fundamentalist" mode, and on the relative language and symbols. Given the existing conflict, the question is, however, whether these shared principles meant the same things and operated in the same way for both sides.

"The Appalachian character," says Harlan journalist Ewell Balltrip, is "fiercely patriotic. These people, the people who settled Appalachia were the dregs of society from England and Scotland and Ireland, you know; and they were the very people who were waving the flag of glory, you know, when the declaration of independence was signed. Sure, you know—to hell with Great Britain. And so the ancestry of the people in this area, you can trace it directly back to the . . . the patriotic beginnings of this country." From the revolutionary era to the world wars and Vietnam, from the Watauga Association and the battle of King's Mountain to the legendary war hero from Appalachia, Sergeant Alvin Cullum York, Appalachia indeed boasts "more than our share of heroes."[10]

Describing strike meetings in Harlan County, John Dos Passos stressed these revolutionary associations: "I never felt the actuality of the American revolution so intensely." NMU organizer Jim Garland sees a typological relationship between his struggle and the American revolution, when he sings that if police and thugs try to get him "there'll be another Boston Tea Party." Findlay "Red Ore" Donaldson, a miner and a Holiness preacher, told a strike meeting that "The National Miners Union stands for the principles that our forefathers fought for at Bunker Hill." Mary Nick, a 13-year-old miner's daughter, wrote a song, *The Miner's Blues*, in which she claimed, "We must all be united/We will march through the land/ Then we will be free Americans and get our full demands."[11]

However, while Attorney Smith claimed that the people of Harlan and Bell "approve . . . the government of the United States as it is now administered" (the New Deal was yet to come), Findlay "Red Ore" Donaldson declared to cheering miners that "our nation and country [are being] handled by corrupt men," and added "I love my children today ten thousand times better than I love Herbert Hoover."

Although both sides appeal to the Constitution as a source of authority and to democracy as an ideal, they interpret them in sharply contrasting ways. We also believe in freedom of speech, freedom of the press, and freedom of movement," wrote Smith to Hays; however, the people of Bell County "do not approve th[e] doctrines [of the American Civil Liberties Union], nor do they acknowledge that any man, or any such organization, or any group of persons representing it have any Constitutional rights in Bell County, that any person is bound to respect." On the other hand, Findlay "Red Ore" Donaldson told the strikers:

> I love the flag of the United States—I love the name of America, but I want to tell you what I hate. I hate the men that handles this country of ours . . . I want to say to you my friends, that the miners of the State of Kentucky is today being worse mistreated than Slaves in Slave Times. You are denied the privilege of meeting out and discussing ways and means

whereby you might make the condition better for your neighbor and your neighbor's little children . . . You are denied every privilege that the United States gives you by unjust judges, [who] forbid us every privilege that the Constitution of the United States guarantees a man.

Precisely this discovery that "all your rights have been taken away," as a speaker put it to a mass meeting at Pineville, startled and enraged the miners. "You see, people were so steeped in this idea that people have equal rights. And they come to find out, by God, they didn't have rights. See, they didn't understand, that they was bein' . . . that they was in the hands of the state," says Tillman Cadle. The lesson was soon learned by the sympathizers who came to bring assistance to the strikers.

TILLMAN CADLE. They put all the members of this committee, you see, they put them under house arrest, and a bunch of vigilantes and thugs and things, they took them to the state line and beat them up, and they had a lawyer there, he'd come in from New York, to see that they got their constitutional rights, and they just poked fun at them about their constitutional rights. They would say to one before they beat him up, they would say, maybe you'd like to get your attorney to give . . . make you a . . . an address on your constitutional rights. Just making fun of the Constitution, you see. And, so, [the strikers] had an old song 'bout "come on mama and go my bail, take me out of this buggy jail"—well, then, they added a verse on, there. "Come on mama and go my bail, take me out of this buggy jail, 'cause all of my rights been taken away" . . . They had broken all the laws, there was no laws for us whatever . . . What you get to feelin', that your whole country has betrayed you.

To some of the miners, as contemporary news stories reported, this betrayal seemed final. "One miner, a veteran of the World War, spent his bonus check for a supply of rifles. A mountaineer of Anglo-Saxon lineage, he made no secret about it. He told the court he preferred living in Russia to Harlan County."[12] Commenting on the breaking up of a parade of miners marching under the Stars and Stripes, one miner said, "By God, if they won't let us march under the American flag, we'll march under the Red flag."[13]

The very verbal extremism of some of these statements, however, has the sound of angry, intentional blasphemy rather than ideological alternative; they sound as if they were passionately denying what they still passionately believed. A few were radicalized in a more or less permanent way. Tillman Cadle recalls telling a professor from New York who asked him what books he had read "about the role of the state; 'I haven't been reading books,' I said. 'I didn't have to read it,' I said. 'Mister: the damn thing fell and hit me right on top of the head.' "

As we have seen, Molly Jackson contrasted the "big red, white, and blue" with the miners' flag "dipped in blood"; her half sister Sara Ogan wrote a song called *I Hate the Capitalist System*. But these were difficult thoughts to hold on to and live with permanently. Later, Molly Jackson replaced "Join the NMU" with "Join the CIO" and tried to downplay her radicalism.[14] Sara Ogan for a time changed "capitalist system" to "company bosses." Jim Garland's song about the murder of NMU organizer Harry Simms ended with "Let's sink this rotten system/to the deepest pits of hell"; later, he added a milder final verse (though by the end of their lives, both he and Sara Ogan were again singing the original versions).[15] Even at their most radical, however, these individuals never felt that they were breaking with America and what it stood for. After all, even those who retained some links with the organized Left were exposed then to Earl Browder's idea that "Communism is twentieth-century Americanism."

The majority of the strikers in fact attempted to reconcile their actions with their patriotism, by proving that they, not the judges and operators, were the "real" Americans and that the union fulfilled the Constitution—while the operators and the judges were claiming the same values and authorities for themselves. Thus, they became involved in a cultural as well as a material class struggle, fought with symbols as well as guns. The question was: Who has the right to control the shared system of symbols and signifiers? Who has the right to formulate interpretations and ascribe meanings? Together with the question of "Who owns the land and its wealth?" the strike also raised the question of "Who owns the symbols of the land?"

RED-BLOODED AMERICANS

I love my flag, but I don't understand why they let them get away with all that stuff.

Sudie Crusenberry, Brookside, Harlan County, Kentucky (1989)

When the Evarts miners came up for trial, their very use of the American flag was turned against them. The attorney for the prosecution claimed that their leader, W. B. Jones, "carried an American flag, but the red flag . . . was in his heart."[16] It was essential for the prosecution to prove that the striking miners had stepped beyond the commonly recognized cultural boundaries, and therefore out of the protection guaranteed by the authority of the Constitution and the symbol of the flag.

While strikers were denied the use of this symbol, the courts wrapped themselves in it. As Circuit Judge D. C. Jones instructed the jury that was trying Theodore Dreiser after his unfortunate trip to Harlan and Pineville to investigate the strike:

> You have two parties in America . . . If one party is not functioning, kick it out and put in another. You don't have to haul down the Stars and Stripes and put up the red flag of Russia to do it . . . Every thread of the Stars and Stripes was purchased at the greatest price ever paid for any flag. . . . It is a disgrace not only to you but to the dead that sleeps in the grave [if] you get wobbledy in your patriotism just because a little depression has hit you.[17]

Incidently, the Evarts strike leader W. B. Jones was never a "red," and was often attacked by the Communists; but the strategy of denying the legitimacy of the workers' use of national symbols to label them with hostile, un-American ones was too attractive.

Long before the NMU ever came into Harlan County, the red threat was being agitated by the local authorities and press; whether they belonged to the Communist party or not, these striking miners were not "free Americans," as young Mary Nick claimed, but "Rooshian reds." "If you are hungry, you are a red," a miner told a visiting committee of churchmen, "and if you tell your neighbor that you are hungry that is criminal syndicalism."[18]

"I've been framed up and accused of being a red, when I did not understand what they meant," said Molly Jackson years later. Though she was certainly overstating the case when she said, "I never heard tell of a Communist until I left Kentucky," she made a telling point by claiming that "I got all my progressive ideas from my hard tough struggles, and nowhere else."[19] Mountain people had only a vague idea of who these "reds" were. "Ninety percent of these people," says Tillman Cadle, "wouldn't know the difference between communism and rheumatism." Some linked communism to a vague idea of "community," and called them "Commù-nists." "If you had at this time said to a group of average mountain people 'I'm a Communist'," " wrote Jim Garland later, "they more than likely would have answered 'I'm a Baptist' or 'I'm a Mason'."[20]

The NMU organizers concentrated on the immediate, material needs of the strikers, without putting their ideology up front (although the strikers did adopt such words as "comrade" or "capitalism"); and this choice later furnished the basis for the charge of having deceived the workers. At first, miners did not seem to feel that the issue was too important, anyway. They were "grabbing at straws," and anybody's help was welcome. When the question of communism came up, writes John Gaventa, it was "usually interpreted in terms of the local culture." The nickname, "reds," was a useful handle, as it tied in with a whole cluster of symbols of local and national identity and pride.

The most important is blood—again, a symbol invoked by both sides in conflict. "One drop of pure Kentucky blood is worth more and is more sacred than an entire river of Communist blood" said Attorney W. B. Smith; and Judge D. C. Jones announced that he would "use the full power of my court to prevent these human rattlesnakes from injecting the virus of Communism into the veins of the American workingman."[21] This might have been Findlay Donaldson's reply:

> It is the voice and mouth of every coal-operator-sympathizer that the Russian Red is abroad in the State of Kentucky. When you starve me down and deny me the food and raiment that is required to take care of my body and the little children that I claim to be the father of, I want to tell you that you are putting Red Blood into me as sure as you live.

What Attorney Smith failed to perceive was that "pure" Kentucky or American blood is just naturally "red." "I am a true American and can't be beat," said NMU local secretary Billie Meeks, at the same meeting; "And I am a red-blooded one." Sara Ogan Gunning used blood symbolism to reverse the charge of un-Americanism, by referring to the "blue" blood of Kentucky's "dirty rich aristocrats." The same process extended to other "red" symbols. Charles R. Walker's article entitled " 'Red' Blood in Kentucky" quotes a miner who said, "They call us 'Rooshun Red Necks . . . I wonder why that is? My folks have been in Kentucky for five generations, but one of 'em was a red Cherokee Indian. Maybe that's why I'm a Red."[22]

The operators' side had claimed to be the real "Believer[s] in America," the "100-percent American" representatives of government institutions. By casting themselves as pure red-blooded Americans and Kentuckians, these Red Indian Rednecks turned the table on the operators and changed the tainting epithet to a symbol of legitimacy. On the other hand, by denying them the legitimate use of national symbols (the flag) and associating them with foreign ideologies ("Rooshian") and outside agitators, the operators claimed the exclusive right to use the symbols of national and local identity. "To Hell with Russia and all the Communists and Bolsheviks in New York City," was Attorney Smith's battle cry. While journalists like Herndon J. Evans stirred resentments against "outsiders" coming in from New York to investigate Kentucky (and even proposed a counter-delegation to investigate crime and prostitution in New York), the union organizers pointed out that much of the local mining wealth was actually owned by outsiders. While the law-and-order element systematically called them "Russians," they sometimes reacted by calling deputy sheriffs "Kaiser."[23]

We should not, however, extend the symmetry too far. It is important, in fact, to bear in mind that the confrontation took place on ground chosen and defined by the operators and their supporters. Therefore, the operators campaigned aggressively, while the strikers were mostly on the defensive. There was more emphasis on proving that the strike was not un-American than in proving the "un-Americanism" of the operators, nor was any attempt made to reject this ground of confrontation altogether. This can be partly explained by the fact that the operators controlled most of the places of public discourse from newspapers to courts and the more respectable churches. But it is also apparent that, while the strikers insisted on the operators' lawlessness, they did feel vulnerable to the charges of anti-patriotism brought against themselves.

Therefore, a recurrent rhetorical device in the strikers' discourse is the claim that their goals are limited, that all they ask for is a living. "I don't want your millions, mister," sang Jim Garland later; "All I want is food for my babies/Give me back my job again." "What we want," said Donaldson, "[is] a protection that we are entitled to according to the Constitution of the United States and then we will be satisfied."

The flags that the miners waved really had two sides: one toward their own side, to rally supporters around the struggle; and the other toward the operators and the law, to prove that the strike was not really subversive—as if, by proving it to the other side, the strikers could also convince themselves.

CROSSING THE RED SEA

There are three things I believe in: the Bible, the Union, and God.

Sudie Crusenberry, Brookside, Harlan County,
Kentucky (1989)

"I am a good Christian and a member of the Christian church," one operator was quoted as saying, "but I would just as soon tie a Communist in a sack and throw him into the river as do anything else I know."[24] On the other hand, preacher Findlay Donaldson gave the struggle a religious sanction. "A man who won't support his children is worse than an Infidel, and there is no place for that man but Hell."

Religion was the other shared signifier which became a battleground in the struggle for the control of symbols and meanings. Again the operators' side claimed that the strikers had stepped out of the pale of acceptable cultural behavior, thus forfeiting all their rights as Christians. The strikers, on the other hand, sought religious justifications to their actions. Like the Constitution, the Bible was invoked by both sides. When Ronald Niebuhr came to Kentucky with a committee of churchmen, he found that all the urban and mainline churches in Pineville (as well as the Episcopal bishop of Lexington) opposed him; but he also discovered that "miners are more religious than any similar body of proletarians. The religious character of these proletarians would offer a splendid opportunity for the emergence of a real proletarian religion."[25]

"The little preachers that didn't get paid for preachin' who worked, worked for a livin', you'd get along well with them, because they was part of it," says Tillman Cadle. "They was preachin' because of their conviction. They wasn't preachin' for money. But you couldn't get along with these guys that had to have a big salary to preach, because he wasn't interested." The essential distinction did not appear to be a theological one, between liberal and conservative denominations, but a social one between urban and rural, middle-class and working-class churches. Myles Horton, a student of Niebuhr who helped establish unions in the South and created the Highlander Folk School, says:

They had mountain religion. It would be the conservative, more literalist sort of religion with a predominantly Pentecostalist people, the kind of religion I would describe as the

Regular Old Baptist dominated at the time you're talking
about. Not that church necessarily, but that kind of . . . that
kind of religion. They . . . their teachers, their preachers were
nonpaid, volunteer preachers; some of them couldn't read, but
they were . . . they were fervid in their religion, and they were
working class. It wasn't the kind of religion that city folks or
mainstream folks thought of. And some of the preachers from
the Old Regular Baptist Church were the leaders in the struggle. They'd preach on Sunday, this fundamentalist religion,
then go out on the picket line all week. And some of the
preachers in the cities were talking liberal theology, liberalism,
all the modern, you know, interpretations of religion, yet they
would side with the [operators] . . . It was a class division.

Thus, while the First Baptist Church in Pineville held meetings to denounce the Communist influences in the NMU, and the
middle-class based Red Cross refused (on grounds of "neutrality")
to feed the hungry miners' families, rural churches were lent to the
strikers for meetings and soup kitchens, and many preachers were
active in the struggle—from Holiness preacher Findlay Donaldson
to former snake-handler and NMU activist Harvey Valentine; from
Baptist pastor Rev. Frank Martin, who was jailed for criminal syndicalism to the black preacher Gill Green who, "while helping the
miners in their efforts to organize . . . conducted a revival and had
over a hundred converts, all of whom were baptized."[26]

TILLMAN CADLE: And one day, we was havin' a big mass
meeting in Pineville, and they was a fellow they called him
the "cussing preacher." His name was Randalls, Randolphs, I
guess; he was a preacher but he could talk very violently
sometimes; and he was the last speaker at this meetin'. And
when he started to close his speech he said "Well, I guess
we'll all be gathering back here next weekend for another
meetin'," and they began clamoring back out in the crowd,
"What's the use to go home if you can't take any food to your
family." He asked, how many there was in that crowd there
that didn't have any food in their homes for supper; and a
whole gang of hands just went up like that. He jumped down
off of the steps, and he said, "Foller me." And he made a
break for the A&P store: and by God, they was all follerin'
him, too.

Eventually, Cadle says, the A&P agreed to feed the miners if they would also raid their competitors. Led by the "cussing preacher," the miners duly obliged.

Of course, it would be wrong to generalize. The "other-worldly" approach still prevailed in many Holiness churches, and preachers in the coal camps were often under the direct control of the operators. On the other hand, some town ministers did sympathize with the unions. Rev. C. E. Vogel, a Harlan Methodist minister, discussed the miners' plight in his church, protested against the deputy sheriffs' violence in the UMWA drive, and was finally removed from his church after his middle-class congregation complained of his pro-union stance.[27]

But the general distinction holds, with both sides quoting the usual Biblical cliches. While company preachers might teach "somethin' 'bout some will be masters and some be servants," (Cadle), Rev. Hugh Cowans, a black miner and later a preacher from Verda, warns that "there's a passage in the Scripture. It said if you don't work, you don't eat, you know. And I think I kinda halfway go along with that."

The miners' religion, in fact, seemed to oscillate in perpetual tension between otherworldly resignation and radical criticism of this world, and between subordination to the status quo and egalitarian solidarity. These attitudes can be detected, for instance, in the miners' songs, ranging from religious consolation for mine deaths to representations of the union as an extension of the church and a step toward a unionized heaven.[28]

In times of conflict, "fatalist" religion gives way, at least temporarily, to the religion of the union; and the old-time folk religion supplies the language and forms for the new ideas. All the great strike songs—from Molly Jackson's *Join the NMU* to Florence Reece's *Which Side Are You On?* and Sara Ogan's *Dreadful Memories*—are based on hymn tunes. Findlay Donaldson spoke "like an old time hell-roaring evangelist."[29] Billie Meeks addressed the Straight Creek meeting as "service," interchanged "comrades" with "congregation," and wove the words and images of the Biblical sermon together with those of the revolutionary agitator:

> The time is presented to you in the days when the Children of Israel was under bondage, when Moses went to lead them out and he came to the Red Sea and the Children got scared . . . and they thought they could not go through, they walked through dry-shod, and Pharoah's hosts came on and

the water closed up on them. . . . We have the same opportunity presented to us, laboring men, by the National Miners Union to walk out as the Children of Israel did, and if you don't drown these Capitalists and this Capitalism, it is your own bad luck. You can't blame any one but yourself.

In the same meeting, Aunt Molly Jackson not only quarried the Bible for words and images, but cast the whole struggle in neat theological terms, with the union as a "second cause," as one of God's "means" of intervention in the world. "Now, we are under bondage. We have been under bondage for a long time but God is going to redeem his people. He is fixing a way and a plan for them to be redeemed from this bondage through this great organization."

Some went as far as viewing even the Communists as some kind of church. "They was trying to get something started, to have an organization, so that people could have something to live on," a miner's wife recalled. "They even gave'em clothes . . . like the Church of Christ . . . like when they started the Church here."[30] "The local people, they [the operators] might tell them that I didn't believe in religion or something like that," Tillman Cadle says, "but you see, the people all knowed me, and they'd say 'why, we know he's not against it, if we wanna believe in religion,' because they knowed my family's background, you see."

In fact, some have their religious identity severely shaken. Jim Garland was a religious man, a deacon of the church, and came from a religious family. "But when a person gets involved, truly involved, in a labor struggle," he writes, "it's hard to keep his religious beliefs primary, mainly because he gets so damn mad." "I've had two days' work since August and no money," Chester Hoskins, a miner and a former church member, told a journalist. "I don't know much about this Communism and I ain't worrying about God, but if the Communists can get me something to eat, I'm for 'em." A black preacher named Johnson told his fellow workers on the eve of the battle of Evarts, that his religious beliefs would not allow him to fight, but he would pray for them. The black activist Elzie Phillips replied, "You'll get no results from prayer."[31]

Yet, the church remained an essential part of these people's identity. Jim Garland, who moved away from Kentucky after the strike, wrote later that, though he seldom went to church now, he made a point of attending when he visited his native region, because "this is the mountain life . . . and the sociability I have returned for." Long after the strike, Sara Ogan still sang with pride:

> My daddy was a preacher
> But he loaded coal as well
> My mother was a Christian
> And she served God all her life
> She worked hard for her children
> And she was a miner's wife.[32]

A twofold ambiguity characterizes the role of religion in the strike. On the one hand, the same traditional Christian religion is shared by both sides. On the other hand, while the operators hardly entertain a doubt about their own righteousness, the miners are again uncertain, ambivalent, and in constant need of justification. Their religion tells them that what they are doing is both righteous and sinful; and this contradiction is the lever which the operators use to finally break the precarious continuity between the old the new, the actions and the beliefs, leaving the defeated miners culturally powerless, sinful in their own eyes.

THE RELIGION OF THE WORKERS

In February, 1932, nine NMU organizers were on trial in Pineville for criminal syndicalism. Almost a thousand miners "marched around the Pineville courthouse expressing protest and solidarity with the nine jailed revolutionaries as they knew how—singing hymns, carrying American flags, led by a fundamentalist preacher."[33] When NMU secretary Doris Parks took the stand, Attorney W. B. Smith began the interrogation. The magistrate's first question was: "Do you believe in any form of religion?"

Let us consider Doris Parks' quandary. She knows that a negative answer will damn her. On the other hand, she does not wish to deny her beliefs. Perhaps, Communist as she is, she still retains some vestige of patriotic and religious education, and thinks that church and state are separate under the United States Constitution and that religion is a personal matter; she might also have some vague notion of bearing witness to her faith. Be that as it may, she answered, "I believe in the religion of the workers"—meaning, as she explained under further questioning, "the working class and their right to organize and to teach [that] they can be led out of this oppression by the Communist party."

"Once Herndon Evans reproduced this statement in the *Pineville Sun* and called Doris Parks and the entire NMU atheistic," writes Jim Garland, "we lost more than half of our members."[34]

When Findlay Donaldson addressed the Straight Creek meeting, he had said:

> We don't want to get rich. I hate the name of money because it led me into a bad life. I used to have some money and it led me down in Sin further than anything that ever happened. There is four things that the Nation and American people must [dislike: the typescript says "like," but it is clearly an error]; that is, Degradation, Privation, Starvation, and Sin. If you put a man in privation you are driving him into sin, but if you give him something to live on, he can stand up to help the Christian world, but if you deprive him of food and raiment, you cause that man to commit in his heart, murder and robbery and stealing, and they have almost starved me.

If Theodore Dreiser and John Dos Passos, who both heard him speak, had relied on their writers' ear for language and words rather than on their ideological preconceptions, they might have helped the NMU avoid some tragic mistakes. They might have realized that Donaldson not only *spoke* like a "hell-roaring evangelist," but he *was* one, and obscurely sensed that his radical rebellion was somehow tied to a sense of sin "in his heart." "Today, friends, I would not ask much to steal a good square meal, haven't had one in so long," he said. To the outside radicals, this meant that Donaldson was on his way to challenging private property; to him, it also meant he was on his way to hell. The strike was an inevitable risk for the soul as well as the body, which the miners had not chosen to take but which had been foisted upon them by the operators. Dreiser and Dos Passos might have understood this if they had given a thought to what a tough fighting rebel like Aunt Molly Jackson might have meant when she took for her text "Blessed is the peacemaker and cursed is the peace breaker," and invoked "all the promises that God had promised to the obedient."

Fascinated as they were by the miners' songs and eloquence, however, these urban intellectuals never really listened to what they said; or perhaps they ascribed it paternalistically to the miners' rural naivety, charming but not serious. Thus, when the Communist party began to bring strike leaders North for political training, the results were disastrous. In an affidavit filed in the Bell County courthouse, and widely circulated through the local press and in leaflet form with those of other former NMU members, Findlay Donaldson stated:

>   Fellow workers and citizens, the teachings of the Com-
> munist party would destroy our religious beliefs, our govern-
> ment and our homes. In their teachings they demand their
> members to teach their children [that] there is no God; no
> Jesus; no Hereafter . . . I heard them in a mass meeting and
> a big demonstration while in Chicago denounce our govern-
> ment and our flag and our religion . . . I saw them who were
> believers in the Communist Party with great applause give
> honor to Soviet Russia by honoring and saluting the Red
> Flag. The Communist party believes in white and coloured
> marrying each other and if you refuse for the negro men to
> keep company with your daughter you cannot be a friend to
> Soviet Russia.[35]

Discussing his organizing work in the 1930s, Myles Horton
commented, "We learned very early that you cannot make people
do something which they consider evil, a sin. You must know how
people are, and what they believe in. And then they can change."
The northern organizers had not learned what these people were
like and what they believed in, although they had come with great
generosity and great personal risk to help them. On the other hand,
as John Gaventa notes, the local elite knew them, and even shared
some of the same ideas and beliefs.

While they thought they could reconcile the strike to their
beliefs, miners fought against both the deputies' guns and their
own misgivings and guilt. But when they found that these same
actions were interpreted by their new allies as part of a wholly different and conflicting system of values and beliefs, they withdrew
in fear. "Lean miners look levelly through solemn eyes and say, 'I
couldn't deny my God'," reported a writer for *The New York Times
Magazine*. "Religion in this case is on the side of the strike-
breakers."[36] Until a few weeks before, the strikers had thought it
could still be on theirs.

I WILL NOT FIGHT MY GOVERNMENT

Let us go back to the three armies with the same flag, which we left
facing one another in Logan County. Fred Mooney, one of the leaders of the strike, wrote in his autobiography:

>   When the miners surrendered their arms to Brigadier
> General H. H. Bandholz in September, 1921, and said to the

grizzled veteran of many battles, "General, we are not fighting our government," it was similar only to the signing of the Magna Carta [Mooney's spelling] by King John on the battlefield of Runnymede. Thus was established beyond question the fact that they were not in revolt against constituted authority but had taken to arms because they believed there was no other way to correct the wrongs perpetrated upon them by a conspiracy between the law and unlawful violence.[37]

"Boys, we can't fight Uncle Sam" was the word, echoing the words with which John L. Lewis had ended the national coal strike two years before. "I will not fight my government, the greatest government on earth."[38] In a different mood from Mooney, Frank Blizzard, a miner from Cabin Creek, West Virginia, reminisced:

> And then the governor called in the U.S. troops . . . We surrendered. We wouldn't fight the regulars. If they hadn't brought Uncle Sam in there, there wouldn't have been a thug left in Logan County. Well, it broke our local, broke our district, came damn near to breaking our International.[39]

In his discussion of the ethnic use of national and religious symbols, Werner Sollors notes that "people who sing very similar anthems or wave flags all of which contain the colors red, white, and blue need not be pursuing the same goals" and that "the consensus ritual of speaking with the Bible . . . did not make the speakers of a shared rethoric uniform in spirit."[40] The shared signifier may be ultimately more powerful than the conflicting signifieds; in fact, in "rituals," the signifier itself tends to become the signified. Furthermore, the way in which different meanings attach themselves to the same symbols depends to a large extent on the context of power relationships. The powerless, the poor, the unschooled grope toward interpretations of their own, but are constantly exposed to the powerful interpretations of the elites. They may risk the lonesome and doubtful effort of creating their own meanings; but when this fails, it is too easy and tempting to go back to the warmth and security of those authorized interpretations which even the insurgents carried inside them all the time anyway. The "surrender" which, according to Frank Blizzard, almost destroyed the union, becomes a victory comparable to the signing of the Magna Charta—as if the miners had conquered those democratic rights which, in fact, were effectively denied them. The most representative song which came from the Harlan strike, written by Florence Reece, said: "They say in Harlan County/there are no neutrals there," and asked the question, "Which Side Are You On?" The miners were finally defeated by the one-sided neutrality of powers—the churches' God, the nation's President—which they had thought could be on *their* side.

The extent to which the cultural class conflict is waged upon the attribution of meaning to shared texts and symbols is one of the specificities of the American labor movement. If we compare with the Italian experience, we find that, to a large extent, the cultural class struggle there has been a conflict between, not within, symbolic systems. Although patriotism, religion, and family are important parts of Italian working-class culture, yet a number of historical circumstances have made it both necessary and possible for the organized workers to sanction their own actions largely according to independent sets of signifiers, symbols and texts. Among these factors were the relative weakness of national identity, the recognizable class nature of the State, the fact that democracy is seen as a result and not a condition of working-class struggles, and the undemocratic structure and often hostile position of the Catholic Church. This symbolic autonomy allowed Italian workers to preserve some of their alternative consciousness in forms that were stable and self-sufficient, if often staid and bureaucratic, with a conformism of their own. The greatest threat to this autonomy has come, recently, from the shared symbols and signifiers of mass media and consumer culture.[41] In the United States, on the other hand, explicitly antagonistic symbolic clusters have surfaced mostly in the context of exceptional conflicts, with an incomparably intense emotional appeal but a limited staying power.

Findlay "Red Ore" Donaldson's affidavit breathes with a sense of relief, as if he had at last come in from the cold. "I feel at this time that the great capitalists and officials of this great nation of ours which I deem second to none, in some way will give relief and assistance to our poor starving humanity, which is now suffering in America." There are echoes in Donaldson's statement of "DivineRight" George F. Baer, the industrialist who claimed in 1903 that "The rights and interests of the laboring man" would be "protected and cared for . . . by the Christian men to whom God, in His infinite wisdom, has given the control of property interests."[42] Donaldson's affidavit also contains an inverted signifier—the word "capitalists," no longer hostile but protective: they will find "some way." Donaldson does not know how; but what he now knows is that finding the way is no longer his responsibility. He had tried for a while to take his life in his hands; now it is safely back in the hands of the "capitalists"—a demonstration of how "fatalism" and other such traits attributed to folk cultures are not necessarily inherent in them, but are often actively created and enforced by the framework of power relationships.

WOULD YOU LET YOUR DAUGHTER MARRY ONE?

In his recollection of the interrogation of Doris Parks, Tillman Cadle adds a detail which is not confirmed by other sources. Attorney Smith, he says, first asked her about her religion, "and then he brought up the question of marriage. He says: 'You wouldn't want your daughter to marry a nigger, would you?' She said, 'I don't tell my daughter who she should marry. I think my daughter can decide that for herself'."[43] Whether this exchange actually took place or not, Cadle's story underlines the role of another shared signifier—race.

When both sides contended for the right to call themselves "100-percent Americans," they agreed on one essential thing: freedom of speech is inherent to being "100-percent Americans." By invoking "blood" symbolism to legitimize the "red" stigma, they automatically and implicitly excluded Afro-Americans and immigrants. By another turn of the screw, their own blood symbolism turned against them, in the form of the most frightening of southern taboos: racial blood mixing, or miscegenation.

"Mixed marriages, even mixed dances, were virtually unheard of, but, as one would expect, some mixing was done on the sly. Sometimes the white boys would try to make time with the black girls," writes Jim Garland. "And I'll tell you, anytime, anytime that they wanted to have trouble . . . bring trouble with the minorities, they'd use a black man and a white woman," says Julia Cowans, the wife of a black miner and preacher. Interracial affairs, in fact, were the cause of at least one major riot in the 1920s; and Iverson Minters, a musician from Mississippi (also known as "Louisiana Red"), tells about his father, who worked at Lynch, being killed around 1940 by a mob who thought his light-skinned wife was a white woman. Months before Donaldson and the others took their trip North, a local minister explained to the Middlesboro Kiwanis Club that communism means: "(1) hatred of God, (2) destruction of property, (3) social and racial equality and class hatred."[44] Race, however, hardly surfaced as an issue in the strike. Perhaps, Tillman Cadle's version of the Doris Parks episode should be interpreted to mean that, though dormant, it had been there implicitly all along, ready to surface again when the strike broke down.

As we have seen, Donaldson's affidavit lists interracial marriage as one of the offensive tenets of the Communist party. This motif recurs in most of the other statements by disaffected NMU members. "They believed and said in their meetings that they just as leave their girls to marry a negro as a white man, let the girls be pleased." (H. L. Doan). "They teach that there is no God, that a white woman is equal to a colored woman, that a negro has a right to marry a white woman . . ." (Harvey Collett).

Black and white miners had been quick to recognize that their interests were the same in the struggle with coal operators. Reverend Hugh Cowans recalls that, when he became active in the UMWA drive:

> My father . . . he's passed and gone now . . . he told me . . . says . . . uh . . . "You're crazy to go on those pickets lines. You'll get killed." He said, "It's not going to benefit anybody but the white man." I says, "Well, I know it will benefit him more than it benefits me, but I see some good in that for you, and I see some in it for me."

On this basis, black miners joined the struggle and the union. The UMWA was in the vanguard of American unions in formally rejecting segregation; and several black miners and preachers had taken an active role in the Evarts movement. Black miners, including Elzie Phillips (later a defendant in the trial for the Battle of Evarts) and preacher Gill Green had been included in committees and delegations. The NMU, of course, made it a point of including black miners, both in the first group of delegates who attended the union's convention in Pittsburgh in the summer of 1931 and in the central committee of the strike.[45]

Segregation and racism, however, were part of the region's heritage, though more attenuated than in other parts of the South. "Way back when I was just a kid," says Tillman Cadle, who was born in Tennessee near the Bell County line in 1902, "they had signs up in all those little old communities, 'nigger don't let the sun set on you here' and things—oh, yeah." Julia Cowans recalls that in the 1930s "We were up in a place called Louellen. And you come down going to Harlan, which is the county seat, and you go through two or three communities where blacks wasn't allowed to live."

Even among unionized miners, whatever limited integration took place was restricted to the workplace and to union business. Jim Garland writes that "Once the work day ended, blacks and whites were separated, living in different coal camps, attending different churches and schools."[46] Critical though we must be of the Communists' errors concerning patriotism and religion, one can hardly blame them for trying to interfere with this aspect of the traditional culture, insisting, if not on interracial marriages, at least on integrated soup kitchens. In fact, miners did not seem to mind the socializing while both blacks and whites were equally hungry. Sara Ogan sang:

> Really friends, it does not matter
> Whether you are black or white
> The only way we'll ever change things
> Is to fight, and fight, and fight.[47]

When the crisis occurs, color matters again. Donaldson and the others seem to imply a shifting of borders from *class* back to *race:* from class conflict and race integration, back to race discrimination and class "harmony". In fact, the NMU itself had been a "mixed marriage" of sorts. The miners found the courage to join with others who were unlike themselves in color and background, but who shared their interests. When the strike collapsed, they rejoined those who were very much like them in color and background, but whose interests were opposite to theirs. For some reason, the fact that Doris Parks did not believe in God and would not mind her daughter marrying a black man authorized the Harlan County Coal Operators Association to continue its "reign of terror" and starvation.

A LONG WAY FROM HARLAN

Myles Horton came to Harlan, in the guise of a Federal Press reporter when the strike was virtually over. Asked if he had a visual memory of what he saw, he answered:

> That is very easy. It was hunger . . . hunger in the faces of the people, you know, gaunt-faced children and parents, people that you could see that they hadn't had enough to eat.

And lifelessness. You know, this kind of—you know, givin' up; this kind of sense of no struggle left; there's no road that they could take that gave 'em any hope. No future. Organization was the only road to any kind of decent life and that had failed, so there's nothing. So there's kind of a sense of despair. It was tragic, it was really tragic. I used to go to bed and cry. I just couldn't take it. After seeing and talking to those people. So it was . . . it was the epitome of poverty and hopelessness. The kind of despair that you have when there's no hope. People with no hope will not do anything. And they weren't doing anything.

The struggle in Harlan wasn't decided by Doris Parks's misguided earnestness or by Findlay Donaldson's culture shock. The strike wasn't defeated by the cultural class struggle—it was probably already lost by the time the NMU stepped in, anyway. But the cultural struggle defeated the men and the women. Not only did they lose the strike, but they lost their reasons for it. "Most of those who joined the NMU in 1931," writes Bill Bishop, "now bow their heads or avert their eyes when asked about the Communists . . . Some even look away and say no group called the National Miners Union ever entered Kentucky."[48]

Again, it would be wrong to generalize. "That Harlan experience," says Myles Horton, "as disastrous as it turned out to be, was a seed bed of a lot of real solid radicalism in the mountains. It had some bad effects, but it also had some . . . it radicalized a lot of people." Some joined in the new effort to organize the UMWA a few years later, when the union was officially allowed to appropriate the national symbols in John L. Lewis's slogan "The President wants you to join the union."[49] Others, perhaps the most politicized—the Garlands, Tillman Cadle, Florence Reece and her husband Sam—were forced to continue their lives and their struggles elsewhere, gaining more audience among urban radicals and intellectuals than among their own people. It was many years before Jim Garland was able to return to Harlan without finding sheriffs and thugs ready "to welcome the traveler home."

III. THE INTERDISCIPLINARY APPROACH

12

The Oral Shape of the Law:
The "April 7 Case"*

... At the morning session on October 22, 1969,
during argument on a motion of attorney William
Kunstler for leave to withdraw as counsel for the defendant [Bobby] Seale, the following discussion occurred in open court.
MR. SEALE: Can I speak and answer his argument?
THE COURT: No. This is not your motion, sir. Your
motion has been decided.
MR. SEALE: In other words, I can't speak on behalf of
myself?
THE COURT: Not at this time, sir.[1]

Judge Severino Santiapichi was forced, over and
over, to remind the defendant and witness for the
prosecution, Mauro Borromeo, that he was supposed to repeat his version of events in court, rather
than just refer back to the transcript of his pretrial
testimony. "Otherwise, you understand, we might
as well carry out the trial in writing."[2]

HISTORY OF THE TRIAL

In the Beginning Was the Voice

On 16 March 1978, Aldo Moro, former Italian prime minister and
leader of the Christian Democrat party, was kidnapped in Rome by

---

*Published as "Oral Testimony, the Law and the Making of History: The
'April 7' Murder Trial," *History Workshop Journal* [Oxford, England], 20 (Autumn, 1985), 5–35.

a Left-wing terrorist group called *Brigate Rosse* (Red Brigades). The five men of his body guard were massacred; Moro himself was murdered after being held captive for almost two months.

While they were holding him, the Red Brigades called his family on the phone. The conversation was recorded and later broadcast and televised. According to a judicial reconstruction, "Certain individuals, who had previously met and talked with Antonio Negri and remembered his phonic characteristics . . . identified him as the probable author of the call."[3]

Antonio Negri was a professor of political theory at Padua University, and also taught at the Sorbonne in Paris. He was a leading figure in the ultra-Left movement known as *Autonomia Operaia* (Workers' Autonomy), and had been a leader of the dissolved New Left group *Potere Operaio* (Workers' Power). On 7 April 1979, Negri and other current and former activists and leaders in *Autonomia* and *Potere Operaio* were arrested on orders from the Padua state attorney, Pietro Calogero. They were accused of being the leaders of the Red Brigades and (through the legal front of *Autonomia* and *Potere Operaio*) the organizers and instigators of the wave of terrorism that had spread through Italy in the late 1970s. On the same day, Negri was also indicted by a judge in Rome for the murder of Aldo Moro. The indictment also included the charge of promoting an insurrection against the state, and linked him with several crimes attributed to the Red Brigades. From the date of the arrest of the first group of defendants, the case came to be known as the "April 7 Case."[4]

An American specialist in voice identification, appointed by the court, testified that the voice on the Red Brigades' phone call was indeed Negri's. A few months later, however, a self-acknowledged leader of the Red Brigades, Patrizio Peci, was arrested. Peci decided to cooperate with the prosecution, and stated that Negri had nothing to do with the Red Brigades; the voice on the recording belonged to somebody else.[5]

The other real leaders of the Red Brigades were later arrested and tried for Moro's murder, and charges relating the April 7 defendants to that crime were quietly dropped, but not forgotten. Instead, new charges were immediately brought against the same defendants and other members of their political organizations and movements, with successive indictments from courts in Padua and Rome.[6]

After much shifting of charges and evidence, seventy-one individuals were brought to trial (four years after their arrest, a time which most of them spent in jail) for promoting an insurrection; forming a subversive organization and an armed band; performing several actions related to political violence; and being instigators and abetters of two murders. One victim was Carlo Saronio, a *Potere Operaio* activist from a wealthy family who had been kidnapped (allegedly, to finance the group) and died while in his kidnappers' hands. The other was *carabiniere* [military policeman] Lombardini, killed during an attempted bank robbery near Bologna, also allegedly intended to finance a political group close to Negri. It was another sixteen months before a verdict was reached.

It was appropriate that the case should begin with an attempt to use the voice as evidence of guilt. In most criminal trials, much of the evidence comes, in fact, from "oral testimony." In this case, the oral witnesses were of a special kind: the so called *pentiti.* These are "repented" former terrorists who demonstrate their change of heart by giving evidence against their former associates, and who are encouraged to do so by "emergency" legislation granting them lighter sentences or, in some cases, impunity. After being introduced in terrorism trials and used in the April 7 Case, the *pentiti* have become one of the backbones of the Italian judicial system. Later, the same type of witnesses supplied most of the evidence for the prosecution also in major mafia and organized-crime cases.

The specific criminal charges brought against defendants in the April 7 Case were secondary to a broader hypothesis on the history of Italian terrorism and New Left insurgency. It was assumed that, from the early 1970s, a single secret organization had "coordinated" the different forms of terrorism, linking them in a coherent subversive strategy with outwardly legal mass movements and struggles. This alleged organization was supposed to have gone through many outward changes, splits, and apparent dissolutions, but always preserving a continuous core of leaders and theorists, of whom Antonio Negri was the most important. From the name of its staunchest proponent, Padua State Attorney Pietro Calogero, this interpretation of history came to be known as the "Calogero theorem."

The defendants were no blue-eyed innocents. They certainly were involved in much of the political violence linked to Left radicalism in the 1970s, but denied that they had any relationship to terrorism. "I am a political activist, a subversive, a person who thought he was changing society," said defendant Emilio Vesce. "My actions may have been penally reprehensible, but there is nothing in my background which may be related to terrorism."

Negri also acknowledged, according to newspaper reports, that "the aims of his organization were subversive, and that it did commit actions which come under the jurisdiction of penal courts. These actions include sabotage and expropriations; they, however, never included terrorism. The organization never had an armed structure."[7]

Advocacy and practice of violence are attested to through much of the history of *Potere Operaio* and *Autonomia Operaia;*[8] on the other hand, the same has been true of most other New Left organizations, the differences being mostly of degree. Through *Potere Operaio* and *Autonomia*, in fact, the judiciary was charging all the radical movements in post-1968 Italy with being linked to or inspired by terrorism. This explains why activists and groups who had been politically at odds with the defendants supported them during the trial. It also explains the votes which elected Negri to Parliament while he was in jail—and the gravity of the blow he inflicted to the entire Left, as well as to the other defendants, when he jumped bail and escaped to France after an unprecedented decision by Parliament had made his rearrest pending trial possible.

The case was a crucial test for the so-called "emergency" legislation passed to combat terrorism. Much of this legislation had seriously curtailed the rights of the defense. It had upset the balance and neutrality of the procedure by making the *pentiti* the principal instrument of the trial. It had also set an unheard-of maximum of twelve years of pretrial detention for suspects of terrorism.

Criticism of this legislation was common also outside the circle of the defendants' political sympathizers. Doubts about the constitutional standing of the emergency legislation were, however, waived aside on the grounds of its effectiveness in combating terrorism. It became, therefore, politically important that these laws and procedures—and the *pentiti* most of all—prove their usefulness by securing convictions.

The Politics of Judicial Orality

Judge Severino Santiapichi, who was in charge of the courtroom phase of the April 7 Case, knew what he was talking about when he defended the role of orality in the proceedings. For one thing, his own role was inextricably linked to it.

The distinction between orality and writing marks two forms of the criminal trial and two stages of criminal procedure. The *inquisitory trial (which survives in the pretrial phase) is based on writing and secrecy, and on the identification of the judge with the prosecution. The *accusatory* trial is based on orality, publicity, debate, cross-examination, and neutrality of the judge—characteristics which are meant to ensure, at least in theory, "equality between the parties."[9]

Therefore, most procedures which (as is the case in Italy) maintain secrecy and writing in pretrial phase also provide that the evidence thus gathered must be rehearsed orally in court in order to be valid.[10] In recent times, however, there has been a tendency to transfer the pretrial record mechanically into the courtroom record by merely asking witnesses whether they confirm their statements made during the pretrial investigation.

While this makes trials move more quickly—an all-important consideration given the painfully slow operation of the Italian system—it also means that the writing and secrecy of the inquisitory model are received into the supposedly oral and public courtroom phase. The inquisitory model, thus, embraces the entire trial, with serious consequences.[11]

> Writing—says Walter J. Ong—fosters abstractions that disengage knowledge from the arena where human beings struggle with one another. It separates the knower from the known. By keeping knowledge embedded in the human life-world, orality situates knowledge within a context of struggle.[12]

The courtroom is one such arena of struggle.[13] The function of the spoken word there is to permit the trial to be conducted in as nearly a democratic fashion as possible. Orality makes it possible for two discourses—in this case, that of the defense and that of the prosecution—to go on at the same time, intersecting and modifying each other. Face-to-face confrontation allows greater flexibility, and publicity (more easily connected to orality than writing) allows the defendant specific forms of control. Some essential functions of a rational and sane society—the corrective of publicity over the secrecy of office, and the equality of the parties in court—are linked to certain functions of judicial orality.

"On October 29 [1969]," writes Philip S. Foner, "Seale was chained hand and foot to a metal chair and a gag of muslin was put in his mouth so that he could not continue to challenge the judge and interrupt the proceedings. During the next few days, the gag was strengthened."[14] This picture ought to be kept in mind during the rest of this discussion, together with the image of Carlo Fioroni, the most important witness for the prosecution in the April 7 Case. Fioroni refused to appear to speak in court and his transcribed pretrial testimony was read to replace his absent body and voice. This testimony was a cornerstone of the verdict.

THE TRIAL AS HISTORY

Theory

There is cruelty in the abolition of memory.
Giuliano Spazzali, defense lawyer in the April 7 Case[15]

"It was only natural," writes Giuliano Scarpari, "that the judiciary should be entrusted with the reconstruction of fragments of this history (of the New Left), especially of those which eventuated in terrorism. . . . It is however a grave and meaningful fact that the judiciary was left alone to perform this task, with no help from historians and politicians."[16]

The April 7 Case was history in many ways. First of all, more than ten years elapsed between some of the events considered and the time when a verdict was rendered. This was due partly to the slowness of Italian tribunals, but also to the fact that legal action was initiated long after the event, when both *Autonomia Operaia* and *Potere Operaio* had been dissolved for some years.

Many of the actions and words which came to the attention of the magistrates had not appeared equally criminal at the time they were publicly performed or expressed. It was only after a change in the political and cultural atmosphere that judicial considerations prevailed over political ones in the judgment of those times and events, and a whole movement was redefined in terms of a criminal conspiracy.

The magistrates were thus involved in reconstructing the past, redefining its meaning, and attempting an overall interpretation. These are historical tasks, and it is appropriate to examine the way they were performed from the point of view of the theory and method of history—oral history specifically, given the nature of most sources used.

Reminiscing about the early stages of the investigation, Pietro Calogero told a journalist:

> I'll tell you how it happened. I had been studying the language of terrorist leaflets and literature, and was not convinced that it was, as some said, mere ranting and raving. No, sir, I said to myself: there's a mind behind this, a criminal but intelligent plan. So I told my wife, "I can feel the hand of someone here, who is very familiar with constitutional law." She ups and says, "Look, Pietro, have you ever read about this

Oral Shape of the Law   247

man Toni Negri, who teaches in the University? His classes are all but political harangues. You ought to keep an eye on him." . . . So I began to read his books and articles . . .[17]

Jurist Luigi Ferrajoli has written that "The historical method exhibited by Calogero's brief and [Francesco] Amato's [the judge in Rome] indictment is coherent with a specific mode of the criminal trial: inquisition. Charges, arrests, briefs, and indictments are based on a preconceived version of history."[18]

"The logical model you can discern in the way the case was conducted," says defendant Paolo Virno, "is the one that [Karl] Popper describes, where he says that if you make a statement you will always find evidence to support it. What they never consider is that, under certain conditions, if certain events happen, your statement may also be falsified."

In a 1979 interview, Pietro Calogero said, "It would be naive and mistaken to expect tangible evidence of specific facts. What we have are not the hoodlums of terrorism, but leaders and instigators. By definition, leaders of these organizations do not go around shooting or planting bombs . . . Therefore, in this case one must not expect evidence of individual terrorist acts."[19]

Conversely, Rome State Attorney Giorgio Ciampani claimed that Negri's leadership was proven by his "participation in common crimes," which in turn was proven by "his position as the O[rganization's] leader" and "the assumption that, as a leader . . . he must have approved [of criminal actions]."[20]

If evidence of single criminal actions was not to be expected, proof that the Organization existed and that the defendants belonged to it was also hard to obtain. Calogero insisted on its "informal" nature, which made it, in his own words, "very difficult to delineate and pin down." Philosopher Massimo Cacciari pointed out how "Lack of evidence is itself used as evidence of the ability with which the terrorists concealed themselves."[21]

Dr. Calogero and his colleagues were not entirely without assistance from professional historians in developing their reconstruction of the past and a method by which to substantiate it. Some of the essential points for the prosecution were outlined and anticipated by Padua historian Angelo Ventura.

The crucial point in Ventura's reconstruction was a definition of "terrorism" as any act of politically motivated violence, from murder to rough picketing. Terrorism (thus defined) is then described by Ventura as a conspiracy, rather than a social movement; its leadership, in spite of alleged splits and dissolutions, was assumed to have been continuous from *Potere Operaio* to *Autonomia Operaia* to the Red Brigades. Mass struggles and the armed underground were thus represented as parts of one coherent strategic design.[22]

This version of history was also related by Ventura to a critique of current methods of historical enquiry. "Explaining history as a conspiracy," he wrote ironically, "does not look like good social history, either of the *macro* or *micro* variety. It is not *longue durée*. It is a brutally *événementiel* approach. In other words, it is neither elegant nor fashionable." It is however, he maintained, true to the facts.

This theoretical approach had a bearing on sources. A conspiracy can be reconstructed only by the methods of political history, by looking at the actions and ideas of leaders and elite groups. Therefore, the main historical sources are to be found in the written record left behind by the leaders of the "conspiracy."

Documents

Seven hundred and thirty pages into his reconstruction of the history of the 1970s, Dr. Calogero grappled with a crucial question. From a lengthy reading and analysis of literature from or related to *Autonomia, Potere Operaio,* and adjacent individuals and groups, he derived the conclusion that terrorism was led by an underground armed Organization (or Party) and carried out by a military structure connected to these groups. Given that these structures existed, he goes on to ask, "How is it that they are never mentioned by the so-called 'repented terrorists' who, given their position, should know them better than anyone else?" Can we answer this dilemma, Calogero continues, by the "simplistic method" of saying that, since all the witnesses, including those for the prosecution, deny that these structures existed, then perhaps they did not exist?

This crucial discrepancy between (his reading of) the written record, and the oral information of witnesses on whom he otherwise relied throughout the investigation, led Dr. Calogero to make a methodological statement concerning the hierarchy of historical sources. "Reality," he wrote, "must be reconstructed, as far as possible, with the help of documents . . . The testimony of the *pentiti* is to be used [exclusively] to fill voids that cannot be filled by documentary analysis, or to validate and broaden the results of this analysis."

In this Dr. Calogero aligned himself with the long-honored practice of considering oral sources "subordinate and ancillary to written ones."[23] Renzo De Felice, one of Italy's foremost conserva-tive historians, has written, "This writer is by no means a fan of oral history. I believe, in fact, that oral sources may be valuable only as a subsidiary to coeval ones," or when used "to clarify individual roles and histories."[24] Calogero's methodological statement can be seen, then, as a part of the tradition which considers oral sources useful in matters of detail, but never allows them to contradict writ-ten ones.   *primacy of written over oral testimony*

The examining judge, Giovanni Palombarini, who refuted Calo-gero's conclusions only to be reversed in turn by a higher court, argued that, while each statement by the witnesses must be care-fully verified, it was wrong to "presume a primacy of documentary analysis over the facts reported by witnesses or defendants . . . as if the role of facts were only that of filling gaps in documents."[25]

Paul Thompson has written that in most nineteenth-century historiography, "the notion that the document is not mere paper, but reality, is . . . converted into a macabre gothic delusion, a ro-mantic nightmare."[26] "The semantic ambiguity of 'document' and 'documentary analysis'," Ferrajoli commented, led the prosecution to believe that writings "document the facts, rather than represent their authors' ideology and dreams."[27]

Palombarini pointed out that, in the April 7 Case, the usual "ambiguity of the relationship between facts and writings" was heightened by "the ambivalence of [the defendants'] political lan-guage, with its heavy burden of tactical bluff, ideology and com-placent optimism." Negri complained in court of the "damning pretense, which runs through all our writings," and added that theirs was "the language of the Marxist tradition, but it carries a residue of simulation that creates a distorted redundancy." Much New Left literature, especially propaganda, is filled with exag-geration and wishful thinking; reading it literally, Palombarini concludes, one is apt to take "purely ideological expression" for "factual truth."

For instance, Negri and his group hailed a 1974 demonstration at the Fiat Mirafiori plant as the beginning of a new level of struggle and organization, the birth of the "Mirafiori party" which would lead the masses to armed rebellion. According to Palombarini, the "Mirafiori Party" was "a metaphor" which never materialized; Calo-gero, on the other hand, referred to it several times as an existing and functioning organization. Incidentally, while Negri's group spoke of an "armed takeover" of the Fiat plant by the workers, Bianca Guidetti Serra (a long-time Turin activist, a member of the

April 7 Case defense counsel, and an oral historian) saw the episode as merely a show of solidarity to the Fiat workers' struggle for a new contract and a "political defeat" for *Potere Operaio*.

Authentic and Authorized: From Oral to Written

In the introduction to *The Scarlet Letter*, Nathaniel Hawthorne writes that he found the story in an old manuscript in the Salem customhouse. "It should be borne carefully in mind," he continues, "that the main facts of the story are authorized and authenticated by the document." Ironically, he then informs the reader that the document was in turn based on "oral testimony."

Hawthorne was well aware of the hierarchy of sources: his claim to authenticity would have carried much less authority had he claimed access to the first-hand, oral sources, rather than to a second-hand, but written one.[28] Hawthorne's allusive use of legal terminology illuminates the predicament of Dr. Calogero and his colleagues in the April 7 Case: though their ideology was based on the primacy of writing and "documents," their accusations were "authorized and authenticated" mostly by "oral testimony."

The usual method, when "drawing from oral evidence to serve reconstructions of history of the *évenementiel* type" is "a fusion/confusion of oral with the written testimony."[29] In the April 7 Case, the prosecution followed the course of assimilating "oral sources" by turning them into written documents: the records of pretrial testimony and interrogations, once committed to the transcript became "documents" which were consigned to the courtroom judges and adopted wholesale—to the point that the oral testimony of courtroom witnesses was never allowed to contradict the now-written pre-trial testimony.

This complicates further the traditionally thorny problem of transcription.[30] For instance, in Calogero's report, prosecution witness Antonio Romito appears to have listed *Potere Operaio*'s working-class contacts as follows, by town and factory:

MARGHERA: Petrolchimico (Montedison and Chatillon),
PORDENONE: Zanussi (Rex)
ROVIGO: personal contacts with P[otere] O[peraio] groups in the Adria (lower Po delta) region, in a number of plants and textile workshops . . .
GENOA: Ansaldo;
ROME: Fatme;

BAGNOLI (Naples): Italsider and Italcantieri;
GERMANY: Ford and Volkswagen . . .

Jack Goody has shown that the very concept of a list depends on writing. In a culture of secondary orality like ours, it is quite possible for lists to be composed and delivered orally (as was Romito's case) without the help of chanting and other traditional mnemonic devices.[31] It is however impossible to distinguish an oral list from the rest of discourse by such typographic means as spacing and indentation. It is also unlikely that a list that has none of the rhythmic devices mentioned above may be delivered with no false starts or hesitations, or without such connectives as "at" Rovigo, or "there were" contacts . . . It is also unlikely that the location of small towns would be specified orally in parentheses as is done in official documents or on letter envelopes.

The typographic and syntactic arrangement of Romito's testimony must be seen, then, as the contribution of the transcriber. This does not imply falsifications of contents; if anything, it sets out facts more clearly. This is, however, the point: by assimilating the list typographically to a written document it makes it easier to perceive the testimony as fact rather than words. Cognitive manipulation is achieved with no factual manipulation.

Italian legal procedure in the pretrial phase (and, officially, in the courtroom as well) ignores the tape recorder: the authority of the magistrate cannot be subjected to verification by a machine. Also, given the secret nature of pretrial proceedings, there is no need for permanent documentation. Therefore, words are recorded as dictated by the magistrate, who is not expected to follow the witness's actual wording, but rather to rephrase it in formal legal terminology. Thus, the degree of interpretation is much higher than in normal transcripts, and the complexity of experience is tendentially reduced to descrete legal categories in forms that, at times, actually anticipate the verdict.[32]

A portion of the testimony of Carlo Casirati (a common criminal who participated in the Saronio kidnapping and murder) reads: "I first realized how effective the Organization in Padua was . . . the Organization was very serious . . ." It is difficult to distinguish, orally, a capital "O" from a lower case one. However, Organization with a capital initial (often abbreviated as "the O") was the form used by the Rome magistrates to designate the alleged secret terrorist group headed by Negri. Since the spelling of the word is the responsibility of the transcriber, we may conclude that, rather than basing his interpretation of history on the testimony, the judge was writing his preconceived version into the witness's words.

In fact, when Patrizio Peci—the most important of the former terrorists who turned state's evidence—uses the word "organization" to refer to the Red Brigades, the interrogation record always spells it with a lower-case initial. However, when he refers to Negri's circle, Dr. Calogero transcribes it with a capital "O." We have no way of telling whether this change reflects a shift in Peci's intonation when pronouncing the word, or Dr. Calogero's belief that the Red Brigades were only a subordinate part of Negri's elusive Organization.

The problem of transcription came up several times in court. Witness Mauro Borromeo explained a contradiction between his pretrial and courtroom testimonies by saying that his earlier statements must have been transcribed incorrectly. Another witness remembered that his testimony had not been transcribed immediately, but only a few days later and on the basis of notes taken by the magistrate.

Political History and the Pentito Perspective

Witness Antonio Romito described in his testimony the differences between Negri and Franco Piperno (another April 7 Case defendant) which led to the dissolution of *Potere Operaio* at its 1973 convention. While Negri is said to have favored a long-term strategy of mass struggle, Piperno opened the meeting by "announcing that 1974 would be the year of the insurrection." Romito went on to say that, "from the fact that the armed insurrection advocated by Piperno did not take place, while mass working-class struggles grew wider and more intense, I presumed" that Negri's line had prevailed and was also being followed by Piperno in spite of apparent differences.

Like historian Angelo Ventura and magistrate Pietro Calogero, prosecution witness Romito favors political over social history: mass struggles or insurrections do not depend upon the masses or on broad social causes, but on the secret dealings of leaders—whose influence on the working class was never more than marginal anyway.[33]

Though Romito was not a *pentito* in the technical sense (he had been a member of *Potere Operaio*, but never joined the terrorist underground), his conspiracy theory of history fits well with the *pentiti*'s testimony. While it circumscribes and defines the evil from

(Conspiracy)

which they have separated, the image of the conspiracy also allows them to feel that they are at the center of history. The heroic role that some *pentiti* felt they were playing after their conversion continued their earlier heroic image of themselves as underground fighters.[34]

Christopher Lasch has pointed out how ex-Communists in the "cultural cold war" of the 1950s were quick to subscribe to an image of communism as conspiracy, which squared with the crudely elitist version of Leninism which they had followed before their conversion.[35] The conspiracy theory also squares with the elitist nature of terrorism, which sees small secret vanguard groups rather than social movements as the decisive forces of history.

Finally, the conspiracy theory enhanced the importance of the "inside" information which the *pentiti* were able to supply.

Patrizio Peci, who had been a leader in the Red Brigades, was offended at Dr. Calogero's suggestion that there might have been a higher level of command above his own. This tendency was reinforced by the fact that the investigating magistrates were apt—as all reluctant oral historians are—to try to elicit from their oral sources the same type of information that they looked for in written documents.[36]

Mutability, Memory and the Professional Witness

A testimony is the sum of all the statements of an informant which relate to the same referent.

Jan Vansina[37]

Mutability is an inherent character of oral sources. This appeared in several discrepancies between individual witnesses' testimonies in the pretrial and the courtroom phases.

Key prosecution witness Carlo Fioroni first said that he *thought* that defendant Alberto Magnaghi had been at a certain meeting where crimes were supposed to have planned; he then grew more assertive each time until, on his fourth interrogation, he said he was *sure* Magnaghi had attended. This allowed the prosecution to order Magnaghi's arrest.[38]

We might define this as "incremental testimony": the same story is told over and over again, with additional detail. Incremental testimony in the April 7 Case derives from a multiplicity of causes, some inherent in the mutability of memory itself, and others peculiar to this case and to the social function of the *pentiti*.

In the first place, memory is not an instantaneous act of recall—as the prosecution sometimes tended to believe—but rather a process and a generator of meaning.[39] In the trial, the reconstruction of events varied according to the changes that had occurred in the witnesses' view of history and of themselves.

Also, the record offers several cases in which "collective" memory is used as a source. When second-hand information was allowed, some of the processes of transmission and change of oral folklore were introduced in the record. Actual folklore can also occasionally be found. *Pentito* Carlo Alberto Pozzan, for instance, testified that "in order to join the Red Brigades, candidates were required to prove themselves by stealing a gun with their bare hands."

Like memory, repentance is a process, not an event. Before the April 7 Case began, Carlo Fioroni had been sentenced to 27 years for the murder of Carlo Saronio; when he appealed this sentence and began to incriminate his former comrades, the appeal judge justified the fact that he had not told the "truth" at his own trial by saying that his contradictions were themselves evidence of his "complex path to redemption."[40] In a later terrorism trial, defendant Roberto Vitelli admitted to having been a member of the *Prima Linea* underground group; but only at the very last moment could he bring himself to confess that he had participated in an action which resulted in murder. The difference between these two examples of incremental repentance lies in the fact that Fioroni incrementally incriminated others and exonerated himself, while Vitelli incrementally incriminated only himself. Since the emergency legislation grants *pentiti* benefits only to those who incriminate others, Fioroni was allowed to go free and seek refuge abroad with a special passport released to him by the government. Vitelli, on the other hand, received a life sentence.

This allows us to perceive the memory effects of the social role of *pentiti*. David Caute has shown that a sort of incremental testimony occurred with the American ex-Communists who set themselves up as paid consultants to firms and agencies on Communist infiltration.[41] The *pentiti*'s information was not being repaid in money, but in freedom; and they knew that their continuing usefulness to the prosecution depended on their always having new information to supply. "They were professionals, in their own small way," recalled defendant Paolo Virno;[42] and the incremental nature of their testimony was incentivated by its exchange value. For instance, Michele Galati refused to continue his testimony in court because, he complained, his contribution to other trials "was strangely underrated," although it had helped secure convictions.[43] Star witness Roberto Sandalo complained:

> I have no job, I am unemployed . . . Three years ago we [*pentiti*] were heroes; now, perhaps, no more. Terrorism is forgotten . . . I am more clandestine now than before, nobody will give me a job . . . Now that, it seems, they say, that terrorism in this country has been defeated, I am as clandestine as when I was in *Prima Linea*.[44]

The philology of oral sources has developed techniques which take account of mutability. According to Jan Vansina:

> No attempt should be made to reconstruct a so-called original text . . . variants are valuable because of the opportunity they provide for judging the informant's confidence in the reliability of his statements and his psychological attitude toward his testimony, and sometimes also for detecting errors and lies.[45]

The judicial processing of oral sources has obvious points of contact with this situation, including the "practical" need (in Vansina's terms) to settle on a "final text" in view of "publication." However, the prosecution in the April 7 Case hardly attempted to take advantage of the mutability of testimony for the purposes outlined by Vansina; they simply seemed to assume that the most incriminating version was the more accurate one. In the case of Fioroni's testimony on Magnaghi, it happened to be the last version given. In the case of Romito's testimony on the "top ranking" of defendant Lisi Del Re in *Autonomia*, the prosecution stuck to the first version[46] though, in a later one, Romito said he might have been wrong.

Sincere and Disinterested: Subjectivity, Narrative, and Testimony

Giorgio Roverato, a university colleague of Negri's, testified that "it was a common belief" that the defendants belonged to *Autonomia Operaia*; that Negri "was believed by everyone to be the leader"; that "acquaintances told [me] that Negri had taught guerrilla classes in the students' dorms"; and that "a great impression was created" by Negri's arrest at a demonstration—ten years before. Hearsay and rumor are not allowed by law as evidence; however, almost every page of the pretrial record contains such formulaic expressions as "according to what I heard," "it was generally believed," "it was my impression," "from this I inferred that," and so on, with usually no attempt to seek the original source. Roverato's "acquaintances" are described as "students who lived in the dorms," but the record shows no attempt to have him identify them or to have them summoned.

Oral historians consider hearsay, opinion, beliefs, value judgments, and even errors as part of the peculiar usefulness of oral sources. This is why it is more correct to speak of "narrative" and "narrators," rather than "testimony" and "informants"—terms for which full semantic implications are revealed by the present context. "Narrative" implies an awareness of the role of verbal organization and of the inherent ambiguity and connotative aura of language, which can be rendered less ambiguous only at the price of heavy loss of information. "Narrator," on the other hand, spotlights the speaker's subjective presence.

Subjectivity has been considered both the prize and the bane of oral history. While it is helpful in reconstructing the speakers' own mentalities and the cultural and political atmosphere, its appropriate cognitive status can only be appreciated if it is recognized *as* subjective, and if attempts are made to keep it as methodologically distinct as possible from straight factual information and intermediate forms.[47]

This principle was often disregarded by the April 7 Case's prosecution. Once oral sources were assimilated to written "documents," they were granted the same presumptive literal credibility. Thus, Dr. Calogero and his colleague in Rome, Amato, seemed to accept opinion and hearsay as evidence not of the witness/narrators' mentality (as oral historians do), but of actual events. As Scarpari noted, "The authority of the document is replaced by that of the *pentiti*."[48]

Narratives were consequently treated as if they were pure *testimony*. Let us consider, for example, Fioroni's testimony on his role in the kidnapping of his friend and comrade Carlo Saronio, who was later murdered:

> I still don't understand how I was persuaded to give information about Saronio, and to accept the very idea of kidnapping him . . . Carlo Saronio was one of my best friends, and in the absurd world of the organization, he had created with me the most humane and sincere relationship. I

believe that the reason why I was implicated and used was that this friendship would have kept Saronio from prosecuting afterwards.

Fioroni explained his actions by his feelings of friendship for the victim and of "liking" and "awe" for Carlo Casirati, the common criminal who actually carried out the act. He always described himself as passive ("implicated and used"); ignorant ("all this time, I though he was still alive"); and weak ("I hesitate to speak of moral subjugation" to Casirati—but he does). He tried to convey the image of the weak petty bourgeois revolutionary fascinated by the tough underground figure. Like other witnesses, Fioroni invoked his own psychological weakness to exculpate himself. "I would not have been implicated and used if I had not been going through a time of psychological disarray and existential unbalance." //

In one of Fioroni's earlier trials, the judges excused his reticence by saying that "a man who incriminates himself must be allowed to retain at least a remnant of self-respect in the depths of his degradation."[49] Self-derogation and expressions of guilt are rhetorical requisites to prove repentance, which is, in turn, a requisite to credibility: "As a corollary of his sincere and disinterested desire to separate himself from the armed struggle," wrote Dr. Calogero, Fioroni "revealed many facts which fully validate the prosecution's position." Fioroni's statements were said to be proven by the sincerity of his conversion; in turn the sincerity of his conversion was "proven" by the statements he makes. "Sincere and disinterested" became almost formulaic when referring to the "brave and responsible witnesses" for the prosecution.

On the other hand, each time a *pentito* contradicted the prosecution, his sincerity and disinterestedness were questioned. Those who denied that there was such a thing as the secret top leadership headed by Negri became, in Dr. Calogero's words, "so-called *pentiti*." "In cases of terrorism," he wrote, one could never be sure that witnesses did not "alter reality" in order to cover up for the real leaders. If a *pentito* contradicted a judge, his sincerity was dubious[50], as when Peci insisted that Negri had never been the supreme leader of the Red Brigades, and Calogero warned him that he might lose his *pentito* benefits.

There is no reason to doubt the actual sincerity of the repentance and horror which many former terrorists felt for their crimes. Fioroni's lawyer insisted that his client was sincere.[51] The law, however, makes it impossible to evaluate actual sincerity, since it recognizes as *pentiti* only those who turn evidence against others, and rewards them with very tangible benefits, thus casting doubts on the lack of self-interest of even the most authentic conversion.

The Plural Authorship of Sources: Interrogations and Interviews

A statement made in reply to a number of questions must be regarded as the work of two informants: the questioner and the person questioned. The testimony consists, in fact, not only of the replies, but also of the questions.

Jan Vansina[52]

The shared root of *inter*view and *inter*rogation indicates that interaction is the shared structuring factor in field work and in judicial testimony; oral historians and magistrates shape their own sources by means of interactive processes. Bruno Leuzzi, Negri's counsel in the pretrial phase, recalled:

Negri's interrogations were accurately staged and conducted. He was always asked questions that were fragments of a picture which existed in its entirety only inside the judge's mind. He never knew the intention behind those questions, so he was easily led to conceal, utter half-truths, [and] contradict himself. They never confronted him, as the law says they're supposed to do, with the actions of which he was accused and with the evidence against him. If the transcript shows that Negri gave crazy answers, it's because he was asked crazy questions.

Vansina describes two types of interviews: one in which "the questioner merely creates the occasion for giving the testimony," and the other in which "the reply is already suggested by the questions." There are two ways, Vansina shows, of asking for the same information. For example, "Who reigned before Mbong aleng?" versus "Did Shyaam reign before Mbong aleng?" From what we can reconstruct in the transcripts, questions of the second type prevailed: not "Who were the leaders of the Red Brigades?", but rather "Were the defendants leaders of the Red Brigades?"

Most courtroom interrogations consisted in reading extensive portions of the witnesses' pretrial testimony, and merely asking whether they confirmed it. As Vansina says, "If the question contains material which is repeated in the reply," the testimony consists largely "of projections of information already in the possession of the questioner." Vansina concludes that "statements of this kind are generally unreliable."[53] In fact, even a *pentito*, Antonio Savasta, complained of the "ideological" nature of his pretrial interrogations, which consisted of "ideological questions" encouraging him to express judgments and opinions.[54]

The Plural Authorship of Oral Sources: Power

'Give your evidence,' said the King, 'and don't be nervous, or I'll have you executed on the spot.'
                    Lewis Carroll, *Alice's Adventures in Wonderland*

Mauro De Rossi, witness for the prosecution, testified in court that, "During my first interrogation, I was very upset, very nervous. I was inaccurate. When Dr. Calogero interrogated me again in 1983, I explained that my first testimony was mostly hearsay." However, the second transcript contains no trace of these corrections.

All field workers have come across the bias introduced into the testimony by power relationships between the observer and the observed. In the best of cases, this results in the interviewee's polite tendency to give the interviewer what he or she thinks the interviewer wants. In the worst cases, it results in the interviewers forcing interviewees to say what they want to hear. Many intermediate cases result in half-truths, silences, and concealed information.

Many prosecution witnesses were either in jail or threatened by the possibility of arrest when interrogated, and chances of clearance or liberation depended on the usefulness of their testimony. This created a state of dependency. Rather than working around it, magistrates often chose to accentuate it, as shown by Dr. Calogero's threats to Peci. "If I didn't trust the courts so much", said *pentito* Borromeo, "I should think that the fact that they had me arrested again before the trial was a move intended to put pressure on me."[55] Antonio Lombino, also a witness for the prosecution, wrote in a letter to a newspaper that "the clever maneuvers of certain magistrates, who kept me in solitary for a year, induced me to give testimony" which was instrumental in incriminating others.

The intersubjective authorship of oral sources has consequences also at the stages of selection and interpretation. While quantitative samples have been used successfully at times by oral historians,[56] oral sources have a basically qualitative character. Their representativity depends on the breadth and scope of the interviews. The magistrates in the April 7 Case, however, relied mostly on the network/grapevine sampling method, one limitation of which is that witnesses lead investigators to others similar to themselves who will supply basically the same type of information.

The witnesses for the prosecution came from two basic networks: *pentiti,* and university acquaintances of Negri and the others. Other testimony was discouraged or excluded; the 71 defendants were allowed to call only 17 courtroom witnesses altogether, and their own testimony was subjected to grave limitations. Some spent years in jail without being interrogated; others never had an opportunity to testify about the facts of which they were accused.[57]

In his final brief, Dr. Calogero hardly quoted information contained in the defendants' testimony, though he quoted at length their earlier political writings. As always, the level of "publication" is where authorship is subtracted from the narrators and concentrated in the investigator. In this case, quoting only one set of testimony can hardly result in an unbiased synthesis.

Finally, interpretation completes the historian's appropriation of the words of the sources. Especially after being transcribed—thus acquiring the supposed objectivity of "documents"—words can be detached from their context and used independently of the original intention.

For instance, witness Ennio Di Nolfo said that the defendant Guido Bianchini was close to the leadership of *Autonomia,* but "in a vaguer position." Di Nolfo later wrote Dr. Calogero a letter to explain that he did not mean to say that there was a structured hierarchy but only a loose intellectual and charismatic leadership; and that Bianchini's "vaguer position" meant that he was only loosely involved with the group's violent activities and often critical. Dr. Calogero insisted that hierarchy and leadership are the same thing, and interpreted Di Nolfo's words about Bianchini's "vague" role to mean that "his activity was . . . less perceptible at first sight" and therefore, far from being more peripheral, he was part of the secret core group. He entirely disregarded Di Nolfo's explanation of his own words.

Antonio Savasta insisted that, in interpreting his testimony, the courts had "flattened out" his distinctions between opinion and fact and his explanations of the meaning of political terms in their historical context. "Everybody was using my testimony to their own advantage, rather than to seek the truth," he said. "Every time I enter a courtroom, I wonder whether I made the right choice when I laid down arms and decided to cooperate."[58]

ARENA OF STRUGGLE: THE COURTROOM

Disruptions and Interruptions

'This can't go on. There's a whole lot of confusion here!' For
the first time, Toni Negri's voice rang out in the April 7 courtroom.

Corriere della Sera, March 31, 1983

The April 7 prisoners had looked forward to the trial as to a
sort of liberation. 'A trial now' was their initial demand. When
it finally started, they demanded 'a fair trial' . . . They
thought the moment of truth had come, when at last their
voices would be heard.

Luigi Ferrajoli[59]

"There were great expectations," says Paolo Virno. "There was
a yearning to come out in the open at last; to defend ourselves, in
political and in legal terms. But the first round of witnesses, the
first couple of months in the courtroom, was enough for us to realize that we could do nothing, that the court would continue along
the same path, that it would yield on nothing."

The most emphatically oral moment in the courtroom trial is
the confrontation between prosecution witnesses and defendants. It
is a subspecies of what Vansina calls "dispute between informants,"
one of the situations in which the "antagonistic" character of orality
(Walter J. Ong) is most visible. We might also view it as a case of
"group interview," a technique for validating testimony.[60]

In the April 7 Case trial, the antagonistic aspect prevailed
over the cooperative possibility of dialogue. Each side maintained
its version, and prosecution witnesses often sought refuge in the
pretrial record. This made these confrontations highly charged
with emotion. Mario Dalmaviva was accused of promoting an insurrection, but had never been interrogated about it, although
he had spent years in jail. When he was finally granted an opportunity to confront the prosecution witnesses, he blew his top. "The
witness keeps saying," he shouted, "that we talked of sabotage, ar-
son, shooting. Can he describe one fact, only one fact, that we actually perpetrated?" Romito's reply was, "I confirm my [pretrial]
statement."

Chicco Funaro was charged with teaching the use of weapons
and guerrilla techniques to a group of high school students in Mi-

lan, some of whom later used this information to commit terrorist actions. In court, Funaro faced one of them—Marco Barbone, a confirmed murderer but also a *pentito* who had been set free as a reward for his cooperation. Observers contrasted Barbone's "calm and chilly," "cold and professor-like" behavior with Funaro's emotional delivery. Funaro told his version of the meetings with Barbone and the other students, saying that he taught politics and economics, not guerrilla tactics. He insisted in recalling his friendship with and affection for them then—and perhaps even now:

> I knew them well . . . it was only natural to have with these kids not just a political relationship but also some human warmth, mutual knowledge, as always happens between people who are normally civil, in spite of age differences . . . You must consider, your honor, that in those years it was not a crime to feel friendship and warmth for people who were not your age. It was not a crime! It was part of a political style that overcame age differences, [with no need for] indoctrination.[61]

Halfway through Funaro's testimony, Barbone was bothered by his emotion: "Take it easy, you're shouting all over me," he said. A voice from the defendants' cage answered. "Easy? You're free, and we've spent five years in jail!"

Throughout the court sessions, voices from the cage rang out anonymously and collectively. As is possible only in oral performance, they talked back, and all at once. "Voices without power," Virno said about the disruptions and interruptions of a discourse that concerned them but excluded them.

When Romito said that the 1973 *Potere Operaio* convention applauded certain kidnappings in Milan and Genoa, "an ironic voice from the cage reminded him" that these facts had taken place four and six months *after* the convention. The judge, according to Virno, shut down the disturbance. Again, when prosecutor Antonio Marini read from the *Potere Operaio* magazine an attack on the judicial system and added that many of those magistrates "were later kidnapped, shot at, killed!", a protest rose from the cage: "Certainly not by the defendants in this trial!" According to M. S. Ball, "Disorderly conduct may occur as an anguished protest against injustice and an appeal for justice":

> One of the characteristics of judicial theatre is its ordered sequences and exchanges. Disruption of the order may make it

into something else or may expose the fact that it has already been made into something else—perhaps theatre of the absurd, a categorization suggested for the Chicago conspiracy trial. . . .[62]

Dialogue

"We did have a chance to talk freely, even *too* freely," said Paolo Virno. "In fact, the court considered what we had to say of our background and personal history to be merely ornamental, ritual. As soon as it was over, they would start asking questions that had no connection with what we had just said. You could tell that they weren't interested, that there was a visible selection in listening patterns. That discouraged us."

Some observers detected a pattern of open-ended questions from the court to prosecution witnesses, as opposed to very narrow question-and-answer techniques with defendants and defense witnesses. "We are not historians, we are magistrates," courtroom Judge Severino Santiapichi said over and over when defendants "digressed"; but prosecution witnesses were allowed to speak more freely and broadly.[63] Hence, a tendency on the part of the defense to step over the boundaries set by the interrogation. For instance, defendant Lucio Castellano was described as "more talkative" than the questions entailed: he was trying to explain to the court the meaning of words and expressions that were used as evidence against him.

According to Virno, those defendants who were accused of no specific crimes but only charged with membership in subversive groups were handled with the "how-could-you-not-know" approach, an up-to-date version of guilt by association. As the editor of a magazine at which another defendant, Oreste Scalzone, also worked, Virno says that he was automatically held responsible for Scalzone's actions. "How could you not know that Scalzone was [supposed to be] organizing robberies, trading arms in the Middle East, and so on? How could you not know? It was always, 'how could you not know'—given your acquaintances, the acquaintances of your acquaintances, former acquaintances . . .'"

Negri was charged with the murder of the *carabiniere* Lombardini, at which he was admittedly not even present, simply because, since the actual killers had a loose political connection with him, he *must* have known and approved.[64]

On the other hand, those who also had to answer charges of specific criminal acts were interrogated only on matters of detail.

"The court was not interested in whether these details were part of a broader picture. They reserved connections for themselves."

Pentiti, instead, were allowed both to expand on the broad political and historical picture and to specify details, the two levels reinforcing each other. "Since they made specific charges, they were allowed to talk of philosophy and history," Virno said. "And since they provided a broad outline, their specific charges were believed." The defense was overwhelmed by this circularity.

Paper

Two years into the case, defendant Oreste Scalzone took a look at the material plight of the defense:

> The pretrial record includes [so far] forty-nine thousand pages. To prepare our defense we need urgent photocopies, at a cost of 450 *lire* each. That makes 22 million *lire* [about $18,000]. Then we need about ten more copies, one for each four or five lawyers. This runs into 50 millions more . . . The more urgent photocopies will be delivered in two or three weeks; it takes twice as long for the others, provided there is enough equipment available. Next, we need to study and analyze the record, and prepare our briefs. We will be allowed no more than thirty days for this (which is already a concession: the laws provides a five-day term).

For three more years, paper kept piling higher. Its very bulk made the defense hard to manage. The sheer length and size of the trial loaded it with writing. Even the introduction of the tape recorder in the courtroom eventually resulted in thousands of pages of transcript, too many for the jury to really go over while considering the verdict. They were probably used to check specific points, but the synthesis and selection of the relevant aspects of the trial were largely left to the judges and to the pretrial documents.[65]

The primacy of writing played against the defense in the courtroom. In a nearly random example, Judge Santiapichi conducted his interrogation of *pentito* Leonio Bozzato as follows:

> THE COURT: You have stated that, 'Early in 1974 . . . [The judge reads two pages from Bozzato's pretrial testimony.] . . . Is it so?
>
> BOZZATO: Yes.

This pattern continues throughout. Bozzato is never asked to speak, but only to confirm the transcript. In twenty pages of the transcribed courtroom interrogation, Bozzato's statements extend for more than five lines only five times [the longest is eight lines]. About sixty of his answers are one-liners, or less.[66] *Pentito* Michele Galati repeated "I confirm the transcript" so often and even out of context that he was asked to explain what he meant. "I have been in so many trials and heard it used so often that I thought it was a ritual formula."[67]

The contrast between defense and prosecution often took the shape of a conflict between orality and writing. "If we were here only to confirm the transcript," counsel Alberto Pisani argued, "we might as well not be here at all."[68] Discrepancies between courtroom and pretrial testimony arose, therefore, mostly during counter-interrogation by the defense. Occasionally, the judge also stepped in, to defend not so much the oral nature of the proceedings per se, as his own role: the depreciation of orality also depreciated the phase of the trial over which he presided. A typical exchange occurred when a discrepancy arose between Bozzato's testimony in court and his earlier statements:

> THE COURT: . . . the truth, which is the truth?
>
> BOZZATO: What I said in the transcript.
>
> THE COURT: And what you're saying to me now, what is it?
>
> PROSECUTOR: [It seems] that the pretrial transcript is being considered worthless. I am sorry, but I must step in . . . The oral debate is all very well, but we must also bring up the witness's pretrial testimony, and it is my duty as the prosecutor to consider it.
>
> THE COURT: Will the prosecutor kindly let me know when I may be allowed to continue doing my job? Court is suspended.

Court was resumed ten minutes later—with a lengthy reading of pretrial transcripts.[69]

Like the oracle or the prophet [writes Walter J. Ong] the book relays an utterance from a source, the one who really "said" or wrote the book. The author might be challenged if only he or she could be reached, but the author cannot be reached in any book. There is no way directly to refute a text. After absolutely total and devastating refutation, it says exactly the same thing as before.[70]

At the crucial moment of the trial, the person "who really said" the heaviest words was emphatically beyond reach. Carlo Fioroni, whose testimony linked Negri and others to the death of Carlo Saronio, had been set free two years before, and when the court summoned him to repeat his testimony at the trial, he was nowhere to be found. The chief of police told the court that Fioroni had been given a false passport by the secret service, on directions from the prime minister.

From his undisclosed residence abroad, Fioroni sent word that he would not come. The defense asked that his testimony be excluded from the record, since it had been impossible to cross-examine him: the pretrial phase had been conducted in secret, and he was absent from the public proceedings. The court ruled, however, that in absence of Fioroni's oral testimony, the written transcript would stand. Fioroni's story was submitted to what amounted to a "total and devastating refutation" (even his own lawyer informed the court that he had reason to believe that the defendants were not guilty on the most serious counts); but at the end his written testimony still said "exactly the same thing as before." Says Paolo Virno:

> It was a peculiar thing. Here was an oral voice, a witness from the early 70s, who had become written in secret, in the absence of counter-interrogation and control. Once it was turned into a written source, the writing prevailed over the lack of its oral repetition. There was a whole system of stratification—in fact, a perverse mixture—between the oral voice of the *pentiti* and the written sources. The court relied entirely on Fioroni, who refused to come, and on Casirati, who refused to answer the defense's questions, barely answered the prosecution's, and refused to face the defendants. On the basis of these two testimonies—one absent, one reticent—the court handed down guilty verdicts for the death of Carlo Saronio.

Oratory and Silence

According to a reporter for the Left-wing *Il Manifesto*, the final summing up of Prosecutor Antonio Marini was a display of "oratorical ardor," punctuated by "violent banging of fists and loud shouts." The same newspaper later contrasted Marini's style with the "quiet manners and conversational speech" of defense lawyer Tommaso Mancini.

Though the source is hardly a neutral one, this is a useful description of the role of oral genres in the last phase of the trial. Forensic oratory—once the highest genre of public speaking—has suffered heavily since the advent of print caused rhetorical training to be geared to writing more than orality. The last two parts of classical rhetoric—"memory" and "delivery"—were dropped,[71] and those types of discourse which still depend on orality are practiced, in modern times, with no formal training. The emotional display of Prosecutor Marini is therefore less a characteristic of orality than a consequence of its declension. On the other hand, defense lawyer Mancini tried to use an oral genre, conversation, which was best suited to rational persuasion.

Marini's style was based on the horizontal and vertical varieties of one rhetorical figure: amplification. The sheer length of his summation (which lasted two weeks) and the broadening of the perspective to the whole political history of the 1970s were accompanied by devices of word disposition based on repetition and accumulation. Thus, Negri was described as "false, lying, treacherous, cruel"; the defendants were "thieves, kidnappers, robbers, murderers." As one reporter wrote, "hyperbole"—the most typical figure of vertical amplification—"reigns." Parallel forms of nonverbal amplification were the loudness of the voice and the ample and emotional gestures, the banging fist and the "pointed accusing finger."

The defendants felt, however, that the court's minds were already made up. Even while Marini spoke, Virno had the impression that "the court didn't even pay much attention to him." The defense considered not speaking at all, to call attention to their assessment of the situation. It was finally decided (still according to Virno's narrative) to play the trial straight, and to insist on a fair application of the rules. Before the court retired, the defendants made their final statements.

"I could have escaped abroad a thousand times," said Virno, "between my first and second arrest. But I wanted my freedom to be the result of the ending of the emergency era. Those who have run away merely survive; I want to live."

Arrigo Cavallina said, "I can boast the longest pretrial detention in Italy, in Europe, in the twentieth century: eight years in jail without a trial. I now strongly condemn my past. But I am not willing to prove this change by turning into a merchant of human flesh."

"Those of us who had been outside the cage and free," wrote Rossana Rossanda, "asked one another: Why is it that we never really heard the sound of Arrigo Cavallina's voice?"

TRUTH

Arrigo Cavallina was sentenced to fourteen years, Paolo Virno to twelve (pending appeal, they were granted house arrest rather than jail detention). Neither had ever been charged with even carrying a weapon.

The charge of "armed insurrection against the State" against Negri was dropped at the last moment. Thanks to this, he only received a thirty-year sentence as the instigator of Saronio's murder and for having "morally concurred" in the murder of Lombardini.

Five defendants received sentences above twenty years; nineteen were sentenced to between ten and twenty years; thirty-one were given up to seven years.

"We have finally what is known in legal language as the judicial truth, that is, truth verified by two judges and six jurors of the court. This truth may of course differ from historical truth," wrote jurist Guido Neppi Modona. He might have added another truth, outlined in the editorial pages of the same newspaper where he wrote his comment: that is, media-made truth. "So, *Autonomia*, the one with the capital 'A' described by Calogero five years ago," wrote *Repubblica*, "was an armed band and its members—intellectuals, unionists, and professors—were the 'evil teachers' of subversion in the early 1970s. And they committed robberies, thefts, bombings, shootings, and even two murders."

What Calogero had "described" five years before, actually, was that Negri and the others were not just a subversive organization, but the brains of the Red Brigades. This charge had long been proved false, but Calogero shouted all over the front page, "I was right!" "The theorem has held," said the headline.

The gist of the theorem, in fact, was that these people ought to go to jail for something or other; and they did. They were *all* guilty of "robberies, thefts, bombings, shootings, and even two murders," even though some of them were not even accused of having perpetrated them. But media-made truth, as represented by Italy's then

most respected newspaper, only knows that they were all tried together and were all guilty together.[72] What matters that there was
no such thing as *"Autonomia* . . . with a capital 'A' " in "the early
1970s," since informal groups started calling themselves *"Autonomia"* only after 1974? The political mass-media truth is that in the
1970s there was no social movement; only a political conspiracy.[73]

The distinction between legal and historical truth deserves one
final comment. Historical truth is hardly ever more than a descrip-
tive hypothesis; legal truth, on the other hand, has a performative
nature, measured in years in jail. Also, legal truth has a tendency
to become historical truth, in the sense that future historians will
rely on the court sentence and trial records for their reconstruction
of the political history of the 1970s.

In 1979, Professor Angèlo Ventura was quoted as saying, "an
arbitrary use of oral sources, without controls and scientific guarantees, allows them to be used instrumentally to serve political
ends."[74] These words were intended as a warning to (or against)
young, activist, "barefoot," oral historians; but they may also serve
as a commentary on the judicial use of oral sources in the April 7
Case. This writer has very little sympathy for Antonio Negri, either
politically or morally; and one needs not care about Paolo Virno or
Arrigo Cavallina. History, science and the judicial system, on the
other hand, are all-important to all of us. We might therefore feel
entitled—if only for professional reasons—to suggest that the verification procedures, the "controls and scientific guarantees" which
are normally required for the publication of academic essays about
history, be not disregarded by those whose reconstructions of history result in fifteen- or thirty-year sentences.[75]

13

Absalom, Absalom!: Oral History and Literature*

This chapter is the story of a seminar in American Literature for English-language majors at the University of Rome in 1980–81.

I had been long aware that students found it difficult to relate to literature. They perceived it as something quite apart from their own lives and experiences, which they had to bear with as a burden on the journey toward graduation. This attitude was reinforced by the critical idiom of the day, which stressed literature as, indeed, a separate type of language and experience, to be subjected to strictly technical analysis.

Besides, in Italy, most foreign language majors join the university expecting to study languages, only to learn after enrollment that languages will be merely instrumental to the study of what really counts for the institution—*literature*. The feeling that they are getting something other than what they bargained for heightens their sense of estrangement.

Earlier, I had tried to bridge the gap by teaching readable, socially relevant texts—*The Grapes of Wrath, The Iron Heel,* and so forth. But I met with no more than indifferent success. So I resolved to try another strategy: I would teach a difficult, almost abstruse book, with little or no visible connection to their interests and experience. And I would see if I could make *that* relevant. The choice fell on William Faulkner's 1936 novel, *Absalom, Absalom!*

The novel tells the story of the rise and fall of Thomas Sutpen, from "po' white trash" to rich planter and down again. It is pieced together from memory, conjecture, and inference by young Quentin Compson, forty-three years after the facts. The stratification of nar-

*A first version, "Il discorso quotidiano e il discorso letterario" appeared in F. Mariani, ed., *Letteratura. Percorsi possibili,* Longo Editore, Ravenna 1983, 100–115.

rators, the shifts of temporal planes, the uncertainty between fact and conjecture, as well as Faulkner's highly wrought style make it very difficult reading, especially for foreign students.

I was hoping to show them, however, that their difficulties were not caused by the text's estrangement from ordinary speech and experience, but rather by its close resemblance to them. Where the students expected the orderly sequence of conventional fiction, they were challenged by an apparent chaos resembling the fragmentation and overlapping of voices in everyday conversation, and yet distanced from it by being placed in a new context and medium. I could thus attract the students' attention to medium and context, and help them rediscover the specificity of literature as the result of a learning experience rather than as an *a priori* dogma.

The next step was the identification of a corpus of nonliterary narratives, by ordinary people in everyday speech, which could be used for purposes of comparison. At the time, I was involved in an oral history project in the nearby industrial town of Terni, so I decided to use some of the interviews collected there.

We began with time. The idea was to verify whether the shifting of temporal planes which so perplexed the students had been malignantly concocted by Faulkner in order to confuse his readers, or whether people just naturally told stories that way. Therefore, we looked at the following narrative, from an interview with a factory worker named Alberto Petrini.

PORTELLI: Did your father ever used to tell you what the work was like at the chemical plant [in the 1930s]?

PETRINI: Well, he had a serious accident, and he had to quit. He was in a coma, and spent more than a year in the hospital.

PORTELLI: When was this?

PETRINI: Well, I was a child. I was very small.

PORTELLI: How did it happen?

PETRINI: Well, one of the kilns blew up on him. Later, I worked at the same job myself, same spot, too. I had been working at the steel mill, and I was the [Communist] representative there, you know, so they removed me from there and shifted me to the fertilizer plant, as a punishment. To take me away from things, make me lose contact with the comrades, with the rank-and-file. So they sent me over there for a while. And I worked there—I was about thirty, then—and there I saw, you know, the very place where my father's accident happened. I remember it very well; I was just learning to walk, and after that he supported the family any which way he could.

PORTELLI: How could it happen—how can a kiln blow up on you?

PETRINI: Those were the kilns where the calcium carbide was made. They would take the silica stone down from the mountain, then it was enriched with other minerals and burned. Sometimes there were explosions, gusts of fire [a long technical description follows which is omitted here]. There was *some* protection, but not enough to make it safe for the workers. I have seen people burn like torches, I saw it myself. One morning, I was going in with the 6:00 A.M. shift. I had just been transferred there, and it was nearing May Day, and we were collecting union dues. You see, there was no checkoff in those days, to finance the union; you had to go and collect it from the workers themselves, each time. So I stayed awhile by the locker room stairs below my workplace, waiting for the comrades, asking them for money as they came down the stairs one by one. And I lingered there, and there was this huge explosion upstairs. Those five minutes saved my life. Two of the fellows were—you know, they had wool clothes on, but when that incandescent blast hits you, it burns everything . . . everything burns. And they were rolling on the ground trying to put it out. They scream, they call for help, but when the fire hits you can't go near them, it's like a furnace. You wait for it to abate, but meanwhile they're burning. And people have been killed, people have been crippled for life . . . people who weren't hit as hard, the incandescent mass didn't strike as bad, and these people spent six, eight months in the hospital. The burns remained, but they didn't die. My father's case, it wasn't lethal; but he spent a year, a year . . .

PORTELLI: You were saying he actually caught fire?

PETRINI: Yes, then he was carried to the hospital, and he had a splintered—no, a broken leg. So they carried him to the hospital, and the doctors thought he was going to die, so they didn't do anything about his leg. They said, "He's going to die, no use fixing that leg." But he didn't die. When they saw that he, this poor guy, had survived the critical moment and would live, they went back and were going to break his leg all over again so they could fix it right. But with his other leg, the good one he had left, he kicked the doctor all the way down the hall. He wouldn't let them break his leg again. He was crippled for the rest of his life, but had suffered so much pain that he could not stand it to have his leg broken again, coldly, like that, and then have it fixed . . . go through the whole tribulation once more. You know, he had looked death in the face.

It was easy to discern that the story was articulated upon three intersecting and shifting chronological levels: the 1930s (when Petrini's father had his accident), the 1950s (when Petrini worked at the same place), and the present (evoked by the implicit comparison between the days when there was no checkoff and the union was immediately accountable to its members, and today's bureaucratization).

The time shifts occur in the space of one or two clauses: "I saw . . . the very place where my father's accident happened . . . I was just learning to walk." Narrative time oscillates between singulative and iterative forms: "They were rolling on the ground . . . They scream, they call for help . . ." This enhances the fluidity of the distinction of temporal planes.

I wanted to stress that the manipulation of time is used by the narrator not only to reconstruct the past, but to evaluate it. This story is not a "testimony" but a full-fledged narrative construction. Like Quentin Compson through Sutpen, Alberto Petrini gives meaning to his own experience through his father and his accident.

In order to do so, he departs from chronological sequences and shuttles back and forth in time. With some help from Tzvetan Todorov and some from William Labov,[1] we reached the conclusion that a story is told "naturally" not when it adheres to "objective" chronology but when it departs from it in order to incorporate subjective meaning and judgment. Only a very careful, artificial effort, can keep "facts" and "opinions" separate; in ordinary speech, they are likely to mingle, just as genres mix in most oral speech acts.

In this case, Petrini wanted to indicate both a continuity and a rupture: the continuity of working conditions between the 1930s and the 1950s, and the deterioration of union democracy between the 1950s and the present. The implicit philosophy was a criticism of the myth of progress—which contradicts Petrini's party's conception of history, but rather resembles Faulkner's.

Next, I drew attention to the initial question-and-answer exchange. My question implied the naive belief that Petrini's father had *told* his son about his life, that Petrini had received his heritage through verbal means. As Petrini's answer suggests, this is not the way children learn about their fathers. They pick up knowledge from overheard snatches of conversation among adults, from chance remarks, from seeing how their father looks when he comes in from work, from breathing the factory experience in the atmosphere that surrounds them. Which took us back to our book.

This, in fact, is what *Absalom, Absalom!* is largely about. This is how Quentin learns his first version of Sutpen's story:

> It was a part of his twenty years' heritage of breathing the same air and hearing his father talk about the man Sutpen; a part of the town's—Jefferson's—eighty years' heritage of the same air which the man himself had breathed between this September afternoon in 1909 and that Sunday morning in June in 1833 when he first rode into town out of no discernible past and acquired his land no one knew how and built his house, his mansion, apparently out of nothing and married Ellen Coldfield and begot his two children—the son who widowed the daughter who had not yet been a bride—and so accomplished his allotted course to its violent (Miss Coldfield at least would have said, just) end. Quentin had grown up with that; the mere names were interchangeable and almost myriad. His childhood was full of them; his very body was an empty hall echoing with sonorous defeated names; he was not a being, an entity, he was a commonwealth.[2]

Faulkner insists on this learning process through smells, sounds, and the repetition of stories told *because* the listener already knows: "It was a day of listening, too—the listening, the hearing in 1909 of that which he already knew, since he had been born in and still breathed the same air in which the church bells had rung on that Sunday morning in 1833 and, on Sundays, heard even one of the original three bells in the same steeple . . ."[3] This "breathing the same air" is the very stuff of what we mean when we say "tradition."

The key factor here is repetition, which is one of the things children learn to avoid like the plague in elementary school composition—and which everyone uses normally in conversation. So here was this emphatically *written* literary work of art repeating words, clauses, sentences, whole paragraphs and episodes on every page.

Faulkner's use of repetition reveals a very ambitious project: he is not merely trying to imitate tradition, but to reproduce it. *Ab-*

salom, Absalom! is not *about* tradition, but *becomes* a tradition in itself because its internal structure functions in the same way as tradition does. The reader is placed much in the same condition as the child born into a culture, or the stranger trying to become a part of a culture. Both learn by gleaning information which, like the reader in this book, they only dimly understand at first, they piece together fragments of discourse not addressed to them, edify hypotheses and discard them.

I asked the students to reconstruct the way in which they had learned their own family histories. It turned out that the process was much like the way Quentin learns Sutpen's history—and much like the way they, as readers, learn Quentin's: "entering" the story much as a traveler walks into an unfamiliar town, much as a child enters the world, going from complete bewilderment to total immersion. No one speaks to children, and in this book nobody speaks to the reader. Miss Coldfield speaks to Quentin, Quentin to Shreve, and so on. In each conversation the listener knows something which we, eavesdroppers, ignore; each story will be incomplete for us readers, and we will have to put it together by listening between the lines.

The passage quoted earlier is already a full, self-contained version of Sutpen's story. Though it appears quite early in the book, the story has already been told once, almost in the same words:

> *It seems that this demon—his name was Sutpen—(Colonel Sutpen)—Colonel Sutpen. Who came out of nowhere and without warning upon the land with a band of strange niggers and built a plantation—(Tore violently a plantation, Miss Rosa Coldfield says)—tore violently. And married her sister Ellen and begot a son and a daughter which—(Without gentleness begot, Miss Rosa Coldfield says)—without gentleness. Which should have been the two jewels of his pride and the shield and comfort of his old age, only—(Only they destroyed him or something or he destroyed them or something. And died)—and died. Without regret, Miss Rosa Coldfield says—(Save by her). Yes, save by her. (And by Quentin Compson). Yes. And by Quentin Compson. [Italics in text.]*[4]

There are important differences between these two versions. The one just quoted (but told earlier in the book) represents storytelling as a collective, almost antagonistic process, in which meaning is negotiated through an antiphonal bargaining of collective voices with devices of echo, rhythm, and refrain. The later version is more impersonal, but it contains at least one piece of information which was missing in the earlier one: it begins to explain, though cryptically, *how* it was that Sutpen's children "destroyed" him and (or) themselves.

The insertion of a new detail in a pattern of repetition is known in folklore as "incremental repetition," and is characteristic enough to have been identified as a distinctive aspect of the so-called "ballad style."[5] After familiarizing ourselves with the device by looking at several ballads, we went to work and indexed several hundred occurrences of incremental repetition in *Absalom, Absalom!* The fullest, most developed and yet most self-contained example is the story of the elopement of Miss Coldfield's aunt.

The first we hear about it is that, ten years after Ellen's wedding to Sutpen, she "was still taking revenge" upon the townfolks for not attending the ceremony. Later, we incidentally learn that one night "the aunt climbed out the window and vanished." About twelve pages later, we find out why: "she eloped with the horse-and-mule trader" (*the* trader: it is assumed that whoever is listening to this story already knows about it anyway). On the next page, the two details are pieced together and repeated: she eloped "by climbing out a window one night." Finally, twenty pages after she is first mentioned, the last we and Jefferson hear about her is that she had been seen two years before while trying to cross the Yankee lines to rejoin her husband. The whole story is always mentioned in passing, in other contexts; however, between variants, digressions, and repetitions, we learn it the way Quentin learns it—and the way most of us learn about our own aunts.

In order to understand the functions and consequences of incremental repetition as a form of storytelling, we took up another interview from my oral history project.

This interview happened to tell a story very much like Rosa Coldfield's: both my informant and Faulkner's character repeat obsessively the story of a broken engagement which happened long ago (forty-three years for Miss Coldfield, forty-four for Miss Maggiorina Mattioli). Both live alone; both are seamstresses. Both take the initiative of telling the story. Miss Rosa summons Quentin to set him straight about the whole thing, while Maggiorina Mattioli brings it up and forces it upon an interview which was supposed to be about something else entirely.

I had sought her out because I wanted to hear the story of her dead brother, an important figure in the anti-Fascist underground in the 1920s and 1930s. She, instead, wanted to tell the story of her broken engagement, and introduced it tentatively and by degrees, digressing and tantalizing me with incremental repetition:

> Well, at the age of nineteen I became engaged. To a man who gave me so much pain. God only knows. He kept me in agony for seventeen years. Think of that—seventeen years. A whole life. I was a child before, and then I was an old woman.

I tried to steer the conversation back to her brother but she soon went back to her true subject:

> My brother was just a kid, he'd bring anti-Fascist papers home, that sort of thing. And me—courting with a Fascist! Look: me, the daughter of an anti-Fascist, I couldn't stand those people, and yet I fell in love with a Fascist. I loved him so much. Seventeen years. Seventeen years. A whole life. I was a child, and then I was old. At thirty-six, we broke up.

By then she had won me over. The story she wanted to tell was much more important than the one I was looking for (which happens often, in oral history). In the course of a seemingly endless interview, she told it two more times, with increasing detail and formulaic repetition. "A whole life. I was a child, and than I was old." But the first two versions already contained a classic case of incremental repetition: an essential detail—the political contradiction between herself and her fiance—was withheld the first time and introduced at the second telling.

Mattioli displays a remarkable narrative and conversational skill here. She knows that this information will rivet her listener's attention and divert the conversation from pure politics to the politics of private life and feelings, and from her brother to herself. In fact, in later repetitions, it turns out that politics was only one factor; other reasons why the engagement failed are introduced gradually and incrementally.

Now, the discovery of analogies between "texts" belonging to such different genres, traditions and media as the Mattioli and Petrini interviews on the one side and Faulkner's novel on the other is not a solution, but is, indeed, the heart of the problem. I was not out to prove that all *récits* are the same: my aim was *difference*, the difference which is literature.

I assumed that comparable formal devices and textual results would serve different functions and ends in different genres, media and cultures. Therefore, we set out to analyze the functions of incremental repetition in Maggiorina Mattioli's tale, in order to compare them to those found in *Absalom, Absalom!*

The main function was clearly one of *control*. On the one hand, Maggiorina Mattioli wanted to control her listener by testing my attention. She also wanted control, as narrator, over the subject of conversation.

On the other hand, she was forced to repeat herself several times because she was not sure that she was in full control of the story ("Did I already say this?"). Repetition was her only way of filling in gaps and correcting mistakes, of controlling memory, both of the events and of the earlier parts of the "text." By her use of repetition, both skillful and compulsive, Maggiorina Mattioli conquered the all-important right to speak about herself; and she conquered *time*, because repetition helped her expand the conversation and defer the dreaded moment when it would be over and she would be alone again.

Incremental repetition, then, served two orders of functions: contact and memory. Both groups may in turn be divided into narrator-oriented and narratee-oriented functions:

A. *Contact*
   1. Narrator-oriented: expanding the performance
   2. Narratee-oriented: testing the reception
B. *Memory*
   1. Narrator-oriented: filling gaps, correcting mistakes
   2. Narratee-oriented: securing perception and retention.

Repetition is the vehicle of these functions because the medium is orality. Oral discourse is a constant losing and regaining of control. In its time-determined shape, the spoken word disappears as soon as it is uttered, and can be made to appear again and to achieve some sort of permanence only by being said again and again. Repetition, then, becomes a technical necessity of oral communication.

On the other hand, the writer and reader of written literature (or, more properly, the narrator and narratee) are conventionally assumed to be always in full control. From the point of view of memory (function B), the writer can correct gaps and errors before sending out the text to the printers (or even afterward, in proof), while the reader may go back and reread those sections of the text which he or she has not understood or forgotten. Both may vary the duration of the text and of the performance by changing the pace of reading and of writing.

As for contact (function A), far from testing it, repetition in writing runs the risk of breaking by boredom a contact which is assumed to have been established at the moment of purchase. Repetition—so necessary in an oral performance—becomes technically redundant in a written text.

We might say that the oral event is *unrepeatable*, and therefore can survive only if the repetition is incorporated in the event itself. The written text, on the other hand, includes repetition in its technology. A book can be printed in thousands of absolutely identical copies; it can be preserved to be perused an indefinite number of times. Granted, each reader and each reading make something different out of the text; but the text itself remains the same. Once this relative degree of stability is ensured by the "technology of the word,"[6] the text itself has no inner need to incorporate repetition. Therefore repetition, which appears in orality by *necessity*, appears in writing by *choice* (assuming, of course, the writer's full competence in the medium).

This different genesis points to different ends. Orality and writing are faced by opposite dangers: the spoken word is threatened by impermanence, while writing is threatened by permanence. The oral discourse "runs through our fingers," so to speak, and must be "solidified," "frozen" if we are to hold it, however precariously. Writing, on the other hand, literally fills our hands with solid, already-frozen words. Nothing is lost, but nothing seems to be moving either.

The consequence is a double oxymoron: each medium upholds as values what the other fears as threats; and, consistent with an economic principle of scarcity, each medium values the opposite of what it normally does and inherently consists of. Orality is impermanent, and therefore its values are memory, tradition, conservation, and repetition, while its practice is determined by the difficulty of conserving, remembering and duplicating anything exactly. Writing is stable and permanent, and therefore its values are innovation, change, and experimentation, while its practice consists of prints, libraries, archives and makes it difficult for a typographic culture to ever forget or throw away anything.[7] Not surprisingly, these media beset by opposite dangers recur to the strategy of exchanging weapons.

Repetition (including all types of formalized speech) may be viewed as the implicit way in which orality achieves some of the authority and permanence of writing. The artists of oral expression create an aesthetics based on the very limitations of their medium, on the interplay of necessary repetition and inevitable change, making a virtue of a necessity. Historically, as new forms of preserving words are created, the aesthetic function of these devices becomes independent from their technical functions. Devices created by orality to ensure stability and permanence are adopted by written literature to connote fluidity and improvisation.

One of the functions of literature is, in fact, that of melting the rigidity of material writing. The concepts of innovation, experimentation, and vanguard are time-determined: they are impermanent and temporary. Therefore, a type of discourse which is inherently fluid and impermanent, like the oral discourse, was too good a resource to be ignored. Ironically, however, writing mimics orality by adopting precisely those devices which orality developed to "write" itself—with repetition being foremost—thus creating the impression of a written discourse which is struggling with time as if it were oral.

Let us look at the form of repetition which goes under the name of "paratactic correction," and compare it in William Faulkner and in Alberto Petrini.

Early in *Absalom, Absalom!*, the narrator says that Sutpen's story was "a part of the town's—Jefferson's—eighty years' heritage." We are invited to imagine that, after saying "town," the narrator has realized that the reader might not know which town he is talking about, so he had added the name. In Petrini's interview, on the other hand, at one point, he says that his father "had a splintered—no, a broken leg."

Again, though the two "texts" look similar on the surface, their different histories produce different inner dynamics. Petrini is striving for control: he wants his story to be exact and reliable, so, when he catches himself in error, he adds the correct information. Faulkner, on the other hand, is in full control. He could have stricken out "town" in the manuscript form and replaced it with the more specific "Jefferson." But the impression he wants to convey is that of a blurring of controls. Petrini is striving against time: he wants to recover the event as it really was. Faulkner is striving for time: he wants his text to be infected by the time-oriented impermanence of orality.

Of course, neither literature nor orality ever wish or manage to abolish their original natures and identities. All they do is integrate them, explore their limits and possibilities, and experiment with alternatives. The results are intermediate forms, in which orality and literature may look like each other but still be very different within. Looking at these forms is like looking at a picture of a pond partly covered with ice: it may be a portrait of early winter freezing, or the last traces of spring thawing. In fact, this duplicity is implicit in Faulkner's text. While he injects time in his text through the *dynamics* of orality, he subtracts his text from time through orality as *mythics*. For the reasons of self-defense which I have already outlined, orality strives for timelessness, and is imagined as timeless by the written cultures which place the origins of history at the moment of the invention of "writing."[8] Faulkner is especially concerned with the recovery of this "time before time": even more than *Absalom, Absalom!*, this applies to "The Bear," in which he makes an intensely conscious use of repetition and formulas.[9] Repetition serves both ends: it evokes the intrinsic fluidity of the oral medium, and is used by orality to keep this fluidity under control. By using repetitive and formulaic devices, Faulkner injects and subtracts time at the same time.

Let us go back to the fact that this was originally a didactic experiment. As such, it was basically a failure. It was not that the students got nothing from it: they were interested, participated actively, and wrote excellent papers. But my aims were more ambitious: I was not trying to suggest yet another critical method which they could safely file away along with all the others, but to influence their entire approach to literature and language. And this is where I failed.

For one thing, the material conditions of the teaching of literature must be reckoned with. I had hoped, by concentrating on one book only, that they would all read it quickly and then we could discuss it together. It turned out that, although *Absalom, Absalom!* is printed in Penguin Books, no bookstore in central Italy had a copy. Our department's library was then in its fourth year of inaccessibility due to a sudden move from one campus to another. By the time my own copy was passed around and photocopied (and new copies were ordered from abroad) half the semester was over. Meanwhile, I still had to teach every week; so I wound up doing most of the talking myself. This gave the students a combination of the worst of two academic discourses: the monologue of a lecture course with the unfinished, open approach of the seminar. I ended up giving, as my own discoveries or hypotheses, what I had hoped they would discover for themselves.

They finally wrote excellent papers, in which they confirmed that what I had told them was true—which did not exactly cure them of their addiction to dependence on academic authority. I had underestimated the fact that these students were not *tabula rasa*, but were already set in their ways by years of schooling. I was trying to make them realize that we all *do* speak prose, and they stayed hidden behind the insurmountable walls of aura that school, the university, and criticism have erected around the very concept of prose and poetry. These things are for special people, and common folks like us may approach them only with awe and reverence, and touch them only with a ten-foot pole. Perhaps, this is, in fact, how things now stand; perhaps, all this building of walls has finally succeeded in isolating poetry and prose from our common speech and our daily word.

So, students are always willing to learn new things *about* literature, but they will hardly ever try to do anything *with* it. By the year's end, they knew all about incremental repetition in Faulkner and in ballads; but they were not prepared to recognize it in their own conversation. The hierarchy between general ideas and specific objects—including the book they held in their hands--was still unsurmounted; and the factory worker and the old lady were, at best, a nice novelty or, at worst, just another professor's whim.

The breaking point came when they were asked to compare their own speech with Faulkner's. All their schooling had trained them to believe that language, history, literature, and culture are never something we create, but are entities existing outside of us, already built and finished, and only waiting for us to learn them, to swallow them whole. So, any analogies the students may have discovered between how they talk and how Faulkner writes may have led them, rather than to a new understanding of themselves, to a depreciation of Faulkner.

They may be right—they *will* be right, as long as the dignity of culture, literature, and art is measured by their distance from our own lives.

The Narrators

The table that follows synthesizes information about the narrators quoted in this book, both in the text and in the notes. For reasons of space, I supply here only the basic information which is necessary to place the speakers in terms of time, place, and essential social and political background.

When a name is given in *italics*, it is a pseudonym. Married women are indicated with the name they used to refer to themselves during the interview, whether it is their own or their husbands' names. Some interviewees chose to offer only their first names; they are listed at the end of the list.

Occupations are listed in chronological order; only those which were held for a significant period of time or are in any way influential in shaping the person's background are given. Retirees are referred to by the occupation at which they spent their working lives. For women, the role and occupation of homemaker is always implicit. When the definition "homemaker" is given, it means that the person has not had other employment for significant periods of time. The husband's occupation is indicated when there are no other indicators of social background.

The place where the interview was recorded is supplemented by information (in parenthesis) about the county, province, or region of smaller towns; place of origin, if other than where the interview was done and is relevant to the context, is given in brackets. When more than one interview date is given, it means that all are quoted.

All the interviews were done by the author, with the following exceptions:

Valentino Paparelli interviewed Gildo Bartoletti, Iole Peri, and Ivano Sabatini.

Marcello Ricci: Vincenza Giontella, and Anna Santini.

Agostino Marcucci: the 1978 interview with Arnaldo Lippi.

Gianfranco Canali: the 1980 interview with Vero Zagaglioni, and the 1981 interview with Bruno Zenoni.
Alfredo Martini: Gaetano Bordoni

Last Name	First Name	Birth	Occupation(s) and Remarks	Place and Date of Interview(s)
Androsciani	Agamante	1902	steelworker; partisan	Terni, 21 June 1982
Antonelli	Antonio	1923	steelworker, building contractor; partisan	Terni, 7 June 1973
Balltrip	Ewell	1950	journalist	Harlan, Kentucky, 14 July 1987
Bandinelli	Ferdinando	1911	farmer, poet	Greve in Chianti (Florence, Tuscany), 1 October 1975
Bartoletti	Gildo	1896	steelworker	Terni, 17 February 1974
Bartolini	Dante	1910	steelworker, farmer; partisan, singer, storyteller	Casteldilago (Terni), about 20 sessions, 1971–1976
Bianchi	*Rocco*	1925	steelworker	Terni, 4 January 1976
Bocale	Leonardo	1924	tailor	Genzano (Rome), 26 January 1975
Bordoni	Gaetano	ca. 1915	barber	Rome, 8 April, 1976
Cadle	Tillman	1902	coal miner; active in UMWA, NMU	Townsend, Tennessee, 15 July 1987
Canali	Calfiero	1916	steelworker	Terni, 4 April 1979; 30 August 1982
Cappanera	Santino	1933	steelworker	Terni, 12 September 1979
Carboni	Sante	1901	steelworker	Terni, 18 October 1982
Castelli	Luigi	1948	steel technician	Terni, 9 January 1981

Last Name	First Name	Birth	Occupation(s) and Remarks	Place and Date of Interview(s)
Chiappini	Poliuto	1911	office worker; Christian Democrat local administrator	Terni, 26 June 1984
Colesanti	Diname	1921	textile worker; homemaker	Terni, 28 February; 4 April, 1980
Colombi	Antonina	1913	textile worker; homemaker	Terni, 26 June 1979
Conti	Mario	1925	steelworker	Terni, 5 November 1979
Cowans	Hugh	1915	coal miner, Baptist preacher; UMWA activist	Lexington, Kentucky, 28 September 1983
Cowans	Julia	1916	homemaker; wife of Rev. Hugh Cowans	Lexington, Kentucky, 28 September 1983
Crimi	Alfredo	1897	farmer	Greve in Chianti (Florence, Tuscany), 1 October 1975
Crostella	Raul	1926	steelworker, office worker	Terni, 14 December, 1983
Crusenberry	Sudie	1930	coal miner's wife and daughter; active in Brookside strike (1970s)	Ages (Harlan County, Kentucky), 23 December 1989
Cuppini	Augusto	1911	steelworker	Terni, 30 December 1980
D'Agostino	Tommaso		construction worker	Rome [Polia, Calabria], 14 March; 4 April 1970
Ducci	Tiberio	ca. 1890	farm worker, butcher; farmworkers' union organizer	Genzano (Rome), 24 April; 29 April; 15 April 1976
Fagioletti	Mario	1920	steelworker	Terni, 8 April 1980
Ferri	Emilio	1917	electric worker, cultural organizer	Terni, 17 September 1980

(continued)

Last Name	First Name	Birth	Occupation(s) and Remarks	Place and Date of Interview(s)
Filipponi	Alfredo	1897	tram-car operator, coal merchant; anti-Fascist activist, partisan	Terni, 6 July 1973
Filipponi	Ambrogio	1930	surveyor; son of Alfredo Filipponi	Terni, 11 May 1979
Filipponi	Mario	1924	steelworker, custodian (no relation to Alfredo Filipponi)	Piediluco (Terni), 3 September 1982
Gabrielli	Mario	1925	steel technician	Terni, 3 June 1980
Gabrielli	Rosanna	1958	student; daughter of Mario Gabrielli	Rome [Terni], 19 April 1980
Gabrielli	Solidea	1929	homemaker; Mario Gabrielli's wife	Terni, 3 June 1980
Galeazzi	Aldo	1910	steelworker	Terni, 10 October 1979
Galeazzi	Lucilla	1950	musician; Aldo Galeazzi's niece	Rome, 6 June 1979
Galli	Laura	1921	homemaker; active in Catholic charities; doctor's wife	Terni, 27 March 1984
Giantulli	Vittorio	1937	steel technician	Terni, 3 May 1983
Giontella	Vincenza	1907	seamstress	Terni, n.d., 1979
Grande	Antonia	ca. 1920	homemaker, wife of a construction worker	Rome [Villa Vallelonga, Abruzzi], 25 January 1970
Hall	James H.	1917	coal miner, UMWA member	Lynch (Harlan County, Kentucky), 8 October 1986.

Last Name	First Name	Birth	Occupation(s) and Remarks	Place and Date of Interview(s)
Horton	Myles	1911	educator, founder of Highland Center for Social Research	New Market, Tennessee, 23 September 1983; 16 July 1987
Innocenti	Nello	1915	farmer, poet	Rome, 10 January 1970
Jones	Johnny	1909	coal miner, UMWA member	Lynch (Harlan County, Kentucky), 8 October 1986
King	Hazel	1919	Air Force auxiliary; anti-strip-mine activist	Louellen (Harlan County, Kentucky), 24 October 1988
Laureti	Giuseppe	1924	artisan	Terni, 16 September 1980
Lefevre	Lloyd	1913	coal miner, UMWA member	Louellen (Harlan County, Kentucky), 19 July 1987
Leuzzi	Bruno	1940	lawyer	Rome, 16 October 1984
Lippa	Antonia	ca. 1920	homemaker, wife of a construction worker	Rome [Villa Vallelonga, Abruzzi], January 1970
Lippi	Arnaldo	1899	steelworker, partisan, Communist city councilman	Terni, 30 December 1979; 5 January 1980; 3 September 1982; 15 November 1978
Locci	Angela	1904	textile worker, mother of Claudio Locci	Piediluco (Terni), 12 June 1981
Locci	Claudio	1924	chemical worker, photographer; son of Angela Locci	Terni, 3 March; 5 June 1981

(continued)

Last Name	First Name	Birth	Occupation(s) and Remarks	Place and Date of Interview(s)
Manconi	Riziero	1894	chemical worker	Terni, 16 July, 1980
Maroli	Veniero	1931	chemical worker	Papigno (Terni), 18 June 1979
Matteucci	Amerigo	1919	construction worker; Communist mayor of Polino (Terni)	Polino (Terni), 14 December 1972
Matteucci	Luigi	1924	farm worker	Polino (Terni), 1 May 1973
Mattioli	Maggiorina	1899	seamstress	Terni, 28 February 1980
Minters	Iverson	1926	musician, also known as "Louisiana Red"	Rome [Vicksburg, Mississippi], 27 December 1988
Montini	Donatella	1959	student	Rome [Terni], 8 May 1980
Orientale	Carlotta	1893	textile worker; ex secretary of Terni Syndicalist Labor Council	Rome [Terni], 20 May 1980
Paganelli	Alfeo	1908	steelworker, musician	Terni, 5 January 1980
Peppoloni	Valtèro	1916	steelworker, street sweeper, janitor	Terni, 25 April 1981
Peri	Iole		textile worker	Terni, 9 January 1974
Petrini	Alberto	1925	chemical and steelworker, union and Communist organizer	Terni, 30 December 1980
Piemonti	Settimio	1903	steelworker	Terni, 7 July 1980
Pileri	Pompilio	1905	farmer, shepherd, musician	Arrone and Polino (Terni), about 20 sessions, 1972–76
Pitotti	Trento	1919	steelworker, shoemaker	Labro (Rieti), Terni, about 20 sessions, 1969–76

Last Name	First Name	Birth	Occupation(s) and Remarks	Place and Date of Interview(s)
Porrazzini	Sandro	1953	student, steelworker	Terni, 21 June and 31 August, 1982
Portelli	Salvatore	1913	civil servant; author's father	Gaeta [Rome], 30 August 1979
Proietti	Francesco	1929	coal miner, steelworker	Spoleto (Perugia), 2 January 1981
Ricci	Giorgio	1951	office worker	Terni, 4 and 9 July 1980
Righetti	Remo	1901	factory worker, anti-Fascist activist, Communist city councilman	Terni, 12 September 1979
Sabatini	Ivano	1928	steelworker	Terni, 26 January 1976
Santini	*Anna*	1929	merchant	Terni, no date, 1979
Sassi	Mario	1906	office worker, musician	Terni, 12 January 1983
Spicer	Debbie	1907	homemaker, coal miner's wife	Louellen (Harlan County, Kentucky), 28 October 1988
Spinetti	Dandolo	1909	farmer; father of Silvano Spinetti	Rome [Genzano (Rome)], 13 April 1970
Spinetti	Silvano	—	farmer; Dandolo's son	Genzano (Rome), 9 March 1970
Sweatt	Tommy	1948	coal miner, Methodist minister, UMWA member	Lynch (Harlan County, Kentucky), 7 October 1986
Tobia	Comunardo	1920	chemical worker; union organizer	Terni, 29 December 1982
Trippa	Elchide	1919	office worker, writer of dialect verse	Terni, 29 February 1980
Turner	Earl	1916	coal miner, mine foreman, UMWA member	Lynch (Harlan County, Kentucky), 5 October 1986

(continued)

Last Name	First Name	Birth	Occupation(s) and Remarks	Place and Date of Interview(s)
Valsenti	Alvaro	1924	steelworker, Communist organizer, local administrator	Terni, 8 September, 18 October 1982
Vecchioni	Alfredo	1919	steelworker; merchant	Terni, 5 January 1979
Vella	Mario	1938	steelworker, appliance salesman; Iginio's brother	Terni, 29 April 1984
Vella	Iginio	1944	steelworker, Mario's brother	Terni, 29 April 1984
Virno	Paolo	1952	journalist; defendant, April 7 Case	Rome, 14 October 1984
Zagaglioni	Vero	1913	chemical and steelworker; partisan	Terni, 21 June 1981; 12 November 1980
Zenoni	Bruno	1908	barber; anti-Fascist activist, partisan, Communist local administrator	Terni, 24 June, 6 July 1980; 24 November 1980
Zocchi	Menotti	1931	chemical worker	Terni, 29 December 1982
——	Maddalena	1924	textile worker	Rome [Terni], 24 March 1984
——	Marcello	1957	unemployed; leader of soccer fan club	Terni, 27 May 1981

Notes

CHAPTER 1

1. Walter Benjamin, "The Image of Proust," *Illuminations*, trans. Harry Zohn (New York: Schocken Books, 1969), 202 [*Illuminationen*, Frankfurt am Main: Suhrkamp, 1961].

2. Hans Magnus Enzensberger, *La breve estate dell'anarchia*, translated by Renato Pedio, (Milano: Feltrinelli, 1978), 11–12 [*Der kurze Sommer der Anarchie*, Frankfurt am Main: Suhrkamp Verlag, 1972].

3. *Il Messaggero*, 18 March 1949.

4. *l'Unità*, 18 March 1949. While the conservative paper *Il Messaggero* mistakes the worker's name, (Alvaro instead of Luigi) the workers' paper mistakes the police commissioner's (it was Pezzolano, not Pessolan.)

5. All quotes from the judicial record and testimony are from a mimeographed copy which was prepared and circulated by the Communist party and is in possession of several members. (The copy I consulted was owned by Valentino Paparelli.)

6. The word "jeep" is spelled in a number of ways in official documents: in this case, it is "Ieeps," within quotes.

7. Some of the leaders testified that they expected no parade and were surprised by the action of the rank-and-file. Union Secretary Arnaldo Menichetti insisted that he cooperated with company officials to keep workers on essential jobs and to prevent a raid on the office building.

8. A pseudonym for a narrator who does not wish to be identified.

9. The speech, made on 2 April 1949, is reprinted in Francesco Bogliari, *Tito Oro Nobili* (Perugia: Quaderni Regione dell'Umbria, 1977), 219–228.

10. *l'Unità* reports two such episodes, on 30 November 1948 and 28 March 1950. Though these episodes were denied by the authorities, both oral sources and other coeval news reports (quoted by *l'Unità*) give confirmation.

11. The *celere* is also seen as symbolic of Italy's changing international allegiances. In his Senate speech, Nobili twice puzzlingly described the action of the jeeps as "almost Anglo-Saxon." He probably alluded to the fact that this vehicle had been introduced by the Allies during their occupation, and was therefore identified with lack of national sovereignty—which the Left felt was threatened now by the North Atlantic Treaty. In fact, Nobili wondered "whether the *celere* is one of our own [i.e., Italian] institutions, or was it organized and forced upon us by the winners" (the Americans).

12. Zocchi coherently moves the scene of Trastulli's death from the factory gates to the Town Hall square, where most of the fighting took place. This is why he has Trastulli climb a window, rather than the factory wall.

13. The concept of "adequate causation" versus "accidental causation" is presented by Max Weber in "Kritische Studien auf dem Gebiet des kulturwissenschaftlichen Logik" (1906), in *Gesammelte Aufsätze zur Wissenschaftslehre* (Tübingen: Moher, 1951); Italian trans., *Il metodo nelle scienze storico-sociali* (Milano: Mondadori, 1974), 207–238.

14. *l'Unità*, 13 February and 20 February, 1948.

15. For a full text and a discussion of this song, see chapter 9.

16. Togliatti was wounded in Rome by a young Christian Democrat sympathizer on 14 July 1948. Massive demonstrations, which in certain areas reached almost an insurrectional point, followed. The Communist party and the unions, however, felt that conditions did not exist for a revolutionary action, and endeavored to calm the rank-and-file. See chapter 6.

17. Carlo Martinelli, letter to the author, February 1979.

CHAPTER 2

1. Ernesto De Martino, "Note di viaggio," *Nuovi Argomenti*, 2 (1953), 47–79; reprinted in Pietro Clemente, Maria Luisa Meoni, and Massimo Squillacciotti, eds., *Il dibattito sul folklore in Italia* (Milano: Edizioni di cultura popolare 1976), 383–408.

2. Gianni Bosio, "Lettera a Giuseppe Morandi," published as a preface to G. Bosio, *L'intellettuale rovesciato* (Milano: Edizioni del Gallo, 1967); new enlarged edition (Milano: Edizioni Bella Ciao, 1975), 183–188.

3. Ernesto De Martino, "Etnologia e cultura nazionale negli ultimi dieci anni," *Società*, vol. IX (1953), 3; reprinted in De Martino, *Mondo popolare e magia in Lucania* (Roma-Matera: Basilicata Editrice 1975), 59.

4. See Benedetto Croce, *Etica e politica*, rev. ed. (Bari: Laterza 1945).

5. See Edward Banfield, *The Moral Basis of a Backward Society* (Glencoe, Ill.: The Free Press, 1958); Frederick Friedmann, "Osservazioni sul mondo contadino dell'Italia meridionale," *Quaderni di sociologia*, II, 3 (1952), 148–161; Robert Redfield, *Peasant Society and Culture* (The University of Chicago Press: 1956); and Tullio Tentori, *Ricerche sociali in Italia: 1945–1965*, (Rome: Edizioni AAAI, 1969). For a criticism of this use of social sciences in the context of southern Italy, see Ernesto De Martino's remarks in a letter to the editor of *La Lapa*, 1953: "Some scholars approach Italian ethnology and folklore without knowing anything about them, infatuated as they are with American-applied anthropology and wishing to transplant it here. I have no faith in their efforts; they are alienated from our national culture, and therefore unable to contribute to making folklore an accepted part of it . . . Let us not forget that . . . we must first of all be rooted in our own ground." (Reprinted in Clemente et al., *Il dibattito sul folklore in Italia*, 300).

6. Croce separates human beings who are part of "history" from those who belong to the "inferior reality" of nature. These are "men only zoologically and not historically; like animals, they are to be dominated. They may be tamed and trained; when this proves impossible, they may be allowed to live on at the fringes of civilization, without being the object of any of those cruelties that must be avoided against any form of life, but being allowed as a race to die out like those [native] American races who shrank and died . . . when a civilization they could not withstand moved on upon them." "L'umanitá e la natura," in B. Croce, *Filosofia e storiografia* (Bari: Laterza, 1949), 246 ff.

7. Among the works of Ernesto De Martino (1908–1965), the most important are *Il mondo magico* (1948), *Morte e pianto rituale nel mondo antico* (1958), *Sud e magia* (1959), and *La terra del rimorso* (1961). Most of these works explore the role of magic and ritual as a protection from what he described as "crisis of presence": the constant threat of just "not being there," of vanishing from reality and history, which he recognized as a force in the daily life and attitudes of the poor peasant South. Some of De Martino's writings which are more concerned with the relevance of folklore in the modern world are in *Furore Simbolo Valore* (1962). Many of his shorter articles, dealing with the political and personal problems involved with his work, are collected in Clemente et al., *Il dibattito sul folklore in Italia*.

8. De Martino, "Intorno a una storia del mondo popolare subalterno," *Società*, vol. V, 3 (September 1949), 411–435; repr. in Clemente et al., ibid., 63–81.

9. De Martino, "Note lucane," *Società*, vol. VI, 4 (1950); repr. in De Martino, *Furore simbolo valore*, (Milano: Feltrinelli, 1980), and Clemente et al., *Il dibattito sul folklore in Italia*, 370–382.

10. All the most important works of Rocco Scotellaro (1923–1953) were published after his death. Among them are: *E' fatto giorno* (1954), *Contadini del Sud* (1954), *L'uva puttanella* (1956), and *Uno si distrae al bivio* (1974). I am indebted for some of the remarks in the following discussion to Vincenzo Padiglione, "Osservatore e osservato: problemi di conoscenza e rappresentazione. La vicenda Scotellaro," *Problemi del socialismo*, vol. XX, 15 (1979), 167–209.

11. Scotellaro, *L'uva puttanella* (Bari:Laterza, 1972), 93.

12. De Martino, "Intorno a una storia del mondo popolare subalterno."

13. Antonio Gramsci, "The Formation of the Intellectuals," *Selections from the Prison Notebooks*, ed. and trans. Quintin Hoare and Geoffrey Nowell Smith (London: Laurence & Wishart, 1971), 5, 16. Among Gramsci's concepts relevant to the study of folklore and working-class culture, though beyond the scope of this discussion, are his idea of "hegemony" (the ability of the ruling class to impose its world view on the whole of society), and his pioneering linking of folklore with class in the "Notes on Folklore" included in his prison witings.

14. Gianni Bosio, "Le esperienze del NCI in rapporto con le attivitá di cultura popolare e di massa del movimento operaio" [1966], in *L'intellettuale rovesciato*, 131. (NCI stands for *Nuovo Canzoniere Italiano*, the radical folk revival organization founded by Roberto Leydi and Gianni Bosio, which originated the folk music revival in Italy.)

15. [Antonello Cuzzaniti and Alessandro Portelli], introduction to *I Giorni Cantati. Cultura operaia e contadina a Roma e nel Lazio*, edited by Circolo Gianni Bosio (Milano: Mazzotta, 1978), 8–9. The *Circolo Gianni Bosio* is an independent organization devoted to research in folk music, oral history, and working-class culture which was established in 1972.

16. Most of the writings of Gianni Bosio (1927–1971) were of an occasional, personal, and provisional nature, and were published in book form after his death. The most important are *Giornale di un organizzatore di cultura* (1962); *L'intellettuale rovesciato* (1975); and *Il trattore ad Acquanegra* (1981).

17. Bosio, "Uomo folklorico / uomo storico," *L'intellettuale rovesciato* (1969), 245–262.

18. Bosio, "Lettera a Giuseppe Morandi," 186.

19. Bosio, "Comunicazioni di classe e cultura di classe," *L'intellettuale rovesciato* (1966), 156.

20. Bosio, "Uomo folklorico/uomo storico," *L'intellettuale rovesciato,* 261–2; "Le esperienze del NCI," 141.

21. I have elaborated at greater length on these ideas in the unsigned editorial "Lavoro culturale e intervento politico. Trasformazioni di un rapporto," *I giorni cantati,* 4 (1983), 9–19, and in the introductory chapter of *Biografia di una città* (Torino: Einaudi, 1985).

CHAPTER 3

1. Beniamino Placido in *La Repubblica,* 3 October 1978.

2. One Italian exception is the *Istituto Ernesto De Martino,* an independent radical research organization based in Milan, which has published "sound archives" on long-playing records since the mid-1960s—without anyone in the cultural establishment noticing: see Franco Coggiola, "L'attivitá dell'Istituto Ernesto de Martino," in Diego Carpitella, ed., *L'etnomusicologia in Italia* (Palermo: Flaccovio, 1975), 265–270.

3. Luisa Passerini, "Sull'utilità e il danno delle fonti orali per la storia," introduction to Passerini, ed., *Storia Orale. Vita quotidiana e cultura materiale delle classi subalterne* (Torino: Rosenberg & Sellier, 1978), discusses the relationship of oral history and social history.

4. On musical notation as reproduction of speech sounds, see Giovanna Marini, "Musica popolare e parlato popolare urbano," in *Circolo Gianni Bosio,* ed., *I giorni cantati* (Milano: Mazzotta, 1978), 33–34. Alan Lomax, *Folk Song Styles and Culture,* (Washington, D.C.: American Association for the Advancement of Sciences, 1968), Publication n. 88, discusses electronic representation of vocal styles.

5. See William Labov, "The Logic of Non-Standard English," in Louis Kampf and Paul Lauter, eds., *The Politics of Literature* (New York: Random House, 1970), 194–244 on the expressive qualities of non-standard speech.

6. In this article, I use these terms as defined and used by Gérard Genette, *Figures III* (Paris: Seuil, 1972).

7. On genre distinctions in folk and oral narrative, see Dan Ben-Amos, "Categories analytiques et genres populaires," *Poétique,* 19 (1974), 268–93; and Jan Vansina, *Oral Tradition* (Harmondsworth, Middlesex, U.K.: Penguin Books, 1973 [1961]).

8. For instance, Gaetano Bordoni, Communist activist from Rome, talked about family and community mainly in dialect, but shifted briefly to a more standardized form of Italian whenever he wanted to reaffirm his allegiance to the party. The shift showed that, although he accepted the party's decisions, they remained other than his direct experience. His recurring idiom was, "There's nothing you can do about it." See *Circolo Gianni Bosio, I giorni cantati*, 58–66.

9. On fabula and plot see Boris Tomaševskij, "Sjužetnoe postroenie," in *Teorija literatury. Poetika* (Moscow-Leningrad: 1928); Italian transl., "La costruzione dell'intreccio," in Tzvetan Todorov, ed., *I formalisti russi* (Torino: Einaudi, 1968); published as *Théorie de la littérature* (Paris: Seuil, 1965).

10. These stories are discussed in chapters 1 and 6 in this book.

11. Roman Jakobson and Piotr Bogatyrev, "Le folklore forme spécifique de création," in R. Jakobson, *Questions de poétique* (Paris: Seuil, 1973), 59–72.

CHAPTER 4

1. See Alfredo Filipponi's story discussed in chapter 6.

2. The mnemonic functions of meter and formula are described in Eric C. Havelock, *Preface to Plato* (Cambridge, Mass.: Harvard University Press, 1960); and Albert Lord, *The Singer of Tales* (Cambridge, Mass.: Harvard University Press, 1963).

3. Claude Lévi-Strauss, "How Myths Die," *Structural Anthropology*, vol. II, transl. Monique Layton (London: Allen Lane, 1977), 256–268; *Anthropologie structurale deux* (Paris: Plon, 1963); Vladimir Ja. Propp, "Transformacija vol' šebnych skazok," *Poetika* (Leningrad, 1928); in Tzvetan Todorov, *Théorie de la prose* (Paris: Seuil, 1965).

4. Jurij M. Lotman and Boris A. Uspenskij, "O semioticeskom mechanizme kul'tury" (1971), Italian transl. in Lotman and Uspenskij, *Tipologia della cultura* (Firenze: Bompiani, 1975).

5. See Gérard Genette, *Figures III. Le discours du récit* (Paris: Seuil 1972).

6. Alberto Asor Rosa, "Tempo e nuovo nell'avanguardia, ovvero: l'infinita manipolazione del tempo" in Ruggiero Romano, ed., *Le frontiere del tempo* (Milano: Il Saggiatore, 1981), 78–79.

7. Edith Wharton, "The Lady's Maid's Bell," in *The Collected Short Stories of Edith Wharton*, R. W. B. Lewis, ed. (New York: Charles Scribner's Sons, 1954), 457.

8. Nuto Revelli, *Il mondo dei vinti* (Torino: Einaudi, 1977), 47.

9. William Faulkner, *Absalom, Absalom!* (New York: Vintage Books, 1986), 95.

10. Asor Rosa, "Tempo e nuovo nell'avanguardia," 79.

11. John K. Galbraith, "Intorno al disastro con folle ottimismo," *La Repubblica*, 6 October 1979.

12. Ray Bradbury, *Fahrenheit 451* (New York: Ballantine Books, 1953), 64.

13. On communal "censorship," see Roman Jakobson and Piotr Bogatyrev, "Le folklore, forme spécifique de création," in R. Jakobson, *Questions de poétique* (Paris: Seuil, 1973), 59–72.

14. Jack Goody, *The Domestication of the Savage Mind* (Cambridge, U.K.: Cambridge University Press, 1977), 13–14.

15. Jack Goody and Ian Watt, "The Consequences of Literacy," in J. Goody, ed., *Literacy in Traditional Societies* (Cambridge, U.K.: Cambridge University Press, 1968), 28–68.

16. Asor Rosa, "Tempo e nuovo nell'avanguardia," 93. An eloquent variant on the "my-life-is-a-novel" motif is a character in Aurora Levins Morales and Rosario Morales, *Getting Home Alive* (Ithaca, New York: Firebrand Press, 1986), 169, who claims "Mi vida es como una novela"—that is, like the modern variant of the popular novel and the folktale, the televised soap opera. What makes this analogy interesting is that, unlike the novel but like the life story, the soap opera is open-ended, theoretically endless, and endlessly repetitive.

CHAPTER 5

1. Roman Jakobson and Morris Halle, *Fundamentals of Language* (Den Haag: Mouton, 1956), 17; Roland Barthes, *Elements of Semiology*, in *Writing Degree Zero and Elements of Semiology*, transl. Annette Lavers and Colin Smith, London: Jonathan Cape, 1964, 118–120. [*Eléments de sémiologie* (Paris: Seuil, 1964)].

2. Giovanna Marini, booklet accompanying the record *La Valnerina Ternana. Un'esperanza di ricerca-intervento*, Valentino Paparelli and Alessandro Portelli, ed. (Milano: Dischi del Sole DS 532–34).

3. Francesco Giannattasio, *L'organetto. Uno strumento contadino dell'era industriale* (Rome: Bulzoni, 1979); Marini, notes to the record *La Valnerina Ternana*.

4. The analysis which follows is much indebted to conversations with Giorgio Cardona, professor of Linguistics at the University of Rome, who also helped me formulate my ideas in less impressionistic terms. While the responsibility remains my own, what follows is a token of the friendship and support of a distinguished scholar and wonderful teacher, whose sudden death in the very days in which I was revising this essay was a signal loss to all those who believe that progressive democracy and advanced standards of learning are mutually necessary.

5. Oscar Maurizi, "Per la proprietá del dire," *Gioventù ternana*, January 1943.

6. Which does not exclude, of course, the occurrence of "correct" forms: in our case, for instance, *lamentare* and *quante* (lines 4 and 7). It may be coincidental, but is probably symptomatic, that these "correct" usages contain the /nt/ cluster, and have the same form of the "hypercorrect" ones. There are no occurrences, in this text, of "correct" nasal + voiced stop [e.g., *nd*] clusters.

7. Luciano Canepari, *Introduzione alla fonetica* [Torino: Einaudi, 1979], 13.

8. For a general analysis of this process, see Bruno Morandi, "La carriera, una divinità in declino," *il Manifesto*, 7 January 1982; id., "Partiti, partiti operai, gruppi della nuova sinistra, sindacato," *il Manifesto*, 8 May 1980.

9. Richard Hoggart, *The Uses of Literacy* (Harmondsworth, Middlesex, U.K.: Pelican Books, 1973 [1957]), 149.

10. Luisa Muraro, *L'infamia originaria* (Milano: L'erba voglio, 1977), 89 "When proletarians occupy a house and then furnish it with colonial-style furniture and crystal chandeliers, are they obeying an other-determined bourgeois 'need' or 'necessity,' or expressing—in a distorted, deviated, [and] imaginary form, a right to and an interest in sensuality and aesthetic pleasure?"

11. Marshall Berman, *All That Is Solid Melts Into Air. The Experience of Modernity* (London: Verso, 1983; New York: Simon and Schuster, 1982), 189, describing St. Petersburg in Russia.

12. This interview with an unidentified steelworker from Villaggio Matteotti is one of several published, along with an account of the planning and settling of the new village, in the architecture magazine *Casabella*, 421 (January 1977), 11–35.

CHAPTER 6

1. The two definitions of "uchronia" quoted in the text are from Pierre Versins, comments in Jean Tortel, ed., *Entretiens sur la paralittérature* (Paris: Plon, 1970), 275, and *Collettivo Un'Ambigua Utopia, Nei Labirinti della Fantascienza* (Milano: Feltrinelli, 1979), 75. Among the many science-fiction novels based on uchronia are Philip K. Dick's *The Man in the High Castle*, Norman Spinrad's *The Iron Dream*, both of which describe an alternative history created by a Nazi victory in World War II; and Keith Robert's *Pavane*, in which the Spanish Armada defeats Queen Elizabeth's England.

2. Alfredo Filipponi was born in 1897 at Ferentillo, a village in the Nera river valley of Valnerina, ten miles from Terni. The interview was recorded at his house in Terni, 7 June 1973. Cfr. Alessandro Portelli, "'Gramsci evase con me dal carcere, ci nascondemmo per sei mesi sui monti. . . . ' Tutti i paradossi della 'storia orale,'" *il Manifesto*, 5 November 1979; *Collettivo di ricerca del Circolo Gianni Bosio*, "Osservazioni del folklore su Gramsci," *I Giorni Cantati*, 1 (1981), 32–45.

3. National Archives of the Communist party, Rome, 1945–48, folder 142.

4. The Subiaco story was communicated by Mirella Serri at a 1978 seminar of the *Instituto Storico Romano della Resistenza*. The San Lorenzo episode is a personal communication from Lidia Piccioni and Alfredo Martini, based on their own field work in the 1970's. The episode from Calabria is in Renzo Del Carria, *Proletari senza rivoluzione* (Milano: Edizioni Oriente, 1970), II, 337, note 214.

5. Dandolo Spinetti, a Communist small farmer and traditional singer from Genzano near Rome, believed that *The Internationale* and *La Marseillaise* were written by Karl Marx: *The Marzeillaise* [sic], you see, was called this way because it was made by Marz [sic] at Marseilles": Alessandro Portelli, "La storia non lo vedi marcia verso la libertà," in *Circolo Gianni Bosio, I Giorni Cantati, Cultura operaia e contadina a Roma e nel Lazio* (Milano: Mazzotta, 1980), 150.

6. These verses can be heard in the record *La Valnerina ternana. Un'esperienza di ricerca/intervento*, Valentino Paparelli and Alessandro Portelli, ed., Dischi del Sole DS 523/34.

7. Frederick Douglass, *Narrative of the Life of Frederick Douglass* (Cambridge: Harvard University Press, 1967), 43.

8. Russel Kirk, *The Conservative Mind* (Fabee and Faber, 1954), 18.

9. Claudio Pavone, "Un Togliatti mal trattato," *Indice*, II, 1 (January-February 1985), 13–14.

10. Enrico Berlinguer, interviewed in *Stern*, 34 (August, 1979).

11. Raffaele Rossi, "La storia dell'ultimo trentennio in Umbria. Gli anni difficili. 1947–1953," *Cronache Umbre* [Perugia], II, 1 (January 1977), 63–76.

12. The reorganization which followed the layoffs was much less "deep" than Rossi seems to believe. Franco Bonelli, a competent and impartial historian, says that "the company was unable to seize the opportunity granted by the mass layoffs and the long period of union inactivity which followed in order to create a new company identity." *Lo sviluppo di una grande impresa in Italia. La Terni dal 1884 al 1962*, (Torino: Einaudi, 1975), 288. The all-party committee (which included even the Fascists) achieved very little: at least some of the political parties that were in it were the same that had consented to the layoffs.

13. *Rinascita*, 6 January 1978.

14. The typical example is Renzo Del Carria's *Proletari senza rivoluzione*, volume 1, page 21. This book, which was very popular in the late 1960's, claims that "the absence of revolutionary intellectuals is, in the last analysis, the cause of the missing Italian revolution." The eminent American radical historian Jeremy Brecher also writes, "far from fomenting strikes and rebellions, unions and labor leaders have most often striven to prevent or contain them, while the drive to extend them has generally come from a most undocile 'rank and file.'" [*Strike*, (San Francisco: Straight Arrow Books, 1972)] The unsolved problem is why the revolutionary rank-and-file always manages to generate reformist or sell-out leadership.

15. The two myths are told respectively in Leslie Marmon Silko, *Ceremony* (New York: Viking, 1977), 139–145; and *The Autobiography of Malcolm X*, with the assistance of Alex Haley (Harmondsworth, Middlesex, U.K.: Penguin Books, 1968), 258 ff.

16. Paola Ludovici, "Narrativa indiana contemporanea," in Elemire Zolla, ed., *I contemporanei. Novecento americano* (Rome: Lucarini, 1981), 663–694.

17. Matt Witt, "God's Country," *In Our Blood. Four Coal Mining Families* (Washington, D.C.: Highlander Research and Education Center, 1979), 76.

CHAPTER 7

1. When my book *Biografia di una città*, an oral history of Terni, was first publicly presented in town, a former mayor of Terni, Ezio Ottaviani,

listed Valsenti's fruit-stealing story as one of the passages with which he could most readily identify.

2. Herbert G. Gutman, *Work, Culture and Society in Industrializing America 1815–1919* (New York: Knopf, 1976).

3. Ralph Ellison, *Invisible Man* (Harmondsworth, Middlesex, U.K.: Penguin Books, 1965 [1952]), 94, 98. On *Beruf*, Max Weber's classic description is in *Die protestantische Ethik und der Geist des Kapitalismus*, in *Gesammelte Aufsätze sur Religionssoziologie* (Tübingen: I. C. B. Mohr, 1922), especially chapter 3.

4. Benjamin Franklin, "Agli operai," *L'Unione Liberale* [Terni], 28 August 1881.

CHAPTER 8

1. See the announcement in *Acciaio* (magazine of the Terni Fascist Federation), 13 March 1937; 25 November 1939.

2. *l'Unità* (all references in this chapter come from the Terni edition), 21 October 1948; 14 July 1948; 14 October 1948; Società Terni, *Dopolavoro. Assistenza di fabbrica. Assistenza sanitaria* (Terni: Stabilimento Anterocca, 1937), 131–33.

3. *l'Unità*, 5 August 1946.

4. On *Dopolavoro*, see Victoria De Grazia, *The Culture of Consent: mass organization of leisure in fascist Italy* (Cambridge, U.K.: Cambridge University Press, 1981).

5. *l'Unità*, 15 August 1948. Ironically, Terni was named *città dinamica* ("the dynamic city") by Benito Mussolini in a 1923 speech. The label was later used by all political denominations.

6. Umberto Eco, "La chiacchiera sportiva," *Il costume di casa* (Milano: Bompiani, 1973), 240.

7. The symbolism implicit in the rivalry of the two cycling stars is described in Stefano Pivato, *Sia lodato Bartali. Ideologia, cultura e miti dello sport cattolico (1936–1948)* (Roma: Edizioni Lavoro, 1985); and Giorgio Casadio and Luigi Manconi, eds., *Un uomo solo. Vita e opere di Fausto Coppi* (Milano: Piulibri, 1979).

8. Alberto Provantini, *Quei novemila giorni* (Terni: Edizioni Thyrus, 1984), 19.

9. Maurice Cloes, *Un benemerito industriale da Liegi a Terni. Cassian Bon* (Rome: privately printed, 1982).

10. Alberto Bellavigna, *La Ternana dal '900 al 2000* (Terni: Alterocca, 1967), 32.

11. Christopher Lasch, *The Culture of Narcissism* (New York: W. W. Norton & Co., 1979), chapter V; Thorsten Veblen, *The Theory of the Leisure Class* (New York: New American Library, 1953), chapters 8 and 9.

12. Mario Andrea Bartolini, foreword to Renzo Tomassini, *Borzacchini. L'uomo, il pilota, il suo tempo* (Terni: Cestres, 1983).

13. On this episode, see Enzo Caffarelli, *Una moto per Liberati* (Terni: Arti Grafiche Nobili, 1978), 22.

14. *Il Messaggero*, 4 May 1925.

15. *Il Messaggero*, 26 March 1926.

16. Societá Terni, *Dopolavoro. Assistenza di fabbrica*, 49.

17. Eugene D. Genovese develops this concept in *Roll, Jordan, Roll. The World the Slaves Made* (New York: Pantheon Books, 1974), 146–47.

18. For Borzacchini's baptism, see Tomassini, *Borzacchini. L'uomo, il pilota, il suo tempo;* on the use of his name for the soccer team, cfr. Bellavigna, *La Ternana dal '900 al 2000.*

19. The story was told by Augusto Cuppini. Monsignor Boccoleri, popular and controversial Bishop of Terni in the 1920s, did break a chair on someone's head (or threatened to do so), but on a wholly different occasion: it was when the Fascists attempted to take over the Catholic Church's youth organization in the early 1930s.

20. *l'Unità*, 15 August 1948.

21. Provantini, *Quei novemila giorni*, 19.

22. Quoted in Caffarelli, *Una moto per Liberati*, 39.

23. *Il Messaggero* [Terni edition], 25 January 1983. In 1988, when it seemed that the soccer team might go bankrupt, the parallel with the town's difficult economic situation was standard fare in all newspaper reports.

24. On the parallelism of proverbs, see Alberto Sobrero, "Problemi di ricostruzione della mentalità subalterna: letteratura e circolazione culturale alla fine dell '800," *Studi antropologici italiani e rapporti di classe*, a collection of essays by several authors (Milano: Franco Angeli, 1980).

25. "The Collier Lad," by Johnny Handle, on the long playing record *Along the Coaly Tyne* (London: Topic 12T189).

26. I have developed this point within a broader theoretical and historical framework in "Culture popolari e culture di massa," in Giovanni De Luna, et.al., eds., *Il mondo contemporaneo—Gli strumenti della ricerca 2—Questioni di metodo* (Firenze: La Nuova Italia, 1983), 1470–1490.

27. Antonio Gramsci, "Notes on Folklore," *Selections from the Prison Notebooks* (London: Laurence & Wishart, 1971).

CHAPTER 9

1. Amerigo Matteucci's version can be heard on the record *La Valnerina Ternana*, Valentino Paparelli and Alessandro Portelli, ed. (Milano: Dischi del Sole DS 432/34). Loreta Lippa, Antonia Grande, and Tommaso D'Agostino can be heard performing the songs described in this essay on the record *Roma. La borgata e la lotta per la casa*, Alessandro Portelli ed. (Milano: Dischi del Sole SdL/AS 10).

2. Costantino Nigra, *Canti popolari del Piemonte* (Torino: Einaudi, 1974 [1888]).

3. A religious song found near Terni describes the suffering of Christ on the cross by listing iteratively each part of his body, including the less noble ones, one for each verse. Though there may be no direct relationship with the Spadoni verses, the formal archetype is the same. The graffiti about Spadoni are described in Giampaolo Gallo, *Illustrissmo Signor Direttore. Grande Industria e Società a Terni fra Otto e Novecento* (Foligno: Editoriale Umbra, 1983), 189.

4. A field recording of a brass-band version of the *Inno dei Lavoratori* is in the album *Avanti popolo alla riscossa. Antologia della canzone socialista in Italia* (Milano: Dischi del Sole DS, 158/60 CL).

5. National Archives of the Italian Communist party, 1917–1940, folder 496.

6. Torquato Secci, "Il popolo racconta la serrata," *Indagini* [Terni], 5 (September 1979), 37–40.

7. Roman Jakobson and Piotr Bogatyrev, "Le folklore, forme spécifique de création," in R. Jakobson, *Questions de poétique* (Paris: Seuil, 1976), 59–72.

8. "La nostra società l'è la filanda," sung by Palmira Facchetti from Cologno al Serio (Bergamo, Lombardy), is on the record *Canti del Lavoro—2* (Milano: Dischi del Sole DS 4); on the song of the Centurini workers and its background, see Maria Rosaria Porcaro, "Una lettera, una canzone, una

storia," a supplement to *La storia dell'Umbria dal risorgimento alla liberazione* [Perugia], vol. III (June 1980); on the music and stories of the Tecnedile construction workers, see Alessandro Portelli, "Sempre si canta, pure sul cantiere. La lotta alla Tecnedile," *Il Nuovo Canzoniere Italiano*, III series, 2 (December 1975), 21–27.

9. *La canzone delle Reggiane*, as sung by the Caprara family from Milan, is on the record *I Caprara. Fra città e campagna* (Milano: Dischi del Sole DS 523/25).

10. Maria Goia, "La processione della miseria," *La Turbina* [Terni Socialist paper], 21 January 1905. Valentino Paparelli recorded the song on the joys of Centurini from Adelia Grimani in Collestatte near Terni in 1976.

11. Raffaele Offidani, "Autobiografia di Spartacus Picenus," *Il Nuovo Canzoniere Italiano*, 3 (September 1963), 34–45. Prampolini's song on the air of *Funiculì Funiculà* is on the record *Avanti popolo alla riscossa* (see note 4).

12. *Milano. Lotta operaia alla Crouzet*, Franco Coggiola, ed. (Milano: Dischi del Sole SdL/AS/11). Dante Bartolini's ballad *Il traditore Tanturi* is in *La Sabina*, Alessandro Portelli, ed. (Milano: Dischi del Sole 517/19).

13. *l'Unità*, 23 December 1948; Roberto Sangiuliano, *Quando Roma cantava*, (Roma: Nuova Editrice Spada, 1986), 70–71.

14. *Gruppo Operaio di Pomigliano d'Arco*, "A Flobert," *Tamurriata dell' Alfa Sud* (Milano: Dischi del Sole DS 1072/74). The songs by Della Mae Graham and Woody Guthrie can both be found in Alan Lomax, Woody Guthrie, and Pete Seeger, eds., *Hard-Hitting Songs for Hard-Hit People* (New York: Oak Publications, 1967), 218; 290, and the two British miners' songs are in A. L. Lloyd, *Come All Ye Bold Miners* (London: Lawrence and Wishart, 1918), 186, 290.

15. *Bergamo Redona. Filati Lastex alla riscossa*, Mimmo Boninelli and Franco Coggiola, eds. with the Filati Lastex Factory Council (Milano: Dischi del Sole SdL/AS 12).

16. George Lipsitz, *Class and Culture in Cold War America: "A Rainbow at Midnight"* (South Hadley, Mass.: J. F. Bergin Publishers, 1982), chapter 10; Portelli, "Bruce Springsteen: Working-Class Hero?", *I Giorni Cantati*, III series, n. O (September 1986), 5–11; and Marino Severini, "La banda dei paperi. Autobiografia di un musicista e di un gruppo rock (The Gang)," ibid., 11–16.

17. Both variants of "The Ballad of Harry Simms" are reported in Jim Garland, *Welcome the Traveler Home*, Julia S. Ardery, ed. (Lexington: University Press of Kentucky, 1983), 169–71.

CHAPTER 10

1. United States Congress, Senate, *Violations of Free Speech and Rights of Labor,* Hearings before a Subcommittee of the Committee on Education and Labor—United States Senate, 75th Congress, First Session. Pursuant to Senate Resolution 266 (74th Congress). Hearings conducted at Harlan, Ky., and Washington, D.C., in April 1936 and April-May, 1937. Hereafter, referred to as *Violations.*

2. Coal camps and company towns have been described in a number of sources. For an analysis in terms of power relationships, which has been kept in mind in drafting the present paper, see John Gaventa, *Power and Powerlessness. Quiescence and Rebellion in an Appalachian Valley* (Urbana: University of Illinois Press, 1980), 85–96. For the situation in Harlan County, see U.S. Congress, Senate, *Conditions in Coal Fields in Harlan and Bell Counties,* Hearings before a Subcommittee of the Committee on Manufactures, Senate Resolution 178 (72 Congress). First session (1932).

3. See the testimony of Marshall A. Musick, *Violations,* 3452 ff., and 3809 ff.; Robert E. Lawson, *Violations,* 3833.

4. George J. Titler, *Hell in Harlan* (Beckley, West Virginia, B. J. Printers, no date [probably 1972]), 48–49.

5. UMWA organizer James A. Westmoreland testified to the La Follette Committee that, since Lynch was crossed by a public highway, the company could not keep the organizers out, but had them openly followed in order to intimidate any employees who wished to approach them (*Violations,* 3824 ff.). See also Garland, *Welcome the Traveler Home. Jim Garland's Story of the Kentucky Mountains,* Julia S. Ardery, ed. (Lexington: University Press of Kentucky, 1983), 135.

6. George Davis, *Harlan County Blues,* in the long-playing record *When Kentucky Had No Union Men* (New York: Folkways Records FA 2343).

7. *Violations,* 3833 ff.

8. *Violations,* 3495 (testimony of B. H. Moses); 3809 (M. A. Musick); 3612 (C. E. Vogel).

9. *Twenty Tons,* text by Samuel Boggs, music by Gene Brooks, published in the *United Mine Workers Journal,* 15 March 1957. The song (partly based on Merle Travis' *Sixteen Tons*) had been composed earlier.

10. Field Secretary Lawrence Dwyer describes Smith's beating in a letter to Labor Secretary Frances J. Perkins, 16 November 1934 (UMWA Correspondence Files, Washington, District 19–1934 box—Harlan folder). Musick's conversation with Middleton is reported in Musick's testimony,

Violations, 3809. On Bennett Musick's death, see his mother Mallie Musick's testimony, *Violations,* 4237 ff.

11. Frederick Douglass, *Narrative of the Life of Frederick Douglass* (Cambridge: Harvard University Press, 1967), 43.

12. John W. Hevener, *Which Side Are You On?* (Urbana: University of Illinois Press, 1978), 19.

13. *Violations,* 3809.

14. *Violations,* 4449, 4487, and 4498.

15. On the building of the Terni sports arena and the surrounding controversy, see chapter 8. The quote is from Terni steelworker Augusto Cuppini.

16. *Violations,* 3824.

17. *Violations,* 3847–3859.

18. *United Mine Workers Journal,* 1 November 1949; 12 January 1950; and 15 July 1951.

19. Gaventa, *Power and Powerlessness,* 174. See also Ben A. Franklin, "The Scandal of Death and Injury in the Mines," *The New York Times,* 30 March 1969; reprinted in David S. Walls and John B. Stephenson, eds., *Appalachia in the Sixties* (Lexington: The University Press of Kentucky, 1972), 92–108.

20. *United Mine Workers Journal,* 15 January, 15 September, 1 October

21. *United Mine Workers Journal,* 15 January, 1 March, and 15 May 1949.

22. *United Mine Workers Journal,* 15 January 1950.

23. *United Mine Workers Journal,* 15 November 1948.

24. It is told by Thomas R. Bethell, "Conspiracy in Coal," *The Washington Monthly,* March 1969, reprinted in Walls and Stephenson, eds., *Appalachia in the Sixties,* 76–91; and in Curtis Selzer, *Fire in the Hole—Workers and Management in the American Coal Industry,* (Lexington, Ky.: University Press of Kentucky, 1985), 61–70.

25. Gaventa, *Power and Powerlessness,* chapter 7, "Power within the Organization. Reformism and Anti-Reformism in the United Mine Workers of America," 164–201.

26. Titler, *Hell in Harlan,* 219.

CHAPTER 11

1. David Alan Corbin, *Life, Work and Rebellion in the Coal Fields* (Urbana: University of Illinois Press, 1981), 195–224; and Fred Mooney, *Struggle in the Coal Fields*, J. W. Hess ed. (Morgantown: West Virginia University Library, 1967). Neither source explicitly mentions the use of the flag. In Denise Giardina's novel, *Storming Heaven* (New York: Random House, 1987), the author finds it natural to depict the marchers carrying the flag. Mary "Mother" Jones, who was one of the leaders in the march, appears alongside of American flags in several photographs, including those of her famous "mill children's march"; she is likely to have had a flag in Logan as well.

2. "Report of Governor Laffoon's Investigation Commission," copy in Berea College Appalachian Archives under Coal Mining, UMW, and Harlan Struggle.

3. Bill Bishop, "1931: The Battle of Evarts," *Southern Exposure*, vol. IV, No. 1–2 (1976), 91–101, on which I rely for most of the reconstruction of the episode in Evarts. See also Tony Bubka, "The Harlan County Coal Strike of 1931," *Labor History*, vol 11, n. 1, (Winter, 1970), 41–57.

4. *Join the CIO* (originally *Join the NMU*), in Aunt Molly Jackson, *Library of Congress Recordings*, Alan Lomax, collector (Somerville, Mass.: Rounder Records 1002). See also John Greenway, *American Folksongs of Protest* (New York: Octagon Books 1977), 269–70, for a slightly different version.

5. On the "discovery" of Appalachia an ample bibliography exists. See, among others David Whisnant, *All that Is Native and Fine* (Chapel Hill: University of North Carolina Press, 1983); Jack E. Weller, *Yesterday's People: Life in Contemporary Appalachia* (Lexington: University of Kentucky Press, 1966); Michael Harrington, *The Other America (Poverty in the United States)* (Baltimore: Penguin, 1963); and Henry D. Shapiro, *Appalachia on Our Minds* (Chapel Hill: University of North Carolina Press, 1978).

6. Thomas R. Ford, "The Passing of Provincialism," in *The Southern Appalachian Region. A Survey* (Lexington: University Press of Kentucky, 1966), 9–34.

7. T. N. Bethell, introduction to Jim Garland, *Welcome the Traveler Home*, Julia S. Ardery, ed. (Lexington: University Press of Kentucky, 1983) x.

8. Walter B. Smith, letter to Arthur Garfield Hays, 16 April 1932, in Herndon J. Evans Papers, University of Kentucky, Margaret E. King Library, Special Collections, box 1, folder 6 (hereafter, Evans Papers).

9. Joe Green, "Poverty Back of Mining Turmoil," *New York Times*, 9 May 1932.

10. Ed Price, "More than Our Share of Heroes," *Now and Then*, published by the Center for Appalachian Studies and Services/Institute for Appalachian Affairs of East Tennessee University, Johnson City, vol. 4, no. 3 (Fall 1987). According to official sources quoted by Price, "Soldiers from Appalachia were most likely to die in Vietnam . . . Appalachian soldiers suffered more trauma-related combat stress disorders than soldiers from other regions of the United States." See also Richard G. Stone, *Kentucky Fighting Men* (Lexington: University Press of Kentucky, 1982. For coeval comments, see *The New York Times*, 28 September 1931; and Bruce Crawford, "'What Have We to Lose?' The Story of Harlan, Kentucky," *Labor Age*, December 1981, 7–8.

11. John Dos Passos, "The Free Speech Speakin's" in Theodore Dreiser, *Harlan Miners Speak* (New York: Da Capo Press, 1970), 295–6; Garland, *Welcome the Traveler Home*, 174. Findlay Donaldson's speech and Mary Nick's song are in Evans Papers, box 4. All subsequent quotes from Donaldson's speech come from this source.

12. Louis Stark, "In the Blighted Realm of the Miners," *New York Times Magazine*, 11 October, 1931.

13. Charles R. Walker, "'Red' Blood in Kentucky. Why 100%-Americans Turn Communist," *Forum*, January 1932, 18–23.

14. John Greenway wrote, after he interviewed Aunt Molly Jackson in the early 1950s, "Crippled now and nearly destitute, [she] fears that such thoughtless accusation [of having been a Red] will jeopardize her precarious living." While not hesitating to claim authorship of Jim Garland's *The Death of Harry Simms*, she claimed that some of its most radical lines had "taken on" a "palpable Communist ideology" through "transmission and alteration." (*American Folksongs of Protest*, 260–61).

15. *I Hate the Company Bosses* is on Sara Ogan's record *A Girl of Constant Sorrow* (Sharon, Conn.: Folk Legacy FSA 26 [1965]); she sings *I Hate the Capitalist System* on *The Silver Dagger* (Somerville, Mass.: Rounder 0051); and again in the videotape, *Always Sing My Songs*, Guy and Candie Carawan, eds. (New Market, Tenn.: Highlander Center for Social Research, 1983). Jim Garland includes both endings of his song in *Welcome the Traveler Home*, 169–71.

16. *Bloody Harlan. The Story of Four Miners Serving Life for Daring to Organize a Union—Daring to Strike—Daring to Picket*, published by the Kentucky Miners Defense, 1938. The prosecution brought up the same point against another defendant, Al Benson, a former assistant police chief.

17. "Additional Instructions to Bell County Grand Jury by Judge D. C. Jones, Judge of the Bell County Circuit Court," 9 November 1931, in Evans Papers, box 1, folder 1. On Dreiser's trip to Pineville, besides his own findings in *Harlan Miners Speak*, see Herndon J. Evans, "Two Roads to Harlan," in Evans Papers, box 3, folder 24. Dreiser was framed in an adultery charge (he apparently spent the night in his hotel room in Pineville, Bell County with his secretary, and Evans was instrumental in proving the fact), and later roughly evicted from Bell County.

18. On W. B. Jones, see Bishop, "1931: The Battle of Evarts." Ronald Niebuhr, "Religion and the Class War in Kentucky," *The Christian Century*, 18 May 1932, 637–9, quotes the miner on "criminal syndicalism."

19. Greenway, *American Folksongs of Protest*, 261–2

20. John Gaventa, *Power and Powerlessness. Quiescence and Rebellion in an Appalachian Valley*, (Urbana: University of Illinois Press, 1980), 113 (I have kept Gaventa's book constantly in mind in composing this article) and Garland, *Welcome the Traveler Home*, 152.

21. Smith, quoted in Gaventa, 110; Jones, "Additional Instructions," cit.

22. Evans Papers, box 4, folder 27 (all subsequent quotes from Meeks are from this source); Gertrude Haessler, "In Blue-Blood Kentucky," *Labor Defender*, April 1932, 69 ff.; Sara Ogan, *Always Sing My Songs*; Walker, "'Red' Blood in Kentucky"; and *New York Times* 29 Sept. 1931.

23. While radical journalists continued to describe the miners as "100-percent Americans" (besides Walker's article quoted above, see also Vern Smith, "These Starving 100%-Americans," *Labor Defender*, September 1931, 170), a "100-percent American" sent a note to a Federated Press correspondent ordering her to "leave town by sundown" (Louis Stark, "Harlan War Traced to Pay-Cut Revolt," *New York Times*, 29 September 1931). K. McGuire, president of the Harlan County Coal Operators Associations, signed a May 1932 letter to the Louisville *Courier-Journal* as "A Believer in America" and asked them not to use his name "since many people know that I was one of the most sinister coal operators in Eastern Kentucky" (Evans papers, box 1, folder 7). On Herndon J. Evans's role, especially in the Dreiser case, and on the proposed investigation of New York by Bell County citizens, see Evans papers, box 1, folder 1. The "Kaiser" epithet is mentioned by Stark in "Harlan War."

24. Quoted in Niebuhr, "Religion and the Class War."

25. Ibid.

26. Garland, *Welcome the Traveler Home*, 81–84, 185; and Tess Huff, "Coal War in Kentucky," *Labor Age*, June 1931, 9–11. The active role of

preachers in the union was part of the UMWA tradition in the area. The first UMWA secretary in Harlan County in 1918–19 was a preacher named Frank Keller, and the UMWA drive in the late 1930s was spearheaded by a group of four preachers: George J. Titler, *Hell in Harlan* (Beckley, W. Va.: BJ Printers, no date [probably 1972]), 140.

27. Evans papers, box 1, folder 8; U.S. Congress, Senate, *Violations of Free Speech and Rights of Labor*, Hearings before a Subcommittee of the Committee on Education and Labor, Harlan, Ky., and Washington, D.C., April 1936 and April-May, 1937. Part 10, p. 3612; and Titler, *Hell in Harlan*, 94.

28. George Korson, *Coal Dust on the Fiddle: Songs and Stories of the Bituminous Industry* (Philadelphia: University of Pennsylvania Press, 1943); Korson, *Songs and Ballads of the Bituminous Miners* (Washington, D.C.: Library of Congress—Archive of Folk Song, record L 60); and Archie Green, *Only a Miner. Studies in Recorded Coal Mining Songs* (Urbana: University of Illinois Press, 1972).

29. John Dos Passos, "The Free Speech Speakin's," 294.

30. Evans papers, box 3, folder 24 (for Jackson's speech); and Gaventa, *Power and Powerlessness*, 113.

31. Garland, *Welcome the Traveler Home*, 152–3, 80. Chester Hoskins is quoted from a United Press report by Harry Ferguson, quoted here from the *New York World Telegram*, 5 April 1932; and Elzie Phillips is quoted in *Bloody Harlan*, cit.

32. Ogan, *Always Sing My Songs*, videotape.

33. Gaventa, *Power and Powerlessness*, 116.

34. Garland, *Welcome the Traveler Home*, 58.

35. Evans papers, box 1, folder 4.

36. Malcolm Ross, "Miners, and yet mountaineers at heart," *New York Times Magazine*, 15 May 1932.

37. Mooney, *Struggle in the Coal Fields*, 164–5.

38. Melvyn Dubofsky and Warren Van Tine, *John L. Lewis. A Biography* (Urbana: University of Illinois Press, 1986), 46.

39. Quoted in Anne Lawrence, "On Dark and Bloody Ground: An Oral History of the United Mine Workers of America in Central Appalachia," *UMWA Journal*, 16–31 January 1974.

40. Werner Sollors, *Beyond Ethnicity* (New York-Oxford: Oxford University Press, 1986), 61, 63.

41. See chapter 8 for a discussion of the impact of mass culture on Italian working-class culture.

42. Quoted in Richard O. Boyer and Herbert M. Morais, *Labor's Untold Story* (New York: published by United Electrical, Radio, and Machine Workers of America, 1955), 132.

43. Tillman Cadle's version of Doris Parks's answer on religion also diverges from other sources: he has her reply that religion is a "personal matter."

44. Garland, *Welcome the Traveler Home,* 114; and Gaventa, *Power and Powerlessness,* 110.

45. On black miners in the UMWA, see Herbert R. Northup, "The Coal Mines," in William H. Turner and Ed Cabbell, eds., *Blacks in Appalachia* (Lexington: University Press of Kentucky, 1985), 159–172; and Ronald L. Lewis, "Race and the United Mine Workers' Union in Tennessee," ibid., 173–182. During the strike, Eugene Gordon ["Harlan—and the Negro," *Labor Defender,* October 1931, 208–209] complained that the black press and the middle class it stood for were indifferent to the plight of the miners, including the black miners indicted for the Battle of Evarts. The article was accompanied by an editorial disclaimer.

46. Garland, *Welcome the Traveler Home,* 114.

47. Ogan, *Dreadful Memories, A Girl of Constant Sorrow.*

48. Bishop, "1931: The Battle of Evarts."

49. Elizabeth Levy and Tad Richards, *Struggle and Lose, Struggle and Win: The United Mine Workers* (New York: The Four Winds Press, 1977), 47.

CHAPTER 12

1. Philip S. Foner, ed., *The Black Panthers Speak* (Philadelphia: J. B. Lippincott, 1970), 183.

2. Rossana Rossanda, *il Manifesto,* 29 March 1983.

3. From the indictment of the Rome tribunal, as quoted in *La Repubblica,* 5 April 1981.

4. I refer often to Negri in this discussion, because he was the best-known and controversial figure in the case. This is in no way intended to mean that he was more important, and certainly not more innocent, than the other defendants.

5. According to Bruno Leuzzi, Negri's initial counsel (interviewed in Rome, 16 October 1984), the defense used a socio-linguist, who identified the region from which the speaker on the telephone was later found to have originated. This information, although available, was never used by the prosecution, and the newspapers consistently refused to print it. The defense also stressed that the court's voice identification expert had as much as written in his books that his method was inadequate for legal use. However, that "electronics" should be considered infallible and "human" disciplines, such as linguistics and sociology, irrelevant, fits well with the positivistic approach that characterized the whole case.

6. The literature on the April 7 Case is immense. The best critical summation of the pretrial phase is Luigi Ferrajoli, "Il caso '7 Aprile.' Lineamenti di un processo inquisitorio," *Dei delitti e delle pene*, 1 (1983), 167–204. I have used Ferrajoli's insights, from this and other articles and from an interview, throughout this essay. I have consulted basically two newspapers: *La Repubblica* and *il Manifesto*. They were the only ones that consistently covered the trial and had different positions: *La Repubblica* oscillated between neutral and pro-prosecution; *il Manifesto* was consistently for the defense. Among judicial papers, I have examined the brief submitted by Padua State Attorney Pietro Calogero, 18 May 1981, which is generally considered the fullest statement for the prosecution. I have also been able to see parts of the transcript of the courtroom proceedings, through the kindness of the legal firm of Tommaso Mancini and Antonio Pisano. Paolo Virno, one of the defendants, was interviewed in Rome, 14 October 1984.

7. *La Repubblica*, 11 May 1983; and *Paese Sera*, 30 January 1981.

8. Two random samples, from Calogero's brief. A *Potere Operaio* leaflet: "Absenteeism, sabotage, red terror against capitalistic command are the expression of the communist need for liberation from wage slavery" (451). Testimony of Guido Petter, of Padua University: "On 9 March [1979], Prof. Mazzocco's car was destroyed; on the 10th, a bomb exploded near Prof. Zunica's apartment; on the 11th, Prof. Santinello's car was burned; on the 14th, I was seriously injured by three masked young men who waited for me as I drove home, hit me savagely on the head with iron bars and monkey wrenches, causing a cranial trauma and breaking my right hand." (1217)

9. Giovanni Leone, *Istituzioni di diritto processuale penale* (Napoli: Jovene, 1965), vol. II, 12–13.

10. The pre-trial proceedings (*istruttoria*) are conducted by a *pubblico ministero* (state attorney) who collects the evidence and submits his conclusions as a *requisitoria* (brief) to an examining judge (*giudice istruttore*). The latter evaluates the brief and decides whether to issue an *ordinanza di rinvio a giudizio* (indictment). The next phase takes place in the courtroom (*dibat-*

timento), with a judge (*presidente*), a prosecutor (*pubblico ministero*), and counsel for the defense.

11. Ferrajoli, "Il caso '7 Aprile' "; id. "Il processo penale diffuso," *Dei delitti e delle pene*, I, 2 (May-June, 1983), 381–387.

12. Walter J. Ong, *Orality and Literacy. The Technologizing of the Word* (London and New York: Methuen, 1982), 43–44.

13. This aspect is reflected in the relationship between the trial and the theater. The classic statement is Johann Huizinga, *Homo Ludens* [1939], chapter 4. See also Milner S. Ball, "The Play's the Thing: An Unscientific Reflection on Courts Under the Rubric of Theater," *Stanford Law Review*, vol. 28 (November 1975), 81–115.

14. Foner, *The Black Panthers Speak*, 183.

15. Quoted by Rossanda, *il Manifesto*, 12 April 1984.

16. Giancarlo Scarpari, preface to Giovanni Palombarini, *Il processo e la storia* (Venezia: Arsenale Cooperativa, 1982), 8. The book is based on the historical section of Palombarini's indictment refuting Calogero's theorem.

17. *Corriere della Sera*, 9 October 1984. Apparently, Calogero complained of misrepresentation: the interview was announced as part of a series, which was not continued. The reporter's intentions, however, were friendly.

18. Ferrajoli, "Il caso '7 Aprile'."

19. *Corriere della Sera*, 5 July 1979.

20. Brief of Rome state attorney Giorgio Ciampani, quoted in Ferrajoli, "Insurrezione armata svoltasi in Roma e in altre località," *il Manifesto*, 8 March 1981.

21. *il Manifesto*, 6 June 1981.

22. Angelo Ventura, "Il problema storico del terrorismo italiano," *Rivista storica italiana*, XCII, 1 (March 1980), 125–151. Ventura had firsthand knowledge of the subject. He taught at Padua University, and was beaten, shot at and wounded by *Autonomia* sympathizers. He does not choose to mention this fact in his essay.

23. See Giuliana Bertacchi, "Esperienze didattiche degli istituti della Resistenza e uso delle fonti orali." in *La storia: fonti orali nella scuola*, papers presented at the conference on "Teaching anti-Fascism and the history of Resistance: didactics and oral sources," Venice, 2–15 February 1981 (Venezia: Marsilio, 1982), 44.

24. Renzo De Felice, preface to Sergio Zavoli, *Nascita di una dittatura* (Milano: Mondadori, 1983), 6.

25. Palombarini, *Il processo e la storia*, 50.

26. Paul Thompson, *The Voice of the Past: Oral History* (Oxford: Oxford University Press, 1978), 43.

27. Ferrajoli, "Il caso '7 Aprile'."

28. Nathaniel Hawthorne, *The Scarlet Letter,* in *The Portable Hawthorne,* Malcolm Cowley, ed. (Harmondsworth, Middlesex, U.K.: Penguin Books, 1976), 323–324.

29. Bertacchi, "Esperienze didattiche."

30. See the discussion in Alessandro Portelli, "Traduzione dell'oralitá," *Fonti Orali,* III, 1 (April 1983), 35–41.

31. Jack Goody, *The Domestication of the Savage Mind* (Cambridge: Cambridge University Press, 1977), 74 ff.

32. In 1975, together with the editorial board of the music magazine *Muzak,* I was tried for "attempting the corruption of a minor." We had printed a questionnaire on teenagers' attitudes toward sex. A witness for the defense said that "*today*, these things are accepted; *unfortunately*, change is resisted in some quarters." The judge dictated this statement into the record as follows: "*nowadays* [which has overtones of deprecation], these things are accepted; change, *however*, is resisted in some quarters." The judge's version had reversed the connotations of the witness's testimony. Eventually, a general amnesty caused the case to be dismissed before it came to a verdict.

33. According to Paolo Virno, the theme and the language of "insurrection" were dropped by *Potere Operaio* at least a year earlier. Virno is absolutely certain that Piperno never said those words, but the defendants failed to locate the tapes of the conference, which were known to exist.

34. See the transcript of courtroom session of 15 December 1983: testimony of Roberto Sandalo, 47.

35. Christopher Lasch, "The Cultural Cold War," in *The Agony of the American Left* (New York: Vintage Books, 1969), 67–68.

36. This tendency is noted in Bertacchi, "Esperienze didattiche."

37. Jan Vansina, *Oral Tradition* (Harmondsworth, Middlesex, U.K.: Penguin Books, 1973), 26.

38. See Stefano Rodotà and Massimo Cacciari, "La testimonianza Fioroni, le accuse a Magnaghi," *l'Unità*, 30 December 1981.

39. See Luisa Passerini, "Sette punti sulla memoria per l'interpretazione delle fonti orali," *Italia contemporanea*, XXXIII, 143 (April-June, 1981), 83–92.

40. *Il Giornale*, 4 February 1984.

41. David Caute, *The Great Fear* (Austin, Tex.: S&S Press, 1978).

42. "The majority of the great *pentiti*," says Virno, "maintain a rather high standard of credibility. However, they insert an internal distortion that gives a false meaning even to the truths they do tell. They tell an 80 percent of truth, but the missing 20 percent changes the meaning of the rest."

43. Session of 21 February 1984, testimony of Michele Galati, 6–7.

44. Session of 15 December 1983, 47.

45. Vansina, *Oral Tradition*, 27.

46. *Panorama*, 30 November 1981.

47. The role of subjectivity, narrative form, and imagination in oral history is discussed in chapters 1, 3, 4 in this book.

48. Scarpari, preface to Palombarini, *Il processo e la storia*, 19.

49. *Il Giornale*, 4 February 1984.

50. Dr. Calogero pointed out that Fioroni's incriminating testimony was rendered *before* benefits for *pentiti* were legislated. The first decree on behalf of the *pentiti* was issued, in fact, two weeks later; it had long been under discussion and was known to be likely to be passed.

51. *l'Unità*, 1 January 1984. This was, however, before Fioroni refused to appear in court.

52. Vansina, *Oral Tradition*, 29.

53. Vansina, *Oral Tradition*, 30.

54. Session of 23 January 1984; testimony of Antonio Savasta, 35–36.

55. Rodotà, *La Repubblica*, 3 March 1984. The only witness arrested (in court) for false testimony had appeared voluntarily for the defense, and contradicted two *pentiti*.

56. For instance, in Paul Thompson, *The Edwardians. The Remaking of British Society* (London: Weidenfeld and Nicholson, 1975).

57. Ferrajoli, "Il caso '7 Aprile.' "

58. On Savasta's criticism of the inquest, see session of 20 January 1984, 5; 23 January 1984, 10, 25–26; il Manifesto, 25 January 1984.

59. Ferrajoli, "13 mesi in aula," il Manifesto, 12 April 1984.

60. Vansina, Oral Tradition, 29; Chaim Seligman, "Documenting Oral History," Kibbutz Studies, 11 (November 1983), 10–13; Ong, Orality and Literacy, 43 ff.

61. Session of 12 September 1983, 41–46, testimony of Marco Barbone and confrontation between Barbone and Funaro.

62. Ball, "The Play's the Thing." The concept of theater applies to the case in two senses. One is that of live performance, with dialogue and interaction. The other is the ritual playing out of precast roles: for this interpretation, see Cacciari, il Manifesto, 12 April 1984.

63. Ferrajoli, "13 mesi in aula"; Rossanda, il Manifesto, 2 March 1984.

64. Giorgio Bocca, "Il caso Fioroni e il 7 Aprile," La Repubblica, 7 April 1984.

65. Bruno Leuzzi said in his interview that this practice was common in many large trials with many defendants and complex proceedings.

66. Session of 22 February 1984, 1–25. The exchange quoted above is on pages 6–7; other lengthy readings are on pages 13–15 and passim.

67. Session of 21 February 1984, 5.

68. Session of 23 January 1984, during the testimony of Savasta, 10–11.

69. Session of 22 February 1984, testimony of Bozzato, 24–25. For a similar exchange, see also 27.

70. Ong, Orality and Literacy, 78–79.

71. Ibid., 116.

72. In 1985, a national scandal broke out when cabinet member Gianni De Michelis chanced to meet Oreste Scalzone in Paris, where he had taken refuge, and talked with him for a few minutes. Even President Sandro Pertini condemned De Michelis saying that he would never "shake a murderer's hand." Scalzone was never accused of murder.

73. On the role of the press, see Pasquino Crupi, Processo a mezzo stampa: il 7 Aprile (Roma: Com 2 editrice, 1982).

74. Summary of sessions of the seminar on "National History, History of the Resistance Movement, Local History," organized by the *Istituto Nazionale per la Storia del Movimento di Liberazione*, Rimini, May 25–27 1979, as reported in the *Istituto's* journal, *Italia contemporanea*, July-September 1979, 100–126. At the same meeting, another distinguished progressive historian, Prof. Giuliano Manacorda, warned that "overevaluation of oral sources is often instrumental to polemical attacks against the institutions."

75. In the appeal, in 1987, most sentences were reduced, in most cases by more than half; in several cases, defendants who had spent years in jail awaiting trial were either acquitted or received shorter sentences than the time they had already served. The charge of "insurrection" was abandoned. Negri was cleared of the death of Saronio, but received a 12-year sentence for "moral complicity" in the Lombardini murder. Fioroni did testify, but confrontation with defendants was avoided. In 1988, the appeal sentence was confirmed by the Supreme Court (see the daily papers for 5 October 1988). The appeal and the Supreme Court's decision did not make, by far, the same stir in the news and public opinion as the first trial. By then, the "historical" verdict on *Autonomia* had been passed anyway.

CHAPTER 13

1. Tzvetan Todorov, "Primitive Narrative," *The Poetics of Prose*, Richard Howard, trans. (Ithaca, N.Y.: Cornell University Press), 53–65 (*Poétique de la prose*, Paris: Seuil, 1971); William Labov and Joshua Waletzky, "Narrative Analysis: Oral Versions of Personal Experience," in June Helm, ed., *Essays on the Verbal and Visual Arts*, Proceedings of the 1966 Annual Spring Meeting of the American Ethnological Society (Seattle and London: American Ethnological Society and University of Washington Press, 1967), 12–44.

2. William Faulkner, *Absalom, Absalom!*, (New York: Vintage Books, 1986), 9.

3. Faulkner, *Absalom, Absalom!*, 34.

4. Faulkner, *Absalom, Absalom!*, 5–6.

5. The most concise and accessible introduction to "ballad style" (which was used in the seminar) is the introduction to Albert B. Friedman, *Folk Ballads of the English Speaking World* (New York: Viking Press, 1956).

6. The subtitle to Walter J. Ong's *Orality and Literacy* (London: Methuen, 1982) is "The Technologizing of the Word."

7. On the impossibility of forgetting in written cultures, see Jack Goody and Ian Watt, "The Consequences of Literacy," in Goody, ed., *Liter-*

acy in Traditional Societies (Cambridge, U.K.: Cambridge University Press, 1968), 28–68.

8. The obvious reference, and the reason for the quotation marks around "writing," is from Jacques Derrida, *Of Grammatology,* G. Ch. Spivak, transl. (Baltimore: John Hopkins University Press, 1976).

9. See Mirella Martino, *Oralitá e tempo in* The Bear *di Faulkner,* unpublished dissertation, English department, University of Rome *"La Sapienza,"* 1987–88.

Index

Bakunin, Mikhail, 144, 151
Ball, M. S., 262–3
ballads, 33, 162, 163, 164, 172, 174–75, 177, 181–192, 217, 276, 282
Balltrip, Ewell, 219
Bandholz, Brigadier General H. H., 232
Bandinelli, Ferdinando, 30
Banfield, Edward, 35
Barbone, Marco (witness, April 7 case), 262
Bartali, Gino (cycling star), 145, 155
Barthes, Roland, 81
Bartoletti, Gildo, 105
Bartolini, Dante
  on the death of Luigi Trastulli, 10–1, 17, 19, 21
  as poet and storyteller, 32–34
  poem "Il Partigiano", 82–6
  on historical compromise, 115
  on 1953 strike, 148
  singing style, 172
  partisan song, 174, 188
Bellini, Vincenzo, 190
Benmayor, Rina, xii
Berlinguer, Enrico (Communist Party secretary, 1970s), 16, 111, 112, 115, 125
Berman, Marshall, 97
Bermani, Cesare, viii
Bertaux, Daniel, xi
Bertaux-Wiame, Isabelle, xi
Bethell, Thomas, 218
Bianchi, Rocco, 9, 15, 22
Bianchini, Guido (defendant, April 7 case), 260
Binarelli, Diname (Terni cycling star), 144
Binda, Alfredo (cycling star), 145
Bishop, Bill, 238
blacks, see Afro-Americans
Blizzard, Frank, 233
blues, 68, 82, 98, 165
Bocale, Leonardo, 64–65
body, 5, 18, 124, 147, 158, 164, 168, 172, 178, 186, 231

Bogatyrev, Piotr, 54, 168
Boggs, Samuel (Harlan Co. songwriter), 200, 211, 213, 214
Bologna, Sergio, vii–viii
Bon, Cassian (Terni industrialist), 145
Borderías, Cristina, viii
Borromeo, Mauro (defendant, April 7 case), 241, 252, 259
Borzacchini, Baconin (later, Mario Umberto - auto racing star), 144, 146–47, 151–52, 159
Bosio, Gianni, x, xi, 32, 41, 42
"Circolo Gianni Bosio", 68
bourgeois, bourgeoisie, 68, 74, 88, 92, 136, 153, 159, 178
  petty bourgeoisie, 162, 188, 189, 257
Boyle, Tony (president, United Mine Workers), 214–15
Bozzato, Leonio (witness, April 7 case), 264–65
Bradbury, Ray, 73, 74
Bragg, Billy (rock musician), 180
Browder, Earl (secretary, CPUSA), 222

C

Cacciari, Massimo, 247
Cadle, Tillman, 238
  on civil rights in Harlan (1931–32), 221–22
  on Communists, 223, 229
  on preachers, 226–28
  on racism, 235–36
Calogero, Pietro (judge, April 7 case) 242, 243, 246–47, 248, 249, 250, 252, 253, 256, 257, 259, 260, 268
Canali, Calfiero
  on the death of Luigi Trastulli, 17–8, 22, 23, 107
  on uchronia, 109
  on speedups and accidents, 139–40, 159

"it could have happened to me",
23–4
"my life is a novel", 75–6
"respect", 135, 141
"wrongness of history", 105, 109,
113, 116
"they told us to keep calm", 106,
107, 134
Muraro, Luisa, 95
music, xiii, 81–2, 86, 98, 163, 165–
168, 170, 174, 179, 186, 190–91
country, bluegrass, 177
folk, see folklore - music
gospel, 177
heavy-metal, 181
punk, 181
rock, 180–81
popular, 172, 174, 190
and work, 180
see anthems, hymns, songs
music-hall, 172–3
Musick, Bennett (killed in Harlan
Co.), 200
Musick, Rev. Marshall, A.
testimony to LaFollette
Committee
on Louellen coal camp, 195–96,
198, 199, 205
on Harlan Co. courts, 206
on 1934 strike, 210–11
murder of son Bennett, 200–
201, 204
Mussolini, Benito, 21, 105–06, 114,
115, 120, 148, 151
myths, ix, xiii, 59, 60, 61, 108, 113,
114, 157, 227, 281

N

narrative, vii, xii, 7, 9, 10, 12, 14,
19, 20, 22, 23, 26, 48–50, 52–4,
56–60, 62–5, 67, 69, 70, 76, 87,
89, 100, 105, 109, 113, 127, 130,
132, 137, 164, 191, 202, 205–06,
209, 255–58, 271

modes, 21–5, 70–1
"communal" or "collective,",
24, 70
"personal", 23–4, 70
"political" or "institutional",
21
vs. "testimony", 256
narrators, xi, xii, 5, 8, 10, 12, 14,
15, 16, 17, 18, 21, 22, 23, 24, 25,
41, 48, 49, 50, 52, 53, 54, 55, 56,
59, 60–3, 64, 67–9, 76, 100, 102,
106, 107, 108, 110, 112, 113, 114,
118, 131, 132, 133, 134, 138, 145,
146, 152, 205, 208, 260, 278, 280
time, 70–1
point of view, 71
in literature, 57, 271
vs. "informants", 256
see informants, interviewing,
orality
nationalism, see patriotism
Native Americans
Cherokee, 224–25
Navajo, 114
Pueblo, 113–14
NATO (North Atlantic Treaty Organization), 8, 10, 13, 14, 16, 20,
25–6, 111
Negri, Antonio (defendant, April 7
case), 242–44, 247, 249, 251–52,
255, 257, 258, 260, 261, 264, 266–
67, 268–69
Neppi Modona, Guido, 268
New Deal, 220
New Left, 13, 41, 113, 243, 244, 246,
249
newspapers, 52, 56, 153, 159, 189,
225, 244, 259
Corriere della Sera (Milan), 3, 261
Manifesto, Il (Rome), 266–67
Messaggero, Il, (Rome) 2–3, 18, 156
New York Times, 219, 232
Repubblica, La (Rome), 46, 208–09
[Pineville, Ky.] Sun, 230
Unità, L' (Rome), 6, 16, 20, 142,
144, 147, 153, 154, 172